Lecture Notes in Artificial Intelligence 3416

Edited by J. G. Carbonell and J. Siekmann

Subseries of Lecture Notes in Computer Science

Michael Böhlen   Johann Gamper
Wolfgang Polasek   Maria A. Wimmer (Eds.)

E-Government: Towards Electronic Democracy

International Conference, TCGOV 2005
Bolzano, Italy, March 2-4, 2005
Proceedings

Springer

Series Editors

Jaime G. Carbonell, Carnegie Mellon University, Pittsburgh, PA, USA
Jörg Siekmann, University of Saarland, Saarbrücken, Germany

Volume Editors

Michael Böhlen
Johann Gamper
Free University of Bozen-Bolzano
Faculty of Computer Science
Dominikanerplatz 3, 39100 Bozen, Italy
E-mail: {boehlen, gamper}@inf.unibz.it

Wolfgang Polasek
University of Basel
Institute of Statistics and Economics
Petersplatz 1, 4003 Basel, Switzerland
E-mail: wolfgang.polasek@unibas.ch

Maria A. Wimmer
Federal Chancellery
ICT Unit
Ballhausplatz 2, 1014 Vienna, Austria
E-mail: maria.wimmer@cio.gv.at

Library of Congress Control Number: 2005920700

CR Subject Classification (1998): I.2, K.4, K.5.2, J.1, C.2.4, H.4

ISSN 0302-9743
ISBN 3-540-25016-6 Springer Berlin Heidelberg New York

Springer is a part of Springer Science+Business Media

springeronline.com

Typesetting: Camera-ready by author, data conversion by Scientific Publishing Services, Chennai, India
Printed on acid-free paper SPIN: 11395681 06/3142 5 4 3 2 1 0

Preface

The TCGOV 2005 international conference on e-government was held at the Free University of Bozen-Bolzano during March 2–4, 2005. The conference was initiated by the working group "Towards Electronic Democracy" (TED) of the European Science Foundation and was jointly organized by the Free University of Bozen-Bolzano, the Municipality of Bozen-Bolzano, the TED Working Group, and the IFIP Working Group 8.5.

The conference addressed a large spectrum of issues that are relevant and have to be investigated for a successful transition from the traditional form of government to a new form known as e-government. The main focus was on the following topics:

- improving citizen participation and policy making (e-democracy)
- government application integration
- semantic Web technologies for e-government
- security aspects for e-government services

Two sessions were dedicated to e-democracy, an emerging area within e-government that seeks to enhance democratic processes and provide increased opportunities for individuals and communities to be involved in governmental decisions. The contributions of these two sessions cover more fundamental results and insights as well as experiences from different countries.

Another focus was on government application integration and the use of Semantic Web technologies, which are important technical aspects on the agenda of e-government research. Different architectures for the integration and orchestration of distributed services and processes were presented along with two case studies. Three papers about Semantic Web technologies discussed the use of ontologies in e-government.

An important aspect across e-government and e-democracy is security. The proceedings include three contributions that present new approaches to deal with security issues in the context of e-polling, e-voting, and interorganizational workflows, respectively.

The program was completed with contributions on decision-support systems on the Web, managerial and financial aspects of e-government projects, political and societal implications, and e-procurement.

The technical program included three keynote presentations, given by leading researchers and experts from the field: Prof. Roland Traunmüller from the University of Linz, Prof. David Basin from the ETH Zurich, and Dr. Athanassios Chrissafis from the European Commission, DG Information Society, Unit E-Government.

A total of 92 scientific papers from 26 different countries were submitted to TCGOV 2005. Each submission was evaluated by at least two reviewers, mainly members of the Program Committee. The reviewing process was very selective, and only 28 contributions were accepted as full papers for presentation at the conference and publication in this volume.

Many people and institutions were involved in the joint organization of the conference. We express our thanks to all of them for their support and the smooth collaboration during the preparation of the conference. We are particularly grateful to the members of the Program Committee who selected the best papers that are collected in these proceedings. We greatly appreciate the mentorship given by the TED Working Group and the technical and logistic support provided by the Free University of Bozen-Bolzano.

January 2005

Michael Böhlen
Johann Gamper
Wolfgang Polasek
Maria Wimmer

Organization

TCGOV 2005 was jointly organized by the TED Working Group of the European Science Foundation, the Free University of Bozen-Bolzano, the Municipality of Bozen-Bolzano, and the IFIP Working Group 8.5.

Conference Chairs

Renzo Caramaschi, Municipality of Bozen-Bolzano, Italy
Wolfgang Polasek, University of Basel, Switzerland

Program Committee Chairs

Michael Böhlen, Free University of Bozen-Bolzano, Italy
Johann Gamper, Free University of Bozen-Bolzano, Italy
Maria Wimmer, University of Linz, Austria

Program Committee

Antonio Albano, University of Pisa, Italy
Kim Viborg Andersen, Copenhagen Business School, Denmark
Elisa Bertino, University of Milan, Italy
Jean-Loup Chappelet, Graduate School of Public Administration, Lausanne, Switzerland
Klaus Dittrich, University of Zurich, Switzerland
Mario Fedrizzi, University of Trento, Italy
Simon French, University of Manchester, UK
Gerhard Friedrich, University of Klagenfurt, Austria
Åke Grönlund, Örebro University, Sweden
Pim Hengeveld, Deloitte & Touche, The Netherlands
Marijn Janssen, Delft University of Technology, The Netherlands
Peter Kawalek, University of Manchester, UK
Alfons Kemper, Technical University of Munich, Germany
Mario Jorge Leitao, University of Porto, Portugal
Miriam Lips, Tilburg University, The Netherlands
Ann Macintosh, Napier University, UK
Peter Mambrey, Fraunhofer/FIT, St. Augustin, Germany
Gregoris Mentzas, National Technical University of Athens, Greece
Carl Erik Moe, Agder University College, Norway
Wolfgang Nejdl, University of Hannover, Germany
Aljosa Pasic, Atos Origin, Madrid, Spain

Vassilios Peristeras, Greek National Center for Public Administration, Thessaloniki, Greece
Wolfgang Polasek, University of Basel, Switzerland
Nineta Polemi, University of Piraeus, Greece
Reinhard Riedl, University of Zurich, Switzerland
Fabrizio Ruggeri, CNR-IMATI, Italy
Ahti Saarenpää, University of Lapland, Finland
Gheorghe M. Sandulescu, IPA SA, Bucharest, Romania
Charles A. Shoniregun, University of East London, UK
Maddalena Sorrentino, University of Milan, Italy
Pietro Torasso, University of Turin, Italy
Roland Traunmüller, University of Linz, Austria
Paolo Zuliani, Free University of Bozen-Bolzano, Italy

Organization Chair

Johann Gamper, Free University of Bozen-Bolzano, Italy

Exhibition Chair

Nadine Mair, Free University of Bozen-Bolzano, Italy

Local Organization Committee

Walter Costanzi, Municipality of Bozen-Bolzano, Italy
Cristina Pierotti, Municipality of Bozen-Bolzano, Italy
Danila Sartori, Municipality of Bozen-Bolzano, Italy

Conference Office

Klaudia Verginer, Free University of Bozen-Bolzano, Italy

Honorary Chairs

Ingeborg Bauer-Polo, Town Councilor of Education and Time Policies, Municipality of Bozen-Bolzano, Italy
Roberto Bizzo, Town Councilor of Informatics, Municipality of Bozen-Bolzano, Italy
Friedrich Schmidl, President of the Free University of Bozen-Bolzano, Italy

TED Steering Committee

David Rios Insua (Chair), Universidad Rey Juan Carlos, Spain
Enrique Alvarez Conde, Universidad Rey Juan Carlos, Spain
Simon French, University of Manchester, UK
Raimo Hämäläinen, Helsinki University of Technology, Finland
Miroslav Karny, Academy of Sciences, Prague, Czech Republic
Wolfgang Polasek, University of Basel, Switzerland
Fabrizio Ruggeri, CNR-IMATI, Italy
Philippe Vincke, Université Libre de Bruxelles, Belgium
Simon Wilson, Trinity College Dublin, Ireland

Additional Reviewers

Liliana Ardissono, University of Turin, Italy
Guido Boella, University of Turin, Italy
Suo Cong, University of Zurich, Switzerland
Dario De Jaco, CSI Piemonte (Turin), Italy
Tibor Dekany, University of Zurich, Switzerland
Anca Dobre, University of Zurich, Switzerland
Alexander Felfernig, University of Klagenfurt, Austria
Thomas Hodel, University of Zurich, Switzerland
Dietmar Jannach, University of Klagenfurt, Austria
Jonas Neukomm, University of Zurich, Switzerland
Giovanna Petrone, University of Turin, Italy
Meik Poschen, Fraunhofer FIT, Germany
Christoph Sturm, University of Zurich, Switzerland
Jurate Vysniauskaite, University of Zurich, Switzerland
Markus Zanker, University of Klagenfurt, Austria
Patrick Ziegler, University of Zurich, Switzerland

Sponsoring Institutions

TED Working Group of the European Science Foundation
Free University of Bozen-Bolzano
Municipality of Bozen-Bolzano
Südtiroler Informatik AG - Informatica Alto Adige SpA
Handelskammer Bozen - Camera di commercio Bolzano

Table of Contents

e-Democracy: Improving Citizen Participation and Policy Making

Using Weblogs to Support Local Democracy
Ann Macintosh, Andy McKay-Hubbard, Danae Shell 1

Web-Based Tools for Policy Evaluation
Lasse Berntzen, Marte Winsvold 13

Can Online Map-Based Applications Improve Citizen Participation?
Renate Steinmann, Alenka Krek, Thomas Blaschke 25

e-Democracy: Experiences from Different Countries

Interactive Tools for e-Democracy: Examples from Switzerland
Jean-Loup Chappelet, Pierre Kilchenmann 36

"Public Budget Dialogue" – An Innovative Approach to E-Participation
Stefanie Roeder, Annika Poppenborg, Susanne Michaelis, Oliver Märker, Stefan René Salz 48

Enhancing e-Democracy Via Fiscal Transparency: A Discussion Based on China's Experience
Ling Lan 57

Political and Societal Implications

Third Way e-Government: The Case for Local Devolution
Ailsa Kolsaker 70

"Urban Versus Regional Divide: Comparing and Classifying Digital Divide"
Enrico Ferro, Marco Cantamessa, Emilio Paolucci 81

e-Citizen: Why Waiting for the Governments?
Armando Rech Filho 91

Security for e-Government Services

A Zero Knowledge Proof for Subset Selection from a Family of Sets with Applications to Multiparty/Multicandidate Electronic Elections
Tassos Dimitriou, Dimitris Foteinakis 100

A Protocol for Anonymous and Accurate E-Polling
Danilo Bruschi, Igor Nai Fovino, Andrea Lanzi 112

Model Driven Security for Inter-organizational Workflows in e-Government
Ruth Breu, Michael Hafner, Barbara Weber, Andrea Novak 122

Semantic Web Technologies for e-Government

e-Government: A Legislative Ontology for the *'SIAP'* Parliamentary Management System
Carmen Costilla, Juan P. Palacios, José Cremades, Jorge Vila 134

No (e-)Democracy Without (e-)Knowledge
Giovanni M. Sacco 147

Towards a Semantically-Driven Software Engineering Environment for eGovernment
Dimitris Apostolou, Ljiljana Stojanovic, Tomas Pariente Lobo, Barbara Thoenssen 157

Architectures for Government Application Integration

Towards Requirements for a Reference Model for Process Orchestration in e-Government
Jeffrey Gortmaker, Marijn Janssen, René W. Wagenaar 169

A Distributed Architecture for Supporting e-Government Cooperative Processes
Mariangela Contenti, Massimo Mecella, Alessandro Termini, Roberto Baldoni 181

eGovernment Service Marketplace: Architecture and Implementation
Elena Mugellini, Maria Chiara Pettenati, Omar Abou Khaled, Franco Pirri 193

Case Studies for Government Application Integration

Towards Building E-Government on the Grid
Ying Li, Minglu Li, Yue Chen 205

Applying the ISO RM-ODP Standard in E-Government
B. Meneklis, A. Kaliontzoglou, D. Polemi, C. Douligeris 213

Decision Support Systems

Quixote: Supporting Group Decisions Through the Web
J.A. Rubio, D. Rios Insua, J. Rios, E. Fernandez 225

UNICAP*: Efficient Decision Support for Academic Resource and Capacity Management
Svetlana Vinnik, Marc H. Scholl 235

A Methodology Framework for Calculating the Cost of e-Government Services
Elias A. Hadzilias 247

Managerial and Financial Aspects of E-Government Projects

Good Practice in e-Government: Management over Methods?
Lee Anthony Eddowes 257

Participatory Budget Formation Through the Web
J. Rios, D. Rios Insua, E. Fernandez, J.A. Rivero 268

On the Transition to an Open Source Solution for Desktop Office Automation
Bruno Rossi, Barbara Russo, Paolo Zuliani, Giancarlo Succi 277

e-Procurement

Public eProcurement in Action: Policies, Practices and Technologies
Catherine Hardy, Susan P. Williams 286

An Integrated Approach in Healthcare e-Procurement: The Case-Study of the ASL of Viterbo
Tommaso Federici 298

Author Index 311

Using Weblogs to Support Local Democracy

Ann Macintosh, Andy McKay-Hubbard, and Danae Shell

International Teledemocracy Centre, Napier University,
10 Colinton Road, Edinburgh, EH10 5DT, Scotland, UK
(a.macintosh, a.mckay-hubbard, d.shell)@napier.ac.uk

Abstract. This paper addresses the important aspect of democracy at the local community level and the need for e-democracy tools. Communities require easy to use ways of accessing and sharing information and ideas, responding to consultations and participating in policy formulation. In this paper we focus on Community Councils which are the smallest local tier of the statutory framework of democracy in Scotland. The councillors live in the community they serve, know personally many of the issues and can readily judge the impact of new or changed policies and suggestions from government. Currently they represent their communities as best they can, relying on word-of-mouth and may therefore not be as inclusive as they otherwise might be.

The rapidly expanding public access to the internet and the increasing popularity of weblogs offer an opportunity for both the councillors and the communities to discuss issues together and lobby government for policy changes.

1 Introduction

There is a need to develop e-participation tools to create new opportunities for democratic participation at the community level. The notion of e-participation and responsible citizenship brings attention to bear on access to information, the nature of participation in public debate and opportunities for communities to provide input to political decision-making and policy formulation (OECD, 2004). The overarching objective of our work is to investigate renewing local democracy by enabling elected councillors and the communities they represent to have greater influence over factors affecting their lives. We address this objective by investigating how weblogs can enable the renewal of democracy at the local level.

Much previous work to engage people in government initiated consultations and public debate using technology has been based on discussion boards. For example, Macintosh and Smith (2002) describe an online participation study to consult citizens on environmental policy issues and Luhrs, et al (2003) describe a large scale participation exercise in the City of Hamburg - both using specially developed discussion boards. On the other hand, Coleman and Gøtze (2001) have described a number of technologies for online engagement, ranging from email to chat rooms. It is now well accepted that technical, social and political factors need to be considered when developing technology to support e-democracy and using ICT to enhance democracy is a challenging task (Mambrey, 2004).

M. Böhlen et al. (Eds.): TCGOV 2005, LNAI 3416, pp. 1–12, 2005.

This paper is based on a project "The e-Community Council" which started on 1st February 2004 and is funded by the Scottish Executive. The aim is to design technology to support Community Councils to engage with the community and participate in decision making by government and service providers. Community councils are the local tier of the statutory framework of democracy in Scotland. They are small, local groups and there are 1160 Community Councils across Scotland. They typically each have 12 elected members who represent a small population spread across both small and large geographical areas, depending on the urban or rural nature of their location. By law, they are made up of members of their own community, giving them direct access to their constituents at a more detailed daily level than most politicians or local authority councillors could ever hope to achieve. They live in the community they serve, know personally many of the issues and can readily judge the impact of new or changed policies and suggestions from government. Currently they represent their constituents as best they can, relying on word-of-mouth and may therefore not be as inclusive as they otherwise might be. They are often given little time to consider fairly major proposals before their considered input is required. This project aims to address these problems by developing and testing a suite of e-participation tools based on weblogs to support Community Councils.

The participating Community Councils are all based in Scotland. They are described in Table 1.

Table 1. The six community councils

Community Council	Population represented	Geographical area covered (sq Km)	Number of councillors
Bannockburn	7150	73.5	15
Cambusbarron	2123	33.1	15
Strathfillan	329	247	11
Stepps	4222	-	21
Thornhill & Blairdrummond	673	54.5	12
Torbrex	1723	0.5	9

The project has two phases each lasting one year and each with its own aims and deliverables. In this first phase, version 1 of the e-Community Council toolkit has been developed for a target community council that is currently familiar with, and using IT to conduct some aspects of their work. This is the Strathfillan Community Council. By focusing on this IT literate group the impact of some of the known variables - in particular access to and familiarity with technology - is minimised. At the end of year one, and after piloting and evaluation, the initial toolkit will be generalised and tested again with the five other Community Councils with varying degrees of literacy and covering both urban and rural communities. The results of this second phase will allow an overall roll out mechanism for Community Councils and other community groups in a region to be developed.

Community councils have the statutory role set out in the 1973 act section 51 :

"to ascertain, co-ordinate and express to the local authorities for its area, and to public authorities, the views of the community which it represents, in relation to matters for which these authorities are responsible, and to take such action in the interests of that community as appears to it to be expedient and practicable".

(For a description of Community Councils see http://www.scotland.gov.uk/cru/kd01/comm-01.htm)

More specifically, and as result of legislation tangential to that covering directly the community council, they have some powers in relation to consultation over liquor licensing and planning applications. The 1976 Licensing (Scotland) Act gave community councils the right to object to the granting, renewal or transfer of liquor licenses. In 1996, community councils were given a specific role as consultees in relation to applications for planning permission. Local planning authorities must consult community councils on planning applications affecting their areas and are required to send community councils a weekly list of all planning applications. It is also a statutory obligation of local authorities to ensure that community councils have ready access to planning information affecting their community.

Each Local Authority provides a model constitution for its Community Councils. A typical constitution would have the following set of objectives for the community council:

- to ascertain, co-ordinate and reflect the views of the community which it represents, to liaise with other community groups within the area, and to fairly express the diversity of opinions and outlooks of the people.
- to express the views of the community to the Local Authority for the area, to public authorities and other organisations;
- to take such action in the interests of the community as appears to it to be desirable and practicable;
- to promote the well-being of the community and to foster a community spirit;
- to be a means whereby the people of the area shall be able to voice their opinions on any matter affecting their lives, their welfare, their environment, its development and amenity.

Therefore the effectiveness of community councils is dependent on the Community Councillors:

- being aware of, and having the ability to obtain, the opinions of the community on a variety of consultative issues that could effect the community;
- having the ability to gather and respond to the views and ideas of the community to both sustain and develop the community.

2 User Requirements Gathering

The general aim of the e-Community Council toolkit is to support Community Councillors to engage with individuals and groups by facilitating:

- Access through a range of ICT-based devices to allow promotion of any engagement initiative at the earliest possible stage – *awareness*
- Fast, easy access to information to support issues – *information provision*
- Informed responses from individuals and groups - *consultation*
- Deliberative dialogue with and amongst groups through interactive facilities - *dialogue*
- Feedback to individuals and groups of progress and outcomes – *information provision*
- Participative (non-legally binding) voting and lobbying – *participation and lobbying*
- Co-ordination of the Community Council workload.

In order to determine the overall user requirements for the toolkit we set ourselves 5 main questions.

- What engagement activities could the toolkit realistically support?
- How are those activities currently carried out, by which actors and groups of citizens, and using what methods?
- Why did these activities need to be enhanced using the toolkit?
- What are the current technical capabilities of the Community Councils who would be using the toolkit?
- What IT skills and infrastructure issues may affect deployment and require training or awareness-raising?

These questions have been addressed and the user requirements defined by using questionnaires, observations, semi-structured interviews and demonstrating mock-ups and early prototypes of the system. It was important to involve the community councillors right from the start of the project in the design of the toolkit so as to encourage effective use and ownership of the resulting system.

3 Requirements Gathering Tools

The following describes the main requirements gathering tools.

3.1 Questionnaires

Questionnaire 1 was distributed to project partners who represented the 6 participating Community Councils. This sought an overview of the type of area and population size that the Community Council is representing and the typical internet connectivity and IT infrastructure of the area.

There were 16 questions grouped under 2 headings:- About the Community? About the Community Council?. These questions aimed to develop a picture of the current overall situation in each of the participating Community Councils. This would provide material for understanding the type of community represented by the Community Council and information regarding the baseline technical requirements.

Questionnaire 2 was distributed to all elected members of the 6 participating Community Councils. This contained detailed questions concerning the tasks carried out by the Councillors and sought their perceptions on the relevant importance and also difficulty of these.

There were 27 questions grouped under 6 headings:- personal perspective on their work; communication strategies; responding to policy considerations and consultations; about public meetings; Internet access, and their wish list.

This questionnaire aimed to develop a picture of community council work, providing material for understanding the type of tasks undertaken, their level of difficulty and their relevance for inclusion in the toolkit.

3.2 Observation

The development team attended a regular monthly meeting of Strathfillan Community Council to observe and appreciate the level and type of work undertaken by each member and the need for communication between members and other communication links.

3.3 Semi-structured Interviews

Three members of Strathfillan Community Council - the Chair person, the Secretary and a member responsible for undertaking a number of consultations - were interviewed. The purpose of this was to support and extend information gained from the questionnaires as a means of understanding the nature of community councils and their activities.

The 'guiding' questions which helped shaped the interview were based around 4 headings. The aim was to gather more detailed information on how the Community Council reacted to consultations and other communications.

The guiding questions were:

General: Overview of duties, activities and workload; any sub committee structure and how it works; secretary's workload; other time commitments.

Planning consultations: How the community council receives planning proposals; How the community council is required to publicise them; How they collect local views; What supporting information is available; What effect can or has the community council had on the planning process; If there are objections, what affect these have on the planning proposal.

Other consultations: What sort of material is included; How are these publicised;
In what manner do the public respond; Level of incoming consultations, requests, etc. and how are these organised; What would make dealing with this work load easier; Do they get feed back from the consulting body.

Communication: Their level of contact with the Local Authority; What letter writing and lobbying activities they engage in; Whether there are regular publicity activities; Do they need to communicate with each other regularly and how this currently done.

3.4 Prototype Demonstrations

Prototype demonstration 1 was an initial demonstration of version 1 of the e-community council toolkit to project partners who represented the 6 participating Community Councils. Drawing on the responses to the questionnaires and observations an initial mock-up of the end-user system containing an events diary and a fictional planning consultation was used, with fictional characters, to illustrate how the toolkit could support communication activities. Comments were sought from the audience, on what was desirable and feasible from their perspective. The intention was to gather reaction from this group on the general look and feel of the toolkit and also its intended functionality.

Prototype demonstration 2 was a 'walk-through' of version 2 of the e-community council toolkit to members of Strathfillan Community Council. It used information based on the actual work of Strathfillan Community Council, including a survey questionnaire recently conducted by them. It also had some fictional consultations, characters and events. This time the toolkit was demonstrated from both the end-user and Community Councillor perspectives. During the walk-through the members were asked a series of questions to ascertain what was desirable and acceptable and what was required to be amended for them to be able to use the toolkit to support their work.

4 Activities the Toolkit Should Support and Why

Most community councillors viewed representation of the community, advocacy for the community, and being a voice for the community as their most important tasks. Many felt that keeping an interest in community affairs and being aware of them was also highly important.

However, there was also consensus that communication in general was seen to be problematic, within the community council and both with the community and the local authority. Communication between all stakeholders was the most commonly given response by community Councillors to the question "What is the most difficult activity?". There is a need to improve communication with the community.

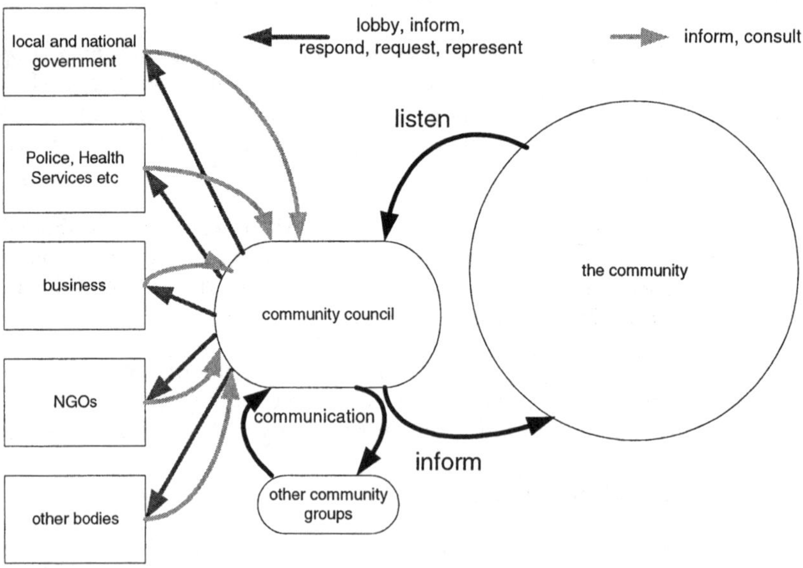

Fig. 1. Overview of communication activities

The most prevalent responses to the "wish list" question were those concerned with improving communication and contact between the community council and the community it serves. Linked to this was the desire to improve community involvement and lessen community apathy.

Figure 1 provides an overview of the communication links and activities for a typical community council.

4.5 Support the Consultation Process

The main activity, in terms of time and effort involved, is responding to consultations originating from local government. These include policy proposals and planning applications, the latter being the most extensive and regular. There is also the need to respond to consultations from the Scottish Executive and other public agencies. Even though it is generally agreed that their major role is as a consultee, there is no standard guidance as to how this is to be carried out in practice. All Community Councils agree that the workload associated with consultations and planning applications is considerable and problematic. Indeed it is seen as creating a barrier to effectively conveying the views of the community back to the local authority. The problem is partly a result of the shear volume of paper work accompanying each consultation and partly a problem of the number of consultations and timescales involved. The consensus is that they are currently struggling to cope and many consultations do not receive the level of attention they require.

Currently the community councils seek the opinion of the community on consultations in a limited manner, often responding themselves to a consultation, or simply posting their response to a planning proposal, for example, on a community notice board, and then collecting any few comments there may be. There is a consensus that the consultative workload, as it is currently undertaken, does not permit a deeper level of consultation. Only on very sensitive community issues are deeper methods employed.

While the toolkit cannot address the issue of the volumes of paper produced by external bodies and the frequency of consultancy demands, it can support the management of consultations and support the community council to respond to them more effectively.

4.6 Support Gathering of Community Views

Bottom-up ideas, initiatives and complaints raised by the community are communicated to the Community Council by word of mouth, telephone and letters, with e-mail being used to a small extent in some councils. This communication is almost exclusively issue based. Currently the public convey their views to the community council in a sporadic manner. Most councils agree that some means of keeping in touch with the community would be beneficial.

Depending on the issue, results to paper-based surveys are typically low. Similarly with turn out at public meetings, if the issue to be addressed is controversial and community wide, then a broad section of the community is likely to attend. By the same token, narrower issues, if they result in any public interest at all, will attract a much narrower section of the community. The average level of attendance at public meetings is variable and very much depends on what issues the community council is discussing. The general consensus is that public attendance is low and consequently this is not an effective method of gathering community views.

4.7 Support Information Dissemination and Communication Links

Providing mechanisms to raise awareness of community council's activities and "success stories" about their achievements was viewed as one way to improve communications with the community. Typically, such achievements are not regularly publicised, and in general it was felt that the community do not pay much attention to publicity material provided by the community council. Current communication methods used by community councils to raise awareness within the community and disseminate information varies, but commonly include a newsletter, a community notice board and use of the local press. The toolkit can add to these delivery mechanisms by providing an online notice board for the community and publicising meetings and newsletters through lists of news and events.

There are a large number of bodies that interact with the community council, but by far the most common is the relevant local authority. Others range from the National Park Authority to Public Transport companies. The toolkit could provide contact details for such organisations.

5 The e-Community Toolkit

The resulting e-Community Council toolkit comprises a number of integrated weblog based tools. Its overall purpose can be defined as to facilitate the work of Community Councillors supporting their engagement with the community and representing its views. It does this through supporting the councillors to:

- Respond to consultations
- Support bottom-up participation
- Access and disseminate information
- Communicate with each other
- Co-ordinate the workload of the Community Council
- The toolkit is being used as a centrally managed web-based service, aimed at: -
- Community Councillors accessing from their home, library or community centre;
- Residents in the community accessing from their home, library or community centre;
- Representatives from government departments and public agencies accessing from their work place.;
- Local authority councillors and local MSPs accessing from their work place.

Because of this diverse spread of users the toolkit has to be usable on either a PC or Apple Macintosh platform. The respective minimum specifications are: -

- PC: Intel 486 or equivalent, 400 Mhz, 64Mb RAM
- Apple: G3, 300Mhz, 64Mb RAM

and a minimum screen resolution of 800 x 600 is assumed.

All user interfaces to the toolkit are provided via industry-standard web browsers and it is possible for a user to perform all toolkit functions using MS Internet Explorer or Netscape (version 5 or above). Because of the rural communities involved in the project broadband connections to the internet cannot be assumed. Therefore under normal circumstances users should not have to wait more than 20 seconds, and on average no more than 10 seconds, for toolkit web content to load at 56kbps. Animated graphics, video and audio clips may exceptionally take more than 20 seconds but no more than 30 seconds to download at this speed. The toolkit web pages are compliant with the Web Content Accessibility Guidelines version 1.0 available at: http://www.w3.org/TR/WAI-WEBCONTENT.

Weblogs were chosen because of their ease of use and maintenance. Basically, a weblog can be considered as frequently modified web pages in which dated entries are listed in reverse chronological sequence. The prototypical weblog is focused around links to other sites of interest (or other weblogs) with blogger commentary for added value. Posts are primarily textual, but they may contain photos or other multimedia content. Most weblogs can also provide hypertext links to other Internet sites (see for example: Herring et al. 2004 and Nardi et al. 2004). Research by others on the community building aspect of weblogs has shown that they can create public space (Huffaker 2004) and build a relationship between the weblogger, readers and the domain (Nichani 2004). Blogging has been characterized as socially interactive and community like in nature (Herring et al. 2004) and therefore highly suitable to support the work of the community councils. The Hansard Society report (Ferguson and Howell, 2004) on weblogs discusses their uses and impact on politics, it concludes:

"From the perspective of politics or, more specifically, political awareness and participation in the UK, blogging is fresh and exciting." (p23).

The toolkit comprises:

- Community Council (public) web pages (e.g. the Strathfillan Community Council) with associated weblogs and
- Community Councillor (private) web pages with associated weblogs.

Figure 2 is a screen dump of the prototype community council public web page.

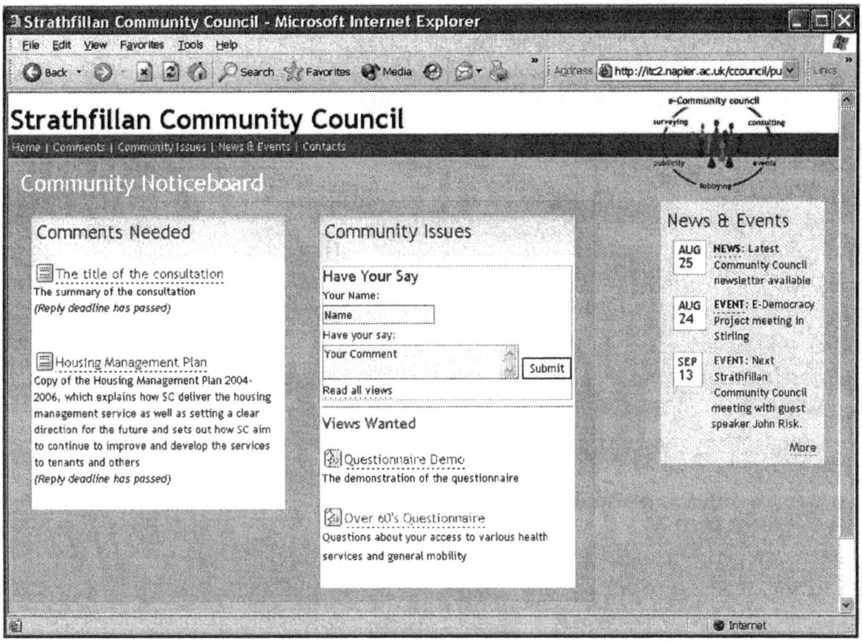

Fig. 2. Community Council public home page

With regard to functionality, the toolkit has:

Top-down consultation functionality – "Comments needed"

This will assist the community councillors in managing and responding to consultations and planning proposals emanating from government or other consulting bodies. In this instance, communication is initiated by the consulting body, in a top-down manner. Currently community councils are inundated with consultative material, from bespoke, single-issue consultations to planning applications. The tool provides a means of managing this workload, facilitating internal discussion around each consultation and enabling direct community involvement in responding to consultations, something that is currently rare.

Bottom-up views gathering functionality – "Community Issues"

This will assist the community council in gathering information directly from the community in a bottom-up manner. In this sense it provides facilities through which members of the community can raise their own issues for consideration by the community council. These issues could then seed further initiatives and lobbying activity on the part of the community council. It also includes a means of creating and publishing on-line questionnaires and collecting their responses. These questionnaires would be authored directly by the community councils in keeping with the bottom-up perspective of this tool.

News and Events lists

This supports the community council promote its activities. It enables Community Councillors to maintain a detailed list of activities and also serve as a vehicle for publicising community news and events. Announcements of meeting, such as Public Meetings, along with their minutes and agendas, can be made available through this list as well as any newsletter the Community Council publishes.

Contact lists

This comprises two distinct sections. One publicly viewable area with summary contact details of the community councillors and also website addresses of relevant organisations useful for that community. The other section is restricted to the Community Council. Here the councillors maintain and share their working contacts. These would include details of individuals within government and relevant NGO as well as website addresses providing useful information for the community council.

The e-community toolkit is not meant to replace completely existing communication and participation channels and in all cases, conventional media and face-to-face events will continue to be used alongside the e-community council toolkit.

6 Conclusions

The next stage of project is to evaluate the usefulness and effectiveness of the e-community council toolkit within the first community council. The overall success criteria are defined from two perspectives, firstly from the perspective of the Community Councillors, and secondly from the perspective of the project partners.

From the Community Councillors' perspective the benefits sought are: -

- Ease of co-ordination of consultations
- Ease of access to and provision of information
- Informed comments to top-down consultations by residents in the community
- Better appreciation of the bottom-up opinions and ideas of residents in the community.
- From the project partners' perspective the benefits sought are: -
- Take-up by the Community Councillors
- Take-up by a cross-section of residents in the community
- Increased ability for Community Councils to obtain and disseminate the views of the community to local authorities and other public bodies.

The first stage of the evaluation is due to be completed by December 2004.

To conclude, international, national and local governments and agencies make decisions which fundamentally affect the lives of citizens. Organisational complexity and an increasing pace of change are making it increasingly difficult for individuals and community groups to even know about, far less engage in, decision making processes. Communities require easy to use ways of accessing and sharing information and ideas, responding to consultations and participating in policy formulation. The rapidly expanding public access to the internet and the increasing popularity of weblogs offer an opportunity to individuals and community groups to discuss issues together and lobby government for policy changes. The research work we are undertaking has the potential to provide a framework for e-participation at local community, and in so doing contribute knowledge to a broad range of strategy and planning policies.

Acknowledgements

This project is being conducted in partnership with the Association of Community Councils for the Loch Lomond & Trossachs National Park area, Stirling Assembly, the Association of Scottish Community Councils, Stirling Council and with the support of Dr Sylvia Jackson MSP. We acknowledge the support of our partners in writing this paper.

References

1. Ferguson, R. and Howell, M. (2004) "Polictical Blogs – Craze or Convention"; Hansard Society, UK
2. Herring, S., Ann Scheidt Lois, Sabrina Bonus, and Elijah Wright. (2004) Bridging the Gap: A Genre Analysis of Weblogs. *Hawaii International Conference on Systems Science HICSS-37*
3. Huffaker, D. (2004) *Spinning yarns around the digital fire: Storytelling and dialogue among youth on the Internet.* First Monday 9. Web page, [accessed 16 April 2004]. Available at http://www.firstmonday.org/issues/issue9_1/huffaker/index.html

4. Luhrs, R., Albrecht, S., Lubcke, M and Hohberg, B. (2003) How to Grow? Online Consultation about Growth in the City of Hanburg: Methos, Technuies, Success Factors; in: R.Traunmuller (Ed); Electronic Government, Second International Conference, EGOV 2003, Prague, Czech Republic, September 1-5, 2003 Proceedings. Springer (Lecture Notes in Computer Science; Vol. 2739)
5. Macintosh, A. and Smith, E. (2002) Citizen Participation in Public Affairs; In: R.Traunmuller and K.Lenk (Eds); Electronic Government, First International Conference; proceedings / EGOVS 2002, Aix-en-Provence, France, September 2002. Springer (Lecture Notes in Computer Science; Vol. 2456). pp256-264
6. Mambrey, P. (2004) Networked ICT to foster e-demcoracy; in: R.Traunmuller (Ed); Electronic Government, Third International Conference, EGOV 2004, Spain, 2004 Proceedings. Springer (Lecture Notes in Computer Science; Vol. 2739)
7. Nardi, Bonnie, Diane Schiano, and Michelle Gumbrecht. (2004) Blogging as Social Activity, or, Would You Let 900 Million People Read Your Diary? *Proceedings of Computer Supported Cooperative Work 2004*. Chicago: ACM
8. Nichani, Maish. (2004) *How to use weblogs to create engaging learning experiences*. Web page, [accessed 16 April 2004]. Available at: http://learnscope.flexiblelearning.net.au/learnscope/golearn.asp?category=12&DocumentId=5723
9. OECD, (2004). *Promises and problems of e-democracy; Challenges of Citizen on-line Engagement*. OECD, Paris

Web-Based Tools for Policy Evaluation[1]

Lasse Berntzen and Marte Winsvold

[1] Faculty of Social Science, Vestfold University College,
P.O. Box 2243, 3103 Tønsberg, Norway
lasse.berntzen@hive.no
[2] Norwegian Institute for Urban and Regional Research,
P.O. Box 44, Blindern, 0313 Oslo, Norway
marte.winsvold@nibr.no

Abstract. Current research in e-democracy has so far focused on the early stages of political decision making. Information- and communication technology (ICT) has been shown to facilitate participation in agenda setting and alternative selection. But ICT also has the potential to facilitate evaluation of existing policies. This paper examines policy evaluation from local politicians view. What web-based tools are useful for policy evaluation, and what kind of information do these tools provide?

1 Introduction

The political decision making process is often modelled as an iterative process consisting of the following stages [1]:

- Issue emergence. The point at which an issue becomes more visible and important to citizens and policy makers, when some stirrings of government and interest group activity begin to be evident. Often issues emerge when national policies are seeking a local implementation, or when the local administration wants to rewrite current policy because it does not longer work according to the initial assumptions.
- Agenda setting. The process by which problems and alternative solutions gain or lose public and elite attention, or the activities of various actors and groups to gain greater attention or to prevent them from gaining attention.
- Alternative selection. The analysis and construction of policy alternatives.
- Enactment. The act of putting a decision into effect. Typically when the local government vote on an issue.
- Execution. The local administration implements the decision, and the policy is put to work
- Evaluation. At some time the administration or local government decides too evaluate if the policy is working according to the initial assumptions.

[1] The authors want to thank the following persons for their help with preparation of this paper: Erik Dahl (City ombud, Bergen), Geir Halstensen (KS), Ivar Johansen (Oslo SV), Torill Lønningdal (9K), Jan Wølneberg (Kommuneforlaget).

M. Böhlen et al. (Eds.): TCGOV 2005, LNAI 3416, pp. 13 – 24, 2005.

Figure 1 illustrates the political decision making process.

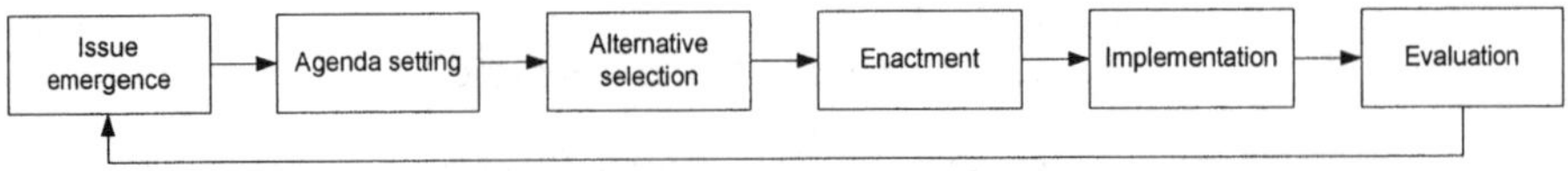

Fig. 1. Political decision making process

Information and communication technology (ICT) tools may be used to support the political decision making at all stages [2]. This paper is written from a local politicians view. Therefore emphasis is put on how local politicians can use technology to become better politicians. ICT may also be used to increase citizen participation and influence. This has been discussed by several authors, e.g. Ted Becker and Christa Slaton [3], Kevin A. Hill and John E. Hughes [4], and Anthony G. Wilhelm [5], and will not be discussed here.

Another dimension is the division of responsibility between local government and local administration. We assume that local government is responsible for bringing new technology into the political decision process, even if politicians are not actively involved in all stages.

Different tools apply in/fit different stages in the political process. At the first two stages, tools that support unstructured communication may be used by politicians to listen for emerging political issues and ideas, and gathering support for bringing issues or ideas into the political arena. Examples of such tools are discussion forums, e-petitions, e-panels, and virtual town hall meetings.

At the alternative selection stage politicians may use e-consultations, opinion polls and even e-voting to ask citizens what they think of different alternatives.

Enactment may be done by e-voting.

During the execution stage, ICT may be used for service provision. Politicians are not involved in the actual provision of services. Decisions must be evaluated to find out if they work according to assumptions made before the decision was made.

ICT provides for faster and even continuous evaluation of the results of decisions. This opens up for a reformulation of the model presented earlier (Figure 2):

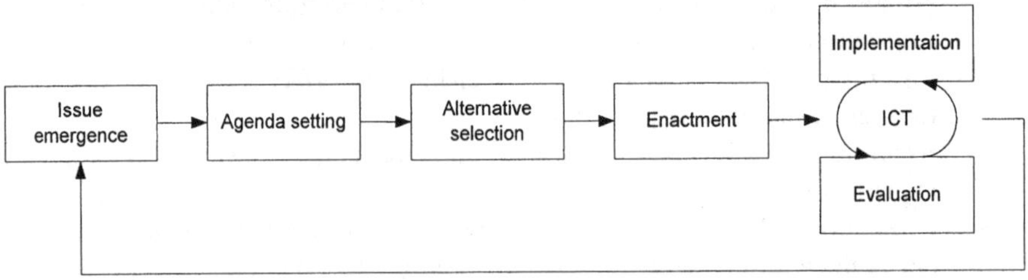

Fig. 2. Revised political decision making process

How can then ICT be used by politicians for evaluating decisions? We argue that ICT provides some powerful tools for evaluation of political decisions. One such tool is benchmarking by use of web-based tools connected to databases. Benchmarking makes it possible to compare different values related to demography, use of resources (money, people), and outcome. Another tool is web-based user satisfaction surveys. Such surveys are used to find out what citizens think about the services and the service provision. If user satisfaction surveys are asking the same questions, the results may be used for benchmarking as well. Benchmarking and user satisfaction surveys are initiated by politicians. We also see a need for citizens taking the initiative when policies are not working according to their assumptions. Therefore, we propose a third tool, an e-ombudsman, to alert decision makers when necessary.

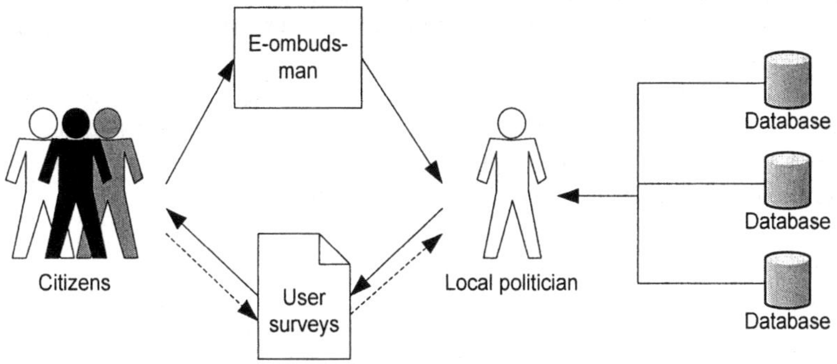

Fig. 3. Different web-based tools for policy evaluation

2 Methodology and Related Research

So far, research has focused on the use of ICT-based tools in the early stages of the political decision process. Several papers have been published on the use of discussion forums, e-consultations and e-voting to include citizens in the decision making process.

Ann Macintosh [2] also uses a model of the political decision making models to map tools to stages, but her examples are focused on the early stages. Interestingly, in her model, she has replaced "evaluation" by monitoring", probably to emphasize the idea of evaluation as a continuous activity.

In their proposed framework of e-democracy development, Wichian Chutimaskul and Suree Funilkul [6] introduced "e-complaints" as a tool for use by citizens during the evaluation period, but they did not elaborate on this.

Stephen Coleman [7] proposed a set of political mechanisms to make a step towards direct public participation. One such mechanism was online evaluation. His idea was to use some kind of standing focus groups. Such groups may cover a broad area and give their recommendations.

This paper aims to describe the current state of the art for web-based evaluation of political decisions in Norway. Even if the tools described may be used by citizens in general, we have focused on local politicians' need for evaluating political decisions.

The remaining part of the paper will discusse the use of existing tools and initiatives for web-based benchmarking and user-surveys, and the development of an e-ombudsman. The research is mainly based on examination of current tools, literature studies (evaluation reports and working papers) and interviews with local politicians, administrators, and persons involved in implementation of the tools.

3 Benchmarking

Benchmarking [8] is a technique to measure the performance and quality of one municipality compared to other municipalities. The comparison is based on data reported by each municipality. The most common data are related to people, expenses and results. By using a database located on an Internet-connected server, it is possible to give access to such data, not only to administrators, but also to local politicians and citizens in general.

We will now describe one Norwegian benchmarking database and one portal connected to several databases. Both are accessible through the Internet, and are good examples of the current state of the art of benchmarking. The description is followed by a discussion of pitfalls and possible improvements.

3.1 KOSTRA

KOSTRA[2] is a database administered by Statistics Norway. From 2001 all municipalities are required to submit data to KOSTRA. A wide range of data related to service provision, resources, and expenses is collected from the municipalities. Such data includes: Municipal fees, purchase of external services, property management, financial key numbers, kindergartens, public schools, health, care, social services, children protective services, environment, culture, churches, water, renovation, public transport, municipal housing, commercial sector support, and fire protection.

KOSTRA includes an advanced web-based reporting application. This application makes it possible to select a number of municipalities and generate results as tables. Tables may be downloaded to personal computers in several formats (e.g. Excel) for further analysis.

We will now show some real life benchmarking examples:

The local government of Sande is about to vote on a new four year plan for kindergartens. One local politician is concerned with the quality of the kindergartens, and asks KOSTRA for information on the ratio of employees with a degree in kindergarten teaching. She also includes three other municipalities in the same geographical area, and gets the following results (Table 1):

She observes that the number of employees with degrees has dropped and is now the lowest among the four municipalities. Based on these numbers, she proposes to the local government that future recruitments should prioritize teachers with a degree in kindergarten teaching, and that the municipality should start a development program for existing employees.

---

[2] http://www.ssb.no/kostra/

Table 1. Example of information returned by KOSTRA

	Employees with degree in kindergarten education (percent)		
	2003	2002	2001
0701 Horten	40.0	39.9	38.7
0702 Holmestrand	33.3	27.9	30.7
0713 Sande	28.3	37.8	37.5
0714 Hof	30.8	31.4	33.3

During the local election, one local party group in Horten promised to prioritize public education. The local party leader wants this to influence the budgeting process, and ask KOSTRA how much of the total budget other municipalities in the same area are using on public schools. Armed with the following numbers (Table 2), he confronts the rest of the local party's representatives, and manages to increase the school budget.

Table 2. Example of information returned by KOSTRA

	Percent of total municipal expenses spent on public schools	
	2003	2002
0701 Horten	27.2	26.2
0702 Holmestrand	28.0	27.4
0713 Sande	33.4	35.0
0714 Hof	31.7	31.6

Holmestrand local government wants to discuss the organization of the public library. KOSTRA reports the following (Table 3):

Table 3. Example of information returned by KOSTRA

	Net. expenses public library / citizen (NOK)			Average loans / citizen		
	2003	2002	2001	2003	2002	2001
0701 Horten	262	279	268	6.1	6.1	5.9
0702 Holmestrand	308	382	370	3.9	3.7	4.0

Based on the numbers, the politicians sit down to discuss why the average loans per citizen are so much lower, finds out that the public library of Horten is more accessible during evenings, and then decide to do something about the opening hours.

3.2 Skoleporten.no[3] (School Portal)

Skoleporten.no has recently been launched by the Ministry of Education and Research as a national web portal for issues related to education. The portal uses an underlying data warehouse collecting data from several other sources.

One important source is the **National Information System for Primary Education**[4]. This database contains all statistical information collected by the Ministry of Education and Research, and is made available to all citizens and politicians.

Key information includes the number of pupils, teacher/pupil ratio, teaching hours per pupil, size of teaching groups etc.

Another important source is the **National Grade Database**[5] maintained by the Norwegian Board of Education (Læringssenteret). This database contains the final grade statistics for all public schools, and can be used to compare individual schools to each other.

Recently, Norway introduced national tests in the public schools. Results from these tests are also available on the portal.

Compared to KOSTRA, skoleporten.no has a much narrower scope. The portal is primarily developed for decision makers (including local politicians, school leaders, teachers and national education authorities), but also as resource for teachers, pupils and citizens in general.

3.3 Discussion

There is no doubt that benchmarking may give politicians and citizens valuable information. Still, we need to stress some common pitfalls:

- Reporting errors due to differences in organization and accounting practices [9]. One example is the reporting of administrative overhead. Some municipalities report such expenses as an integrated part of each administrative unit, while other municipalities report some of these expenses as central administration. It may therefore look like one municipality is using more money on administration and less on service provision, even if they are in fact delivering the same services. The same happens with property. Some municipalities charge each unit for the use of municipal property, while others do not.
- Lack of granularity. We do not always see what is behind the numbers. If we look at the ratio of people working in the home health care to the number of patients, we can find that one municipality is spending more money on home health care than another municipality. But the real reason may be that the first municipality has two or three housing units with 24 hour supervision, and limited home health care provision, while the other municipality may have centralized their home health care homes, and is in fact providing much better services in the homes. Due to the granularity of the reporting, it is not possible to find out what is actually happening behind the numbers.

---

[3] www.skoleporten.no

[4] http://www.wis.no/gsi/

[5] http://www.ls.no/stati/stati.asp

Reporting errors may be avoided by providing clearer guidelines, better granularity, and by increasing the competence among those reporting information.

It is important to stress that benchmarking should be used with care. Still, differences may trigger an urge to find out why the differences appear. Politicians may therefore get a better understanding by using benchmarking.

There have been several newspaper discussions on the use of both KOSTRA and the public school databases. The discussion about KOSTRA has concentrated on reporting errors and granularity, while the discussion regarding the public education databases has been much more concerned with the effects of benchmarking. One wing embraces this information and will use it to improve the educational system, while others fear that a ranking system that will increase differences within the educational system. It is still too early to draw any conclusions from this ongoing debate.

Even if there has been some criticism of quality of reported data, we believe that the quality eventually will improve. By making better guidelines and improving granularity, such information will be valuable resources for local politicians and citizens trying to find out how their municipality and schools measures up.

4 User Satisfaction Surveys

Web-based surveys represent an opportunity to collect information from citizens with less expenses and more frequency than is possible by using traditional paper based surveys.

Web-based surveys have so far mainly been used for evaluating schools. One system has been used by pupils; another system has been used by parents to answer how satisfied they are with different aspects of the school.

4.1 Effektiviseringsnettverket (Efficiency Network)

The project "Effektiviseringsnettverket" founded by The Norwegian Association of Local and Regional Authorities (KS) has developed a set of manuals explaining how to conduct user surveys in different areas together with a set of evaluation criteria for each area. These were originally used as basis for paper based surveys, but are now used for making ICT-based surveys.

A web-based application, **bedrekommuner.no**, (better municipalities) gives local administrators the possibility to initiate and administer electronic surveys. Some results from 2002 and 2003 are present in the database, but these results come from paper based surveys, except for some trials performed by public schools.

This year citizens may provide their answers directly through a web-based interface, by using a password received in the mail. The results are stored directly into the database. An option is to let the municipality register the data on behalf of the users. This may be appropriate when users lack the necessary ability or competence to fill out an electronic form.

Since several municipalities are using the same questions and the same database, the data not only reveals user satisfaction, but also facilitates benchmarking among the municipalities.

Currently 167 municipalities are registered users of the web-based application. The municipalities are performing user surveys within the following fields: Public school (parents), kindergartens, children protective services, building permits, care (three different sub-surveys), and social services.

Today, September 27th, 2004, more than 12000 questionnaires have been answered and put into the database. The results will be available later this autumn.

One example is Tinn municipality. Tinn used a web-based survey to measure the user satisfaction among parents of kindergarten children. The municipality received 297 answers, which is 81% of the parents. This is a very good return rate. Effektiviseringsnettverket reports that normal return rate for paper based surveys within this sector are around 60%.

4.2 Elevinspektørene (Pupil Inspectors)

The Ministry of Education and Research has developed a web-based survey "elevinspektørene"[6] to measure user satisfaction among public school pupils. The survey was made mandatory for 7th and 10th grade this year, and the results for all public schools are now available on their website. The survey was answered by 86% of all public schools. The rest either had technical problems, used the wrong survey (a demo), or was not able to complete the survey within the preset timeframe.

The survey contains questions about motivation, well-being, victimization, participation, school democracy, and physical environment.

Table 4 shows a translated example for 7th grade of one school:

Table 4. Example of information returned by Elevinspektørene

Facts	2003
Motivation	3,0
Well-being	3,4
Victimization	3,7
Participation	2,0
School democracy	3,3
Physical environment	3,1

Higher values mean better results. In this school, we observe that participation is ranked considerably lower than the other areas. It is possible to examine the underlying numbers, shown in Table 5 (questions are translated):

Table 5. Example of information returned by Eleveinspektørene

Facts	2003
Are you allowed to participate in the planning?	1,5
Are you allowed to participate in the selection of different types of assignments in the different subjects?	2,0
Are you allowed to participate in decisions on how you should work on the subjects?	2,5

[6] http://www.elevinspektorene.no/

In 7th grade the pupils are supposed to take part in planning their own education. In this case, we see that the school still has some work to do on this question.

4.3 Discussion

User satisfaction surveys give valuable information on the how the users perceive the different services. If such surveys are done in several municipalities, it is possible to use these results for benchmarking as well.

Critical comments on the use of user satisfaction surveys have been concerned with the questions asked and the selection of citizens. Are the right questions asked to the right users? It will always be a decision whether to use the surveys developed by Effektiviseringsnettverket or to make own, localized surveys. The advantage of using the first alternative is benchmarking, the advantage of the second alternative is the possibility to focus on local issues.

5 E-Ombudsman

Benchmarking and user satisfaction surveys are valuable tools for assessing policy decisions. But both methods have in common that they must be initiated by local government or administration.

There is also a need for some kind of mechanism to insure that local government is made aware of policies not working according to their intentions.

Norway has long traditions of appointing ombudsmen to oversee government. Ombudsmen receive complaints, give advice, investigate, make recommendations, and report to the parliament.

Norway currently has several ombudsmen:

- The Parliamentary Ombudsman for Public Administration
- The Gender Equality Ombud
- Ombudsman for the Armed Forces
- The Ombudsman for Children
- The Consumer Ombudsman

Some cities have adopted the idea. The city of Oslo has a dedicated ombud for users of health- and social services, while the city of Bergen has a general purpose city ombud.

The city of Bergen, Norway, established a city ombud [10] in 1992. The city ombud is an independent control body. The city ombud has a special responsibility to protect citizens against mischief, and that municipal employees do not make errors or neglect their duties to the citizens. Today, most enquiries are made by telephone.

The 2003 annual report shows the increase in number of enquiries during the last four years (Table 6).

Table 6. Number of enquiries received by the City ombud of Bergen

2003	2002	2001	2000
349	243	263	155

Again, such ombudsmen are independent from administration, and act on behalf of citizens. Therefore ombudsman is a good metaphor for an e-service aiming to funnel complaints and reports of malfunctioning policies to the local politicians.

The idea is not original. A local government representative, Ivar Johansen of Oslo, established his own website **osloombudet.no**[7] two years ago. He reports that he has received around 100 enquiries since the web-site was launched.

The e-ombudsman would complement benchmarking and user satisfaction surveys, and give citizens the opportunity to raise issues not being handled by formal complaint processes.

5.1 E-Ombudsman Implementation

Citizens have the possibility to contact both local administration and politicians when they are dissatisfied with aspects of the services. In practice this is often done by using telephone, letter, e-mail or other means of communication. In some municipalities the mayor and other politicians makes themselves available by keeping an open door policy, and some even conduct regular visiting hours in a cafe, a park or other locations.

The E-ombudsman would serve as a complement to such traditional channels. From time to time, citizens require anonymity. The E-ombudsman could also protect the anonymity of the citizens, but at the same time facilitate communication between the citizen and the local politicians volunteering for the ombudsman role.

The problem caused by anonymity is insufficient information. It is impossible to communicate with an anonymous letter writer to clarify certain points. By using ICT is it possible to develop an application that makes it possible to communicate anonymously.

The proposed E-ombudsman (Figure 4) is an application that acts as a mediator between a citizen making a complaint and one or several politicians acting as ombudsmen. They receive the complaint, and have the possibility to get back to the person complaining to ask for more information.

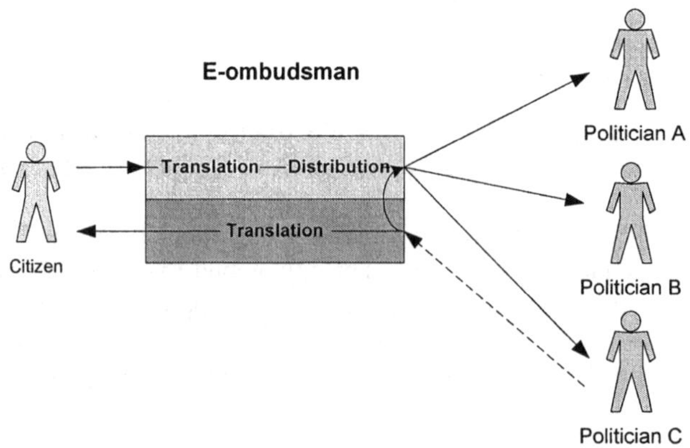

Fig. 4. Implementation of an E-ombudsman

7 http://osloombudet.no

Example of use: Nina, the single mother of a twelve year old boy, has received a letter from the local school about a school trip and that every pupil has to pay for transport and accommodation. She knows that the law says that education is free, and even if the amount is not that big, it will make some minor economic problems. She does not want to address this issue in person, since she may be accused for destroying the fun for the rest of the pupils. She could contact a politician, but would really like to be anonymous. She could of course write an anonymous letter to one of the politicians, but would then be unable to answer any further questions.

The E-ombudsman application translates the identity (e-mail address or user ID) into a new identity used in the communication with the politicians. Next, the application sends the complaint to a list of politicians. Any politician may ask further questions, and these questions are sent to the e-ombudsman, which translates the address back to the original address, but also to the other politicians taking part in the process.

There are still many problems to be resolved, both organizational and technical. Trust is one important issue. The application should probably be managed by some trusted third party. We are currently developing a prototype to try out the idea in practice.

6 Discussion

This paper shows different ways to evaluate political decisions by using web-based tools. Web-based tools make it possible to collect and use information faster and more often than with traditional evaluations.

We have presented a model using three different tools: Benchmarking by extracting information from databases containing statistical information, user satisfaction surveys, and a tool to capture alerts from citizens being concerned about the effects of policy decisions.

We have given some practical examples of use, and pointed out problems with benchmarking and user satisfaction surveys. We have also introduced the idea of an application called an E-ombudsman to capture citizen alerts.

References

1. Birkland, T.A. An Introduction to the Policy Process: Theories, Concepts, and Models of Public Policy Making, M. E. Sharpe Inc., Armonk, New York, 2001, p. 295
2. Macintosh, A. "Characterizing E-Participation in Policy Making," 37th Annual Hawaii International Conference on System Sciences (HICSS '04), 2004 , pp.
3. Becker, T., and Slaton, C.D. The Future of Teledemocracy Praeger Publishers, 2000
4. Hill, K.A., and Hughes, J.E. Cyberpolitics: Citizen Activism in the Age of the Internet Rowman and Littlefield Publishers, Lanham, Maryland, 1998
5. Wilhelm, A.G. Democracy in the Digital Age Routledge, New York, 2000
6. Chutimaskul, W., and Funilkul, S. "The Framework of e-Democracy Development," Third International Conference on Electronic Government (EGOV 2004), Springer Verlag, Zaragoza, Spain, 2004, pp. 27-30

7. Coleman, S. "Cutting out the middle man: from virtual representation to direct deliberation," in: Digital Democracy : Discourse and Decision Making in the Information Age, B.N. Hague and B. Loader (eds.), Routledge, London, 1999, pp. 195-210.
8. Karlöf, B., and Östblom, S. Benchmarking: Veiviser til forbedret produktivitet og kvalitet ad Notam Gyldendal, Oslo, 1993
9. Cap_Gemini "Evaluering av KOSTRA (KOSTRA Evaluation)," 2002, p. 125
10. Dahl, E. "Årsmelding 2003 Byombudet (Annual report 2003 The city ombud)," Bergen, p. 16

Can Online Map-Based Applications Improve Citizen Participation?

Renate Steinmann[1], Alenka Krek[1], and Thomas Blaschke[2]

[1] Salzburg Research Forschungsgesellschaft mbH,
Jakob-Haringer Str. 5/III, 5020 Salzburg, Austria
{renate.steinmann, alenka.krek}@salzburgresearch.at
http://salzburgresearch.at
[2] Z_GIS, Zentrum für Geoinformatik Salzburg,
Hellbrunnerstr. 34, 5020 Salzburg, Austria
thomas.blaschke@sbg.ac.at
http://www.zgis.at

Abstract. Public participatory geographic information systems (PP GIS) aim at enlarging citizen's involvement and participation in decision-making processes. In this paper we review existing online PP GIS applications and present the framework of our analysis. We concentrate on the aspects of interactivity of such applications and the GIS functionalities needed for their operation. First results of ongoing research exhibit that a vast majority of applications only deliver information to the citizen in a one-way communication process. Although the technology is available, only few applications fulfill criteria of our analysis to be classified as two-way communication tools. We conclude the paper with directions for our further research.

1 Introduction

Geographic Information Systems (GIS) are technically mature and widely used at all levels of administration and planning. Considerable effort has been devoted over the years to utilize GIS for public participatory processes. GIS spatial visualization techniques combined with participatory functionalities form a novel way for the presentation of spatial issues to the general public. They aim at improving the interaction and communication between the citizens and decision-makers. Virtual environments and 3D designed city environment spaces can be used to show the current and future situation in a near realistic way [9]. The aim of public participatory GIS (PP GIS) is to enlarge the level of citizens' involvement in decision-making and to improve access to relevant tools, data and information. The Internet generates a new public sphere that supports interaction, debate and new forms of democracy [10]. Online PP GIS applications can be used as a mean to augment traditional methods of participation such as for example public meetings and consultation documents, or to enhance the existing classical participatory methods. Thus far, research on broadening a basis for planning was dissected into technological and societal research. While the first is sometimes criticized for being too positivistic the latter is generally very critical. This paper demonstrates that the potential of GIS to support public

M. Böhlen et al. (Eds.): TCGOV 2005, LNAI 3416, pp. 25–35, 2005.

participation planning processes and to broaden the basis for participation is significant. While most GIS research focus on the technical functionalities of such systems, there are almost no empirical studies on the problem of potential exclusions of the citizens with poor computer literacy or computer aversion by certain social groups, especially elderly people.

This paper critically reviews selected online PP GIS applications, develops a framework for our analysis and presents the first results. The following questions are central to our research: "When does an online GIS application become a public participatory GIS application?", "What are the necessary conditions for that?", and "Which GIS functionalities are needed for an online PP GIS application?" In the analysis we concentrate on different degrees of interactivity which determine the interaction between the user and an online PP GIS application. Special attention is devoted to the GIS operations. This is a first step within an ongoing research initiative of the new Centre of Excellence for Map-Based Online Public Participation Map[3] (http://map3.salzburgresearch.at), which focuses on interactivity of PP GIS applications, spatial visualization, information access and social and economic aspects of online map-based public participation.

2 Online Map-Based Participation

2.1 GIS and PP GIS

Increasingly, online public participation in spatial planning utilizes Geographic Information Systems (GIS) and the Internet. A GIS can in this context be defined as "a system of hardware, software, data, people, organisations and institutional arrangements for collecting, storing, analyzing and disseminating information about areas of the earth" [3]. A geographical information system used to support public participation is often referred to as public participatory GIS (PP GIS). In general, PP GIS applications range from Internet-dependent spatial multimedia systems to conventional field-based participatory development methods with a modest GIS component [5]. These applications have the linking of community participation and geographic information systems in a diversity of social and environmental contexts in common. In this section we provide an overview of PP GIS definitions, and concentrate on the differences between GIS and PP GIS. We discuss theoretical foundations for interactivity of PP GIS applications, and GIS functions included in most of currently available PP GIS applications.

The term public participation GIS was coined at the I-19 Initiative workshop of the *National Center for Geographic Information and Analysis* (NCGIA) in the United States. At the time, PP GIS was defined as "a variety of approaches to make GIS and other spatial decision-making tools available and accessible to all those with a stack in official decisions" [11]. Talen [14] stresses the importance of the community integrated or neighbourhood GIS (sometime called CiGIS) that provide better access to Geographic Information technologies and opens up the opportunities for collaboration and participation in planning processes. Craig [5] identifies "PP GIS as a broad tent with multiple meanings and a global reach made of emerging forms of community interaction with GIS that are linked to the social and geographic context of GIS production and implementation." Haklay and Tobon [6] consider PP GIS a research field that focuses on the use of GIS by the general public with the aim to involve citizens in spatial planning processes. A new and novel development of PP GIS increasingly uses the possibilities of the Internet. So-called online PP GIS are being used to facilitate the delivery of spatial information to participants and allow them to return their information for inclusion in the database [5].

Table 1. Difference between GIS and PP GIS [8]

GIS	DIMENSION	PP GIS
Technology	*Focus*	People and technology
Facilitate official policy-making	*Goal*	Empower Communities
Rigid, hierarchical and bureaucratic	*Organisational structure*	Flexible and open
Specified by technologists and GIS experts	*Details*	Specified by users, focus groups
Led by independent specialists	*Applications*	Led by facilitators, group leaders
General, multipurpose applications	*Functions*	Specific, project-level activities
Top-down	*Approach*	Bottom-up

We are particularly interested in the differences between 'classical' GIS and PP GIS, how PP GIS applications differ from the classical GIS applications and what makes them so special. Kyem [8] summarises the topology of differences between GIS and PP GIS. We have modified these differences in table 1. In Kyem's approach the technology becomes an integral part of the bottom-up spatial decision-making process. This approach differs from Schroeder's [11] view who suggests GIS to be employed by interests groups to support the official policy-making interest and to empower the process as such and the participants in the decision-making.

2.2 Interactivity of PP GIS Applications

Interactivity implies that some action of the user generates a response either from another human being at the other end of the connection or from a program or application residing on a computer. In the framework of a PP GIS application interactivity refers to the user's interaction with the application [4], [7] using a computer. In our analysis, we refer to the e-participation ladder after Smyth [13] that we modified for our analysis. The e-participation ladder provides a structured overview of different forms of online participation and focuses particularly on the degree of interactivity. We distinguish between the following four stages of interactivity:

Information Delivery
At the bottom stage of the ladder, participation exists in an entirely passive mode and can be described as "the public right to know". This stage represents the delivery of online services to the user in one-way direction and has some sort of informative status for the users. The users can extract geographic information by using the PP GIS application and the data stored in the database.

Online Discussion
In this stage, the participation has a higher degree of interactivity which is achieved through the two-way exchange of information and the participant's suggestions and comments. This stage includes online discussions among the participants, planning offices and planning authorities. The participants can, for example, write an email to the planning office in which they attach a specific map extent and write their suggestions and comments in an e-mail. The possibility of drawing changes on a map is not included in this stage.

Map-Based Discussion
PP GIS applications that correspond to this stage provide the user with the possibility of communication on the basis of an online map. The participants can graphically express suggestions for changes or can make comments on specific objects in the selected map. A PP GIS application and its specific tools enable the participants to send their personal map version together with annotations or additional material to the planning authorities. This level of participation uses maps as a communication tool. Participants send their suggestions to the responsible persons, but are not actively involved in the decision-making process through iterative processes or feedback-loops.

Involvement in Decision-Making
In the highest stage of the ladder participants can actively contribute to the decision-making process and participate in the final planning processes and, consequently, in the decision making. An example of such decision-making process is voting for the most suitable alternative or predefined planning scenario. An example would be the case where the planning office presents alternative locations for bus stations to the citizens who can then vote for the most needed and desirable location. The location for the bus station that gets the most votes is then finally selected by the planning office and included in the plan.

2.3 GIS Functionalities Included in PP GIS Applications

PP GIS applications include different GIS functionalities ranging from basic operations such as zoom, pan, copy and paste themes between views, spatial queries or simple calculations to more complex operations such as 3D visualisation or statistic calculations. Some GIS operations also allow for "personalized views" of the data sets and enable the user to access information on specific topics.

The GIS functionalities explained in this chapter are standard in all GIS and are usually needed for PP GIS applications. They present a core subset of basic GIS functionalities and they serve as a benchmark for the selected online PP GIS applications.

Topological Overlay
A geographical information system is traditionally organized in different layers. Examples of such layers are land use, soil hydrology, streets, and buildings. Different layers can then be combined in a customised map. Topological overlay is an analysis procedure for determining the spatial coincidence of geographic features presented in the layers integrated in a GIS.

Information Retrieval
In a GIS, graphic data are related to the attribute data describing their characteristics. Attribute data can be a qualitative description of the object or a number describing the features of the object. With a simple mouse click on a spatial element the user may retrieve attribute data about the selected object. Such queries are basic functionalities of standard GIS. Their results are being displayed on the screen and, for instance, selected objects or data may be highlighted using a specific colour.

Query
Performing a query implies that the user can retrieve the data according to the related terms, phrases or features chosen. The GIS displays the data that match the respective query and highlight them in the resulting map using specific colours or symbols.

Data Selection
Data selection tool enables the user to select spatial objects on the specified thematic data layer. This function is used for instance if the participant submits a comment related to the object or perhaps question the characteristics of the selected object.

Zoom and Pan
The zooming buttons within a GIS usually show zoom in (a +) or zoom out (a –) symbol. Even occasional Internet users are familiar with enlargement or shrinking of map extents in applications like route planning systems. These tools enable the users to change their view and the level of detail by clicking on a location or by dragging a box to define a particular extent. With the pan functionality they can move the map on the screen into the position they like focusing on the part of the map that is of interest to them.

Distance Measure
The distance measure function enables the user e.g. to measure the distance between two locations or the total distance of a route, with multiple stops. The calculation is performed in the background and the result of the measurement is displayed on the map or underneath.

3 Analysis Framework and First Results

The analysis is three-tiered. First we selected twelve online PP GIS examples which were accessible and operational at the time of our survey. The second step was the definition of the following analysis criteria: interactivity, visualisation, usability, and GIS functionalities. We designed a questionnaire and interviewed a group of experts by concentrating on visualisation and usability criteria. First results of these interviews were documented in a recent paper [12]. Here, we concentrate on the interactivity aspect and the GIS functionalities.

3.1 Selected Online PP GIS Applications

Table 2 shows twelve selected currently available online PP GIS applications which we have found on the Internet. The first seven were developed in US, the following three in UK and the last two in Germany.

Table 2. Online PP GIS applications

	Project name	*Internet Link*
US1	Pilsen Project – Urban Design Visualization of Pilsen	http://www.evl.uic.edu/sopark/new/RA/#sub1
US2	Orange County Interactive Mapping, developed by the city of Orlando – Florida	http://www.cityoforlando.net/public_works/esd/gis/interactive_mapping.htm
US3	Resource Management Mapping Service	http://space1.itcs.uiuc.edu/website/rmms/
US4	Wyoming Oil and Gas Resource Assessment Mapper	http://wogra.wygisc.uwyo.edu/wyoims2/wims2awogra.html
US5	Erie International Airport	http://gis.csengineers.com/erie/viewer.htm
US6	Town of Clover Planning Analyst	http://www.lic.wisc.edu/clover_web/history_bkgrnd.htm
US7	I-map Delaware River Basin	http://bassriver.state.nj.us/imap_delbasin/
UK1	Virtual Slaithwaite Project	http://www.ccg.leeds.ac.uk/slaithwaite/
UK2	Bradford Community Statistics Project	http://www.bcsp-web.org/mapguide_site/maingeo.cfm
UK3	"Openspace" of Salford University	http://www.ties.salford.ac.uk/pg/xiao/openspace-main.html
DE1	„Bürgerbeteiligung Online" – landscape plan Königslutter	http://thuja.land.uni-hannover.de/entera/mapserv.phtml
DE2	„Vernetzter Bebauungsplan" – Landkreis Freising	http://fs.mapsailor.de

The *Pilsen Project* was initiated by the University of Illionis at Chicago and community leaders of the Pilsen community. Within this project the resources of a Geographical Information System were combined with the talents of a graphic artist. *Orange County Interactive Mapping* is an application which was developed by the city of Orlando. *The Resource Management Mapping Service* is a project developed by the College of Agricultural, Consumer and Environmental Sciences. The application is based on ESRI technology using ArcIMS 4.0. The *Wyoming Oil and Gas Resource* Assessment (WOGRA) is an interagency project with the intention to provide information oil and gas resources throughout Wyoming. The company C&S developed *Erie International Airport.* This is a facilitated public involvement approach to environmental and community decision. The *Town of Clover* project wants to support managed residential development that will meet the town's future housing needs. The results of this public participation process are published on the

Internet. *I-Map Delaware River Basin* is an interactive mapping application that gives responses to basic questions of the users about recreational activities in the Basin area. *Virtual Slaithwaite* is one of the most often quoted PP GIS applications. This project was developed by the School of Geography, University of Leeds. It is a model application for public participation in urban planning. The system is based on the open source Java mapping toolkit GeoTools. The *Bradford Community Statistics Project* provides us with statistical information about the community Bradford. *Openspace* PP GIS application developed by Salford University uses a 3D model for the visualisation of the environment. It is created with the adoption of the virtual reality modelling language (VRML) and Java programming languages. One of the two German examples is the *Interactive landscape plan Königslutter* which was developed by two private companies in cooperation with the University of Hannover. The State of Bavaria, Germany, supported the *Landkreis Freising* to publish a set of development plans on the Internet.

3.2 How Interactive Are PP GIS Applications?

In our analysis of interactivity we use the concept of the e-participation ladder as explained above and apply it to the criterion interactivity (figure 1). The following three applications offer one-way communication: *Erie International Airport, I-Map Delaware* and the *Bradford Community Statistics Project.* They serve as examples for the lowest stage of the ladder. Erie International Airport allows users to view maps of proposed projects, letting nearby residents to see how their properties might be affected. This means that the users are able to observe different planning scenarios, but they are not able to make comments on them. *I-Map Delaware* and *Bradford Community Statistics Project* are simple information systems with no opportunity for the users to take part in the participation process. In this stage of the ladder we could include also numerous GIS applications which simply deliver geoinformation to the users and help them to improve their decision-making processes. A huge number of such applications can be found on the Internet. Most of them are webmapping applications based on the popular ArcIMS map server. In all these examples, the users do not have the possibility to actively contribute to the planning decisions. The applications lack two-way communication and do not allow the users of the application to comment on specific decisions or suggestions presented online on a map.

The majority of the analysed PP GIS applications sample falls into the stages online discussion or map-based discussion. Online discussion level of interactivity is included in five analysed online PP GIS applications. *Orange County Interactive Mapping* offers the opportunity to define user specific areas on which comments can be stated into the map. The result can be mailed in a form of an attached .pdf file to the Orange County Board of County Commissioners. The "*Resource Management Mapping Service*" application allows the users to write comments into the map and mail then a specific map extent to anybody they want to. "*Landkreis Freising – Vernetzter Bebauungsplan*" provides development plans where the participants can have a look at the actual stock and also on the planning proposal. If they want to make comments on the plans, they have the possibility to write a standard e-mail. *Wyoming Oil and Gas Resource Assessment Mapper* and the *Town of Clover Planning Analyst* also offer the possibility to express opinions in form of e-mails.

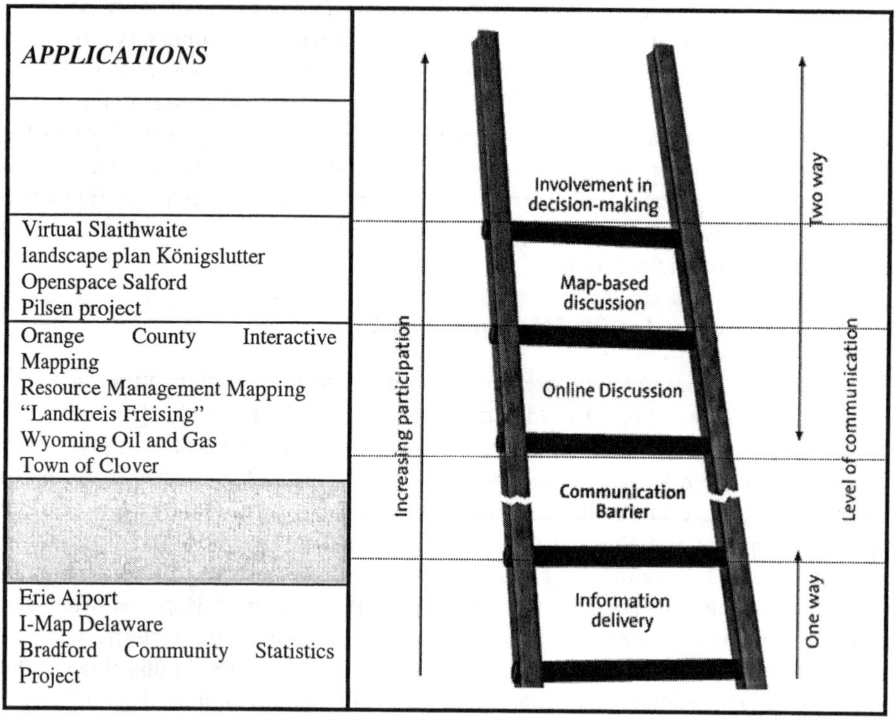

Fig. 1. Interactivity of the selected PP GIS applications

Map-based discussion is provided within four of the selected PP GIS applications. The *Virtual Slaithwaite* application enables the participants in planning to write their own ideas in a separate window on the basis of selected features and then submit them to the responsible persons. "*Openspace*" of Salford University lets the user either walk or fly through the virtual city. The application enables exploration of different viewpoints and walking speeds. The participant can also submit a comment at any spatial location. Within the application *Landscape plan Königslutter* the users can work on self-defined map extents which means that they can draw polygons into the map, comment the planning situation and send their opinion and analysis results to the planning authority. Although only parts of the *Pilsen project* are realized by now, we were able to classify the project regarding a project description of Al-Kodmany [1]. This project allowed participants to truly participate in designing revitalization projects in their neighbourhood.

3.3 Which GIS Functionalities Are Included in PP GIS Applications?

Table 3 shows the results of the GIS functionality analysis for the selected online PP GIS applications. Vertical column include topological overlay, query, information retrieval, data selection, zoom and pan, and distance measure function. Vertical columns represent the PP GIS applications from table 2. "x" implies that a particular PP GIS application offers the respective GIS operation.

Table 3. GIS operations included in PP GIS applications

	US 1	*US 2*	*US 3*	*US 4*	*US 5*	*US 6*	*US 7*	*UK 1*	*UK 2*	*UK 3*	*DE 1*	*DE 2*
Topological overlay		x	x	x	x		x		x		x	x
Query		x	x				x					
Information retrieval		x	x	x	x		x				x	
Data selection		x	x				x	x	x			
Zoom and Pan		x	x		x		x	x	x	x	x	x
Distance measure		x	x				x					x

Only three applications include all six GIS functionality categories identified in this paper. These PP GIS applications are the *Resource Management Mapping Service* (US1) application, the *Orange County Interactive Mapping application* (US3) and the *I-Map Delaware River Basin* (US7). This type of application provides general GIS functions like zoom and pan or the user is able to identify objects and to query the attributes of the respective object. Basic navigation functions like zoom and pan are included in all analysed applications but only these three applications provide the powerful "Query" functionality. The *Pilsen project* and the *Town of Clover Planning Analyst* have not been considered in this analysis, because the *Pilsen project* was not consistently available online throughout the analysis and the *Planning Analyst* was not categorized as to be an online GIS application.

We conclude that nearly all selected online PP GIS applications fulfil primary functions like topological overlay and navigation functions, but most of them lack querying, selecting and identifying options. The majority of applications do not provide attribute information to their users. In the next step of our analysis we will link the interactivity and GIS functionalities criteria and observe the complexity of PP

GIS applications and how it is related to the use in a practical participatory process. This will enable us to study the relation between the needs for interaction and the number of GIS functionalities.

4 Conclusions and Further Work

In general, we can conclude that currently available PP GIS applications vary strongly concerning their included GIS functionalities and their complexity. Basedow [2] observes that the selection of the GIS functionalities in a PP GIS application depends very much on the application area and the software that is used for the development of the application. A potential danger is that if the GIS functionalities increase in a PP GIS application, also the complexity of a system may increase. High complexity of an application might prevent elderly and less computer skilled people from using it. The range of computer skills of the participants is probably the most important factor for a PP GIS user's requirements analysis [7]. The complexity also strongly depends on the nature of the decision-making process itself and related possible level of interactivity. Technically, PP GIS applications can be designed in a relatively simple way in the cases of one-way communication where the planning authority only informs the participating people about the planned actions. Complexity and needed GIS functionalities is higher in the cases of map-based discussion and involvement in decision-making. There is a lack of practical, user-based testing of such applications where a minimum set of needed GIS functionalities can be defined and tested. Further development of PP GIS applications should be based on the principles of intelligent user interfaces and decision making support systems that offer personalized information and the possibility of communication with the citizens.

Our research dealt in the first step with the comparison of selected online PP GIS applications. The results of our study are partially presented in this paper. The next activities include the development of an online web-based PP GIS application for a study case in the Salzburg region where public participation is needed. We will intensively deal with the user requirements and the usability of a user friendly PP GIS application. We will analyze novel visualization techniques and innovative spatio-temporal communication approaches. Our planned research projects will include different types of media such as outdoor touch screen installations and for example collaborative planning meetings that are monitored with videos or sketch map techniques. Within the evaluation phase these applications will be tested by a large number of expert and non-expert users. We will also analyze sociological issues that are closely related to map-based online public participation with the focus on user-based testing and recommendations for user friendly PP GIS applications.

References

1. Al-Kodmany K., (1999): Combining Artistry and Technology in Participatory Community Planning, Berkely Planning Journal 13, p. 28-36
2. Basedow S., (2001): Web-basierte GIS Funktionalitäten für die Öffentlichkeitsbeteiligung in Planungsverfahren, Diplomarbeit im Fachbereich Geowissenschaften der Westfälischen Wilhelms-Universität Münster, 79 pages

3. Chrisman N.R., (1997): Exploring Geographic Information Systems, New York
4. Chua Y. L. (2002): Data Intermediation and Beyond: How the Web modifies the Dissemination of GIS Information, online located at: http://www.urisa.org/PPGIS/2002/papers/SWong.pdf
5. Craig W.J., T.M. Harris and D. Weiner (Eds., 2002): Community Participation and Geographic Information Systems, Taylor & Francis, London.
6. Haklay M. and C. Tobón, (2003): Usability Engineering and PP GIS: towards a Learning-improving Cycle, online located at: http://www.casa.ucl.ac.uk/muki/pdf/Haklay-Tobon-URISA-PPGIS.pdf
7. Kingston et al., (1999): Virtual Decision Making in Spatial Planning: Web-based Geographical Information Systems for Public Participation in Environmental Decision Making, online located at: http://www.geog.leeds.ac.uk/papers/99-9/index.html
8. Kyem P.A.K., (2000): Embedding GIS applications into resource management and planning activities of local and indigenous communities: a desirable innovation or a destabilizing enterprise? online located at: http://www.socsci.umn.edu/~bongman/gisoc99/new/kyem.htm.
9. Pleizier I. et al, (2004): Using virtual reality as information tool in spatial planning. In: Proceed. EuroConference on methods to support interaction in geovisualisation environments
10. Sadagopan G., (2000): Web-based Geographic Information Systems. Public Participation in Virtual Decision Making Environments, online located at: http://scholar.lib.vt.edu/theses/available/etd-05232000-11100031/unrestricted/MajorPaper.pdf
11. Schroeder P., (1996): Report on Public Participation GIS Workshop. NCGIA Technical Report 96-97, Scientific Report for Initiative 19 Specialist Meeting
12. Steinmann R., Krek A. and Blaschke T., (2004): Analysis of online public participatory GIS applications with respect to the differences between the US and Europe, UDMS, Chioggia, online located at: http://map3.salzburgresearch.at/research_publications.html
13. Smyth E., (2001): Would the Internet widen public participation?, unpublished master thesis, University of Leeds
14. Talen E., (1999): Constructing Neighbourhoods from the Bottom Up: the Case for Resident Generated GIS, Environment and Planning B, 26, p. 533-55

Interactive Tools for e-Democracy: Examples from Switzerland

Jean-Loup Chappelet and Pierre Kilchenmann

IDHEAP Swiss Graduate School of Public Administration,
21 Route de la Maladière,
CH-1022 Chavannes-Lausanne, Switzerland
{Jean-Loup.Chappelet, Pierre.Kilchenmann}@idheap.unil.ch

Abstract. Democracy is based on freedom of voting but also on meaningful discussions about matters that are put to the vote or about people who wish to be elected. E-democracy cannot therefore be reduced to e-voting. It should also include Internet-based services that facilitate online interaction between voters, candidates and supporters of various opinions. This paper presents a series of interactive tools that can be used to support such a virtual dialogue. A matrix is proposed to categorize these tools. Examples of such tools used in Switzerland are given. The most sophisticated tools and websites recently developed for Swiss elections or referendums are described in some detail. Possible future research on the impact of these tools is outlined.

1 Introduction

Many lay discussions and scientific papers about e-democracy have concentrated on the various forms of e-voting, and in particular, remote e-voting i.e. an Internet-based form of voting by using a computer that is not under the physical control of election officials (Alvarez & Hall 2004). In fact, e-voting is only one of the three steps in the electronically supported democratic process. There is a post-voting step in which results can be quickly published and discussed on the Internet, and there should be a pre-voting step whereby citizens can find information on the Web about the issues and candidates on which they are called upon to vote, electronically or otherwise. This paper concentrates on the pre-voting phase (Kies & Kriesi 2004) and its recent Internet developments in Switzerland, a country where many matters are put to the vote four times a year at all three levels of government (so-called direct democracy), in addition to regular or exceptional elections of executive and legislative bodies. Switzerland is also one of the few countries where e-voting experiments have been actively pursued by the Federal government and some cantons (Chancellerie fédérale 2004).

Within this pre-voting phase, it is possible to distinguish two stages (Figure 1) if we consider e-democracy as a subcategory of e-government and if we refer to the traditional three-stage model of e-government: publication, interaction, transaction (see for example Dempsey, 2003). The transaction stage corresponds to e-voting itself, which involves the same technical difficulties as other online services requiring

M. Böhlen et al. (Eds.): TCGOV 2005, LNAI 3416, pp. 36 – 47, 2005.

high security (identification, authentication, etc). The publication stage consists of the Web posting of data, information and documents about matters submitted to voting. It also includes the publication of detailed results after (e-)voting (the post-voting step mentioned above). The interaction stage consists of all possible Internet-mediated communications between the citizen who will eventually vote and those publishing information about voting matters. Research has been carried out on this stage (sometime referred as e-engagement or e-participation) especially in the United Kingdom (e.g. Kearns et al. 2002).

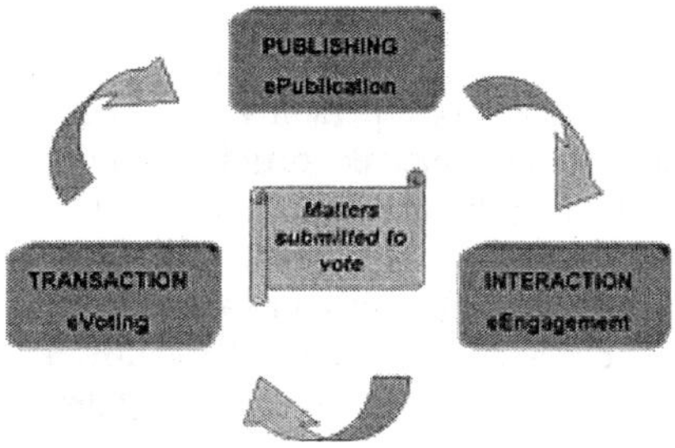

Fig. 1. Three stages of e-democracy

The potential of online communication and interaction for changing offline politics has been recognized by several authors (e.g. Rushkoff 2003, Gibson et al 2004, Jeitziner 2004). This paper will present an overview of the voting assistance tools phenomenon, and will attempt to categorize these tools according to their sophistication and type of authors / publishers.

The paper is organized as follows: Section 2 presents the three main political actors who can offer voting assistance tools for an interaction with the citizen on electoral matters (2.1). It outlines the various Internet-based tools and techniques available for such a purpose (2.2). A matrix is proposed to categorize these tools, and presents examples of voting assistance tools recently used in Switzerland (2.3). Section 3 describes, in some detail, the most sophisticated tools offered on non-volatile Swiss websites from different types of actors. In the conclusion, the possible effects of these tools are outlined and further research is proposed.

2 Voting Assistance Tool Functionalities and Actors

We first describe the political actors able to provide these tools on their websites and then the Internet-based functionalities that can be put to use.

2.1 Actors

It is necessary to distinguish three main political actors: governments, advocates and third parties.

Governments. The executive and legislative bodies (and the judicial sphere in some countries where judges are elected) are obviously involved in electoral and voting matters. They can present their views on these matters in an interactive way in order to supplement the purely informative approach used by most of them today on their official websites. All levels can be involved: local, regional, national and even international as some e-votes have been organized at world level by international organizations such as ICANN (Internet Corporation for Assigned Names and Numbers) (Ahlert 2003). Governments can only take an (online) official position (e.g. in a referendum) or no position at all (e.g. in a parliamentary election), but this position can lend to some interaction with the citizens.

Advocates. This category of actors includes all those who take a clear stand for or against a matter that is put to vote or a person who is seeking to be elected. It includes candidates for election, (already) elected officials, political parties, factions, action committees for or against a particular vote, unions, NGOs, etc. Some of these persons or organizations have permanent websites; others have a web presence that is limited to the period prior to the vote and that disappears shortly afterwards, making it more difficult to study. Easy access to the Internet has allowed previously obscure advocates or opponents to convey their views to wider audiences in ways that are at times highly innovative and interactive.

Third Parties. In this category of actors, we place all the observers, commentators and researchers who provide websites dealing totally or partially with matters put to votes or candidates seeking to be elected. Third parties include online media, regular media with websites, independent organizations and individuals, many of them political scholars who conduct experiments and surveys. Most of the time, third parties have a neutral position concerning the vote, although they can sometimes indicate a preference (in particular the media, via editorials). The third parties' websites are often volatile, since many are only experimental or do not have an archive section.

2.2 Functionalities

Because interaction can be considered as a continuum between information and transaction, it is possible to list the voting assistance tool functionalities from the least to the most interactive ones, i.e. from games to simulations.

Games are proposed to citizens to complement a purely informative website and to offer them an entertaining way of discovering facts about a matter to be voted on or the voting process itself. Sometimes, they take the form of an e-learning tool. The interaction is built into the tool and the netizen has little leeway except to choose between predefined options by clicking on some buttons or boxes. The tool returns some kind of predefined "answer". An example is the quiz that was proposed by the European Union and partners for the European Parliament elections of 2004 (www.europaquiz.org).

E-mail is an obvious way of providing citizens with the means to interact with governments, advocates or third parties. Most of these political actors' websites do provide one or more e-mail addresses to send a personal question or comment, although a response is never guaranteed. Sometimes this form of interaction simply serves to build a data base of constituents' e-mails. Bill Clinton, as President of the United States, is arguably the first head of State to have interacted with his electors through e-mail (president@whitehouse.gov). It is said that a large staff at the White House was recruited to answer his e-mails in a personalized way. Recently, the European Commission upgraded its "Dialogue with Citizens" service. Users can now obtain personalized help in any of the 20 official languages by e-mailing services such as "Europe Direct" and "Citizens Signpost service" (IDA 2004).

Forums and Web "blogs" go a step further than e-mails. The questions or comments sent by citizens can be seen by all those who consult the website hosting a particular forum. These users can in turn post their own answers and remarks. Political and also other forums have been known to attract unsuitable comments (racist, sexual, etc.) and must usually be moderated if the website owner does not want to be held responsible. Forums can be organised by topics structuring the debate about political issues put to vote, and are thus a form of (asynchronous) dialogue between citizens. The Suffolk Online Project, within the British Wired up Communities pilot projects, is a well known example of how a forum can be organized for democratic discussions of political issues (Hansard Society 2002). Web logs or "blogs" (online journals) are a more recent form of interaction. During the American elections of November 2004, the phenomenon of blogs rose to become one of the major opinion making factors. Both presidential candidates had their own official blogs and many unofficial ones (www. watchblog.com). The fact that many moderators of these blogs at times obtained the same status as journalists shows the impact of this upcoming information channel.

Chats are basically synchronous forums. They have been used more rarely than forums for voting matters, for example in Sweden (Rosen 2001). They provide a higher level of interaction although a very ephemeral one. A moderator is almost indispensable. In 2002, Telecom Austria invited politicians for a "special Election 2002" chat on its website (Pressetext Schweiz 2002). A current example is the website of the European Union (www.europa.eu.int/comm/chat/index_en.htm) which offers a server for chatting in 11 languages of the European Union and proposes transcripts of previous chats. SMSs can also be considered as a type of chat; they have been used by parties to urgently call back their members for a parliamentary vote, and by radio and TV shows to let their audience interact with a live political debate.

Polls about issues to be voted on can be a very effective form of interaction if their results are continuously provided online, meaning that the netizen can see the influence of his/her vote. They require the completion of an online form with at least one question, but often have several. Such polls by questionnaire have no scientific validity, as they are usually not based on a representative panel of citizens who can vote. They have been known to be prone to "hijacking" by advocates. The Webocrat system developed within the EC-funded 5th Framework Programme includes polling and forum functionalities (www.webocrat.org). Polls can sometimes take the form of rating devices for elected officials, or markets for pending elections. The Iowa Electronic Markets are a sophisticated example of this peculiar type of polls (www.biz.uiowa.edu/iem).

Simulation tools are so far the most sophisticated form of interaction that can be provided on the Internet for citizens who wish to see the effect of their vote on their own particular situation (on fiscal matters for example). They sometimes try to match voters' political opinions with candidates' positions. Simulation tools allow for innovative ways of selecting candidates, because they provide the possibility of scanning candidates and parties more systematically and choosing those that are the closest to the voter's own political preferences, beyond party affiliation or single issue position. A precursor of this type of tool was in 1998: the "Stemwijzer" in the Netherlands (www.votingindicator.net). This functionality has also been experimented with in other countries such as Austria (www.wahlkabine.at), Germany (www.wahl.o-mat.de), Sweden (Aidemak 2003) and the USA (www.vote-smart.org).

2.3 Actor-Functionality Matrix

An actor-functionality matrix can help clarify the already crowded field of voting assistance tools. It is filled with Swiss examples (table 1), some of which are briefly described below. The examples marked in bold are discussed in section 3.

Table 1. Examples of Swiss interactive political websites (Autumn 2004)

	Governments	*Advocates*	*Third parties*
Games	**www.parlament.ch (>CiviCampus)**	www.postfueralle.ch	www.lacourseauconseilfederal .com
E-mail	**www.parlament.ch** www.calmy-rey.admin.ch	**www.prd.ch** www.gruene.ch www.olivierfeller.ch www.zisyadis.ch	www.infrarouge.tsr.ch www.rsr.ch (>Programmes >Forums)
Forums & Blogs	**www.parlament.ch**	**www.radical.ch/forum** www.rene-vaudroz.ch www.postfueralle.ch	www.infrarouge.tsr.ch forum.swissinfo.org/swiss-abroad www.fimm.ch www.freegoat.org
Chats	www.edi.admin.ch (with Swiss President)	www.fdp-live.ch	
Polls		www.blocher.ch **www.prd.ch** www.pssuisse.ch	www.24heures.ch/home/agora www.swisspolitics.org **www.politarena.ch** www.wahlen.ch
Simulation	www.calcul-impot.ch	www.avs-oui.ch www.non-au-paquet-fiscal.ch	www.candidats.ch **www.smartvote.ch** **www.parlarating.ch** www.comparis.ch

In the **games** category, a good example is the website of those in favour of the Swiss post initiative (www.postfueralle.ch) which proposed a Pac-Man type of game in which the player had to "eat" positive votes without being captured by the ghosts (Figure 2). The end score shows how many votes the player obtained. Although the game is not directly trying to convince the player to vote in favour of the initiative, the netizen might remember having enjoyed it, and at the end of the day, this may influence his or her voting behaviour. Another example of the game category is the politician's puzzle offered on www.swisspolitics.org (Figure 2).

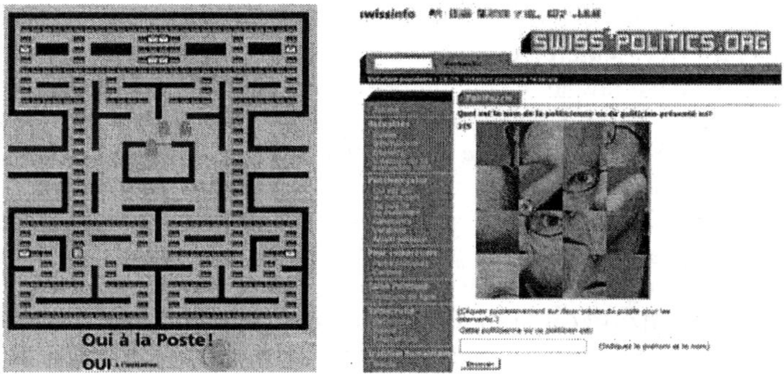

Fig. 2. "Pac-Man": www.postfueralle.ch and « Puzzle »: www.swisspolitics.org

Another noteworthy website that can be classified under the games category was created for the election of the Federal Council (Swiss Government) on 10 December 2003 (see Figure 3). This game permitted netizens to "vote" for Federal ministers, although in reality, only members of Parliament can vote. The principle was similar to a stock exchange; each candidate for the Federal Council represented a company with shares. The share quotation was based on factors such as popularity surveys or number of public debates. Netizens could buy or sell shares with virtual money by following their "broker instinct" (cf. www.lacourseauconseilfederal.com [the race for the Federal Government]).

Fig. 3. www.lecourseauconseilfederal.com

At least one **e-mail** address is present on most Swiss political websites to provide the netizen with some opportunity for communication. Whether mail sent to these addresses is answered is another matter. A quick survey of the websites of the candidates for the Federal elections in October 2003 has shown that most of them do not answer, or only do so after a long delay (Seydtaghia 2004). Almost all members of the Federal parliament have a published e-mail address (often in the form: firstname.surname@parl.ch) and about 30% have a website (Chappelet 2004). This is also the case for the 7 members of the Federal Council. E-mail is also used more and more by the media to let the audience directly interact in talk shows, and in addition to the telephone. The Infrarouge@tsr.ch (television) or Forums@rsr.ch (radio) addresses are two examples among many others.

Forums and "blogs" are another asynchronous way of exchanging and communicating on voting matters. Forums have been initiated, with limited success, by the Swiss Parliament (NZZ 2002) or by regional governments (e.g. the Canton of Vaud which was forced to close its forum in 1998 following racist comments). This functionality is much more widely featured on the websites of advocates or third parties. Nearly all the Swiss parties and initiative committees have a permanent forum on their website. The forums set up by initiative committees only exist during the few months preceding the vote (e.g. www.postfueralle.ch for the maintenance of post offices in all communes, or www.oeuvres-sociales-sures.ch against improved maternity insurance). Some politicians have their own forums (e.g. MP Vaudoz's forum in Figure 4). Radio and television websites usually feature forums related to their political debates or talk-shows (e.g. Infrarouge.tsr.ch). There are also websites powered by media companies (e.g. forum.swissinfo.org/swissabroad). Concerning "blogs", the discussions generated by this type of communication is usually more fragmented than in forums and the sense of community between netizens and public officials is seldom existent (cf. www.freegoat.org).

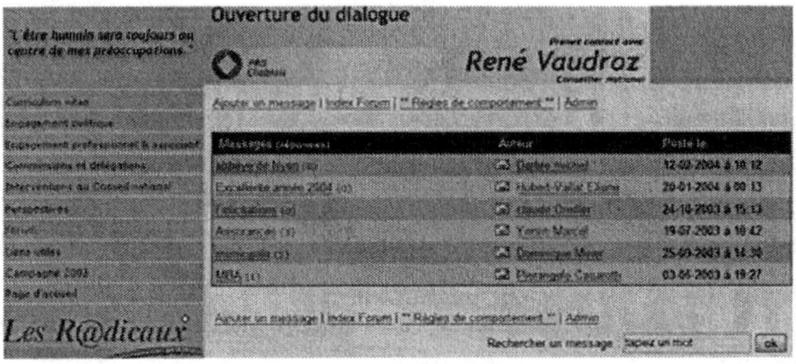

Fig. 4. An MP's forum at www.rene-vaudroz.ch

Chats provide synchronous interaction between netizens, but are rarely used in Swiss political debates. One of the first experiences of this functionality in Switzerland was a one-hour chat with the President of the Swiss Confederation in 1999. For 60 minutes, President Ruth Dreifuss had the opportunity to answer more than 300 questions from citizens (NZZ 1999). On 23 June 2001, the Liberal Democratic Party (FDP) organized its first "e-Party Day". During that day, an *ad hoc* website proposed forums and chats with FDP politicians (NZZ 2001). Radio and television rarely use chats because they could compete with their own live talk shows.

Polls are often used in political websites with the exception of those initiated by governments, which must refrain from influencing final results with intermediate predictions. One of the first Swiss politicians to introduce a poll on his website was Christoph Blocher, who is now a member of the Federal Government (www.blocher.ch). It consisted of a simple monthly question to be answered by yes or no. The permanent online outcome was shown by using a thumb pointed either up or down. Political parties also use online polls to evaluate the trends of public opinion. Newspapers often propose sophisticated polls with several questions on their homepage. The Lausanne-based daily "24 heures" used weekly polls to address local questions. In April 2004, it launched an online poll about the reintroduction of marks in Cantonal schools, a hot political topic at the time and the subject of a Cantonal initiative. Those in favour of not reintroducing marks voted heavily in this poll and biasedits outcome. After this experience, the daily decided to stop its political polls (Moginier 2004). Another interesting interactive tool is www.wahlen.ch, which polls many pending national voting items and shows the current results online. This third party website even proposes contests to guess the result of real votes (e.g. which party will win the Cantonal elections in Basel in October 2004?).

Simulations have been used on Swiss websites since 1999 to compare insurance and banking services (www.comparis.ch is the most well known of these sites). Such a functionality has now been introduced for political matters. Comparis.ch used its simulation engine to help voters compute the rent they would pay if a new law was accepted by popular vote in February 2004. (It was refused.) For the May 2004 votes, a website was created in support of a change to the Swiss pension system (www.avs-oui.ch). Citizens had the opportunity to simulate their pension at retirement age, with or without the proposed modifications to the system. (The change was refused.)

Simulation tools are rarely created by governments. A rare example is the website provided to calculate one's income tax if a 2003 proposal by the Swiss government was accepted. The netizen had to introduce different variables such as income, number of children and marital status (Figure 5). Within seconds, the screen displayed the tax to be paid with the existing and proposed systems.

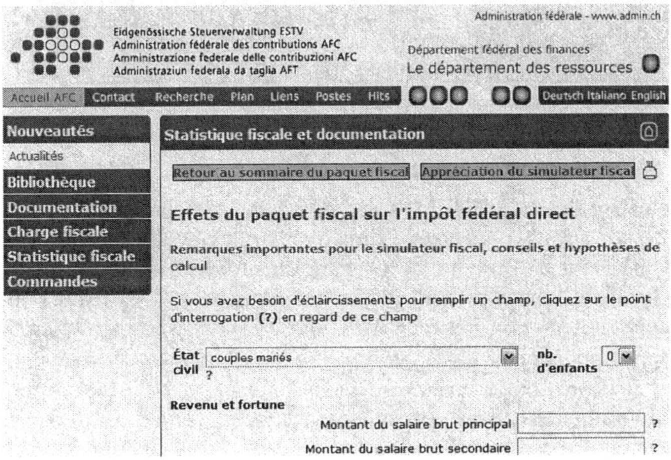

Fig. 5. www.calcul-impot.ch

3 Analysis of Some Swiss Websites with Voting Assistance Tools

We shall now describe some of the permanent Swiss websites that feature several voting assistance tools and that are published by different types of political actors.

3.1 Parlament.ch

The portal of the Swiss Parliament (two legislative chambers) aims at providing both MPs and citizens with information about the Federal legislative process. Its main interactive functionalities are: game, e-mail and forum.

The **game** category is represented by an e-learning application entitled "Civi-Campus". Switzerland being a direct democracy, its citizens not only elect the

Parliament, but also vote on matters such as amendments to the constitution, initiatives (proposals for a new legal feature) or referendums (against a law voted by Parliament). CiviCampus is a simple and fast way to refresh knowledge or to learn about the basic political rights of a Swiss citizen, and is available in French, German and Italian (Figure 6).

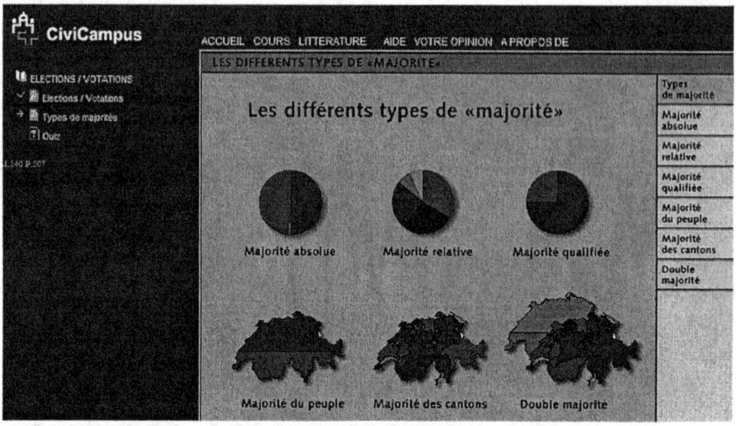

Fig. 6. www.parlament.ch ("CiviCampus")

The **e-mail** addresses of all MPs are provided in alphabetical or Cantonal order. These addresses are also accessible directly by clicking on the MP's name when it appears in the Official Bulletin of the Parliament which records (in text, voice and video form) all the speeches held in the two chambers. This feature of the Official Bulletin invites interaction between MPs and citizens, who can voice their opinions after having read or heard an MP's comments. But it is not well known.

The first **forum** offered on the Swiss Parliament website (about the adhesion of Switzerland to the UN) was a resounding success. Over 300 contributions were posted, many addressed to or written by elected officials. The following forum (on abortion) was rather disappointing, with no more than 50 contributions. For the Parliament website, forums are an interesting form of communication, although not an entirely suitable one. The reason for this is simple: most Swiss MPs are not full time politicians, and hardly have time to answer all the comments received. The idea of continuing with forums on the Parliament website for important debates in the future is however being considered (Schaffner 2002).

3.2 Prd.ch

The website of the Liberal Democratic Party (LDP) aims at providing both members of the LDP and other citizens with all the information required for the political process, based on the point of view of this centre right party. Its main interactive functionalities are e-mail, forum and poll.

The LDP party can be contacted by **e-mail**, as can most of its cantonal sections and (elected) personnel through the website, which serves as an electronic directory.

The **forums** indirectly offered by the LDP national website are fragmented over the party's various Cantonal websites. The advantage of this fragmentation is that the local politicians can discuss locally relevant problems with the local netizens. These forums are organized by current political subjects, and moderators supervise the debates to avoid inappropriate comments.

The **poll** featured on the LDP website is a first in Switzerland. It allows global consultation of LDP members in order to define the future of the party (www.f.avenir-radical.ch). The consultation procedure was addressed primarily to the members of the party, but sympathizers or any other interested parties could participate. In two months, (21 June to 21 August 2004) two thousand people did so. 90% of those responding gave their opinion via the website. By the end of the poll, the party received more than 5,000 comments. The participants were given the possibility to appreciate the various party projects according to a scale ranging from 0 to 5 on the one hand and based on three criteria (important – right – liberal) on the other. The final results were presented at the party's national assembly and will be integrated in its vision statement.

3.3 Smartvote.ch

This website aims to provide citizens with all the information required to make an appropriate electoral choice. It has two main functions: the smartvote choice assistance tool itself (which is a simulation) and the myvote online choice tool (a poll).

Smartvote was the first national-scale system to give Swiss citizens the opportunity of comparing via the Internet their opinions with those of most candidates for the 2003 Federal elections. For Andreas Ladner, a political scientist, this system allows an individualisation of the vote and reduces the importance of the parties in the composition of electoral lists. In future, it could revolutionize election campaigns and the selection of the elected officials (Petignat 2003).

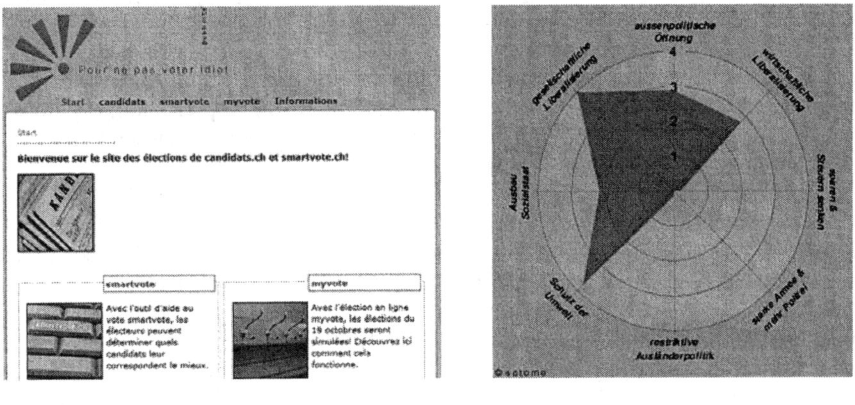

Fig. 7. www.smartvote.ch (Homepage and "smartspider")

Smartvote.ch has been online since 1 August 2003, and is also accessible through candidats.ch and myvote.ch. It allows the netizen to give his/her opinion on a number of political subjects, and in particular the fields of education, safety, health, environment or economy. The user can choose between the full version, which consists of 70 questions and takes about fifteen minutes to fill in, and a lighter version (24 questions, less than 5 minutes). The candidates for the Federal elections were asked to fill in the complete questionnaire and had to answer additional questions to reveal possible areas where their position differed from that of their party. After having filled in their questionnaires, netizens can then visualize, for each Canton and each chamber, a list of those candidates sharing more or less the same political views. A graph similar to a cobweb, named "smartspider", indicates exactly those domains for which the netizen and the candidate share opinions (figure 7).

The myvote displays the results of National Council and Council of States elections based on the netizen's online vote. The bank of candidates included almost all 3,000 candidates for both chambers in the 2003 elections.

Smartvote.ch has been generally praised as being a way of regenerating some debate. A few observers, however, have criticized it as an ersatz for real political debate, a little in the same way as the TV show "Loft Story" faked real life interactions (e.g. Zendali 2003).

4 Conclusion

The aim of this paper was to describe an emerging phenomenon in Switzerland, a country that prides itself on its direct democracy – a system that implies voting at least four times a year. It has provided an overview of the field of interactive tools for enhancing electoral choice and presented the most sophisticated tools, in particular those used in the Swiss Federal election year of 2003 and in 2004. The influence of such tools on voters' behavior and choice remains largely unknown. Do they increase citizens' participation? Do they incite them to vote, whether electronically or not? Do these tools make citizens decide differently from what their party affiliation would suggest? What are the consequences for the candidates and political parties? Have the quality of the opinion-forming process and the level of information among the electorate improved? Do such tools make politics more visible and thus lead to a new type of democracy wherein live discussions would be replaced by forms of virtual interaction?

It is also necessary to ensure that the interactive e-participation tools, and in particular online polls, strengthen rather than undermine the representative nature of modern democracy and do not replace this by a "government by referendums", even in Switzerland where "direct democracy" is sacred.

Empirically founded research is needed to explore all these issues, and to assess whether interactive tools constitute an opportunity or a threat for democracy as we know it. A first step would be to create an online observatory for such tools. However, as in the case of e-voting itself (e.g. Norris 2003), caution must certainly be taken regarding the great expectations which are placed by some authors on the phenomenon of voting assistance tools (e.g. Rushkoff 2003).

References

1. Ahlert C. (2003), Weltweite Wahlen im Internet: Möglichkeiten und Grenzen transnationaler Demokratie. Frankfurt: Campus Verlag.
2. Aidemak J. (2003), A Knowledge Perspective on E-Democracy. In: Traunmüller R. (Ed.): EGOV 2003, Berlin: Springer-Verlag, pp. 319-324.

3. Alvarez R. & Hall T. (2004), Point, Click, and Vote: The Future of Internet Voting. Washington DC: Brookings Institution Press.
4. Chancellerie fédérale (2004), Le vote électronique dans sa phase pilote, Bern.
5. Chappelet J.-L. (2004), The appropriation of e-mail and Internet by members of the Swiss Parliament. Information Polity, vol. 9, number 1-2, p. 89-102.
6. Christin T. & Trechsel A. (2004), Who votes via the Internet ? A scientific approach to polling in Carouge and Meyrin. Published at : http://edc.unige.ch (25.11.2004).
7. Dempsey J. (2003), How E-Government Interacts With Its Citizens. Published at http://www.worldbank.org/transitionnewsletter/janfebmar03/pgs39-41.htm (17.9.2004).
8. Gibson R., Römmele A. & Ward S. (eds) (2004), Electronic Democracy: Mobilisation and Participation Online. London: Routledge.
9. Hansard Society (2002). Published at www.intelligentcommunities.org.uk/edemocracy.
10. IDA (2004), European Commission upgrades "Dialogue with Citizens" service. IDA eGovernment Observatory News. http://europa.eu.int/ida/en/document/3265/194 (17.9.2004).
11. Jeitziner B. (2004), "Wahlen im Internetzeithalter: Informationsvermittler als politische Berater von Wählern und Politikern", in Perspektiven der Wirtschaftspolitik (Schaltegger C. & Schaltegger S, Hrsg), Zurich: vdf Hochschulverlag.
12. Kearns I., Bend J. & Stern B. (2002), e-participation in local government. London: PPG.
13. Kies R. & Kriesi H. (2004), "Designing Internet Voting: The Potential Impact of a Pre-Voting Public Sphere on Pre-Electoral Opinion Formation", in The European Union and E-voting (Trechsel A. & Mendez F., Eds), London: Routledge.
14. Moginier D. (2004), "L'école vaudoise tue le Coup de sonde", Lausanne: 24Heures, 13.3.04.
15. Norris P. (2003), Preaching to the Converted? Pluralism, Participation and Party Websites. Party Politics 9/1, p. 21-45.
16. NZZ (1999), Ausbau der Online-Dientse bei Parlament und Bund. www.nzz.ch (17.9.04).
17. NZZ (2001), Erster "E-Parteitag" in der Schweiz. www.nzz.ch (17.9.2004).
18. NZZ (2002), Internet-Diskussionsforum zur Uno. www.nzz.ch (17.9.2004).
19. NZZ (2002), Im Internet über Politik streiten. www.nzz.ch (17.9.2004).
20. Pressetext Schweiz (2002), Politiker chatten mit Rauch-Kallat am 15.11.2002. Published at: www.pressetext.ch/pte.mc?pte=021114023 (17.9.2004).
21. Petignat Y. (2003), Avec Smartvote.ch, votez futé aux élections fédérales. Genève : Le Temps, 21.9.2004.
22. Rosen T. (2001), E-democracy in practice: Swedish experiences of a new tool. Published at: www.svekom.se/skvad/E-democracy-en.pdf (17.9.2004).
23. Rouiller S. et al (2004), Wahlumfrage 2003: Eine Umfrage unter den Benutzerinnen und Benutzer der Online-Wahlhilfe „smartvote", Published at: www.politools.net (17.9.2004).
24. Rushkoff D. (2003), Open Source Democracy. London: Demos.
25. Schaffner D. (2002), Trotz positiver Erfahrung sollen auf der Website des eidg. Parlaments in Zukunft nur selten Diskussionen stattfinden, www.tagesanzeiger.ch (17.9.04).
26. Seydtaghia A. (2004), Peu interactifs, les sites Web des candidats serviraient-ils avant tout à flatter leur ego? www.letemps.ch (17.9.2004).
27. Waaijenberg A. (2003), "Wahlen im Internet: Das Ende der Qual der Wahl – die Wahlplattform smarvote.ch/kandidaten.ch", www.sgvw.ch (17.9.2004).
28. Zendali M. (2003), Le "Loft" fédéral, Lausanne: Le Matin, 24.08.2003.

"Public Budget Dialogue" – An Innovative Approach to E-Participation

Stefanie Roeder, Annika Poppenborg, Susanne Michaelis, Oliver Märker, and Stefan René Salz

Fraunhofer-Institute AIS,
Schloss Birlinghoven, D-53754 Sankt Augustin
{stefanie.roeder, annika.poppenborg, susanne.michaelis, oliver.maerker, stefan.salz}@ais.fraunhofer.de

Abstract. The potential of the internet has been recognised to enhance government initiated citizen communication. Despite limited experience so far, some lessons for designing online-participation have been learned: Ensuring the external and internal relevance of online consultation processes seems crucial. Some measurements to ensure the external and internal relevance will be set out in a description of an e-participation process in Esslingen, Germany, the first project to use web-based discussion forums as an instrument to inform and consult the public about the municipal budget.

1 Introduction

The discourse on the potential of e-government often focuses on the digital availability of municipal administrative processes and on the possibility to provide internet-based access to those processes. The internet is increasingly used as an instrument to inform the citizens about municipal affairs, based on a paradigm in which public administration is steadily transformed from a "service community" into a "citizen community". In addition to its potential to deliver information, the internet also offers new methods of engaging citizens in political discourse and especially of involving large numbers of relevant stakeholders into the discourse processes. While the potential benefits of the internet may have been recognised, little knowledge exists on how internet-based participation processes may be designed to tap its full potential. The Fraunhofer-Institute AIS developed a model for the design of successful internet-based participation. This paper illustrates the model on the basis of a case study in the city of Esslingen, Germany. The Esslingen case is doubly innovative: not only was the internet used for a public participation, but also was the topic 'public budget' an immensely complex subject for a discussion amongst the lay citizens. Critically assessing the case study, the model for successful internet-based participation will be used to highlight the measures to utilize the internet's full potential.

2 Benefits of Internet-Based Participation

In the context of e-democracy, the internet is often discussed as a tool for the 'direct and democratic' participation of citizens [1]. However, often these discussions revolve

M. Böhlen et al. (Eds.): TCGOV 2005, LNAI 3416, pp. 48–56, 2005.

around internet-based voting procedures or the availability of forms. Here, e-Participation is defined as *'the process, in which policy makers involve citizens via internet in preparing a decision. (...) Citizens' experience and expertise are used to generate knowledge in order to solve complex problems'* [2]. The underlying concept of e-participation presents internet-based participation as an offer rather than legislation. This is comparable to traditional informal consultations in which citizens are involved in the process of discussing, assessing and evaluating issues, but not in the decision itself.

For citizens, administration and politics, the benefit of participation is, that the citizens' insight into governmental processes can lead to stronger acceptance of political and administrative decisions. The acceptance of political decisions mainly increases, since citizens who are strongly involved in the decision making process are more likely to accept its outcomes.

Various advantages of internet-based participation methods and processes were identified by Wesselmann [3], Kubicek, Westholm and Wind [4] as well as Friedrichs, Hart and Schmidt [5]: The internet provides a low-barrier threshold and offers 24/7 access to relevant political information. Hence, wider sections of a population can be informed without them having to attend a public meeting or to consult with politicians at a specific date and time. Since the spatial location is irrelevant for internet access, participants may be spatially distributed but still have the same possibilities of attendance. Thus, the number of potential participants increases again. Another advantage is that internet-based participation is text based and thus more transparent than the conventional participation process. Especially the more complex topics require a high level of transparency, which is considered a value in democratic processes. The deliberative democratic approach initiates communication in order to discuss different viewpoints on a topic. Compared to traditional public discussions, participants in internet-based discussions are able to refer to all other contributions. This leads to a more thorough and complex discussion. With asynchronous online discussions communication decelerates. Relevance and objectivity of the contributions may increase, as more information can be taken into account. New knowledge can be generated and integrated into the political process through the participation of many - citizens as well as experts.

Regardless the benefits and the discursive potential of the internet, the reality is disillusioning. Coleman and Gøtze [6] point out, that *'there are very few examples anywhere of the internet being used to involve citizens in policy deliberation. Where examples can be found, they are of an experimental nature; online public participation is still in its infancy.'* With regard to their examination of case studies in twelve different countries, they conclude that all projects are frustrated by the same two problems: *'Too few people know about them and governments fail to integrate them into the policy process or respond to them effectively.'* Similarly to Coleman and Goetze, Pflüger et al. [6] regret that to date opportunities for internet-based citizen participation have been developed mainly from a technical perspective.

3 Success Factors for Internet-Based Participation

Fraunhofer AIS has developed a model for internet-based participation, which describes success factors that should be taken into account in the design of the process. A detailed description of the model can be found in Märker et al. [7].

The basis of the model is to ensure the 'external and internal relevance' of the participation process. The term 'external relevance' describes the embedding of the internet-based participation process into the users' and government's environments. This means, that not only do the new internet-based procedures have to be technically adaptable but they also have to be integrated into political-institutional, organisational, cultural and economical structures [8]. Within the framework of e-governance the need for integration has already been recognised as significant, and some good-practice examples and guidelines have been realized [9]. If measures for the external relevance are taken seriously before and during the internet-based participation, it is more likely that citizens will be motivated to participate in the process. Michaelis [10] identified 22 criteria to ensure the external relevance. They include for example the degree of involvement of decision makers, how to select the optimum phase for the consultation during a policy cycle, how to ensure the accessibility for participants and the feedback through governmental bodies. Not only are the measures leading to good external relevance important, those ensuring good internal relevance are also significant for a successful process. The term 'internal relevance' describes all measures to enhance the productivity of the discourse. This includes especially measures that increase the trust regarding the productivity of the process from the participants' point of view. Internal relevance targets a goal-, and results-oriented discussion. Michaelis [10] has identified 12 criteria to achieve internal relevance. Acland [11] regards the concept as the key challenge in designing successful public consultation processes because *'electronic processes have the effect of magnifying conceptual and design failures'*. Regarding the state of the art, it has to be acknowledged that there is less known about internal relevance and affecting criteria than about external relevance.

4 The Case 'Public Budget Dialogue in Esslingen'

Esslingen is a city located southeast of Stuttgart in south Germany with about 90,000 inhabitants. Esslingen participates in the German federal multimedia project 'Media@Komm', which supports comprehensive e-government and e-democracy activities. The city aims to use information and communication technologies (ICT) to transform the traditional bureaucracy into a modern service organisation by optimising administrative processes and services for citizens and businesses. The processes to be optimized include online-administration services as well as citizens' consultation. The integration of internet-based participation into standard procedures and practices has become one of Esslingen's goals. Since 2001 the City strives to implement a permanent online participation infrastructure. However, similar to other public internet forums the first attempts were not accepted by the public and lacked participants and contributions. It became clear that the sole existence of discussion forums is not sufficient, even if supervised like in Esslingen. In 2003 Esslingen was given the chance to start a new approach on internet-based participation due to the Media@Komm project. Esslingen decided to involve the citizens in the preparation of the municipal budget and the distribution of the cities' financial resources.

The municipal budget is a central instrument of political governance and is based on a complex process of relating finances with political agenda. Therefore municipalities usually determine their budgets with the help of political experts. In Europe, citizens have rarely been involved in the process of the development f the municipal budget. In South America, however, the "public budget process" is a successful participatory approach to deal with the problems of minimal financial resources in large cities. The "public budget process" has its origin in Porto Allegre, Brazil. Since 1989, the citizens of Porto Allegre (1.3 million inhabitants) have been consulted on a regular basis on the distribution and investment of municipal funds. Their input has served as a basis for the decisions of the municipal council of Porto Allegre. Involving citizens in developing the municipal budget has led to significant improvements of the quality of life in Porto Allegre. The Porto Allegre approach is a successful model of participation and a growing interest can be recognized, even though it is known to be difficult to transfer experiences of the South to the North, especially if they concern representative model of democracy. We can see, for example, first attempts to emulate features of the Brazilian experience in many European countries. Currently the Marc Bloch Institute in Germany runs a research project that compares such projects in Europe.

The public budget dialogue in Esslingen is one of the first European projects to use an internet-based discussion forum as an instrument to inform and consult the public about the municipal budget. Esslingen assigned the Fraunhofer Institute AIS to support the conceptual and technical realization of the internet-based participation.

The process design started in May 2003. The first step towards the process design was an analysis of the initial situation in Esslingen regarding its municipal budget. The analysis identified scope and suitable topics for the public consultation. The main part of the process planning addressed the identification of the stakeholders' interests and their opinions about the internet-based process. Fraunhofer AIS interviewed all stakeholders and representatives of the municipality over a period of three weeks. Additionally, questionnaires were sent to other relevant concerned parties and committed citizens. In this manner, all relevant persons could contribute and name risks and benefits from their viewpoint.

The topic "budget" had been assessed a risk by the politicians. They believed it to be too complex for a public discussion. Another identified threat was the potential of misuse of political influence and lobbyism. The municipal council identified the risk of losing power regarding decisions about the budget. The lord mayor supported the project despite the political and administrative concerns. The questioned citizens anticipated higher transparency regarding the decision about the municipal budget. Further anticipated benefits from the experts' point of view were that the discussion could generate new ideas and even proposals on how to balance budget deficits, as well as the possibility to initiate a learning process about municipal structures for all participating parties. Identified factors for a successful outcome were the accessibility of the forum (e.g., internet access for all citizens), the transparency of the process, the facilitation of the discussion by an impartial institution, and the transparency of the utilization of the discussions outcomes.

The public budget discourse was divided in to two online phases. The first phase was mostly information-dedicated. The second phase concentrated on the development of ideas and proposals regarding saving financial resources.

The first phase of the internet-based discussion lasted four weeks and was initiated with a public meeting in the old town hall of Esslingen. The forum started with a discussion on several topics in the main forum. Topics were for example the basic parameters of the municipal budget, the financial situation in Esslingen and municipal traffic expenses. During the course of the discussion sub-forums, dealing with the refurbishment of schools, major investment projects, and saving measures for the administrative budgets were set up. Outcome of the first online phase were about 20 proposals. They ranged from initiating a list of people interested in voluntary community services, to switching off traffic lights to save energy at night.

Within the first online-phase 156 users registered and about 150 contributions, not counting the moderators contributions, were posted. The website (www.haushalt-esslingen.de) counted about 8,000 hits and the page of the main forum was directly accessed more than 4,500 times. In comparison to other internet-based public participation processes, these figures can be assessed as quite positive, considering the complex subject of the discussion, and the low number of citizens who usually get engaged in information and discussion about the municipal budget.

At the end of the first online-phase the results were summarized and published in the internet. Further, a questionnaire was sent out to the participants via email. They were invited to provide feedback addressing the moderation and usability of the forum, and to suggest topics for the second online-phase.

The time between the two discussion phases was used to analyse the questionnaire; the suggestions for topics for the second phase were given to the online-moderation team. The outcomes of the first phase, namely the proposals for saving financial resources, were compared to an existing list of "saving measures" of an official municipal budgetary commission. The lists partly matched each other in several thematic budgeting areas. On the basis of these results topics for the second internet-based discussion were identified.

Additionally, Fraunhofer AIS held a workshop on online moderation in Esslingen, aimed to build up moderation capabilities in Esslingen for future internet-based discussion processes. During the second online phase the 12 participants of the workshop had the possibility to get actively involved in the discussion as moderators. They were supervised by the Fraunhofer AIS moderation team and supported by an adviser in Esslingen.

The second discussion phase lasted two weeks. It was designed to deepen the discussion on specific topics, especially the "saving measures" of the official budgetary commission. Similar to the first phase, the internet forum was initiated by a kick-off meeting at the city hall. Discussed categories of "saving measures" were for example energy, services, fees, and alternative sources of revenue. During the second discussion phase, 27 ideas and proposals were developed, ranging from "citizen loans" to increasing parking fees. Half way through the discussion, a two hour online-chat with the lord mayor and the mayor of finances was offered and attracted many participants.

During the second phase 171 participants were registered and about 110 contributions were written (not counting the moderators' contributions). About 4,000 hits on to the homepage and more than 1,600 direct accesses to the main forum were counted. These figures show, that not only the number of registered participants had increased, but also the relative number of contributions. The interest for information and participation did not decrease despite holiday time and less public relations for the second discussion phase.

5 Success Factors 'External and Internal Relevance'

The external relevance can be assessed as relatively low. Although the Lord Mayor and the Mayor of finances assigned the project and were campaigning for it, a political relevance could barely be established. Integration into the political-administrative process did not occur, which was a direct result of the concerns of the municipal council to lose power over financial decisions, and to be confronted with impossible requests. Measures to integrate the project into the political-administrative structures, for example by scheduling the procedure according to the policy cycle of the municipal budget or including the suggestions of the official budgetary commission did not improve the involvement of the political groups. So far it is uncertain if Esslingen will repeat the public budget dialogue, although citizen initiatives are highly supportive of the idea.

The internal relevance can be assessed by taking into account three factors: process planning, moderation and software. In the following, some criteria for internal relevance will be described and applied to the experiences throughout the public budget dialogue.

5.1 Process Planning

Definition of objectives and collection of basic information: A clear definition of what the consultation shall achieve is important information for the municipal council and a motivation for the citizens [11]. A thorough collection of basic information is necessary in order to tailor the process according to the interests of all stakeholders. In the case of Esslingen the goal was to inform and consult citizens about the municipal budget. All information concerning the budget was provided in user-friendly form in the internet. A survey at the end of the consultation process showed a general contentment with the provision and quality of information [12].

Timing of the consultation: Generally, internet-based participation procedures should be carried out as early in the respective process as possible [9], [13]. Existing guidelines about the duration of a consultation vary from three weeks [14] to 12 weeks [15]. Consultations are best carried out in multi-stage processes [11]. In the case of Esslingen the internet-based discussion lasted six weeks, divided into a four-week and a two-week phase. Between these two phases was a two-month summer break. The schedule acknowledged the policy cycle of the municipal budget.

Process type and tools: Märker et al. [7] emphasise the advantage of hybrid processes which means the combination of web-based elements and traditional offline participation processes (e.g., public meetings). Bremer [14] highlights the benefit of a mix of elements, including other interactive elements like polls, surveys or expert interviews as well. Especially these events help building up a "discourse-dramaturgy" and increase the attention and motivation of the participants [16]. The consultation in Esslingen was a hybrid process, since both online-phases were initiated by public events. For the discussion, the asynchronous, web-based discourse software Dito® was used. The online-chat with the lord mayor and the mayor of finances was a synchronous event.

5.2 Moderation

Previous pilot projects and evaluation reports emphasise moderation as a fundamental success factor for internet-based cooperation-, and participation processes [7], [11], [16] and [6]. Moderation by a neutral third party guarantees the trust of the participants, and seems to have a strong impact on their motivation [16], [14]. In the case of Esslingen an active moderation style was applied, which means that the moderators actively shaped the communication process, phrased opening questions and responded to contributions. One member of the moderation team had an editorial function and was responsible for forwarding technical questions about the budget or municipal structures to the relevant offices and to retrieve and edit their responses. This made sure all information was compiled in user-friendly form and stored in the online library of the forum. Another asset were the citizens, who participated in the offered day's workshop on online moderation. They successfully supported the moderation team in the second online phase.

5.3 Software

A platform for internet-based discussions needs to be flexible in the sense that it can be tailored to the demands of each particular project procedure. The platform especially needs features for moderation. Equally important is the usability of the software for the participants. They have to be able to find their own submissions and see how they are allocated in the context. It proved to be an advantage to have easily navigable, multi-threaded and cross-referenced contributions [17]. For the public budget discourse in Esslingen, the web-based discourse software Dito® was used. Dito® offers a wide range of moderation features, for example changing the structure of discussion threads and a notification feature that automatically informed the moderators by e-mail about new contributions in the forum. While everyone, including unregistered guests, was allowed to read the contributions, only the moderators' team was able to modify them.

6 Conclusion and Outlook

The case of Esslingen has to be classified as an e-participation project with relatively high internal relevance and a rather low external relevance. Given that the context of e-participation is essentially of a political nature, we conclude that in this context the process cannot be deemed successful. The low external relevance influenced the overall assessment negatively, or vice versa, the successful elements of the process would have had more impact with a higher external relevance. A stronger external relevance may lead to changes in the common communication processes among the triangle of politicians, citizens and administration, and thereby lead to more modern and sustainable decision making processes. However, introducing external relevance to participation processes is a long-term goal depending on the overall planning and participation culture. Through public participation that regards the success factors 'internal and external relevance', new knowledge can be produced, which can catalyse the sustainable solution of complex problems. Using the internet, as a communication medium with high participative and communicative potential, may initiate the transformation of institutional and organisational structures in the municipal administration and policy.

Future research could investigate the impact of city scale on the model for internet-based participation, as well as the influence of cultural factors throughout Europe.

References

1. Siedschlag, A., A. Rogg, and C. Welzel, *Digitale Demokratie. Willensbildung und Partizipation per Internet.* 2002, Opladen: Leske + Budrich
2. Märker, O., M. Trénel, and A. Poppenborg, *Ungenutztes Wissen. Einleitungsbeitrag des Themenhefts 'e-Partizipation. Wegbereiter einer neuen Planungskultur?'* Kommune21. e-Government, Internet und Informationstechnik, 2003. **2003**(9): p. 18-20
3. Wesselmann, C., *Internet und Partizipation in Kommunen. Strategien des optimalen Kommunikations-Mix.* Sozialwissenschaft. 2002, Wiesbaden: Deutscher Universitäts-Verlag
4. Kubicek, H., W. Westholm, and M. Wind, *Stand und Perspektiven der Bürgerbeteiligung via Internet. Von verstreuten Einzelangeboten zur mandantenfähigen Beteiligungsplattform.* Verwaltung und Management, 2003. **9 (2003)**(2): p. 68-77
5. Friedrichs, S., T. Hart, and O. Schmidt, *Die Bürgernähe auf dem Schirm: Verwalten und Regieren nach dem Balanced-E-Government-Ansatz*, in *E-Government. Effizient verwalten - demokratisch regieren*, S. Friedrichs, T. Hart, and O. Schmidt, Editors. 2002, Verlag Bertelsmann Stiftung: Gütersloh
6. Coleman, S. and J. Gøtze, *Bowling Together: Online Public Engagement in Policy Deliberation.* 2001, London: Hansard Society
7. Märker, O., et al., *Erfolgsfaktoren der ePartizipation. Ansätze zur Entwicklung einer Systematik der ePartizipation*, in *CORP 2003. 8. internationales Symposion zur Rolle der IT in der und für die Planung sowie zu den Wechselwirkungen zwischen realem und virtuellem Raum*, M. Schrenk, Editor. 2003, Selbstverlag des Instituts für EDV-gestützte Methoden in Architektur und Raumplanung der Technischen Universität Wien: Wien. p. 433-442
8. Westholm, W., *»Adaptability« in online democratic engagement: A multi-channel strategy to enhance deliberative policie.* Communications, 2003. **2003**(28): p. 205-227
9. Macintosh, A. and E. Smith. *Citizen Participation in Public Affairs.* in *Electronic Government. First International Conference, EGOV 2002, Aix-en-Provence, France, September 2002, Proceedings.* 2002. Berlin, Heidelberg, New York, u.a.: Springer
10. Michaelis, S., *E-Partizipation als neues Instrument der Stadtplanung. Eine Analyse der internen und externen Relevanz am Beispiel der Projekte Berlin Alexanderplatz und Esslinger „Haushalt im Dialog".* in *Geographisches Institut Bonn; Fraunhofer Insitut AIS.* 2004, Universität Bonn; Fraunhofer Institut Autonome Intelligente Systeme: Bonn; Sankt Augustin

11. Acland, A., *Designing and Managing Electronic Consultation Processes*. 2003, Dialogue by Design Ltd
12. Märker, O. and A. Poppenborg, *Computerunterstützte Mediation als Instrument für eine nachhaltige Stadt- und Regionalplanung*, in *Online-Mediation. Neue Medien in der Konfliktvermittlung – mit Beispielen aus Politik und Wirtschaft*, O. Märker and M. Trénel, Editors. 2003, edition sigma: Berlin. p. 287-314
13. OECD, *Engaging Citizens Online for Better Policy-making*. Policy Brief OECD, 2003. **2003**(March 2003): p. 1-9
14. Bremer, C., *Gestaltung und Unterstützung von Online Diskursen*, in *Moderierter Online-Diskurs grüne Gentechnik. Machbarkeitsstudie*, T.v. Schell and A. Tyroller, Editors. 2003, Akademie für Technikfolgenabschätzung in Baden-Württemberg: Stuttgart. p. 47-67
15. UK-Cabinett-Office, *Code of Practice on written consultation. http://www.cabinet-office.gov.uk/regulation/Consultation/Code2000.htm (April 2004)*. 2004
16. Clift, S., *Online-Consultation and Events- Top Ten Tips for Government and Civic Hosts*. 2002
17. Märker, O., M. Trénel, and H. Hagedorn, *Internet-basierte Bürgerbeteiligung Esslingen. Relevanz - Moderation - Software*, in *MEDIA@Komm - Bürgerkommune im Netz. Tagungsband des 2. Fachkongresses am 11./12.6.2001 in Esslingen*, Bundesministerium für Wirtschaft und Technologie (BMWi), Editor. 2001, BMWi: Esslingen. p. 259-274

Enhancing e-Democracy Via Fiscal Transparency: A Discussion Based on China's Experience*

Ling Lan

Tianjin University of Finance & Economics Tianjin, China
llinglan@eyou.com

Abstract. The transition process from E-government to e-democracy involves a number of complex government changes, among which one of the important reforms for China, lies in the fundamental transform of its public finance regime from a "secret tradition" which has been holding for centuries long, towards a modern democratic open process. From 2003, Chinese government decided to release the Audit Report of its central and local budget to the public; this unprecedented event had stirred a so-called "Audit Storm" in the country. This paper therefore explores the significant meaning of fiscal transparence in China, analyzes the relationship between fiscal transparency and government accountability. Hereby argues that fiscal transparence can service as a catalyst both to e-government and open government process. Finally the paper points out China should follow the Code of Good Practices on Fiscal Transparency edited by IMF, enhancing e-democracy via fiscal transparency.

1 Introduction

E-government, the use of information and communication technologies (ICT) to transfer government by making it more accessible, effective and accountable , is not an end in itself, but a means to facilitate E-democracy-----A new fashion of democracy of modern information age, in which ICT empower citizens and human society to accelerate and ultimately realize the Elysium of a unprecedented democratic society .

From theoretical and historical perspectives, democracy is an evolving concept; the word derived from two Greek words: demos (the people) and kratia (rule), proving the Greek city-states in the 6th century BC was the first democratic forms of government. Then in Athens all citizens, whether rich or poor, participated fully in government activities. Hereby, Webster's dictionary defined **democracy** as "a government in which the supreme power is vested in the people and exercised by them directly or indirectly through a system of representation." Democracy is thus distinct from government controlled by a particular social class or group as oligarchy or a single person as dictatorship and monarchy. Since the time of ancient Greece,

* This paper is one of the results of Chinese national social science research programs. No.04BZZ040.

M. Böhlen et al. (Eds.): TCGOV 2005, LNAI 3416, pp. 57–69, 2005.

democracy has attracted support throughout history, because it represents an ideal of justice as well as a form of optimal government. The ideal is the belief that freedom and equality are sacred and that democratic participation in governance enhances human dignity. Nowadays, when we put an "e" in front of democracy is by no means we should draw any substance out of democracy, but to enhance or perfect it by a more powerful engine. Government equipping with digital technology, should be supposed to be driving by a powerful engine, it should run with high speed on the road of democracy.

However, if we remember what Thomas Hobbes compared government to Leviathan in 17 century[1], what James M. Buchanan, Gordon Tullock and other public choice scholars explain government "cures" often cause more harm than good, and how interest groups seek favors from government at enormous costs to society; also we may keep in mind the words Ronald Reagan spoke in his president inauguration that government is not a solution to our problem, government is the problem, etc, then we should logically reach the similar conclusion that e-government is not a panacea, not a royal road smoothly leading to e-democracy. Great ancient philosopher Aristotle once convincingly argued that any selfish abuse of power can cause different kinds of governments, including democratic origin, deteriorate into tyranny, oligarchy, and even inferior mob rule[2]. Therefore government should be restricted, monitored and subject to the will of its people. Any malfeasance of government agencies, such as bribery, cronyism, embezzlement, extortion, fraud, graft and so forth should be punished severely according to state law. In information age what digital revolution has imparted to people is the edge tool of public participation by which people can share information, disclose scandal, enjoy and radiate sunshine of e-democracy.

The paper is divided into five parts: Part two dwells briefly on the far-reaching event in China----from 2003 government began to publish audit report of its central and local government via e-government project----a so called "audit storm" had been stirred with the exposure. Analysis the interdependent and co-existence of fiscal transparence and government accountability is the subject of part three. The possible consequences or impact of open budget in China, and the implication in which fiscal transparency could promote open government and e-democracy is the main contents of part four. Concluding comments reviews the opportunities and challenges entailed

---

[1] In his political treatise Leviathan (1651), the English philosopher Thomas Hobbes compares the state, with its innumerable competing members, to the largest of natural organisms-- the whale, or leviathan, one of the names of the primeval dragon subdued by Jehovah at the outset of creation. By this analogy Hobbes argued that the state, like the monster, requires a single controlling intelligence to direct its motion.

[2] Aristotle distinguished three kinds of government: monarchies, aristocracies, and democracies, in his famous book Politics（335 BC）, The differences among them chiefly concerned whether power was held by one, by a few, or by many. He also argued that the selfish abuse of power caused each type to become perverted, respectively, into tyranny, oligarchy, and a lower form of democracy characterized by mob rule. Monarchy tended to become tyrannical because it vested authority in a single ruler. Aristocracy, a government based on birth and privilege, in which the rulers governed for the good of the whole society, tended to become oligarchy as a consequence of restricting political power to a special social and economic class; only a few members of the class would have enough drive and ability to acquire the power to govern. The polity, likewise, would deteriorate into ochlocracy, or mob rule, if the citizens pursued only their selfish interests.

in the implementation of open government and e-democracy in China, the critical issue of whether Chinese government has a strong volition to carry e-government and e-Democracy through.

2 E-Government Project Stirred Audit Storm

Public finance sector has long been a notorious locus of government corruption since early history of nation-state. Slavery or feudalistic monarchies, had taken advantage of state treasures, usurped and prioritized public money to augment benefits and preserve wealth for themselves and royal families; meanwhile malfeasants up and down whole bureaucratic hierarchy competed each other vigorously for stealing public money from state treasury[3]. Comptroller or Audit Agency, although existed as some watchdog institution in many dynasties, however they merely served the monarchies, so that fiscal transparency and government accountability were limited only to one person, i.e. the king. Great Athenian democratic state pioneered in the way to keep public treasure and fiscal transparency under a nascent democracy of people's representative regimes. Ancient China, unfortunately, had not founded similar organizations to authorize public purse or keep fiscal transparency to the people in spite of the fact that auditing theory and practice in China can be traced as long as some 3,000 years in history[4].

Thus, we have inferred from above analysis that exposure information of public revenue and expenditure, i.e. holding fiscal transparency is one of the importance elements for good governance in China. Along that routemap another crucial necessary reform is the auditing system, because it is the auditing agency, rather than any other institution, which can expedite process of fiscal transparency, enforcing the auditing system will win the victory against ascending corruption in the country.

Pursuant to schedule of China's e-government framework drew by the State Council, a so called" Golden Auditing Project"[5] was launched and kept improving since 2000 in tandem with other parallel e-government projects covering the field of public finance, tax collection, customs duty and social security, etc. The "Golden Auditing Project" aimed to

---

3 One such example in Chinese history is in Qianlong aged, Qing dynasty 18 century. Heshen, an emperor's former bodyguard had lulled Qianlong emperor's trust, was authorized with various government affairs. Heshen availed himself of emperor's trust and lavish his arbitrary power to build up his personal fortune. The blind Qianlong emperor, although is regarded as a sage emperor in Chinese history, was let-alone Heshen's whatever behaviors. The extent of Heshen's corruption came to light immediately after Qianlong died. Rough accounting, Heshen had accumulated gold bowls, silver bullion, land, and pawnshops, the total was valued at half of what the state collected in revenues over a 20-year period. Heshen was forced to commit suicide, but the dynasty had difficulty recovering from the damage. The story had been vividly represented by a series TV drama in recent years.

4 Auditing system in China has a long history. A rudimentary form of auditing emerged as early as the Western Zhou Dynasty, 3,000 years ago; a royal audit court was set up in the Song Dynasty in 992 A.D. From then on, every dynasty established specific institutions or offices in charge of monitoring state revenues and expenditures.

5 According to Chinese ancient tradition, golden color is noble and auspicious that the use of the color was restricted to some kind of special occasions. Giving the name of "Golden projects" to e-government projects, indicating Chinese government has attached great importance to the projects and taken strong commitment to carry them through.

establish an auditing information system that enables the effective monitor and supervision over the government revenue and expenditure by a new online auditing model. One mighty advances promoting fiscal transparency by China National Audit Office (CNAO) is to release full text of auditing reports of central and local governments to the public via CNAO's internet website (http://www.audit.gov.cn) from the year of 2003.Before that year the CNAO only reported to the State Council and the National People's Congress, but not to the public by keeping full texts of almost all audit reports as secret with only some abstract summaries be occasionally published in some occasions.

The first open budgeting audit report issued on June 25, 2003, it focused on the budgeting of 2002 fiscal year. Based on a great number of auditing data, the report was sharply critical of the improper activities of the Ministry of Finance, of state-owned banks, of large state-owned enterprises and some other ministries. For instance, the report exposed serious problems ranging from the Ministry of Finance's mishandling of pension funds to fraudulent loans granted by dozens of local branches of the China Construction Bank.

The releasing of the national auditing report through e-government project was a prelude to a significant reform toward fiscal transparency and e-democracy, just like a thunderbolt, the audit results drew wide media attentions, shook the whole nation, and consequently resulted in a so-called "Audit Storm" all over the country. According to 2003 fiscal year's audit report, financial malpractice was discovered at 41 of the 55 surveyed departments in the central government and its affiliates. The misused money amounted to 1.4 billion yuan (US$170 million) in 2003's budget, and the situation is so serious that even emergency funds earmarked for disaster-relief programs were defaulted. During the period between 2003 and 1983, when the CNAO was established, the CNAO has examined more than 3 million institutions throughout the country, and exposed extensive misuse of public funds by some government departments, seized illegal and suspect funds worth 130 billion Yuan (US$15.7 billion).

The "Audit Storm" was sweeping rapidly from central to provincial levels, Guangdong province, once again acted as a precursor in leading the movement of fiscal transparency[6]. The province had adopted a more detailed department budget report method since 2001, intending to provide delegates of local People's Congress with more concrete information for checking and ratifying. It had reported that during the latest session of local congress of Guangdong province, delegates noticed four kindergartens affiliated with government agencies, which were reserved for children of government employees, were allocated more than 20 million yuan (US$2.41 million), thus delegates demanded an explanation as to why taxpayers' money could be used to raise civil servants' children without approval or even inform to taxpayers. Other problems detected by local audit body and delegates include the lack of a feasibility study before commencing a constriction project, poor accounting, inadequate management, shortcomings in bidding process, low efficiency and legal violations and so forth.

---

[6] Guangdong province is a place teemed with revolutionary tradition economically and politically. At dawn of last century, the revolutionary movement led by Sun Zhongshan, gained momentum and overthrew the last feudalist dynasty in the province, since then China became a republic. Beginning from 1979, foreign investment led to spectacular economic development in Guangdong province, particularly in the three Special Economic Zones regions of Shenzhen （near Hong Kong, Zhuhai (near Macao), and Shantou (near Taiwan).

Spurred by process of open budget and fiscal transparency, the fight against corruption has been intensified in recent years all over the country. The Supreme People' Court of China, the juridical section of the government, also has playing an active role in fighting corruption. In 2003 Chinese courts at all levels concluded investigation into 5,687,905 cases which involved a sum of 768.5 billion yuan, and six former ministerial-level officials were sentenced on charges of job-related crimes[7]. The penalties on them range from death sentence with a reprieve, life imprisonment, to 12 and 15 years behind bars, according to China's chief justice report.

It is a worldwide movement towards open government and fiscal transparency---- an international consensus based on the facts that financial crisis bred in part due to fiscal practices that were not open to scrutiny----putting an urgent emphasis on public participation and supervision of government behavior, among which, the most crucial matter is certainly how government spend public money. The "Audit Storm" inspired by China's e-government "Golden Auditing Project", however, is only a small advance compare with many other countries' best practices, but in fact, it is already a great leap forward from a remote scratch line in China's "secret budget history", it is also a path-breaking endeavor towards e-governance and e-democracy.

3 Fiscal Transparence Strengthen Government Accountability

It was observed that fiscal transparence and government accountability are interdependent. There could be no government accountability without achieving fiscal transparency, neither could be fiscal transparency without government making strong commitment to mobilize citizens involving in budget process by holding public hearing, facilitating public discourse, and dispatching budget priorities according to citizen's preference of public good and service. All that activities manifests the best practices of government accountability.

Briefly speaking, government accountability can be simply understood as answerability for government performance in that, taxpayers expect and are entitled to the best possible value for their tax money, they must have assurances that the tax money they paid are being spent wisely and effectively, government in turn, should give them a satisfied answer. Besides auditing arrangement, government accountability embeds in the public finance system itself. Many disciplines and frameworks, which have hitherto been related to public expenditure management and fiscal transparence, are gradually becoming international criterions[8]. Among which two influencing documents are *the Manual on Fiscal Transparency* and *the Code of Good Practices on Fiscal Transparency* edited by the Fiscal affairs Department of International Monetary Fund.

7 The six former high-ranking officials were former governor of Yunnan Province Li Jiating, former vice chairman of the Shandong Provincial Committee of the Chinese People's Political Consultative Conference Pan Guangtian, former president of the Liaoning Provincial Higher People's Court Tian Fengqi, former deputy governor of Hebei Province Cong Fukui, former deputy governor of Zhejiang Province Wang Zhongli, and former governor of the China Construction Bank Wang Xuebing.

8 From the mid-1990s, the IMF has been leading efforts to develop and implement Code of Good Practices on Fiscal Transparency, and the Manual on Fiscal Transparency, This was done in response to a clear consensus that good governance is of central importance to achieving macroeconomic stability and high-quality growth, and obviously that fiscal transparency is a key aspect of good governance.

The Good Practices on Fiscal Transparency, according to that Manual, include the following basic principles:

- Clarity of Roles and Responsibilities.
- Public Availability of Information.
- Open Budget Preparation, Execution, and Reporting.
- Assurances of Integrity.

From the basic principles of best practice in fiscal transparency above, we can recognize that the progression the "Audit Storm" in China has been accelerated, although a significant step forward in our own country, is only a starting phase, along this roadway there are still many challenges, even barriers lies ahead. It is no use to have well designed and written auditing law and regulation that are not followed, and it is no meaning either if after audit report release to the public whereas little has done by government to address exposed malfeasance, and the base line for punishment be kept lifting higher and higher. Because it will send a wrong message to some person informing them that it is really does not matter even if someone is caught for wrongdoing. Obviously sufficient punishment should be meted out so as to stop others from doing the same thing. In China, further open budget process such as public hearing, public debate and discourse and more dynamic citizen participation still fare very poor, we should not merely applaud over the "Audit Storm" therefore, the fundamental problem we have to seriously consider for next step reform is how to put into practice some more sound and specific measures to enforce fiscal transparency and government accountability succeed the "Audit Storm".

Premchand（2001）had interpreted government accountability to be of two kinds ----vertical accountability and horizontal accountability. The former has relevance to the pyramidal structures of governments and essentially refers to the accountability of the lower levels to the higher levels. The latter refers to the patterns of relationships between governments and the legislatures as well as to the public. Romzek and Dubnick gave a more complicated matrix in 1987 (See Figure.1), they also articulated four types of government accountability .All of their analytical frameworks are relevant to our open government and fiscal transparent discussion.

		Source of Expectations and/or Control	
		External	**Internal**
Degree of Autonomy	**Low**	**Hierarchical**	**Legal**
	High	**Professional**	**Political**

Source: International Public Management Journal Vol.6, No.1, 2003,P20

Fig. 1. Government Accountability Framework

In Figure 1 Romzek and Dubnick distinguished four kinds of government accountabilities: Hierarchical, Professional, Legal and Political; and measured the degree to which government agencies have a low or high autonomy, and the origin of control or expectation coming from internal or external forces. It is self-evident that Hierarchical and Professional Accountabilities are endogenous; they exhibit a gradual increase of autonomy vertically. Contrarily, Legal and Political Accountability are extraneous, but the autonomous degree of theirs is also increase vertically. Public budget is more than simply technical tools for allocating public expenditures; it is also a social and institutional arrangement that shape public life, state institutions and promote good governance in a country. Form a theoretical perspective, we shall discuss below on how fiscal transparency will facilitate the implementation of these four kinds of government accountabilities.

Firstly, government Professional Accountability entails assigning the professional budget tasks to professional persons who are experts based on special knowledge, background, experiences or training, such as accountant, auditor, tax collector, computer engineer and programmer etc. To empower them with high degree of autonomy is equivalent to reinforcing their Professional Accountability simultaneously. Process of fiscal transparence, especially under certain comprehensive e-government project, is undoubtedly a pivot point for a great democratic undertaking that will mobilize all sorts of professionals, with each doing his best according to his abilities. Professional Accountability will be enhanced by various tasks in framework of best practices of fiscal transparence, for example, to make budget information more understandable to wider range of readers by giving non-technical explanations of term and jargon; supportive charts, graphics, sometimes a navigation etc, will summon many talent experts and strengthen their responsibility automatically.

Secondly, government Hierarchical Accountability requires a clear definition of government structure and function that is coincident with the request of clarity roles of government responsibility for fiscal transparency that require the budget document to reveal details about government units, including descriptions of their activities, performance standards and achievements. Fiscal transparency will certainly bring about a performance motivation, evaluation and supervision mechanism, both for government agencies and for civilian persons, under this reasonable and distinctive pyramid of responsibility assignment, Hierarchical Accountability within government bureaucracy will eventually be strengthened.

Thirdly, government Political Accountability refers to responsiveness to the concerns of key stakeholders, mainly supervisors, elected officials, and general citizens according to western tradition. Although in China, the system of checks and balances is not so strong and sharp-edged by nature, it is the citizens who are exclusive beneficiary of government service are beyond question. Thus budget report, as one of important policy documentations, should be prepared and presented within some long-term assumptions, comprehensive macroeconomic frameworks, and so forth. In order to respond citizen upon how enforced budget is being implemented a monthly, quarterly or at least mid-year report on budget developments should be presented to the legislature as well as to the public. Despite government Political Accountability has a relatively larger room for political manipulation, a responsible government must take crucial measure to strengthen its accountability to the public and expedite the tasks of fiscal transparency.

Fourthly, government Legal Accountability involves some strong supervision from outside, demanding government compliance with the established budget mandates, budget policy and program. Fiscal transparency can enhance government Legal Accountability by government releasing budget reports timely and actually, and confirm that public money is not allocated by a few oligarchies, but under strict monitor, being spent in a legal and efficient manner. The best practices of fiscal transparency provide many regulations, mandates and rules to intensify government Legal Accountability.

Fiscal transparency is a prerequisite for government Hierarchic, Professional Legal and Political Accountability. To be brief, if budget information were not available, the public could not have a chance to discuss it, thus not only budget policies but also national macroeconomic strategy could not be assessed and analyzed, under that situation fiscal policy could never lead to efficient resources allocation. Fiscal transparency also facilitates the identification of governmental weaknesses, promoting the adoption of needed reforms. Adherence to fiscal transparency can increase faith in governments; it can also contribute to build consensus on and commitment to social trade-offs that is an impetus to macroeconomic stability, because it prevents the build-up of a crisis in secret, introducing any smaller adjustments as soon as possible. The increased faith in and support of a transparent government can also attract international investors, which is especially important to China, since fiscal transparency and government accountability are valuable elements of healthy investment atmospheres within a country.

4 Government Accountability Induce E-Democracy

Nowadays as e-democracy is in its beginning stages in China, there is much confusion about what it encompasses and how to clearly define it. Steven Clift, an acknowledged expert and leader in the worldwide e-democracy campaign, describes e-democracy as "how the Internet can be used to enhance our democratic processes and provide increased opportunities for individuals and communities to interact with government and for the government to seek input from the community" (democracy online http://www.dowire.org). From his statement we can get the core of e-democracy is to strengthen democracy through the use of innovative ICT to deliver improved democratic decision-making processes, to increasing citizen participation.

How about the evolution from e-government to e-democracy? The Institute for Electronic Government（IEG）has designed a four-stage model of "e-development" (see Figure 2), which mapped four progressive scenarios from an informed to an engaged citizenry. It also serves as a scorecard of digital savvy----how successfully a government entity interprets and responds to the digital world and exploits technology accordingly to advance influence. There are two axes in the Figure, one axis measures the degree of engagement, the other measures influence.

Figure 2 depicts a life cycle of e-government, from initial stage of asynchronous information dissemination to a higher level of two-way communications, then an even higher level of collaborative, interactive and transaction between government and citizens, and finally, the most advanced level of e-democracy. Some people think that now in China even e-government is still in its early phase, hence e-democracy is a more marginal occurrence. This opinion only focuses on extent of ICT use and development, but neglect the soul of e-democracy. We believe, certainly the technological limitation does not discount e-democracy's potential, which requires us pay more attention to democratic processes and institutional innovation in our country. As we argued above, fiscal transparency ----one ingredient of advanced phase of e-democracy (see Quadrant Four in Figure 2)----will enforce government accountability, and consequently induce e-democracy. we can speed the process of citizen engagement in policy-making and gain e-democracy by virtue of ICT and e-government infrastructure, (Cullen and Houghton 2000), we can also increase trust in government (Heichelbech 2002) ,promote predictability in public service performance (United Nations 2001), and promote credibility through better incorporation of citizen needs and access to information (Martin and Feldman 1998;Roberts 1999), as well as encourage oversights in the fight against corruption (Radics et al 2001).

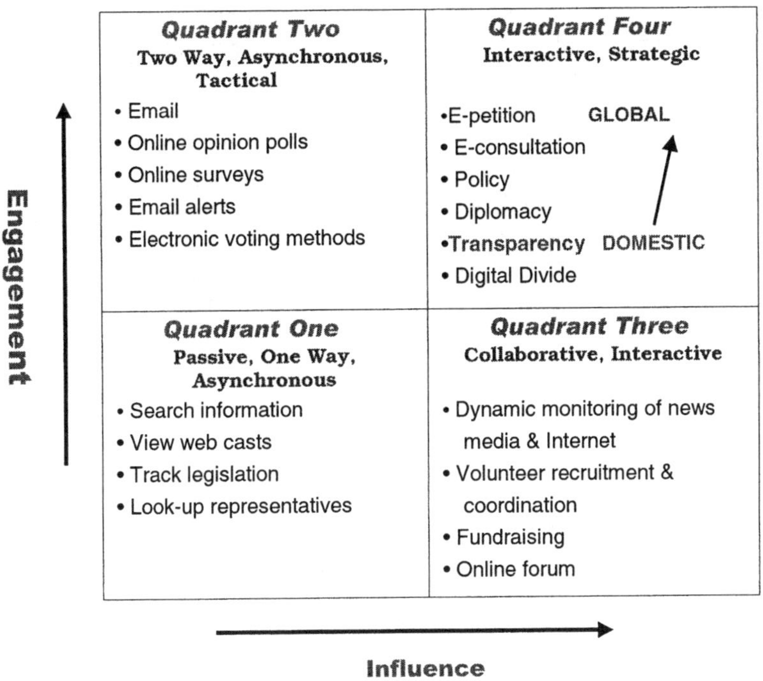

Source: E-democracy: Putting Down Global Roots Janet Caldow January, 2004,P.5

Fig. 2. E—Democracy Model (IEG)

Government, a Leviathan as Thomas Hobbes's imagery, plays both positive and negative roles in society. Many research found out that government----through over-bearing regulation or taxation, waste and outright corruption----could be a serious impediment to economic development. In China, for example, the cases of bribery, cronyism, embezzlement, extortion, fraud, graft, nepotism and even bureaucratic corruption are seemingly going up in recent years. Of which there are many occurred in government subsidies, public procurement, state owned enterprise and tax expenditures. Thus public financial activities if not subject to transparency and accountability, will create high stakes for political rent seeking and corruption will stifle entrepreneurship, innovation and market adjustment and fail to achieve social, environmental and economic goals. Expose public finance performance to public supervision will curb corruption in government activities.

Based on above arguments, the following list of core measures for fiscal transparence and government accountability should be taken by Chinese government:

Continue to make an effort to construct effective and practical audit network based on e-government projects, connect audit institutions to the major audited bodies nationwide, and develop a suite of auditing application software that satisfies requirements of audit tasks. Install a group of economic and practical computer facilities and infrastructure to facilitate scrutiny and monitor work over public revenue and expenditure; Meanwhile, construct a group of databases (working platforms) to support audit assignments and provide general public with annual national audit report on budget as well as other audit report on a regular basis, create a transparent environment for effective public decision-making.

Continue to promote the reform of budget process, ensure that government budget may function as a policy document, financial plan, operational guide and a communication device. Take initiative in public hearing, public participating, budget debate and other budget discourse activities. Cast away the old tradition of "budget secrecy" by inviting citizen participation. Government should reveal financial and economic information on regular basis. Budget report should be comprehensive, including all quasi-fiscal activities, financial and non-financial assets held by government, contingent and future liabilities, and tax expenditures. In order to facilitate ordinary people understand budget terms and programs, a "citizen's budget" should be provided for the help of a wider audience.

Continue to deepen public participation in democracy by strengthening the connection between citizens and delegate of National People's Congress, citizens and government agencies as well as groups of citizens in civil society, highlights the importance of ensuring the integration of online and traditional methods for citizen engagement in policy-making, open up new channels for democratic communication to encourage involvement by people who in the past may have felt excluded from the democratic process or unable to participate. Use the Internet and other ICT tools; to encourage citizens' engagement in e-discussion, e voting, e-consultation, e-petition e-scrutiny and many other e-activities within more comprehensive e-government framework. People, who for various reasons had not use traditional democratic forums and channels, should be empowered to use new technologies to make their voices be heard.

Continue to experiment with performance-targeted or result-oriented management reform in government organization and public sectors, especially "performance-based budgeting", linking fiscal expenditure allocations to clarifying and measurable performance targets in government agencies. For the sake of government transparency and accountability, it is necessary to develop ICT software for analyzing public input providing feedback from citizens on how their comments and suggestions have been used in reaching to decisions on budget expenditure and revenue. In order to build a transparent and accountable culture in government institutions, reform designer should focus on such matters as "mainstream" performance budgets by linking allocations to results requirements; develop performance criteria to ensure the relevance readability and realism; clarify accountability relationships by creating results oriented "bottom-lines"; and make accountability relationships enforceable by creating appropriate institutions.

5 Conclusions and Future Challenges

Just the same as "every roads lead to Rome", there are also many approaches leading to e-democracy, However, one of the best approaches for china, a country with centuries long history of "fiscal secrecy", to choose is to open up its budget process, so as to install effective mechanism of good governance in the body of government. The importance of e-transparence in all phases of e-government in general and the fiscal transparence in particular, highlight the urgency of china's budgetary reform. Following the Code of Good Practices on Fiscal Transparency of IMF, China should strive hard to reach this destination.

In light of this statement, China should be prepared to facing barriers and challenges ahead; some crucial gist should be emphasized:

- **Government Commitment:** Chinese government must determine its mind to carry the political reform through, changing governmental structure and function according to the requirement of e-government and e-democracy; this commitment must be enforced stronger and stronger.
- **Strengthen Legal Framework:** Transparent and responsible fiscal management need a legal environment; government should promulgate series of new legislation that promote policy transparency and government accountability.
- **Strengthen Institutional Framework:** The unprecedented degree of interactivity offered by rapid ICT development raises the prerequisite to expand the scope, breadth and depth of government institutional framework concerning some technical, political and governing implications.
- **Eliminate Corruption:** Fiscal transparence is to expose government to the monitor of its citizens. In order to get rid of the" social cancer", government must implement strict self-discipline; penalize any corrupt behavior and activity within government bureaucracy.
- **Moral Integrity:** Integrity is the quality being honest and firm to moral principles and all just causes, a country's moral integrity is a political and administrative system that encourages social equity and justice. Being honest, particularly make sure that all government agencies and public sectors being honest, practical and realistic is the key point to cultivate and keep moral integrity in the whole nation.
- **Awareness of Citizen:** It is the Chinese citizens who will benefit from the reform of open budget and transparent public policy; government should make great efforts to raise awareness of the citizens, to empower them the capacity, with

the edge tool and new channels offered by ICT, to participate the new opportunities of policy-making in e-governance.

- **Technological Supporting:** China is a country with sharp developing discrepancy, therefore, offering citizens, especially those living in remote regions with technological supporting for digital engagement in e-government and e-democracy is primarily important, before that step it is urgently necessary to wipe out illiteracy in all rural areas.

References

1. Andrew Chadwick: E-Government and E-Democracy: A Case For Convergence. Paper for presentation to the panel: Public Policy in the E-Government Era (II) Political Studies Association Annual Conference (2003)
2. China Daily: Audit storm' stirs furore in media.5, July 2004
3. Democracies Online: http://www.mail-archive.com/do-wire@tc.umn.edu/
4. E-Government project, U.S. Senate: http://www.senate.gov/~gov_affairs/egov/
5. IMF: Code of Good Practices on Fiscal Transparency: Declaration on Principle (1998) and Manual on Fiscal Transparency (2001) http://www.imf.org
6. James E. Alt et al: Fiscal Transparency and fiscal policy Outcomes in OECD Countries, presentation at the EPRU-Network conference on Danish and International Economic Policy. University of Copenhagen (2002)
7. Janet Caldow: E-Democracy: Putting Down Global Roots. Institute for Electronic Government, IBM (2004)
8. Kurt Thurmaier: The Role of Budget reform in the Accountability of Polish and Ukrainian Local Governments. International Public Management journal, Vol.6 No.1 (2003)
9. Ling lan: E-government: A Catalyst to Good Governance In China. Maria Wimmer (eds.): Proceedings of KMGov04.Springer-Verlag Berlin Heidelberg (2004)
10. Meng Xi: Goals set to improve auditing system. China Daily, 10,July 2004
11. OECD: Engaging Citizens Online for Better Policy-making. Policy Brief March (2003)
12. Paul Waller et al: E-Government in the service of Democracy. ICA Information, No.74. General Issue (2001)
13. Premchand: Fiscal Transparency and Accountability: Idea and Reality. Paper prepared for the workshop on Financial Management and Accountability. Rome Nov 28-30 (2001)
14. Putnam, Robert D: Making Democracy Work. Princeton University Press, Princeton. USA. (1993)
15. Roumeen Islam: Do More Transparent Governments Govern Better? World Bank Policy Research Working Paper 3077(2003)
16. Steven Clift: (1) Enhancing E-Democracy in Our Communities (2) Top Ten E-Democracy "To Do List" for Governments Around the World (3) A to Z for E-Government and Democracy. Democracies Online Newswire (2002) http://www.e-democracy.org/do
17. The E-Democracy E-Book: http://www.publicus.net,
18. The International Institute for Democracy and Electoral Assistance: http://www.idea.int/ndex.htm
19. Thoma.B Riley et al: E-government to E-democracy: Examining the Evolution Commonwealth Center for E-Governance. http://www.electronicgov.net (2003)
20. Thomas B.Riley. et al: E-government vs. E-democracy: Examining the Differences in a Changing Public Sector Climate. Commonwealth Center for E-Governance. http://www.electronicgov.net (2003)

21. United Nations: Transparency and Accountability in government Finance management ST/ESA/PAD/SER.E/14(1999.)
22. United Nations: World Public Sector Report2003: E-government at the crossroads (2003)
23. Xinhua News Agency: China to audit more State-funded institutions. July 7, 2004.
24. Xinhua News Agency: Six Ministerial Officials Punished for Corruption in 2003. March 10, 2004
25. Zhou Deming: China's golden Auditing Project. http://www.audit.gov.cn (2003)

Third Way e-Government: The Case for Local Devolution

Ailsa Kolsaker

School of Management, University of Surrey, UK
A.Kolsaker@surrey.ac.uk

Abstract. Governments often embrace the Web as a means of delivering joined-up, citizen-centric services efficiently and cost-effectively. In the UK, despite significant investment both provision and usage of e-services have fallen short of target. In this article the current status of UK e-government is analysed in relation to 'New Labour' Third Way governance. It is concluded that the inherent contradictions of Third Way ideology and the government's favoured command and control style are hindering the development of e-government. It is proposed that greater devolution to local councils may accelerate the provision of participatory, partnership-based e-services. If this is to be successful however, central government must move beyond the popularly prescribed model of transaction-based, bilateral e-services and reconceptualise e-government as an instrument of devolved, communitarian governance.

1 Introduction

It is widely recognised that Internet technology plays a central role in contemporary social transformations. Its capacity to institute change has been seized upon by social analysts (warning of its panoptic properties), businesses (seeking cost-savings), citizens (primarily for communication) and governments (cost savings, improved communications and increased participation). A study of the potential of e-government [1] identified that the Web could not only improve service efficiency but also facilitate new networked relations between the state and its citizens. Recognising this potential governments have invested heavily in the e-government platform. In the UK investment has been significant, yet progress has been slower than planned with portals lacking the functionality of those of other European nations. In a recent survey by the European Commission [2] the UK was ranked sixth in Europe in terms of the availability of online services (at 50%) and eighth in terms of service sophistication (71%). In April -June 2004 the underutilised central government portal, 'ukonline.gov.uk' was replaced by two portals: 'Government Gateway', providing services for businesses, agents and the general public, and 'DirectGov', aimed specifically at the private citizens. Though services are improving, Web technology has not yet delivered the results sought by the government in its 1999 White Paper, *Modernising Government* [3]. It is proposed here that lack of progress is due not to the commonly ascribed problems of unrealistic aims, inadequate resources or the digital divide, but to deep-rooted problems of governmentality centred upon the erosion of state power, the reluctance of central government to devolve decision-making to local authorities and public scepticism.

M. Böhlen et al. (Eds.): TCGOV 2005, LNAI 3416, pp. 70 – 80, 2005.

2 Government Aims: 'Joined Up' and Efficient e-Government

In common with other European countries the UK government mapped out a strategy for the provision of joined-up, citizen-centric, efficient e-services. The three specific aims are as follows (italics added):

- ensure that policy making is *joined up and strategic*
- making sure that public service users, not providers, are the focus, by *matching services more closely to people's lives*
- delivering public service that are *high quality and efficient* (1999:2).

The ambition to develop an e-platform that not only to delivers services efficiently, but in an accessible, convenient and relevant manner is not unique. Additionally, the apparent duality of purpose is accommodated within Third Way ideology which, treading a careful path between Conservative individualism and 'Old Labour' collectivism redefines state / citizen relations in a communitarian model located within a framework of economic rationality [4]. In reality, however, it may simply be impossible to provide services which are both responsive *and* efficient – at least in the short term. Joined-up, responsive e-services are likely to require less central prescription, greater local autonomy, more flexible cross-boundary communication and, importantly, a move away from traditional, protracted, hierarchical decision-making. In contrast, efficiency usually demands standardisation, automation and economies of scale, requiring a relatively high degree of central planning and control. Given the high degree of inherent complexity, conflict may be anticipated between efficiency and responsiveness. Thus, mutually incompatible objectives and the inherent dichotomy of the underlying ideological framework may already be erecting unseen barriers.

2.1 Prioritising Efficiency

Despite the rhetoric of participation, efficiency and cost-effectiveness are afforded high priority in the public sector [5]. Again, this is not unique to the UK, but indicative of the developed world's response to globalisation and intensifying competition. Yet the state has welfare obligations that may impinge upon the achievement of sound financial outcomes, but can not simply be dismissed, for example to serve the greater good, to promote inclusion, and to provide uneconomic public goods. As Jackson [6] illustrates, these obligations lead to fundamental decisions about the balance between efficiency and welfare distribution, for example, whether to pursue a utilitarian policy of the greatest good for the greatest number, or to maximise a weighted sum of each individual's welfare, or to pursue a strategy of maximising the welfare of the least well-off in society. The Weberian state gains its legitimacy precisely from its obligation to address such issues - it is this welfare role that stops the state from degenerating into 'a mere conspiracy for oppression and extortion'[7]. Yet, the UK government, despite its socialist roots and apparently ignorant of the potential conflict between the ideologies of the welfare state on the one hand and the corporate state on the other, continues to propound the now almost universally accepted logic of private sector values.

There is much to suggest, both in government literature and public sector managerialism, that the Third Way has retained many of the core tenets of Conservative neo-liberalism. In *Modernising Government* [3] the corporate world is held up as a role model:

> 'We have seen a revolution over the past decade in the way leading companies across the world do business. They have used networked computing to refocus their activities on the customer. They have used IT to work more closely with their suppliers. They have made innovative use of information to become learning organisations. They have supplied new services, when, where and how the customer wants them. They have developed new delivery channels like call centres and the Internet. They have given their staff the support they need to use IT effectively.'

More recently, the advertisement for the post of Head of e-Government described the role as 'analogous to that of a CIO in a very large and diverse conglomerate', concerned with 'how ICT can transform public services and deliver efficiencies in operations'[8] In Sheptycki's [9] analysis as the power of the state shrivels, the will to govern strengthens, though importantly Cohen [10] observes that as power ebbs away the style of governance changes from macro-interventionist to semi-feudal managerialist. There is much in the current approach that validates this insight, including the artificial creation of internal markets within public sector institutions, the imposition of audit and the introduction of corporate style management structures, practices and vocabulary. Underpinning all of this is an implicit acceptance of the premise that the public sector needs to be reformed – indeed for the last twenty years the most vociferous critic of the state has been the state itself.

3 Central Government's Role in e-Government Development

Reformist critique would argue that the post-social condition allows governments only a facilitatory role in the development of e-government. It is argued widely that the role of the state is diminished, its power eroded and its custodian role all but defunct [11], [12], [13]. The post-social condition embraces a much diminished state which is no longer a driving force but a mode of co-ordination. The decline in the power of the state may be conceptualised as a 'hollowing out' rather than an overall reduction in size. Giddens [14] observes that in most societies the size of the state has remained the same, or continued to grow. In the UK, for example, the public sector has grown steadily since the Labour party was elected, yet there is little doubt that the power of the state and government is much diminished – for example, in May 2004 the High Court gave leave to citizens of the new EU states who had already been granted asylum (or were awaiting the outcome of an appeal) in the UK to challenge the government's decision to stop welfare payments; during the same month the government announced that it would not advise the England cricket team to abstain from touring Zimbabwe, as to become involved in the debate would be 'inappropriate'. Such incidents lead the public to question the role of government in contemporary society. This is not a UK phenomenon, but symptomatic of a broader globalisation and the growing complexities of trans-national regulation, though it must be noted that the UK seems to have moved further and more rapidly down this route than other nations.

3.1 Public Scepticism

At the same time the public is highly sceptical of politicians, the government and civil servants [15], [16], [17]. Recent events, reported at length in the media, have raised questions about the government's integrity - the embellishing of 'evidence' that Iraq possessed WMD in order to justify the imperative of invasion, the implied involvement of the Cabinet in the death of government scientist, Dr. David Kelly, the whitewashed Hutton Report into the case, the debate over whether British troops in Iraq were equipped appropriately, doubts over the legality of the war, and claims of government-sanctioned bugging of the UN. Scepticism towards the apparatus of the state is also increasing, exemplified by public concern over surveillance (databases, speed cameras and the like). State communications do little to reassure, for example the recent television broadcast that car owners who fail to renew annual tax discs will be identified and fined automatically. Such communications are incredibly potent in reinforcing public perceptions of the state as a dominant, coercive power, contradicting many of Prime Minister Blair's statements about the importance of communities, the ideal of co-governance and the state as custodian of the people. In light of the widening gap between the government and the governed it is unsurprising that public has responded with ambivalence to initiatives to improve participation – for example whilst local Citizens' Councils have been created to encourage civic engagement, these tend to attract activists grateful for an avenue along which to pursue their own agendas and have had little effect upon the growing sense of disenfranchisement. According to Warketin et al [18] disaffection with government is likely to affect usage of e-services, thus apparent public ambivalence to the e-platform may in fact be a conscious decision to desist, fuelled by uncertainty about the integrity of both the state and its technology. The prevailing perception of a government out of touch with its citizens and apparently intent upon increasingly interfering in their lives to its own ends presents a significant challenge to the government's ability to engage citizens online.

4 Role of Local Government

At the same time there is little doubt that models of governance which tolerate fragmentation and local representation are in the ascendancy internationally. Like other nations, the UK government has embraced the principle of democratic revival and communitarianism. Its commitment to engaging citizens online is not to be doubted - exemplified not only by the central government portals, but by obliging local government to establish similar portals at local community level. Local e-government strategy is formulated, directed and monitored by the Office of the Deputy Prime Minister, which also administers the 'Local Government Online' (LGOL) fund to assist councils in their development of online services. *However,* at the same time the government appears unwilling to prioritise participation above cost-effectiveness. A statement by the The Institute for Public Policy Research (IPPR) in the 2004 report SOCITM *Local e-Government Now* [19:4] notes:

> 'It seems clear that e-government policy is now at a turning point. On the one hand, more pressure is being placed on local authorities to link e-government activity to the Treasury's Public Service Agreements'... on the other hand, the Efficiency Review is taking centre stage and the potential savings facilitated by e-government are coming centre stage with it.... Central government is now signalling that it wants some serious return on its e-government investment. As a result, the target to get all services online by 2005 is all but dead as a serious framework for shaping future activity'.

Whilst the European Commission's progress report [2] identifies co-ordinated portal solutions and extensive back-office reorganisation as key enablers of e-government, such substantive change requires a significant amount of planning, coordination, resources and time. Given the political imperative of delivering and being seen to deliver outcomes within an elected term these requirements may be treated as luxuries. In its 2003 discussion paper *Managing e-Government* [20:3] the local government Society of Information Management Technology (SOCITM) opines:

> 'The expectation [of central government] is that flexible ICT systems will join up partner organisations at minimum cost with no disruption to existing services and in a very short time frame.....' , however, '...an infrastructure which is low cost normally comes at the expense of flexibility and is, therefore, not very good at joining up to other partners' ICT infrastructure' .

Local government, therefore, is faced with the challenge of constructing an e-government platform which not only delivers its own services, but works in partnership with a range of quasi-private and private agencies to provide services which are not only joined-up but low cost. Despite its desire to reinvent the public sphere and revitalise social democracy, the government has resisted re-nationalising services transferred to the private sector by the Conservatives in the 1980s, opting instead to engage stakeholders by mandating reform of local government political structures, giving councils a statutory duty of public consultation, and developing multi-agency partnerships in key areas (such as health, transport and education) [21]. It has been suggested [22] that there may be a hidden motive – that closeness to the community may not only encourage greater stakeholder participation, but also provide a useful means of exerting pressure for service improvements upon public sector managers, professionals and front line staff – classic neo-liberal outcomes.

4.1 Prevailing Governance Model: 'Centralised Decentralisation'

From the above it is apparent that the New Labour government, far from sweeping away the neo-liberal managerialism of the 1980 – 1990s, has simply superimposed communitarianism upon the existing ideological framework. Newman [21] opines that the Third Way was created instrumentally as a means of distancing New Labour from its predecessor, from unelectable, socialist Labour party. Once elected, however, the government has faced the task of operationalising an essentially self-contradictory discourse. Perry and Peck's [23] neo-Durkheimian analysis of New Labour's modernisation of the public sector exposes a complex model in which management structures are decentralised whilst power is retained centrally. Despite the rhetoric of communitarianism, in practice the Labour government has consistently displayed a propensity to cling to its favoured 'command and control' style in which it can freely exercise coercive power. The Performance and Innovation Unit's 2000 report *Reaching Out* [24] acknowledged that in the past government structures had 'too often been over-centralised, insufficiently joined up and inadequately attuned to local conditions'. *Reaching Out* concluded that the problem lay not in insufficient devolution, but in central government initiatives being disjointed with little attempt to bring together the 'fragmented networks of regional government'. According to Lee and Woodward [25] Blair did not entertain the possibility that overcentralisation might reflect the absence of political devolution and that implementation deficiencies might be best redressed at the local level. Thus, instead of seeking devolution the government favoured a top-down solution, thereby giving itself the almost impossible task of running in parallel two potentially conflicting models of governance: i) devolved, horizontal, participatory; and, ii) hierarchical, centralised and managerialist.

4.2 Partnership

Newman's text, *Modernising Governance* [21] identifies four distinct models of governance in a quadrant framework which vary along two dimensions: decentralisation/differention – centralisation/vertical integration; and, competitiveness/innovation - continuity/ sustainability. The hierarchical model, characterised by centralisation of executive power and vertical coordination lies diametrically opposite the open systems model, based upon experimentation, innovation and incrementalism. The joined-up, networked, collaborative mode espoused by New Labour lies within the open systems quadrant of the model. Third Way communitarianism encourages partnership and alliances between the public, private and voluntary sectors – the result of which can be seen in the proliferation of PPPs (Public-Private-Partnerships) [see 26]. The involvement of multiple partners in public service has, however, in many instances resulted in expensive over-complexity, poor coordination and culture clashes [for example, 27], and questions are now being asked about the real benefits of PPPs [28]. Lacking devolved power, local government has little clout - 'the discourse of partnership speaks of equality, shared values and high trust, creating an illusory unity which masks fundamental differences of power, and resources and directs attention away from the need to engage with the gritty political realities of divergent interests and conflicting goals [21:117]. Whilst local authorities may wish to prioritise local needs, they can not jettison centrally-determined agendas and authoritarian rule – for example, the forced suspension of the Humberside Chief Constable Westwood in July 2004, demanded by the Home Secretary and pushed through the judicial system, despite the resistance of the Humberside Police Authority. Newman [21] suggests that the interaction between centralisation and decentralisation, between 'controlling' and enabling' strategies involve different sets of norms and assumptions which, if overlaid upon each other produce inconsistencies and tensions which are not easily resolved. The inherent imbalance in power between central government and others may undermine the long-term viability of partnerships and multi-agency collaborations.

Many of the government's multi-agency initiatives require the operationalisation of two dramatically different philosophies - for example, the well-intentioned 'Framework for Multi-agency National Project' (FAME), [29] seeks to develop a framework for information sharing in a multi-agency environment, *however* as intimated, the government has set strict targets for the achievement of e-government and electronic service delivery, recognising that 'if these targets are to be met it is essential that efficient and effective information sharing between local authorities and partner organisations takes place'. Prescription and target-setting counteract the imperative of organic growth at the heart of the open systems model. Similarly, the FAME project contains many of the features of a rational goal model, emphasising control, audit and evaluation, yet simultaneously, recognises the importance of self-governance the framework states:

> 'Local leadership – particularly that of elected councillors – is vital to deliver the benefits of local e-government ', identified as 'service transformation, revitalised democracy, and economic vitality'.

The government's definition of 'partnership' appears confined to central and local government working together with private sector companies where appropriate. Whilst this may encourage enterprise and value for money, it is unclear how the democratic ideal might be pursued within such a constrained definition.

Additionally, the complexity of public-private partnerships may burden public servants with responsibilities which they are ill-equipped to deal with - for example, in 1999 the government launched an initiative entitled 'Computers Within Reach' which aimed to provide 100,000 computers to low-income families. Distribution, installation, training and technical support were outsourced to the private sector. The £15 million initiative collapsed in 2002 amid disputes over delivery, faulty hardware and exorbitant help-line charges, illuminating poor planning, inadequate control and naïveity on the part of public sector managers. A recent study [30] appears to confirm that in relation to rational planning the performance of public servants is affected by a lack of technical resources and expertise.

Newman's [21] analysis of inherent confusion in the Third Way is reflected in the inconsistencies of the current e-government strategy, policy and implementation – the aim of joined-up, responsive, participatory' e-services can only be achieved within an open systems model in which organic growth and local autonomy occupy key positions. It is not easy to reconcile this ideal model with the current rational goal approach based upon prescription, centralisation, target setting, performance measurement and management. Indeed, Stoker [31:418] suggests that New Labour's policies towards local authorities are deliberately designed to be a muddle 'in order to both search for the right reform formula and create a dynamic for change by creating instability'.

The government's apparent ambiguity, on the one hand encouraging partnerships based upon flexibility, innovation and experimentation whilst on the other becoming increasingly prescriptive in a bid to secure short-term targets, is in fact a logical outcome of the self-contradiction of the Third Way in which the compelling narrative of communitarianism is continually tempered by economic and political pragmatism.

5 Devolution – The Way Forward?

Thus, far from facilitating the development of e-government, central government's current approach, whether muddled by design or default, may actually be acting as a brake on progress. Faced with eroding power, difficulties in running a 'decentralised, centralised state' efficiently and growing public scepticism, perhaps the time has come to go beyond decentralisation to a truly devolved model. Analysis of local e-government development suggests that in some localities councils have had great success in developing e-platforms in conjunction with private sector and civil organisation [see 19]. In each case the local council has established partnership networks at two levels: strategic, and service. The council acts as a driver and coordinator, drawing in other public authorities or voluntary and community organisations, or in some cases private companies which provide, for example, ICT or customer care expertise. Local authorities take seriously their obligation to deliver high quality, yet efficient e-services – the SOCITM report *Local e-Government now* [19] states:

> 'It is no longer enough for councils and their partners to look simply at using technologies to deliver individual services or transactions electronically, even though that may deliver improvements in services. The focus now must be on maximising the return on the investments that have been, and are still being made. The value of local e-government must be judged by the return it delivers to all the stakeholders'.

Local successes in the UK mirror those achieved by other EU nations which are pursuing regional and local approaches to e-government [32]. Unlike the European regional developments, however, local authorities in the UK have set themselves an ambitious target to deliver high returns to 'all stakeholders'. Set against the latest, and hitherto most stringent Efficiency Review [5] it is unlikely that local authorities will achieve this target by their own efforts. Ronit [33] observes that the potential role of civil society institutions in contemporary governance has until now been widely neglected. Civil society institutions offer the prospect of a form of governance which relies less on state and market and more on alliances and global networks of private self-regulation. Since public choice theory exposed the 'myth' of public service serving the greater good (claiming instead that it serves only the opportunistic behaviour of bureaucrats and politicians), such a model at least offers the attraction of networks of coordination and cooperation, which may be instrumental in reshaping governance relations. In an analysis of possible regional strategies for e-government development a recent EU report [34] identifies Lombardy as a 'negotiating' region which is developing variable alliances for specific projects and application areas. One of the key objectives in Lombardy is to develop an integrated network connecting local administrations and public agencies. Plans are project-based and 'bottom-up', requiring extensive negotiations with diverse partners. Importantly, the Department of Innovation has created a network of regional competence centres to provide know-how and support for the devolved government. This model of 'negotiating regions' could potentially provide a blueprint for the development of local government in the UK provided central government is willing to 'let go of the reins'.

In a recent paper Lee-Kelley and Kolsaker [35] suggest that e-government success will have to be redefined and measured against criteria which reflect the degree of fit between provision and citizen usage. The reality is that if the public fails to engage in e-government then the state, markets and civil society can not be reconnected as sought in Third Way ideology. Networks of voluntary cooperation may be well placed to improve the degree of fit, without being accused of nanny state interference or Big Brother surveillance. To be successful, central government would have to withdraw from its command and control regime, giving local networks an opportunity to develop e-services which are fit for purpose within the local context. It is argued here that local communities face different challenges and have varying priorities, thus the government's 'one size fits all' approach to the provision of low-cost local e-services, coupled with recent signals that it is seeking serious return on its e-government investment warns of a further drive towards efficiency which may jeopardise participation. It is self-evident that communitarian governance requires the involvement of the community – yet the community is unlikely to be particularly enthusiastic about low-cost, standardised, automated services.

6 Conclusion

In sum, the e-government platform offers much more than the prospect of cost-effective, electronically-enabled government services. It offers also an opportunity to harness the Web to construct a new communitarian, information age model of governance, closing the widening gap between citizens and state, reducing public scepticism and involving civil societies in creative, organic public/private/voluntary collaborations. Ideologically, 'information age governance' chimes well with the Third Way - indeed, socio-political interaction and communitarian collaboration are key elements of Third Way ideology. Yet, whilst Web technology offers a means of facilitating collaborative governance, there is little sign that the UK government is minded to pursue new opportunities. Though lip-service is paid to participation and empowerment, in practice citizens and partners are invited to *deploy* government-prescribed e-services rather then *design and develop* a new model of technology-enabled governance. That the government has chosen not to develop the communitarian potential of the Web suggests one of two things, either visionary myopia and an obsession with low cost delivery, or a conscious decision to exploit technology to maintain the planned muddle of the centralised, decentralised state. Whatever the desired outcome, government should not ignore the potential of new, networked collaborations in post-social society. Thus far there has been little analysis of low usage rates in relation to citizen disengagement and the changing face of democracy. E-government potentially has an important role in governance - the technology is superbly equipped to facilitate new strategic partnerships, communities of interest and synergistic collaborations, but if it is to harness the full potential of the electronic medium the government *must* reconceptualise its e-government strategy in terms of a platform for a new, devolved model of communitarian e-governance.

References

1. La Porte, T., Demchak, C. and de Jong, M.: 'Democracy and Bureaucracy in the Age of the Web: Emprical Findings and Theoretical Speculations', *Administration and Society,* Vol. 34 (4), (2002) pp. 411 – 446
2. European Commission DG Information Society report: *Online Availability of Public Services: How is Europe progressing?,* Cap Gemini Ernst and Young (2004)
3. The Cabinet Office: 'Modernising Government', London, The Stationary Office available from http://www.archive.official-documents.co.uk (1999)
4. Giddens, A.: *The Third Way and its Critics,* Oxford, Polity Press (2000)
5. TSO*Efficiency Review: Releasing resources to the frontline,* Independent Review of Public Sector Efficiency, July (2004), available from http://www.hm-treasury.gov.uk/ media//879E2/efficiency_review120704.pdf
6. Jackson, P.: Public Choice and Public Sector Management, *Public Money and Management,* Winter, (1990) pp. 13 - 20
7. Clapham, C. :The Challenge to the State in a Globalized World, *Development and Change,* Vol. 33 (5) (2002) pp. 775 - 795
8. Sunday Times, 29th February 2004
9. 9..Sheptycki, J.: Transnational policing and the makings of the postmodern state, *British Journal of Criminology,* Vol. 35 (4) (1995) pp. 613 - 635
10. Cohen, S.: Social Control and the politics of reconstruction. In D. Nelken (ed) *The Futures of Criminology,* London, Sage (1994)
11. Peters, G.: Managing the hollow state, In K. Eliassen and J. Kooiman (eds) *Managing Public Organisations: Lessons from Contemporary European Experience,* London, Sage (1993)
12. Rhodes, R.: The hollowing out of the state: the changing nature of public services in Britain, *Political Quarterly,* Spring, (1994) pp. 138 – 151
13. Taylor-Gooby, P. and Lawson, R. (eds): 'Where do we go from here: the new order in welfare'. In P. Taylor-Gooby and R. Lawson *Markets and Managers: New Issues in the Delivery of Welfare,* Buckingham, Open University Press (1993)
14. Giddens, A.: *The Third Way: the Renewal of Social Democracy,* Oxford, Polity Press (1998)
15. Morris, P.J.: The public trust doctors more than politicians, *Bulletin of The Royal College of Surgeons of England,* Vol. 85 (9) (2003) pp. 306 – 308
16. MORI: *Who do we trust? Neither Politicians nor Journalists*! (2003), available from http://www.mori.com/pubinfo/rmw/whomdowetrust.shtml
17. The Times Online: *Public Trust Wanes,* July 18th (2004), available from http://www.timesonline.co.uk/article/0,,15629-1183290,00.html
18. Warkentin, M., Gefen, D., Pavlou, P. and Rose, G.: Encouraging Citizen Adoption, of e-Government by Building Trust, *Electronic Markets*, Vol. 12 (3) (2002) pp. 157 – 162
19. Society of Information Technology Management (SOCITM): 'Local e-government now' (2004), available from: http://www.socitm.gov.uk
20. Society of Information Technology Management (SOCITM): 'Managing e-government' (2003), available from: http://www.socitm.gov.uk
21. Newman, J.: *Modernising Governance,* London, Sage (2001)
22. Foley, P. and Martin, S.: Perceptions of Community Led Regeneration: Community and Government Viewpoints, *Regional Studies,* Vol. 34 Issue 8 (2000) pp.783 - 7885
23. Perry, S and Peck, E.: New Labour's Modernization in the Public Sector: A Neo-Durkheimian Approach and the Case of Mental Health Services, *Public Administration,* Vol. 82 (1) (2004) pp. 83 - 108

24. Performance and Innovation Unit: *Reaching Out: the role of central government at regional and local level,* London, The Stationary Office (2000)
25. Lee, S. and Woodward, R.: Implementing the Third Way: The Delivery of Public Services under the Blair Government, *Public Money and Management,* CIPFA, October – December (2002)
26. see http://www.partnershipsuk.org.uk
27. Stephens, M. and Fowler, G.: Safer Guildford, *Public Management Review,* Vol 6 (1) (2004) pp. 113 – 121
28. Mulder, A. and Van Tulder, R.: PPPs: beneficial to whom?, *European Business Forum,* Vol, 18 (2004) pp. 24 – 27
29. Framework for Multi-Agency National Project (2004), available from http://www.localegov.gov.uk
30. Boyne, G., Gould-Williams, J, Law, J, and Walker R.: Problems of Rational Planning in Public Organisations, *Administration and Society,* Vol. 36 (3) (2004) pp. 328 - 351
31. Stoker, G.: Life is a Lottery: New Labour's strategy for the reform of devolved governance, *Public Administration,* Vol. 80 (3) (2002) pp.417 - 434
32. European Commission: IDA e-Government newsletter, *Bringing a regional and local dimension to the EU's e-government policy.* September (2004), available from www.europa.eu.int/ida
33. Ronit, K.: Institutions of Private Authority in Global Governance: Linking Territorial Forms of Self-Regulation, *Administration and Society,* Vol. 33 (5) (2001) pp. 555 – 579
34. European Union: Socio-Economic Trends Assessment of the digital Revolution (STAR) *Building e-Government: European regions' alternative strategies* report (2004), available from www.databank.it/star/regions
35. Lee-Kelley, E. and Kolsaker, A.: 'e-Government: the 'fit' between supply assumptions and usage drivers, *International Journal of Electronic Government,* Vol. 1 (2) (2004) pp. 130 – 140

"Urban Versus Regional Divide: Comparing and Classifying Digital Divide"

Enrico Ferro[1], Marco Cantamessa[2], and Emilio Paolucci[2]

[1] Istituto Superiore Mario Boella (ISMB), Via Boggio 61, 10138 Turin, Italy
Tel: +39 011 2276201, Fax: + 39 011 2276299
www.enricoferro.com
[2] Politecnico di Torino (POLITO), Cso Duca degli Abruzzi 24,10129, Turin, Italy
Tel: +39 011 5647223, Fax: +39 011 5647299
{marco.cantamessa, emilio.paolucci}@polito.it

Abstract. This paper presents a comparative study on digital divide between a region and its main metropolitan area. The exercise shows how barriers to technology access and usage may vary in terms of both nature and intensity. The paper also proposes a taxonomy of the different types of digital divides that may be present inside a region.

1 Introduction

In recent years, the issue of digital divide has attracted significant interest from both scientists and policy markers. Many papers and reports have been published trying to quantify and describe the phenomenon in terms of who is affected and how.

Researchers that have heretofore dealt with the issue of digital divide may be classified into two main categories. On the one side, there are those that believe digital divide to be a physiological delay inherent in the diffusion of technologies among different geographic areas and social groups [1], [2]. These researchers share the view that digital delays do not require the intervention of public administration since they will eventually be solved by the market.

On the other side, there are researchers that see digital divide as a source of social inequality that mirrors the unbalanced situation in terms of opportunities and quality of life present at global level. For this reason they claim a public intervention to be necessary since the market has shown not to be able to bridge a gap that is profoundly rooted in the structure of society [3], [4].

In spite of the very different views and opinions emerged about the importance and the magnitude of the digital divide in both the short and the long term, a general agreement has been reached on the actual presence of a gap in terms of possibilities and opportunities between people who have access to information and people who do not.

The aim of this paper is not to discuss the importance of digital divide, but simply to raise the awareness of policy makers about some of the aspects that should be kept in due account when assessing its possible presence in a region. It is our firm belief

M. Böhlen et al. (Eds.): TCGOV 2005, LNAI 3416, pp. 81–90, 2005.

that, regardless of its importance, digital divide represents an issue that may potentially jeopardize the homogenous diffusion and development of the information society in a territory and as such it must be carefully monitored and wisely managed by local and regional governments.

2 Context: "The Info-Society Regional Observatory"

The results presented in the following paper are based on the data collected by the Regional Observatory on the Information Society of the Mario Boella Institute. On a yearly basis, the above-mentioned observatory collects data about technology adoption and usage among the main socio-economic actors present on the territory.

The comparative exercise presented below has been carried out using data collected from citizens while the taxonomy proposed in the second part of the paper has been created using the data collected from citizens, municipalities and enterprises.

3 Objectives

The objectives of the paper at hand are mainly two:

1. To help policy makers understand what types of policies may yield the best returns in terms of the Information Society diffusion. Objective that will be pursued by investigating, through a comparative analysis, the context dependency of factors contributing to the creation of digital gaps in areas with similar socio-economic systems.
2. To suggest a taxonomy of different types of digital divide aiming at pointing out the complementary relationship between demand and offer aspects. The acknowledgement of presence of this relationship may represent a key interpretative tool for policy makers in order to create a systemic view of the phenomenon.

4 Methodology

As already mentioned, for the purposes of this paper the data collected by the Regional Observatory on the Information Society of the ISMB was used.

For the identification of the digital divide determinants, two stratified samples of citizens were generated to compare the digital divide present in the region with the one present in the main metropolitan area located in the same region. As it may be noticed from table 1, interviews were distributed as follows: 1000 in the Piedmont region and 700 in the city of Turin. The total number of interviews was thus 1700 out of a total population of about 4.2 million inhabitants.

Table 1. Sample Breakdown

SAMPLING		
Area	**Sample Size**	*Population*
Turin	700	900,987
Piedmont	1000	3,313,690
Total	1700	4,214,677

The variables adopted for the stratification of the sample were: age, gender and size of town of residence. The methodology used for the data collection was CATI (Computer Aided Telephone Interviews).

As per the analysis, the data set used included Boolean variables (broadband adoption and usage) and ordinal categorical variables (explanatory variables). By adopting log-linear models it was possible to identify which categories (i.e.: income/age/education ranges) had a statistically significant probability not to be broadband adopters/users. These probabilities were calculated using odds ratios that are a common measure of association among variables.

From a policy maker point of view this is an extremely interesting result since it allows to single out the population groups that should be targeted in the process of policy design.

Finally, for the creation of the digital divides taxonomy we included the data collected from also enterprises and public administrations in order to have a solid basis of observations representing the most important aspects of the phenomenon.

5 Urban Versus Regional Divide

In this section of the paper, we are going to present the results of a comparative study between the Piedmont region and the city of Turin in terms of digital divide. The exercise has been carried out with the intent to investigate whether and how the determinants of digital divide may vary in terms of nature and intensity even between areas belonging to the same region.

Due to length constrains, we decided to focus our analysis on two variables. Nevertheless we made sure to include both access and usage aspects. The first aspect investigated was the adoption of broadband connections (≥640kbs) among households. The segmentation variables used were: income and number of people in the household. Explanatory variables such as age, education and gender were not used in the analysis of this aspect since the adoption of an Internet connection is a decision influenced by the family composition rather then just some specific characteristics of the person answering the telephone interview.

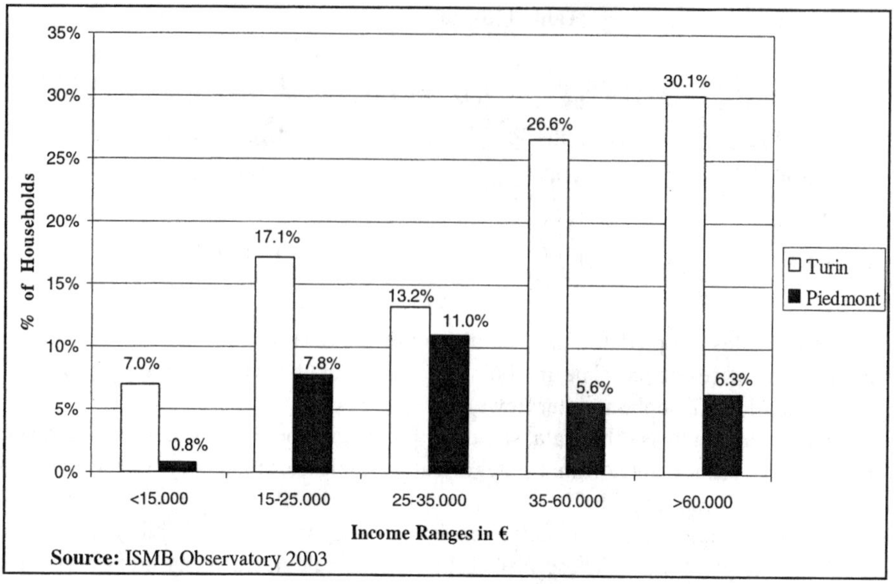

Fig. 1. Households with a Broadband Connection by Income

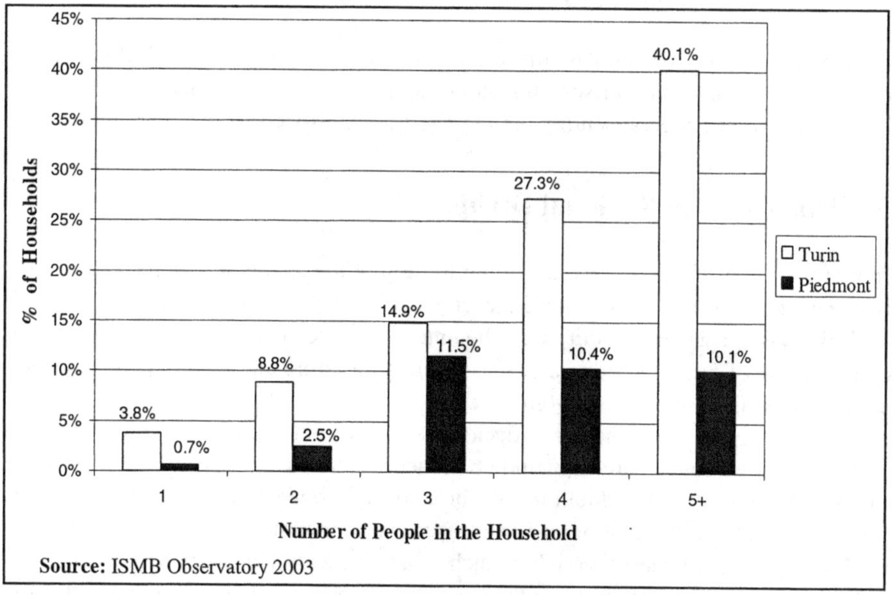

Fig. 2. Households with a Broadband Connection by Size

As it may be noticed by looking at figure 1 and 2 different scenarios may be depicted for the two areas taken into consideration. In Turin both income and family size seem to be important adoption drivers, while the situation is not equally clear in

Piedmont. In order to deepen the understanding of the impact of each segmentation variable, a multivariate analysis was conducted allowing to isolate the effect of age and household size on adoption.

In the log-linear model design, income and family size were set as explanatory variables while broadband adoption was set as outcome.

In Turin, the analysis showed that small and low income households are more likely not to have a broadband connection. (Odds ratios of not owning a broadband connection are respectively 5.39 for households with a yearly net income lower than 15,000€, 6.31 for households with one member and 3.59 for households with two members).

In Piedmont, instead, the situation looks quite different. Income does not exert a statistically significant influence on the adoption of broadband connections while families with one and two members have odd ratios of not having a broadband connection that are respectively 2.4 and 3.7 times higher than the ones found for the city of Turin.

It is also interesting to note that in Turin the odds ratio of one member households not to have broadband connection is 1.76 times higher than those of a household with two members, while in Piedmont are only 1.1 higher. As a caveat, it must be said that the validity of odds ratio comparison holds as long as all the other independent variables are kept constant.

From this first part of the analysis it is already possible to observe some significant differences between the two areas. From a policy maker point of view, being able to identify families with a yearly net income lower than 15.000€ as potential information outcasts represents an important piece of information that could be used to design more effective and better targeted support policies.

Moreover, the fact that income plays a role in broadband adoption in the main city where the infrastructures are available, but it does not in the rest of the region where digital highways are scarce could suggest that an approach simply based on fostering the diffusion of infrastructures will not be enough to contrast the potential diffusion of digital divide.

As far as usage is concerned, the variable used in the analysis was: regular Internet usage, defined as access on at least a weekly basis.

The comparative descriptive statistics presented from figure 3 to 5 provide a first picture of the possible relationships between regular Internet usage and three socio-economic variables: age, education and gender.

At a first glance, the situation present in both areas seems to be similar, but at a closer look reality may be quite different. As already stated, descriptive statistics does not allow to separate the influence of each variable. We thus adopted a multivariate approach again, finding some interesting results.

The log-linear model was designed as follows: regular Internet usage was set as response variable while age, gender and education were used as explanatory variables.

By looking at the results produced by the application of the model at the two areas, it emerged that in Turin the width of digital gaps is wider than in Piedmont. In fact, although in both areas age and education are positively correlated with regular Internet usage, in Turin the odds ratio not to be a regular Internet user of a person between 45 to 54 years old is 9.5 times higher than that of a person between 16 and 24. In Piedmont, instead, people with an age between 45 and 54 have an odds ratio

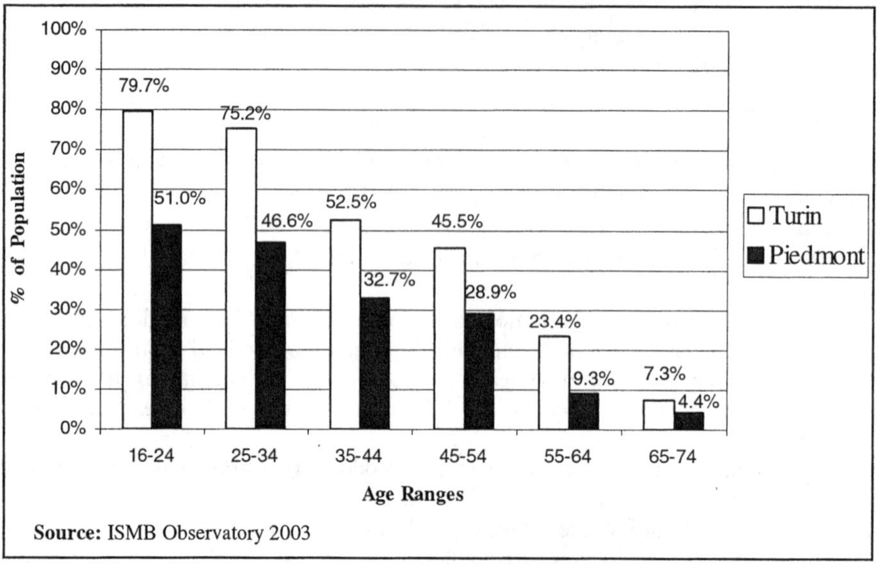

Fig. 3. Regular Internet Users by Age

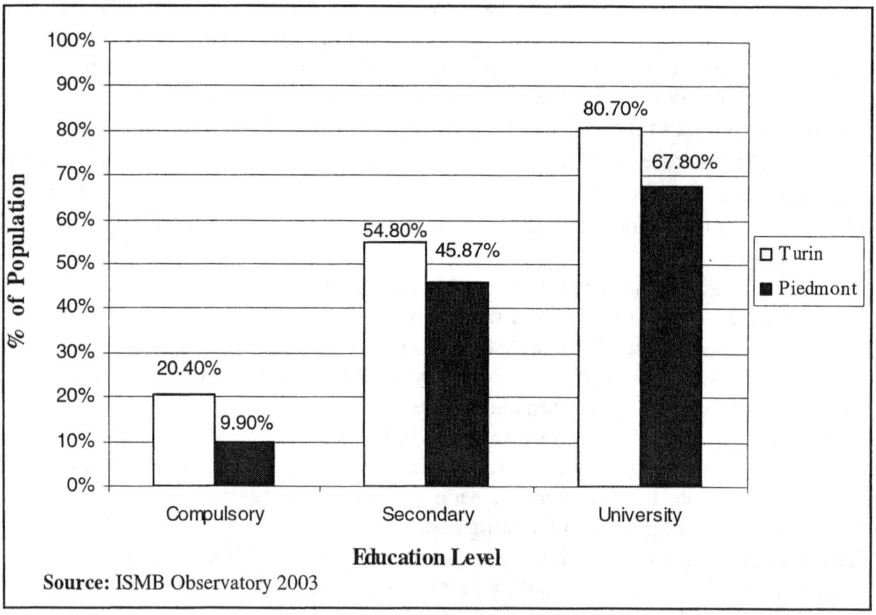

Fig. 4. Regular Internet Users by Education Level

not be a regular internet user that is only 2.5 times higher than that of people between 16 and 24. This, in simple terms, means that the divide present in terms of usage between young and mature people in Turin is considerably wider than in Piedmont.

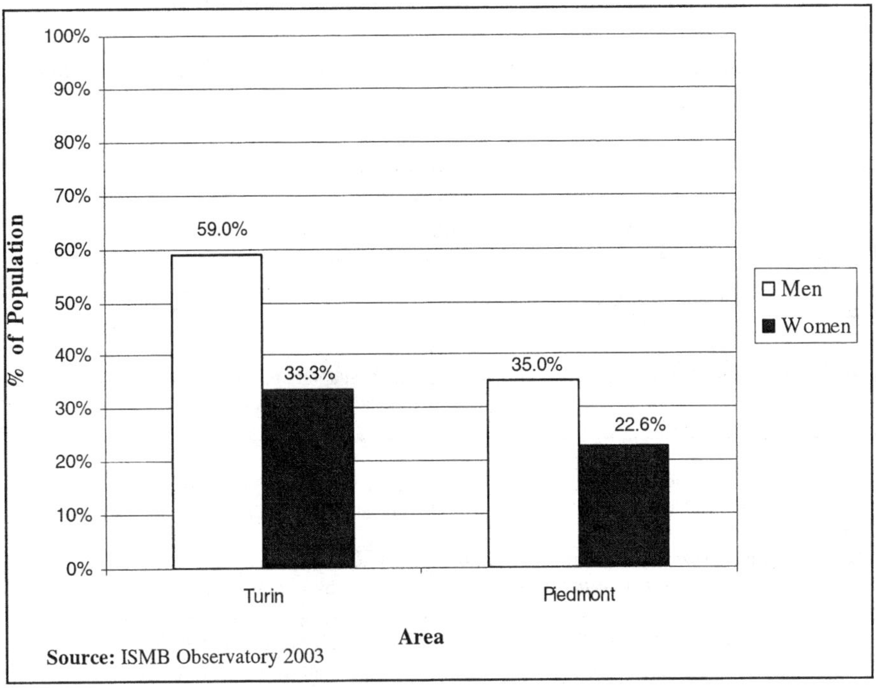

Fig. 5. Regular Internet Users by Gender

As far as gender is concerned, some differences may be found as well. In Turin, women have an odds ratio not to be regular internet users that is twice as high as that of women living outside the main city.

Finally, taking into consideration education, the model mainly confirms what may be noticed from the descriptive statistics. In other words, people with a compulsory education in Turin are twice as less likely to be regular Internet users than those living in the rest of the region.

The correlation between age, gender, education and Internet usage, in itself does not represent a novelty. What may be considered an interesting result, instead, is the fact that digital divide seems to be more severe in areas with higher penetration levels. From a policy maker stand point this represent a challenge since, it reinforces the idea that policies should not only foster infrastructure diffusion but also account for socio-economic divides that arise as the level of adoption increase.

6 Digital Divide Taxonomy

In this final section of the paper, we present a taxonomy that was generated from the observation of different types of digital divide.

The analysis carried out in the first part of this paper showed digital divide as a multifaceted issue that requires articulated solutions. For this reason, the identification of its main dimensions is felt to be an essential step toward the definition of effective policies.

The classification below does not have the ambition to be exhaustive, but should be considered as a first attempt to provide an explicit framework to the different types of digital divide. In particular, it aims to highlight the correlation between demand and offer related aspects.

DIGITAL DIVIDE TAXONOMY

	INTRA-MUNICIPAL (Social Classes)	**INTER-MUNICIPAL (Geographic Areas)**
OFFER	1. Availability of PCs and Internet connections in schools and public places 2. Diffusion of WAI compliant websites	1. Lack of e-Government service provisioning in small municipalities 2. Availability of broadband networks outside metropolitan areas
DEMAND	1. Gap associated to age, gender, education and income 2. Gap associated to enterprise size, sector of activity and type of management	1. Lower penetration of PC and Fast Internet connections in rural vs. metropolitan areas 2. Less training and lower ICT usage in small Public Administrations

Fig. 6. Digital Divide Taxonomy

Figure 6 represents a two by two matrix classifying the different types of digital divides that may be found inside a single region. Along the vertical axis it is possible to distinguish between demand and offer of ICT related products or services. Along the horizontal axis, instead, a distinction is made between gaps present among geographic areas (i.e. urban vs. rural areas, big municipalities vs. small, etc.) and those that are present inside a single municipality. In the case of population, these gaps may be attributed to factors such as income, education, gender. In the case of enterprises, to size, sector of activity, type of management, etc.

The classification work carried out may be considered to be useful for the following reasons. First of all, it shows that digital divide is not a monolithic concept but rather a multifaceted phenomenon determined by the interaction of a set elements with specific features. This view suggests that policies should be designed coherently with the characteristics of the digital divide they are aiming to bridge and that a one-size-fits-all approach will most likely fail in producing effective results.

Secondly, the classification highlights the interdependency relationship between demand related and offer related gaps. Often times, in fact, digital divide is regarded in its entirety as one of the main motivations of slow and heterogeneous diffusion of ICT technologies. Rarely, instead, these motivations have been presented as a combination of demand and offer related causes.

Finally, the classification shows that investment choice may have a tremendous impact on results obtained. Investing in policies aiming at reducing offer related divides may in fact represent a wiser choice since it has an indirect impact on demand related divides as well. To exemplify, an investment aimed at increasing the availability of PCs in schools will also have a positive impact on demand related gaps due to socio-economic variables.

7 Conclusions

From the comparative exercise carried out, the main result that emerged was that in the two areas considered, the barriers to access and usage may differ both in terms of nature and intensity. In fact, it showed that the impact of socio-economic variables on both technology adoption and usage seems to be more severe in the city of Turin, where penetration rates are higher and the broadband infrastructure coverage is complete. This suggests that just investing in physical infrastructures to connect rural areas will only partially solve the issue of digital divide, since it would simply shift the problem from a geographical to a socio-economic sphere.

Moreover, public investments in network infrastructures entail a number problems and risks. Firstly, technological neutrality, although auspicated by EU regulations, is next to impossible to achieve in practice. As a consequence, this type of investments requires a technological choice that is bound to create market perturbations. Secondly, the high level of red tape involved coupled with the high pace of technological innovation, may render the technology chosen obsolete even before its application.

A further confirmation that investments in infrastructures alone do not yield good results may be found in the data about coverage and adoption of broadband services in Piedmont (respectively 70% and 9.1%).

At this point, a legitimate question could arise: what type of intervention would then be necessary? In our opinion, policies aimed at fostering the level of adoption where infrastructures are already available may prove to be more effective since they produce positive effects on both demand and offer related aspects. On the former, the increase of users produces positive network externalities. On the latter, instead, the increase of the adopters' percentage contributes to reduce the threshold of potential customers that municipalities need to meet in order to be reached by telecom operators. Moreover, it also represents an incentive for application providers to increment the amount of content produced.

Concluding, the multidimensional approach adopted should account for the different types of divides present on the territory. As a matter of fact, the choice of which gap to bridge may actually results to be strategically important in order to maximize the impact of the investment on the entire system.

References

1. Adriani F., Becchetti L. (2003), "*Does the Digital Divide Matter? The role of ICT in cross-country level and growth estimates*". CEIS Tor Vergata.
2. Benjamin M., (2001) "*Re-examining the Digital Divide*", Internet and Telecom Consortium, MIT
3. Chin M.D, Fairlie R.W., (2004) "*The determinants of the Global Digital Divide: A Cross-Country Analysis of Computer and Internet Penetration*" Economic Growth Center Yale University

4. Cole J.I., et al., (2004) *"The Digital Future Report"* USC Center for the Digital Future.
5. Christie I and Perry H (1997) "*Wealth and poverty of networks: tackling social exclusion*" Demos, London
6. Foley P., (2004), "*Does the Internet Help to Overcome Social Exclusion*" International Journal of eGovernment Vol. 2 Issue 2 pp.139-146
7. Kim H., Moon J., Yan S., (2004), "*Broadband Penetration and Participatory Politics: South Corea Case*", HICSS conference
8. Norris P., (2000) *"World Wide Digital Divide: Infopoverty, the Internet and Development"*, Johnn F. Kennedy School of Government, Harvard.
9. Peter K. YU., (2002), "*Bridging the Digital Divide: Equality in the Information Age*" Cardozo Law School. http://ssrn.com/abstract_ID=309841
10. Piazolo D. (2001), *"The Digital Divide"* CESifo Forum 2001, Vol.2 No. 3, 29-34.
11. Prieger J.E., (2001), *"The Supply Side of the Digital Divide: Is There Redlining in the Broadband Internet Access Market?"* http://ssrn.com/abstract_ID=309841
12. Xavier P., (2002) "*Bridging the digital divide: issues and policies in OECD countries"*, OCSE, Paris.

e-Citizen: Why Waiting for the Governments?

Armando Rech Filho

BRISA – Information Technology Development Society,
São Paulo, SP, Brazil
armando.rech@brisa.org.br

Abstract. The State of the Art in Electronic Government is the delivering of public services to the Citizen by means of integrated web portals, comprising the public agencies in the different levels of government, aiming to hide from the final user the complexity of the State bureaucracy. Ideally, these portals should be designed according to the mental patterns of the individuals, with their navigation oriented by the life events, and not by the logic of bureaucracy. Besides, the services to be provided must match both the Citizen's and the State's interests. Considering that many e-Government portals do not follow these principles, this article proposes an inversion in the policy of access to public services. By breaking paradigms, it presents the organized society as the drive engine behind the construction of integrated portals, with contents and shape to match citizen's interests, rather than waiting for the government action.

1 The New Context of the Public Services in the Digital Era

The use of Internet has been promoting changes in the way organizations provide services to society. In the last decade the Internet has been solidifying itself as the great propeller of development in the business arena, eliminating barriers of time and space, and bringing convenience and comfort to the individuals. More than ever these individuals want to interact with the organizations at the time, the place and the way they deem adequate, preferably without intermediate steps of any sort. In the competitive world, the waste of personal time is less and less tolerated and the promptness in the replies more and more appreciated [1], [2].

There is an evident change in the relationship between the organizations and their target public, forcing the inclusion of Internet as a service delivery channel in business strategies. The private companies invest on the Internet pursuing continuous cost reduction, quality increase, and product or service differentiation, aiming to seize market share in a global and highly competitive world [3].

From the moment the customers acquire the power in their relationship with the private companies, taking control and conducting business their way [1], [3], [4], they start to feel the need of interacting with the State in the same manner. It must be considered though that the Citizen does not always interact with the State because they like it or want it, but rather because they need it and have no other choice, and also because they have the right to [5]. And provided that the access to the State is financed by tax money, the individuals are not keen on taking on the burden of the inefficiency of the public administration.

M. Böhlen et al. (Eds.): TCGOV 2005, LNAI 3416, pp. 91–99, 2005.

2 The Response Expected by Society

What the society expects from the e-Governments is a web portal of public services that is able to bring to the Citizen the same level of comfort and convenience that they find in the private sector. This portal must be built according to a new philosophy, with a new structure of navigation, emphasizing the way of thinking of the individual and no longer the logic of bureaucracy [5], [6]. In the logic of the common Citizen, they want to start a business, pay a tribute, set an appointment with a doctor or enrol their children in a public school. They do not need to know which level of government the school administration is part of, what public offices are involved in the starting of a business, which division they need to pay their taxes to or who is responsible for the public health care system.

In the same way that place and time are no longer restrictive barriers on the Internet, the hierarchy and departmentalisation of the State have no longer significance, because the structure of the State can work in networks where all the public offices involved in the provision of services are interconnected. The Citizen accesses a web portal which is organized by services representing life events, and no longer by the structure of State. Following the location of the required service by the user, the navigation system takes charge of integrating the several government agencies in a seamless way to conduct the individual to its completion [7]. It becomes unnecessary to understand how the State is organized, as well as which peripheral instruments are needed to complete the process, such as the telephone, the e-mail and personal visits to the respective divisions or public offices. Everything that does not depend on the physical presence of the Citizen can be attained by touching the keyboard of a personal computer.

An integrated web portal of public services focused on the Citizen is conceivable on the grounds that the Citizen is unique in their contrast with the State, thus needing to identify themselves only once to the portal to gain access to all services they require. Once identified, the individual can perform secure online transactions to whichever service, without the need of knowing which department is providing them. A service access gateway drives the communication according to the demands of the user and takes charge of establishing the necessary navigation steps, in case one or more government departments need to be put together for the completion of the task [8].

One of the existing web portals that implement the concept of gateway is of the British Government (www.direct.gov.uk) [8]. A successful example of web portal focused on the Citizen is the Singapore's e-Citizen (www.e-citizen.sg) [1], [7], [9]. In Brazil, the state government of Minas Gerais has recently implemented a new portal based on life events navigation (www.mg.gov.br).

Adopting this new focus in Electronic Government is nothing more than applying the concepts of automated integration of business processes that private companies normally perform, in the pursuit of establishing added value chains and thus caring for their customers in a competitive way, reducing costs, improving quality, increasing the responsiveness of operations and bringing down the time to market [10].

3 Barriers in the Introduction of the New Concepts

The adoption of the new model, however, requires cultural changes and a transformation in the relationship between the government structures, in the same way that private companies have been transforming their processes to overcome the impacts of the Internet competition. The gains for the Citizen will only be achieved through a complete rethinking of the government process, by eliminating the complexities of the off-line world. It is not enough to simply provide the same old services on the internet, on pain of perpetuating bureaucracy. The Internet presents itself as an opportunity for the State to redesign its services to cater for the effective needs of the Citizens and at the same time maintain its structure in a more cost-effective way, making possible a more efficient public governance.

The required transformations, however, are doomed by complexity, calling for considerable effort and political will for their implementation. The service mix is large and its spanning throughout different government departments requires sometimes complex co-operation among them [9], [11]. Besides, in some cases, the service delivery can involve different levels of government, partnerships with non-governmental entities or even with private companies [5]. Those difficulties are not technology-related, but of social, organizational and institutional nature, and their overcoming depends on the capacity of the different players in exploiting the potentiality that technology offers [5], [12].

The technologies of the Internet and the concept of integrated public service portals are more and more vital for the State to accomplish its obligations towards its citizens with the same efficiency in which it levies taxes. However, it needs to be clear that the real transformations will come not only from the availability of services on the Internet, but from a re-design of the State as a whole, putting the Citizen as the centre of attentions [11], [12].

In this sense the Citizen is more and more demanding. He exerts pressure and many governments begin to realize that they need to supply a better service to broaden the democratic participation and give more transparency of its acts to its citizens. With this in mind, governmental institutions invest in programs of e-Government, because the use of the Internet improves the governance and contributes to the full exercise of citizenship by their people [9]. Taking into account that its implementation implies in gains for the society as well as for the economy of the State, it is harder and harder to find justification for the lack of investments in the improvement of the public service delivery on the Internet.

4 Electronic Government Still Privileges the State

Nevertheless, the vast majority of electronic government programs are in their incipient stage [7]. The efforts are still quite isolated between public offices, each one contemplating the Citizen their own way, under their own logic and implementing services according to their own interests. The e-Government portals, unified access points to services and information, are created according to the bureaucratic logic, reflecting this way the very own structure of the State. In order to access a service, it is necessary that the individual knows which departments are responsible for that service. The same way he peregrinates through the counters of bureaucracy to obtain services in the conventional way, the citizen navigates through the guts of the digital bureaucracy until being able to complete (if lucky) his electronic transaction.

A case study conducted to evaluate the public services delivery to the residents of the city of Curitiba, state of Parana, Brazil, revealed that the priority in the implementation of the online public services regards the interest of the State [13]. Analysing the three levels of government (local, state and national) under the viewpoint of the integrated web portals, the tax collecting (68%) and drivers and vehicles licence control (78%) had completion rates significantly higher than health (28%) and education (28%) services. The methodology to evaluate the completion rates took into account the services that can be performed without the physical intervention of the individual, and the possibility of integration between the departments and levels of governments for the provision of each service, and traces a comparison to what is actually found in practice.

The questioning is not towards the high rates obtained by the tax collection services, because those are vital for the well functioning of the State. The easier the control of tax collection is, the more budget there will be, a part of which can be allocated to the supply of public services. The problem the survey shows is that the application of this money does not occur in the same intensity for those services of higher interest to the citizen.

The survey also shows that the concept of service gateway for the authentication and navigation oriented by the mental pattern of the individual and by life events has not been implemented. And there seems to be a long way between this vision and reality.

The methodology applied to the research does not allow for generalizations, but taking into account that the City of Curitiba boasts development indexes and life standards comparable to large cities in more developed countries, it is expected that a similar situation is to be found in the majority of cities throughout the world.

5 Electronic Citizen and Electronic Government

Based on the analysis of the international scenario featuring the public services on the internet, and the results of the above mentioned survey, a new proposition comes to light, and a new emphasis to break the current paradigm becomes more deign of discussion: the concept of *Electronic Citizen*. In contrast with *Electronic Government*, which is used worldwide and prioritises the services in the interest of the State, *Electronic Citizen*, delivered for instance in Singapore [1], [7], [9], puts a higher priority on the Citizen.

There are some governments worldwide working on this concept, focusing the Citizen in the centre of their e-government programs, but the majority are still in the old bureaucratic age, in the earlier stages of services providing. For these governments, that could not achieve yet the new vision, the question to be made is: why waiting for their actions? Why can not society take on the responsibility for having the initiative of the development and the deployment of the service portals emphasising the citizen, organizing them according to their own interests?

The establishment of partnerships for the implementation of e-Government programmes is supported by many researchers as a mean of leveraging their development. All sorts of partners can give their contribution, amongst them the very own public offices, as well as private entities, universities, research centres and non-governmental organizations [5], [14]. These partnership have been proposed as e-government intermediation or government service provision [19].

However, the typical approach is that the government searches those partnerships to carry out its projects established, here again, in order to pursue its own interests. Many governments have been choosing partners for improving their services supplying in many ways like for instance: introducing new technologies, re-engineering business process, training of public employees, deploying new applications, creating or expanding channels for access to the services. Examples can be found in United Kingdom [17] and Italy [18] and other countries worldwide.

The aim herein is not to discuss these cases of typical partnership but to bring as innovation the proposition of a new approach: the society organized by means of non-governmental institutions, for instance, taking charge of searching the desired partnerships, specially with the State, and thereby leading the new services, planning them, deploying the application systems, operating the services portal, training the communities for using and so on. Evidently the State will be always strongly involved in all the processes, but not necessarily should be the one to take the initiative. That is a way of the society to choose by itself the preferable channels to access the public services and moreover to induce the government to deploy new services of its own interests. It does not mean any kind of responsibility transference from the State to the Citizen but a new way of organizing the public services access.

The proposal is for an alternative channel for the Citizen to access public services the same way he does for private companies services. The public services will continue to be provided by the State in the former way to those who can not or do not want to have access by Internet.

6 The Drivers for the New Approach

This proposition is based on the assumption that no technological difficulties are to be overcome for the adoption of the new concepts in electronic government. Every technology adopted by the private sector can be used for the delivery of public services on the internet [3], [9].

Normally governments have many applications for its business processes that are restrained to the internal bureaucracy of its departments. These applications can be kept in the same way they have been implemented, as legacy systems. Running over these processes, an integrated access web portal can be constructed with a unique authentication gateway, and offering to the user a seamless and comprehensible navigation platform reproducing the life events and hiding from the Citizen the complexity of their interconnections. The integration of the legacy systems becomes easier with the adoption of tools such as web services [15], [16] and other technologies [19].

Moreover, the new technologies or solutions already existing on leadings e-government programs are ready to be used by emerging ones worldwide. That means no new technologies and solutions are required for the new approach but those now applied in e-government programs conceived under the traditional concepts. The innovations rely on the changes in the processes for outperforming the services access.

Some fostering issues for the new approach seem to be interesting to discuss as:

1. The new model can be extended also to incorporate services of private organizations on these integrated portals. In this point of view, the Citizen wants to have access to a certain service, but whether this service is provided by the State itself or by a private third party is a mere detail. An e-Citizen portal is capable to address a comprehensive set of services to supply most of the individual needs. This is likely to be a leveraging issue, considering that this kind of action can bring legal difficulties to overcome when started by the government.
2. Many governments have got available resources to invest in electronic government, and as demonstrated in the previously mentioned research [13], the necessary step is to divert those resources to services with more appeal to the Citizen. In democratic governments the society is supposed to be the best partner to dictate which are the priorities for the investments.
3. e-Citizen portals taken over by the organized society can constitute an outstanding instrument for leveraging the concepts of e-Democracy, considering they give the free opportunity to the individuals to participate and to have an active voice to influence the public policies and actions. No restrictions can be imposed by governments that like to listen only they want to.
4. An interesting way to carry the necessary budget to implement e-Citizen portals is the risk contract that can be proposed by organized society, with funding provided by the savings led by the new approach [13]. To convince the elected officials about these savings is a hard issue to cope with, hence the external vision and risk assumption is likely to work well in the decision making. Moreover, governments too often do not have budget enough for investing in new services, even on a perspective of short term payoff.
5. The governments can carry on focusing their investments in the construction of the back-office systems, data bases and processes in order to improve their efficiency, while organized society deploy the front-office applications based on the concept of e-Citizen portals. The existence of comprehensive back-office applications is a basic requirement to provide public services by Internet portals, and the influence of the organized society will push the government for deploying them.
6. The possibility of having a long term planning for public services on the Internet emerges as one of the major motivation for this new approach. Normally the plans are established upon the vision of the short time allocated to the mandates of the elected officials and disruptions will come true when these mandates are over.
7. A new perspective of public services providing comes true while differentiated services can be offered to different segments of society, also implying different fees to be paid for them. This feature is impossible for some kind of governments which consider that all citizens have the same rights, hence they must have the same level of services.

8. The difficulties for the required transformation to come true into the government are focused on the political goodwill and on the sluggishness of the departments supplying public services, which is motivated by the intrinsic organizational culture of the bureaucratic processes. Not always the governments find competition on the supply of services, because the individual has got no choice other then use them the way they are offered. This puts the State in a comfortable situation [9].
9. Another obstacle can be found in the political interest that the public administrators carry over when assuming the responsibility for a department or division in the complex and decentralized public administration. There is no convergence of interests to make feasible the integrations of processes and information available for the generation of services in a unified interface, motivated by the feeling of individual property associated to a political job, as well as the need of preserving the power. The personal interests are major than those corporate [12].

A coordinated effort from outside the government, far apart from the bureaucracy and personal interests of the public administrators – and based on the real demands of society – seems to be an instrument capable of breaking the inhibiting factors and this way bringing to the Citizen the same comfort they feel in their relationship with the private organizations and leveraging the practice of the democracy.

However, legal issues can become great obstacles that society and governors must overcome to allow the disclosure of information from the State to other organizations acting as new channel for public services delivery to the individuals. There is no standard proposition to overcome it so each individual country must coordinate efforts to promote research on how to eliminate the barriers according to the nature of the law on its legislation.

The search for a business model capable of overcoming the legal, political and institutional barriers and funding the operational actions for the maintenance of the e-Citizen integrated portal is a key issue to make feasible the new approach.

7 Conclusion

The proposition presented by this article breaks the paradigms in the relationship between the State and its Citizen, when suggesting that the society should organize itself to gain access to public services with the same comfort as obtained today in the private sector. It differentiates the concepts of *Electronic Government* and *Electronic Citizen* regarding the degree of interest of each one of the parts and allocates the responsibilities of leveraging the processes to the more interested side.

Even if these concepts could suggest a rupture with the installed public power, this is absolutely not the idea, because what is proposed is merely a new way of organizing public services, over which the State still exerts total control and assumes entire responsibility. Some major issues that drive the migration for the new approach have been outlined with the aim of motivating the society actions toward the construction of e-Citizen portals.

As a result, the Citizen will be granted access to public services of their higher interest, such as Health, Education, Security and so on, with the same convenience they find when using online facilities to fulfil their duties and obligations with the State. As an additional gain, the Internet gets closer to one of its promises: to foster a higher democratic participation in the establishment of public policies.

References

1. Cairncross, F.: The Death of Distance - How the Communications Revolution is Changing Our Lives. Boston: HBS Press, 2001.
2. Tapscott, D.: The Digital Economy - Promise and Peril in the Age of Networked Intelligence. New York: McGraw Hill, 1996.
3. Porter, M.: Strategy and Internet. Harward Business Review, Vol. 79, N°.3, pp. 63-78, March 2001.
4. Prahalad, C. K., Ramaswamy, V.: Co-opting Customer Competence. Harward Business Review, Vol. 78, N°.1, pp. 79-87, January/February 2000.
5. Fountain, J. E.: Information, Institutions and Governance: Advancing a Basic Social Science Research Program for Digital Government. Cambrige: Harvard University, National Center for Digital Government, 2003. http://www.ksg.harvard.edu/digitalcenter/research/ working%20papers/rwp03_004_fountain.pdf. (December, 2003).
6. Vintar, M., Kunstelj, M., Leben, A.: Delivering Better Quality Public Services Through Life-Event Portals. In: 10th NISPAcce Annual Conference, 2002, Kracow, Poland. Delivering Public Services in CEE Countries: Trends and Developments. Bratislaw: NISPAcce, 2003. http://www.nispa.sk/news/papers/wg2/vintar.doc. (June, 2004).
7. Ke, W., Wei, K. K.: Successful e-Government in Singapore. Communications of the ACM, Vol. 47, N°. 6, pp. 95-99, June 2004.
8. e-Envoy: Government Gateway. London: Office of the e-Envoy, 2004. http://www.e-envoy.gov.uk/Briefings/Briefings/fs/en. (April, 2004).
9. Symonds, M.: The Next Revolution - A Survey of Government and Internet. The Economist, June 24, 2000. London: The Economist Group. http://www.ebape.fgv.br/e_government/asp/dsp_artigos.asp. (November, 2003).
10. Hammer, M.: The Superefficient Company. Harward Business Review, Vol. 79, N°. 9, pp. 82-91, September 2001.
11. Ongaro, E.: Process Management in the Public Sector - The Experience of One-Stop Shops in Italy. International Journal of Public Sector Management, Vol. 17, N°. 1, pp. 81-107, 2004.
12. Kolsaker, A., Lee-Kelley, L.: Reconceptualising Government in the New E-ra. In: Knowledge Management In Electronic Government – 5th IFIP International Working Conference (KMGOV 2004), Krems, Austria. Lecture Notes in Computer Science 3025. Heildelberg: Springer-Verlag, 2004, pp.18-26.
13. Rech Filho, A.: Public Services on the Internet - Is the Major Interest of the State or of the Citizen? A Case Study of Services to the Citizen of Curitiba. Doctor Thesis, Federal University of Santa Catarina, Brazil, 2004.
14. Barret, P.: E-Government and Joined-up Government. Canberra: Australian National Audit Office, 2002. http://www.anao.gov.au. (January, 2004).

15. Gamper, J., Augsten, N.: The Role of Web Services in Digital Government. In: 2nd International Conference on Electronic Government (EGOV 2003), Prague, Czech Republic. Lecture Notes in Computer Science 2739. Heidelberg: Springer-Verlag, 2003, pp.161-166.
16. Medjahed, B., Bouguettaya, A., Elmagarmid, A. K.: Composing Web Services on the Semantic Web. The International Journal on Very Large Data Bases, Vol. 12, N°. 4, pp. 333-351, 2003.
17. IDA: UK Governments Looking for e-Government Intermediaries. IDA e-Governments News, April, 2004. http://europe.eu.int/ida/eu/document/2416/596. (November, 2004).
18. IDA: e-Government Intermediation: Tobacconists to Deliver Public Services in Italy. IDA e-Governments News, November, 2003. http://europe.eu.int/ida/eu/document/1773/339. (November, 2004).
19. Pasic, A., Sassen, A., Garcia, A.: e-Government Intermediation. In: 3rd International Conference on Electronic Government (EGOV 2004), Zaragoza, Spain. Lecture Notes in Computer Science 3183. Heidelberg: Springer-Verlag, 2004, pp. 88.

A Zero Knowledge Proof for Subset Selection from a Family of Sets with Applications to Multiparty/Multicandidate Electronic Elections

Tassos Dimitriou[1] and Dimitris Foteinakis[2]

[1] Athens Information Technology,
Markopoulo Ave., 19002, Athens, Greece
tdim@ait.gr
http://www.ait.gr

[2] Intracom S.A., Markopoulo Ave.,
19002, Athens, Greece
fotd@intracom.gr
http://www.intracom.gr

Abstract. We present a methodology for proving in Zero Knowledge the validity of selecting a subset of a set belonging to predefined family of sets. We apply this methodology in electronic voting to provide for extended ballot options. Our proposed voting scheme supports multiple parties and the selection of a number of candidates from *one and only one* of these parties. We have implemented this system and provide measures of its computational and communication complexity. We prove that the complexity is linear with respect to the total number of candidates and the number of parties participating in the election.

1 Introduction

With the explosion of growth of the World Wide Web, the increase of computational power, computer memory and the storage capacity, we have the ability to communicate more information faster, cheaper and more reliably. The general trend towards a paperless society has affected the area of voting. Many attempts have been made to create systems that would allow modern computer-based technology to emulate the secure desirable properties valued in centuries of public voting.

Remote electronic voting refers to an election process whereby people can cast their votes over the Internet, from the comfort of their home, or possibly any other location where they can get Internet access. There are many aspects of elections besides security that bring this type of voting into question. The primary ones are:

- *Coercibility*: The danger that outside of a public polling place, a voter could be coerced into voting for a particular candidate.
- *Vote selling*: The opportunity for voters to sell their vote.

M. Böhlen et al. (Eds.): TCGOV 2005, LNAI 3416, pp. 100–111, 2005.

– *Vote solicitation:* The danger that outside of a public polling place, it is much more difficult to control vote solicitation by political parties at the time of voting.
– *Invalid Registration:* The issue of whether or not to allow online registration, and if so, how to control the level of fraud.

The possibility of widely distributed locations where votes can be cast changes many aspects of our carefully controlled elections as we know them. The relevant issues are of great importance and could very well influence whether or not such election processes are desirable. However, in this paper we do not discuss issues like the vulnerability of the Internet to denial of service attacks, the unreliability of the Domain Name Service or the various threats the supporting hosts are liable to, but we focus instead on the security considerations of the *voting process.*

Thanks to the advances in the fields of cryptography an electronic voting system can satisfy the requirements that are considered self-evident for paper based systems and at the same time be efficient and reduce the cost of large scale elections. In [10] Fujioka *et al.* define the properties of a secure, secret election:

– *Completeness*: All valid votes must be counted correctly.
– *Soundness*: The dishonest voter cannot disrupt the voting process.
– *Privacy* and *Integrity*: All votes must be and remain secret and cannot be altered in transit. Hence effective encryption must be used to protect the votes from being disclosed to third parties during transmission.
– *Anonymity*: The voting system must support the voters' right to secrecy of their vote. Hence the vote recording mechanism must not identify the individual voter.
– *Unreusability* and *Eligibility*: No voter can vote twice and no one who isn't allowed to vote can vote.
– *Fairness*: Nothing must affect the voting process. Voters must not be able to affect the system if the supply invalid ballots, colluding or fault authorities must not alter the voting process's results.
– *Verifiability*: Any external party can verify that the result of the election is correct. In particular, this means that votes are recorded as captured and cannot be manipulated when transferred from vote collection to tabulation.

Many voting schemes have been proposed so far that satisfy the above set of requirements, but they are limited by the ballot options they can support. Initial voting systems [1] allowed the voter to select one of two candidates ("yes/no" paradigm) and later systems can accommodate the selection of "t out of n" candidates [3], [4], [6], [8]. Such electoral systems are encountered in the United States and electronic voting systems have already been applied in various State elections. These systems however, cannot be used for elections whose structure is more complicated than a selection of "t out of n" candidates like many electoral systems throughout Europe.

In this work we will present an election system that will accommodate *multiple parties* which in turn consist of *multiple candidates* and will allow a voter to select "t out of n" candidates within a *single party* and prove in zero knowledge manner that this selection is valid.

2 Related Work

An electronic voting scheme consists of a set of protocols which allow voters to cast ballots while a group of authorities collect the votes and output the final tally. Election schemes in [1], [2], [3], [4] were first described by Benaloh [1]. All these schemes mainly discuss the "yes/no" vote scenario. Such schemes utilize a cryptosystem that has the *homomorphic* property (Section 4.1) which allows the computation of the tally without the decryption of individual ballots. Two different election models have been proposed so far.

In Benaloh schemes, a voter shares his vote between n authorities so that t of them can recover it. Each authority computes its encrypted share of the tally and finally t of them need to collaborate to compute the actual tally.

In schemes like [4], the voters send their encrypted votes to a single *combiner*. Using the homomorphic property of the cryptosystems the combiner computes the encrypted tally in a public verifiable way. Then t authorities need to collaborate in order to recover the tally by running a threshold cryptosystem.

Systems described in [3], [4], which are implemented in commercial electronic voting applications, use a variant of the El Gamal cryptosystem exhibiting the homomorphic property and having a threshold version [11]. This cryptosystem requires exponent search in order to compute the final tally from the ballot product, an operation that is computationally *expensive* and may render the system inefficient when the number of voters increases.

Our system uses the Paillier Cryptosystem [5] which exhibits the homomorphic properties needed by the election scheme and more importantly provides an efficient decryption algorithm as well as the largest bandwidth among all cryptosystems using a trapdoor to compute the discrete logarithm. A threshold version of the cryptosystem that appeared in [6], [7] allows its usage in the case of multiple authorities to jointly run a threshold cryptosystem and collaborate in order to decrypt the final tally.

3 Our Contribution

In this paper we present a methodology for proving in a Zero Knowledge manner the validity of *selecting a subset of a set belonging to a predefined family of sets.* More specifically we show how to prove in Zero Knowledge that the voter's selection consists of t elements (candidates) all belonging to the *same* set (party) out of k sets of at most n elements each. We apply this methodology in order to construct an election scheme that will accommodate multiple parties and the selection of t candidates from *one and only one* of those parties. Such election systems are common throughout the world, like in many European countries. Electoral systems with the above mentioned structure are referred to "open party list" systems and are used in many countries, among which are the Netherlands, Norway, Greece, Spain and Slovenia. Electronic voting schemes proposed up to now were limited to the selection of "t out of n" candidates and could not accommodate such a complex system. Our proposal extends existing voting schemes and can be applied to elections which have those requirements.

Furthermore we have implemented a voting system that uses our proposed protocol in order to run an election. Our scheme guarantees the necessary requirements of a voting system mentioned in the introduction: privacy of voters, public verifiability, fairness and soundness, eligibility and unreusability. *Privacy of voters* guarantees that a vote will be kept secret from any collusion of t or less authorities, where t is a system parameter. *Public verifiability* ensures that any external party can verify that the election is fair and that the published tally was computed correctly from the ballots that were correctly cast, through the bulletin board. *Fairness* and *Soundness* ensure that the system can tolerate up to t faulty or colluding authorities without its operation being affected. The existence of the bulletin board and of secure channels via public key cryptography ensures *eligibility* and *unreusability.*

Finally we performed a set of experiments to measure the time taken for creation and verification of the Zero Knowledge proofs, the size of produced ballots as well as the total time needed for a voter to cast a vote in our system, including user and server authentication, ballot creation, transmission and verification, for various system parameters. We prove and validate experimentally that the running time of the algorithm for the creation of the ballot and the Zero Knowledge proofs is linear with respect to the total number of candidates in the elections. Hence our system not only fulfills the basic security requirements but it is also user friendly and practical, an essential characteristic of any voting system that is to be used for public elections.

The outline of the paper is as follows: The next section describes the cryptographic tools that our system uses. We briefly describe the Paillier Cryptosystem and its properties as well as two Zero Knowledge proofs that are used as building blocks for the creation of more complex ones. Section 5 describes the voting protocol, the ballot creation procedure and the Zero Knowledge proofs creation. In Section 6 we describe how the voting system is implemented, the steps needed to cast a ballot as well as the steps for calculating the final result. Furthermore we provide a complexity analysis of the proposed system and measurements of its operation. Finally, we conclude in Section 7.

4 Cryptographic Tools

4.1 The Paillier Cryptosystem

In [5], Paillier proposes a new probabilistic encryption scheme based on computations in the group $\mathcal{Z}^*_{\mathcal{N}^2}$, where $\mathcal{N}$ is an RSA modulus. This scheme has some very attractive properties: It is homomorphic, allows encryption of many bits in one operation with a constant expansion factor and allows efficient decryption. This cryptosystem is based on the *Decisional Composite Residuosity Assumption* (DCRA).

Description of Paillier Scheme

- *Key Generation*: Let $\mathcal{N}$ be an RSA modulus $\mathcal{N} = pq$, where p and q are prime integers. Let g be an integer of order a multiple of $\mathcal{N}$ modulo $\mathcal{N}^2$. The public key is $PK = (N, g)$ and the secret key is $SK = \lambda(\mathcal{N})$ where $\lambda(\mathcal{N})$ is defined as $\lambda(\mathcal{N}) = lcm[(p-1)(q-1)]$. We should note that in [6] Damgraad and Jurik propose that $g = N + 1$ can be used without degrading security. Then the public key will only consist of $\mathcal{N}$.
- *Encryption*: To encrypt a message $M \in \mathcal{Z}_{\mathcal{N}}$ choose a random $r \in \mathcal{Z}^*_{\mathcal{N}}$ and compute the ciphertext $c = g^M r^N \bmod \mathcal{N}^2$.
- *Decryption*: To decrypt a ciphertext c, compute:

$$M = \frac{L(c^{\lambda(\mathcal{N})} \mod \mathcal{N}^2)}{L(g^{\lambda(\mathcal{N})} \mod \mathcal{N}^2)} \mod \mathcal{N}^2, \tag{1}$$

where the L-function receives input from the set $S_{\mathcal{N}} = \{u < \mathcal{N}^2 | u = 1 \bmod \mathcal{N}\}$ and

$$L(u) = \frac{u-1}{\mathcal{N}} . \tag{2}$$

Homomorphic Property

The encryption function has an "algebraic property" which allows computations with the encrypted values without knowing the contents of the ciphertexts. More precisely the encryption function has the following property: $E(M_1 + M_2) = E(M_1) \cdot E(M_2)$ and consequently $E(k \cdot M) = E(M)^k$.

This property is necessary to achieve anonymity as well as universal verifiability since the tally can be computed without the decryption of individual votes by all interested parties. The decryption is performed on the final tally, guaranteeing the privacy of the voters.

In [3] as well as in other voting schemes a variant of the El Gamal encryption scheme is used. In this variant in order to encrypt a message m we compute ($g^k \bmod p$ and $g^m y^k \bmod p$) instead of ($g^k \bmod p$ and $my^k \bmod p$). In this manner the scheme gains the homomorphic property needed for the election schemes. The negative side of this encryption scheme is that no trapdoor exists to compute m given $g^m \bmod p$. Therefore this scheme is only used in "yes/no" schemes, where the message m is either 0 or 1 and therefore g^m lies in limited subset of messages and can be computed using exhaustive search. However, this scheme has been used in several voting systems including some commercial ones. In the case of elections with many candidates and a large number of voters the modified El Gamal scheme becomes inapplicable since exhaustive search or more efficient methods like index calculus cannot efficiently compute the tally.

Threshold Version of Paillier Cryptosystem

A (t, n) threshold scheme does not reveal a secret S unless any t out of the n participants work together. In order to prevent authorities to learn the contents of the votes submitted and to ensure the privacy of the voters a threshold version of the Paillier Cryptosystem can be used. In this case, instead of having a single authority decrypt the encrypted tally, n authorities share the secret, so that at least t are needed to perform the decryption operation. Such versions of the cryptosystem are presented in [6] and [7]. A general description of a threshold decryption model follows:

The scheme includes the following participants: a combiner, a set of n authorities A_i and users.

- In the initialization phase, the authorities run a distributed key generation protocol to create the public key PK and the secret shares SK_i of the private key SK with or without a trusted dealer [12], [13]. Next the authorities publish the verification keys VK, VK_i.
- The user encrypts a message using the private key PK.
- To decrypt a ciphertext c, the combiner forwards c to all the authorities. Using the shares of the secret key SK_i and the verification keys VK and VK_i each authority runs the decryption algorithm and produces a partial decryption c_i, providing a proof of validity for the partial decryption. The combiner can then produce the decryption of ciphertext c, if enough partial decryptions (t or more) are valid.

4.2 Zero Knowledge Proofs

Central to our results is the way to achieve an efficient proof of validity for ballots. The proof of validity shows to any interested party including the tabulation authorities that a ballot actually represents a valid vote. To maintain the privacy of the voters this proof of validity will be a zero knowledge proof. In general, a Zero Knowledge proof allows an all powerful prover to convince a verifier about the validity of statement without leaking any information other than its correctness.

The efficiency of the entire voting scheme depends greatly on the efficiency of the zero knowledge proofs in terms of computational effort and in terms of the required bandwidth. Our goal is to create a zero knowledge proof that the submitted ballot is a selection of t candidates from a *single* party. Since this a complex proof we will use as building blocks the zero knowledge proofs presented in [6] which we include here for completeness. We note that the following protocols are not zero knowledge as they stand; only honest verifier zero knowledge. However, zero knowledge protocols for the same problems can be constructed using standard methods and secondly in our applications we will always use them in a non interactive variant based on the Fiat-Shamir heuristic [9].

In the following protocols, P denotes the prover and V denotes the verifier.

Proof for Power of $\mathcal{N}$

This protocol proves, given:

Input: $\mathcal{N}$ and u

Private input for P: v such that $u = v^{\mathcal{N}} \mod \mathcal{N}^2$

that u is a power of $\mathcal{N}$ modulo $\mathcal{N}^2$. The sequence of steps is:

1. P chooses a random r mod $\mathcal{N}^2$ and sends to V $a = r^N$ mod $\mathcal{N}^2$.
2. V chooses a random k bit number e and sends e to P.
3. P sends $z = rv^e \mod \mathcal{N}^2$ to V and V checks that $z^{\mathcal{N}} = au^e$ mod $\mathcal{N}^2$ and accepts only if and only if this is the case.

Proof for 1-out-of-2 Power of $\mathcal{N}$

This protocol proves, given:

Input: $\mathcal{N}$, u_1, u_2
Private input for P: v_1 such that $u_1 = v_1^N$ mod $\mathcal{N}^2$

that either u_1 or u_2 is a power of $\mathcal{N}$ modulo $\mathcal{N}^2$. The sequence of steps is:

1. P chooses a random r_1 mod $\mathcal{N}^2$. He invokes M on input $\mathcal{N}$, u_2 to get a conversation a_2, e_2, z_2. He sends $a_1 = r_1^N$ mod $\mathcal{N}^2$, a_2 to V.
2. V chooses s, a random t bit number and sends s to P.
3. P computes $e_1 = s - e_2$ mod 2^t, $z_1 = r_1 v_1^{e_1}$ mod $\mathcal{N}^2$ and sends e_1, z_1, e_2, z_2 to V.
4. V checks that $s = e_1 + e_2$ mod 2^t, $z_1^N = a_1 u_1^{e_1}$ mod $\mathcal{N}^2$ and, $z_2^N = a_2 u_2^{e_2}$ mod $\mathcal{N}^2$, and accepts if and only if this is the case.

In the above protocol M denotes the honest-verifier simulator for *proof for power of N* protocol above. Using these proofs as building blocks, we present our construction for selecting in Zero Knowledge a subset of candidates belonging to one and only one party.

5 Voting Protocol

The purpose of the vote is to select t candidates from a single party. Suppose there are K parties participating in the election and let each party have L candidates. The purpose of such an election would be to select a governing party as well as the members of the parliament, or elect a mayor of a municipality and the members of the council. The voter has to prove that the vote is valid, which means that it contains at *most t* positive selections and that all those selections are from the *same* party since one should not be able to vote for candidates belonging to deferent parties.

Since the total number of candidates is $K \times L$ we will hold $K \times L$ parallel "yes/no" votes. In this sense the voter will select "yes" for t candidates and "no" for the rest. If we represent "yes" with "1" and "no" with "0", then the encrypted selection for candidate i will be $E_i = g^1 \times r^{\mathcal{N}} = g \times r^{\mathcal{N}}$ if the selection is "yes" or $E_i = g^0 \times r^{\mathcal{N}} = r^{\mathcal{N}}$ is the selection is "no", for some random $r \in \mathcal{Z}_{\mathcal{N}}^*$.

Along with the encryptions of the "yes/no" selections for the $K \times L$ candidates, the voter needs to send proof of the validity of those encryptions. For this purpose the protocol for *1-out-of-2 power of $\mathcal{N}$* is utilized. Using this protocol, the user proves that either E_i or E_i/g is a power of $\mathcal{N}$ modulo $\mathcal{N}^2$, essentially proving that the vote is either an encryption of "0" or "1". Most importantly, however, the voter has to prove that the t selected candidates come from the same party. For this purpose the voter needs to generate K proofs, one for each party, proving that either E_{p_i} or E_{p_i}/g^t is a power of $\mathcal{N}$ modulo $\mathcal{N}^2$ using the protocol for 1-out-of-2 power of $\mathcal{N}$. E_{p_i} is the product of the encrypted selections for party i:

$$E_{P_i} = \prod_{\text{Party } i} E_j \ . \tag{3}$$

In this manner the voter proves that he has either selected 0 or t candidates from this party. This is due to the homomorphic property of the cryptosystem, since E_{p_i} will either be an encryption of 0 or t. Notice that the voter reveals no information about the party she has voted for, since she proves for *each* party that she has either selected 0 or t candidates from it, which is essential for the validity of the submitted ballot.

Finally the voter needs to prove that she has selected exactly t candidates. In order to do that, the voter uses the *protocol of $\mathcal{N}$ power* in order to prove that $\Pi_i E_i/g^t$ is a power of $\mathcal{N}$ modulo $\mathcal{N}^2$, where $\Pi_i E_i$ is the product of all the encrypted selections. Due to the homomorphic property of the cryptosystem $\Pi_i E_i$ will be an encryption of "t" and $\Pi_i E_i/g^t$ will be a power of $\mathcal{N}$.

Having proven the above properties for the submitted encrypted selections the user successfully shows that she has selected exactly t candidates from a single party and no candidates from the rest of the parties. This is the case since she proves that for every party she has selected t or 0 candidates and that she has selected t candidates in total.

It is easy to generalize the above protocol to allow up to t selections from a single party by adding t "dummy candidates" to the L candidates of each party. The voter will then place the selections she does not wish to use on the "dummy candidates". In the same manner we can accommodate for blank votes be creating a dummy party with t candidates on which the selection will be placed.

6 Voting System Implementation

We will use a hash function h in order to make the proofs used by the above protocol non-interactive according to the Fiat-Shamir [9] heuristic. We will also assume that an instance of threshold version of Paillier's scheme with public key $(\mathcal{N}, g)$ has been set up, with A_i's being the decryption servers. We will also assume that $\mathcal{N}^2 > M$, where M is the number of voters, since $\mathcal{N}$ can always be chosen large enough to satisfy this inequality.

As we have mentioned in the introduction, we will use a general model for election described in [4], which we describe briefly: We have a set of voters $V_1, V_2 \ldots, V_M$, a bulletin board B and a set of tallying authorities $A_1, A_2 \ldots, A_M$. The bulletin board operates as follows: Every voter can write to B and no message can be deleted from B once it has been written there. Everyone can access the messages in B and can identify the origin of each message. This can be implemented in a secure way using existing public key infrastructure. Also assume that we have K parties $P_1, P_2 \ldots, P_K$.

6.1 Voting Procedure

The voting procedure can be summarized with the following steps:

1. Each voter V_i decides on his votes 0 for "no" 1 for "yes" for the $K \times L$ candidates, calculates $E_{ij} = E(v_{ij})$ and creates proofs:
   - Proof that E_{ij} or E_{ij}/g is an $\mathcal{N}$ power modulo $\mathcal{N}^2$ for all $j \in \{1 \dots K \times L\}$ and
   - Proof that $\prod_{j \in P_k} E_{ij}$ or $\prod_{j \in P_k} E_{ij}/g^t$ is an $\mathcal{N}$ power modulo $\mathcal{N}^2$) for all $k \in \{1 \dots K\}$
   - Proof that $(\prod_{j=1}^{K \times L} E_{ij}/g^t$ is an $\mathcal{N}$ power modulo $\mathcal{N}^2$)

   She writes the encrypted votes E_{ij} and all the proofs in B.
2. Each authority A_k sets $\prod E_j = 1$ for all $j \in \{1 \dots K \times L\}$. Then for all voters i
   - Checks the proofs in B for voter V_i and if they are valid sets $\prod E_j = (\prod E_j) \times E_{ij} \bmod \mathcal{N}^2$.
   - Finally A_k executes its part of the threshold decryption protocol, using $\prod E_j$'s as input ciphertext and writes its result to the bulletin board B.
3. From the messages written by the tabulation authorities in B one can now reconstruct the final tally $\prod E_j$ for $j \in \{1 \dots K \times L\}$. Clearly $\prod E_j = \prod_i E(v_{ij}) = E(\sum_i v_{ij})$. Therefore the decryption results will be $\sum_i v_{ij} \bmod \mathcal{N}^2$ for candidates $j \in \{1 \dots K \times L\}$ which is $\sum_i v_i j$ since $\mathcal{N}^2 > M$. One can also easily calculate the votes for each party by summing the votes that the candidates of each party have received and divide them by t:

$$Votes_{Party_k} = \sum_{j \in Party_k} v_{ij}/t \ . \tag{4}$$

The security of this protocol follows from the security of the sub-protocols used and the semantic security of Paillier's Cryptosystem.

6.2 Complexity Analysis

In the analysis that follows we will denote with C the total number of candidates that participate in the election. Without loss of generality we examine the case of K parties with L candidates each and an election that allows up to t selections within a party, so C will be equal to $K \times (L + t)$.

The voter generates C proofs of $1 - out - of - 2$ *power of* $\mathcal{N}$, one for each candidate and K proofs of $1 - out - of - 2$ *power of* $\mathcal{N}$, one for each party. Thus the voter needs to generate $C + K$ proofs in total which is clearly $O(C)$. If k is the bitlength of $\mathcal{N}$ then evidently the size of a vote in this voting protocol is $O(C \times k)$. The same holds for the time needed for the computation and verification of the proofs.

We have implemented a system using the above protocol and made measurements of the running time on a Pentium 4, 2.53GHz machine. In Figure 1 the time needed to create the Zero Knowledge proofs is displayed versus the total number of candidates in the elections. The system behaves linearly to the number

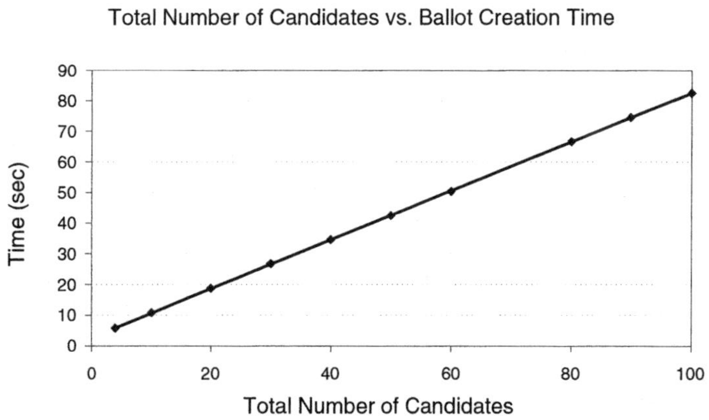

Fig. 1. Proof Creation Time versus Total Number of Candidates participating in the election

of candidates and the computation time is acceptable even when a much larger number of candidates (> 100) is used. For the implementation Java was used, which means that native code will reduce the computation time even further. For the tally computation $O(C \times M)$ verifications of proofs need to be performed, where M is the number of voters as well as $O(C)$ decryption operations on the products of the individual votes. The time to verify the proofs for a single voter is less than that of the proofs' creation time. These operations, as well as the decryption operation can be done offline after the end of the elections without increasing the voter's waiting time.

The size of the ballots created, as we mentioned above, increases linearly to the number of candidates in the elections. In Figure 2 we show how the ballot

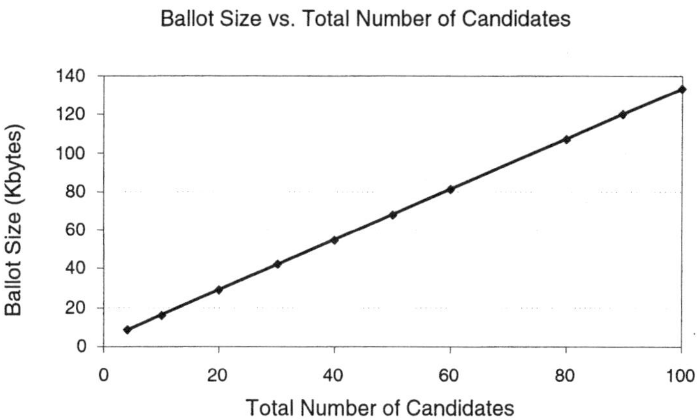

Fig. 2. Ballot Size (in Kbytes) versus Total Number of Candidates participating in the election

size varies with respect to the total number of candidates in our system. As we expected the ballot size doubles when the number of candidates doubles.

We should note that our proposal is not limited to parties that have the *same* number of candidates each. We have used this model so far to simplify the description of the system and not to complicate the notations used in the Zero Knowledge proofs. Our proposal can be applied to elections with *parties that have an arbitrary number of candidates* each and the analysis of the system complexity we made above still holds.

Finally, we provide a formula for the ballot size in our system. In what follows, C is the number of candidates in the system which are distributed (in any manner) in K parties. Let $|H|$ denote the size of the hashed commitments and $|\mathcal{N}^2|$ the size of the modulus used in the Paillier cryptosystem. The size of a vote is then

$$(5|\mathcal{N}^2| + 2|H|) \times C + (4|\mathcal{N}^2| + 2|H|) \times (K + 1) . \quad (5)$$

Evidently the ballot length is $O(C + K)$ and since in most cases $C >> K$ we can say that our system behaves linearly to the number of candidates. In practical applications we may choose $|H| = 80$ and $|\mathcal{N}^2| = 2048$. For an election with 20 candidates and 3 parties the size of a vote is about 30Kbytes.

7 Conclusions and Future Research

In this paper we have presented a methodology for proving in Zero Knowledge the validity of a selection of t elements from one out of k sets of n elements each. We have used this methodology in order to construct an election scheme that can provide more complex ballot options than current existing ones. In particular, our implementation can host elections involving a number of parties each consisting of an *arbitrary number* of candidates with the voter having to select a subset of the candidates from a *single party*, without degrading security or efficiency. Furthermore, the computational and communication complexity is linear with respect to the number of candidates and the proposed voting system satisfies all necessary security requirements.

In our current research, we are examining the possibility to make the complexity of our system (ballot size and computations) proportional to the number of parties *plus* the number of selections the voter is requested to make. This may be achieved possibly by representing a selection as in [8] and coming up with a new set of Zero Knowledge proofs which can correlate the selection with a single party.

References

1. J. Benaloh. Verifiable Secret Ballot Elections. PhD thesis, Yale University 1997
2. J. Benaloh and D. Tuinstra. Receipt-free secret ballot elections. In Proc. 26th Symposium on the Theory of Computing (STOC), pages 544-553 ACM 1994

3. R. Cramer, Y. Frankel, B. Schoenmakers and M. Yung. Multi-Authority Secret-Ballot Elections with Linear Work. In Eurocrypt '96, LNCS 1070, pages 72-83. Springer-Verlag, 1996
4. R. Crammer, R. Gennaro and B. Schoenmakers. A Secure and Optimally Efficient Multi-Authority Election Scheme. In Eurocrypt '97, LNCS 1233, pages 113-118. Springer-Verlag, 1997
5. P. Paillier. Public-Key Cryptosystems Based on Discrete Logarithm Residues. In Eurocrypt '99, LNCS 1592, Springer-Verlag, 1999
6. I. Damgraad and M. Jurik. A Generalization, a Simplification and Some Applications of Paillier's Probabilistic Public-Key System. In PKC '01, LNCS 1992, pages 119-136, Springer-Verlag, 2001
7. P. A. Fouque, G. Poupard and J. Stern. Sharing Decryption in the Context of Voting or Lotteries. In Financial Crypto '00, LNCS, Springer-Verlag, 2000
8. O. Baudron, P.-A. Fouque, D. Pointcheval, G. Pouparde, and J. Stern. Practical Multi-Candidate Election System. Proceedings of the ACM Conference on Principles on Distributed Computing, August 2001, Philadelphia, USA
9. A. Fiat and A. Shamir. How to Prove Yourself: practical solutions of identification and signature problems. In Crypto '86, LNCS 263, pages 186-194, Springer-Verlag, 1987
10. A. Fujioka, T. Okamoto, and K. Ohta. A Practical Secret Voting Scheme for Large Scale Elections, Advances in Cryptology - AUSCRYPT '92
11. T. P. Pedersen. Non-Interactive and information-theoretic secure verifiable secret sharing. In Advances in Cryptology - Crypto '91, volume 576 of Lecture Notes in Computer Science, pages 129-140, Springer-Verlag, 1992
12. I. Damgard and M. Koprowski. Practical Threshold RSA Signatures Without a Trusted Dealer. In Eurocrypt '01, LNCS, Springer - Verlag, 2001
13. P. Fouque and J. Stern. Fully Distributed RSA Signatures under Standard Assumptions. 2001

A Protocol for Anonymous and Accurate E-Polling

Danilo Bruschi, Igor Nai Fovino, and Andrea Lanzi

Dipartimento di Informatica e Comunicazione,
Università degli Studi di Milano, via Comelico 39/41,
I-20135 Milano MI, Italy
{bruschi, nai}@dico.unimi.it
andrew@security.dico.unimi.it

Abstract. E-polling systems are a fundamental component of any e-democracy system as they represent the most appropriate tool for fostering citizens participation to public debates. Contrarily to e-voting protocols, they are characterized by less stringent security requirements in particular they can tolerate errors affecting a small percentage of votes, without the compromision of the final result. Thus the construction of accurate and privacy respectful e-polling protocols is an objective which should be pursued by the research community as it is more close than the construction of practical e-voting protocols. However so far all the research efforts have been spent on the construction of e-voting protocols and the existing e-polling protocols are not respectful of the most elementary security and privacy rules. In this paper we propose a simple protocol for an accurate and anonymous e-polling system. More precisely our protocol satisfies the following properties: a vote cannot be altered, duplicated, or removed without being detected, votes remain anonymous. Moreover voters will be able to measure the level of trust of the process and its accuracy by verifying that their own votes have been counted correctly.

1 Introduction

The milestone of any democracy is participation. Obviously, such a postulate holds even in the case of e-democracy. In such a case the most appropriate tool for fostering citizens participation to public debates is based on electronic polling systems, i.e. systems which enable people to express their opinion on specific issues. The model of direct democracy, which is hindered by nowadays population sizes and state organizations, would then become possible. Besides being a fundamental component of any e-democracy system, e-polling systems are also quite attractive from the technological point of view since they do not have stringent security requirements as the e-voting protocols, thus they can be implemented and deployed more easily. In particular, we remind that the most crucial properties which an e-voting protocol has to satisfy are: *Democracy* i.e. only eligible voters are permitted to vote, and they can do so only once, *Accuracy* i.e. a voter's vote cannot be altered, duplicated, or removed without being

M. Böhlen et al. (Eds.): TCGOV 2005, LNAI 3416, pp. 112–121, 2005.

detected, and *Privacy* i.e. votes remain anonymous. A minimum flaw in the complete satisfaction of any of these requirements will result in an unacceptable e-voting protocol, as either the privacy of citizens or the accuracy of the final result will be compromised. It is the absence of any margin of error which makes very difficult the construction of any practical e-voting protocol. Fortunately, such considerations do not hold in the case of e-polling systems. Such systems are mostly interested in capturing general trends and people orientation, thus they can tolerate errors affecting a small percentage of votes, without the compromission of the final result. Obviously, they have to be designed in order to satisfy all the above mentioned properties (democracy, accuracy and privacy), considering however that some level of imprecision or some misbehavior can be tolerated.

Electronic polling systems have recently appeared on the Internet (e.g. www.epoll.com, www.misterpoll.com). However, such systems are not designed to maintain the level of security and privacy that we would expect, for example there is no way to express an opinion anonymously and there is no way for verifying the accuracy of the results.

In this paper we devise a new protocol for implementing a polling system based on the notion of anonymous credential. We briefly recall that an anonymous credential (introduced in 1985 by Chaum [12]) is an authorization token released by a trusted party, which entitles the owner to perform a specific set of activities on a particular system, without revealing his/her real identity.

Roughly speaking, our protocol works as follows. Any legitimate voter is provided by an anonymous voting credential, released by a Trusted Authority, which enables him to anonymously access to a poll system, once and only once, and to participate to a voting session. Anonymous votes are collected by the system and subsequently counted and published. In order to verify the accuracy and the level of trust of the entire process, a mechanism has been devised which enables any voter to verify that its own vote has not been altered and has been correctly counted in the final tally. The protocol is based on the HTTP protocol and it is transparent to both the browser and the web server, which means that it can be easily implemented using any web server and web browser.

It is not difficult to see that such a protocol satisfies the properties of accuracy and privacy. The accuracy property is satisfied by providing any voter with a mechanism for verifying that his own vote has been correctly counted, while the privacy property is guaranteed by the use of anonymous credentials. However, the use of anonymous credential has a well known drawback know as credential sharing. By credential sharing we mean the possibility that the legitimate user of a credential transfers it to another user which will use it. From the point of view of our protocol this would mean that either a non legitimate user will be able to participate to a poll session or a legitimate user will have the opportunity of voting more than once; in both cases the democracy property will be infringed. This is a very serious problem in the case of voting system, however we believe that it is not in the case of a polling system for the following reasons. In order to influence the final tally of a poll a user should collect too many credentials and the effort would not be comparable with the result, people participate in polling session on a voluntary basis in order to provide their own contribution to a decision process, thus there is no reasons for a user to enroll in a polling session for giving up its own credential to another user.

This paper is organized as follows. Section 2 describes the notation used throughout the paper and provides the definitions of peculiar concepts used for designing the protocol. Section 3 contains a detailed description of the credential system adopted. Section 4 is devoted to the protocol description. Section 5 contains a correctness analysis of the protocol. Section 6 is a brief overview of the state of the art in the field. As so far all the research efforts have been dedicated to voting protocol, and no attention has been deserved to polling protocols, we will briefly describe the most important achievements in the field of voting protocols.

2 Preliminary Definitions

In the paper we will frequently refer to the following terms:

- ***Voters:*** *the subjects interested in participating to a polling . The number of voters is a priori unknown.*
- ***Authentication token:*** *any mechanism used for verify the identity of a user such as password, Digital Certificates, biometric.*
- ***Vote Certificate:*** *a digital certificate which witness the eligibility of a user to participate to a polling session.*
- ***Polling Server:*** *the unit that collects the votes.*
- ***Trusted Third Party (TTP):*** *an entity which guarantees the eligibility of a voter and releases the vote certificates.*

We assume that TTP is provided by a pair of asymmetric keys (public and private) $< K_{pub\_TTP}, K_{priv\_TTP} >$, and K_{pub_TTP} is known to any polling server. By $S^C(m)$ we denote the message m digitally signed by C with RSA algorithm. We also assume that the TTP is able to recognize any of the authentication tokens belonging to the voters and distributes Vote Certificates. In our protocol we will use the blind scheme signature on RSA algorithm, as introduced in [11].

We briefly recall, that through the blind signature operation a party A can obtain a digital signature on a message m from a party B without revealing the content of m. The blind signature of a message m by B will be computed as follows. Let (e, n) and d be respectively the public and private RSA keys of B; initially A chooses a random number $rand$ and sends the following quantity M to B:

$$M = (m * rand^e) \ mod \ n \ . \tag{1}$$

Once B receives M it signs M with its own private key d and sends the result to A, i.e.

$$S^B(M) = (M)^d \ mod \ n \ . \tag{2}$$

Once A receives $S^B(M)$ it performs the following transformations, which will enable him to obtain a "packet" containing the original message m digitally signed by B:

$$S^B(m) = \frac{S^B(M)}{rand} = m^d \; mod \; n \; . \tag{3}$$

3 The Credentials System

As just mentioned we adopted the mechanism of anonymous credential for satisfying the anonymity property. The credential system we devised for our protocol works in the following way.

Any eligible voter , contacts off line, the TTP, which after a face to face authentication, releases to the user a Voting Certificate i.e. a secret random number r, which is stored by the TTP in a database together with a user authentication token (for example the SHA1 of a password or of a X.509 certificate); this random number r is used to unlock the pseudo credential only who knows the secret r (real voter). Once a user has performed such a prescription phase, he is entitled for getting a vote credential. Such a credential is represented by an anonymous certificate signed by the TTP, which enables the bearer to perform a single polling operation.

When a voter needs an anonymous credential for accessing a polling server, he contacts the TTP, and exhibits his Voting Certificate. Subsequently he chooses an integer *cred*, calculates the SHA1(cred) and start the blind signature process on such a quantity equation (1). The TTP, according with the blind signature scheme explained above equation (2), signs the quantity received by the voter and multiply the result by a random number r and sends it to the user, we call such a quantity *pseudo credential*. More formally this is the message exchange among the entities involved in this phase, which we recall is performed on an encrypted channel [10].

User→ TTP : $\{(\text{SHA1}(Voting\_Certificate))\}$
TTP → User : Ack
User → TTP: {M}
TTP→ User: $\{S^{TTP}(M) * r\}$

where:

(e,n) = RSA TTP public key
d = RSA TTP private key
m = SHA1(cred)
rand = random number used to perform the blind signature
M = $(m * rand^e) \; mod \; n$
r = random number used to protect the credential

Once the pseudo credential has been received, the client unlock the pseudo credential dividing by random number **r** and then it performs the last phase of blind signature scheme equation (3) and it obtains:

$$S^{TTP}(m) = \frac{S^{TTP}(M)}{rand} = m^d \ mod \ n \ . \tag{4}$$

Then the user builds the anonymous voting credential, that is equal:

$$(cred, S^{TTP}(m)) \ . \tag{5}$$

At this point the client can verify the TTP signature on the *voting credential* equation (5). Such *voting credential* has some important properties, first of all it does not contain any information about the identity of the user, thus guaranteeing the privacy property, secondly it can be used as one time credential.

4 The Application Architecture

In this section we provide an overview of the e-polling protocol we devised. When a voter decides to participate to a poll session he/she connects to the polling server using his own browser. A proxy installed on the server will intercept the request, and replies with a request for a voting credential. Using the vote certificate the client will apply to the TTP for a "voting credential". The TTP, after the validation of the certificate sends to the voter a pseudo credential, which would be used by the voter for accessing the polling server. More precisely the protocol works as follows.

1. Once a client requests a service, the Credential Proxy (previously installed on the voter machine (see Fig. 1)) forwards the request to the server. If the server site has not a Validation Proxy (installed only on the polling servers), the communication follows the path of a standard connection. Otherwise, if it is the case, it returns the request for a credential to the Credential Proxy.
2. The credential proxy, establishes an encrypted and mutually authenticated channel (e.g TLS [10]) with the TTP, builds the credential and sends to the TTP the digest of the credential adopting a blind signature scheme.

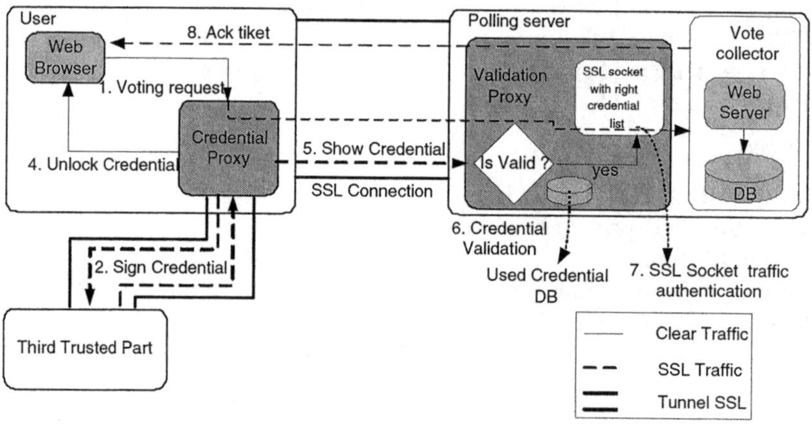

Fig. 1. The Application Logical Scheme

3. The TTP checks if the owner of the *authentication token*(see sec. 3) has the right to vote, if it is the case, the TTP retrieves from the database the random number r associated to the client and it builds the pseudo credential described in the previous section; Finally it sends the pseudo credential to the Credential Proxy.
4. The Credential Proxy unlock the pseudo credential and then it builds the anonymous credential.
5. The Credential Proxy establishes an encrypted communication channel with the polling server (only server side authentication to preserve its anonymity), the poll server sets the state of the connection pending, and then the Credential proxy sends the anonymous credential to the Validation proxy.
6. The Validation proxy (on the Poll server) checks the TTP's sign on the credential, if it is valid it checks if it has been already used, if this is the case the connection will be closed. In the other case, it stores the credential into database and it sets the authorized state into a special memory structure that is used to manage the connections.
7. The voter performs its vote and then the Credential Proxy creates a number (that will be used as *control ticket*) and it sends the digest of this number with the ack ticket request to the Validation proxy, the poll server signs this digest and sends it to the voter. At this point the voter checks the sign on the ack ticket, stores it and closes the connection.
8. At the end of the polling a web page containing all the votes received associated with the relative *control ticket* will be published. The voter in order to control if the vote has not changed during the vote operation, can control if the vote associated to the ticket is right.

5 Correctness Analysis

In this section we show that the protocol we have devised satisfies the properties of accuracy and privacy as defined in Section 2.

Property 1. A voting credential can be used only once

Such a property can be violated only if a vote credential is used more than once, i.e. either when a voter request more vote credentials for the same polling or when a signed credential is used more times.

As explained in Sec. 6 this is not possible as the TTP flags any user which receives a vote credential and the polling server collect all the used credentials in order to discover the multiple use of a credential.

Property 2 (Accuracy violation). The protocol satisfies the accuracy property

Such a property can theoretically be violated in two ways. Either performing a man in the middle attack on the channel connecting the client to the polling server or compromising the polling server itself. However the first attack cannot be performed as we adopted an encrypted channel with mutual authentication.

Instead the second attack is avoided by the release of a receipt, that is the proof that a correct vote operation is performed; thus the voter has the possibility to control in an anonymous way if his vote has been correctly counted.

Property 3 (Privacy violation). The protocol satisfies the privacy property

Two are the possible point in which the privacy property can be violated:

1. *The network between client(voter) and polling server*
   In this case the threat is related to the risk of network sniffing. Adopting encrypted channel (e.g. TLS [10]) it is possible to avoid this threat.
2. *The polling server*
   Assuming that the polling server is corrupted, the voter privacy (at logical level) is guaranteed by the use of the anonymous credential scheme. This scheme is not enough in order to protect the network privacy(e.g. ip address); in this case a solution can be the adoption between client and polling server of a Crowd scheme [9].

In the case in which we assume that the TTP is not really trusted, a collaboration between TTP and polling server must be taken in account. In our system the TTP does not know the credential that he signs (a blind signature scheme is adopted), then the collaboration between the two servers cannot product any type of information that can violate the privacy of the voter.

6 Related Results

As just mentioned, we are not aware of specific papers which address the construction of e-polling protocols, as all of the efforts in such a field has been concentrated on the construction of e-voting protocols. Historically, three are the main approaches adopted to solve the challenge of electronic vote:

- Chaum's Mix-nets scheme [2] based on the concept of network permutation in order to preserve the voter privacy obfuscating the link.
- Chaums's Blind signature[12] in which, as in our case, the notion of blind signature is heavily used.
- Homomorphic schemes in which properties of probabilistic cryptosystems are used [16].

We will now analyze such approaches in the context of e-polling protocols, starting from the consideration that for e-polling protocols, the time efficiency and simplicity are two important goals. For these reasons we believe that approaches based on Mixnet (see for example [15] [17] [18]) and homomorphic functions (see for example [19] [13] [20] [21]) are too complex and time consuming for being adopted in polling systems. In the following we report some of the attempts performed in devising voting systems, which constituted a point of reference for our research on e-polling systems. We will first describe the cryptographic protocols proposed so far and then we will briefly describe the implementations we are aware of.

The first electronic voting protocol was published by Chaum in 1981 [2]. It relies upon public key cryptography as all electronic voting protocols, however it does not guarantee voters' privacy. Chaum then proposed a protocol which unconditionally conceals voters' identity [3] but the entire voting procedure could be disrupted by a single voter. A solution to this problem was suggested by Cohen in [4], but the protocol proposed is not simple (college-level mathematics is required for voters to independently verify election results) nor efficient. In 1994, Benaloh and Tuinstra [1] proposed a voting protocol which allows voters to easily verify the results but voting booths must be used, thus violating the mobility property. Nurmi, Salomaa, and Santean [8] designed a protocol, known as Two Agency Protocol, that preserves the ease of verification properties and relax the "booth" constraint, thus yielding a protocol where voters can easily verify the results. However, it lacked voters' privacy. A breakthrough in the design of electronic voting protocols was realised by Fujioka, Okamoto and Ohta [6], who solved the privacy problem of the Two Agency Protocol using the blind signatures technique introduced in 1982 by Chaum. The Fujioka, Okamoto and Ohta protocol is generally indicated in the literature as the first practical electronic voting scheme. It still does not address the problem of preventing administrators from casting votes for abstained voters. The problem could be solved if abstained voters were forced to cast blank votes, which is clearly a hardly practical solution. Moreover, in this scheme the voter preference is encrypted before to be sent to the vote recipient. This implies during the counting phase that the voter anonymously sends the key to decrypt the vote. The presence of this additional phase in the usual voting scheme is really not practical. Horster, Michaels and Petersen in [14] maintaining the original schema of Fujioka, eliminate this phase adopting a blind multi signature scheme. In this work the presence of more than one administrator (that has the task to sign the vote according the blind scheme) is required. The security in this case is based on the concept that at least one of the administrators is honest. The SENSUS protocol [5], which was implemented and tested with simulated elections, overcomes the abstained voters problem. Karro and Wang [7] proved that SENSUS too suffers from some drawbacks such as the lack of accuracy and proposed another protocol that solves the identified problem. However, from our perspective, neither this protocol satisfies the accuracy property since it is possible to impersonate voters. Furthermore, we note that both protocols [5][7] make some impractical assumptions such as the existence of three or four trusted third parties, which must not collude in order to guarantee the correctness of the protocol, and the existence of a trusted third party that generates the cryptographic keys, which enable the voters to vote but not to cheat.

The design of a flawless electronic voting protocol is very difficult, and no protocols have been designed yet that completely satisfy all the requirements. This negatively influenced the realization of working prototypes. A fairly exhaustive overview of the state of the art regarding voting protocols and their implementations can be found at http://lorrie.cranor.org/voting/hotlist.html. To our knowledge, very little software is available that implements such protocols. Two systems are available, both explicitly written for non-government elections: Sensus and Evox. Sensus is an electronic polling system developed by Lorrie Cranor [5], but after the initial implementation, was never deployed nor maintained. The latter An electronic voting system is under development at MIT based on [6] It was realized by Ronald L. Rivest, Mark Herschberg, Ben Adida, and Randy Milbert. Unlike Sensus, the implementation is being maintained and improved.

References

1. Benaloh, J., and Tuinstra, D. "Receipt-free secret-ballot elections." In Proceedings of the Twenty-sixth Annual ACM Symposium on the Theory of Computing, 1994, pp. 544-553.
2. Chaum,D. "Untraceable electronic mail, return addresses, and digital pseudonyms." Communications of the ACM, 24(2), 1981, pp. 84-88.
3. Chaum, D. "Elections with unconditionally-secret ballots and disruption equivalent to breaking RSA." Lecture Notes in Computer Science, N. 330, Springer-Verlag, 1988, pp. 177-182.
4. Cohen, J. D. "Improving privacy in cryptographic elections." Tech. Rep. YALEU/DCS/TR-454, Yale University, February 1986.
5. Cranor, L. F., and Cytron R. K. "Sensus: A security-Conscious Electronic polling system for Internet." In Proceedings of the Hawaii International Conference on System sciences. Hawaii, 1997.
6. Fujioka, A., Okamoto, T., and Ohta, K. "A practical secret voting scheme for large scale elections." In Advances in Cryptology - AUSCRYPT 92, J. Seberry and Y. Zheng, Eds., Lecture Notes in Computer Science, N. 718, Springer-Verlag, 1993, pp. 244-251.
7. Karro J., and Wang J. "Towards a practical, secure and very large scale online Election." In Proceedings of fifteenth Computer Security Applications Conference, 1999, pp. 161-169.
8. Nurmi, H., Salomaa, A., and Santean, L. "Secret ballot elections in computer networks." Computers & Security, 36(10), 1991, pp. 553-560.
9. Michael K. Reiter and Aviel D. Rubin, Anonymous Web transactions with Crowds, Commun. ACM, vol. 42, number 2, 1999,0001-0782, pag. 32-48, ACM Press,
10. rfc 2246 T. Dierks C. Allen Certicom January 1999
11. Blind signatures for untraceable payments Advances in criptology Cripto '82. LCNS pp. 199-203
12. D. Chaum, Security without identification: transaction systems to make big brother obsolete Communication of the ACM, 1985,vol. 28, number 10, pages 1030, month October
13. M. Hirt, K. Sako Efficient Receipt-free voting based on homomorphic encryption pages 539-556, LNCS 1807, 2000, Springer-Verlag
14. P. Horster, M. Michels, H. Petersen Blind multi-signature schemes and their relevance to electronic voting Proc. 11th Annual Computer Security Applications Conference, New Orleans, IEEE Press, (1995), pp. 149 - 155.
15. C. Park, K Itoh, k. Kurusawa. ALL-nothing Election scheme and anonymous channel. Eurocrypt '93, pages 248-259.Springer-Verlag, LNCS 765, 1993
16. T. ElGamal. A public key cryptosystem and a signature scheme based on discrete logarithms. In Crypto '84, pages 10-18. Springer-Verlag, LNCS 196, 1984

17. K. Sako, J. Kilian. Receipt free mix-type voting scheme. Eurocrypt '95, pages 392-403. Springer-Verlag, LNCS 921, 1995
18. M. Jakobson, A. Juels, R. L. Rivest. Making mix nets robust for electronic voting by randomized partial checking. USENIX '02, D. Boneh editor, pages 339-353, 2002
19. K. Sako, J. Kilian. Secure voting using partial compatible homomorphisms. Crypt'94, pages 248-259. Springer-Verlag, LNCS 839, 1994
20. I. Damgrd, M. Jurik, A Generalisation, a Simplification and Some Applications of Paillier's Probabilistic Public-Key System, PKC 2001, Springer-Verlag, LNCS pg. 119-136, 2001
21. O. Baudron, P. Forque, D. Pointcheval, G Poupard, J. Stern. Practical multi-candidate election system. PODC'01, pages 274-283, ACM 2001

Model Driven Security for Inter-organizational Workflows in e-Government

Ruth Breu[1], Michael Hafner[1], Barbara Weber[1], and Andrea Novak[2]

[1] Universität Innsbruck, Institut für Informatik, Innsbruck, 6020, Österreich
{ruth.breu, m.hafner, barbara.weber}@uibk.ac.at
[2] Austrian Research Center Seibersdorf, Seibersdorf, 2444, Österreich
andrea.novak@arcs.ac.at

Abstract. Model Driven Architecture is an approach to increase the quality of complex software systems by creating high-level system models and automatically generating system architectures and components out of these models. We show how this paradigm can be applied to what we call Model Driven Security for inter-organizational workflows in e-government. Our focus is on the realization of security-critical inter-organizational workflows in the context of web services and web service orchestration. Security requirements are specified at an abstract level using UML diagrams. Out of this specification security relevant artifacts are created for the target reference architecture based on upcoming web service security standards.

1 Introduction

E-government refers to the use of the Internet and other electronic media to improve the collaboration within public agencies and to include citizens and companies in administrative processes. A core aim of e-government is to bring about a digital administration in order to enhance quality of service (e.g., additional online information or service offerings) as well as efficiency (e.g., reduced case processing times, fewer errors or using fewer resources to accomplish the same task).

The implementation of e-government solutions is a very complex task that can only succeed if IT-experts and domain experts co-operate with each other at a high level of abstraction right from the beginning. Security issues rooted in provisions and regulations play a very critical role. These include security requirements of public law (i.e., Austrian Signature Act [1] and the Austrian E-Government Act [2] as well as the Federal Act concerning the Protection of Personal Data [3]), the Austrian Security Manual [4], the OECD Guidelines for the Security of Information Systems and Networks [5] and internal security requirements of the municipalities.

Security requirements must not be considered as an isolated aspect, but during all stages of the software development cycle [6], [7]. As the engineering of security into the overall software design is often neglected, different approaches for integrating security in the system development cycle have been proposed [8], [9]. Nevertheless, they do not yet exploit the potential of a model driven approach.

M. Böhlen et al. (Eds.): TCGOV 2005, LNAI 3416, pp. 122 – 133, 2005.

Model driven software development is particularly appealing in the area of security as many security requirements adhere to certain categories (e.g., integrity) and can be described in implementation-independent models. In most cases, the development of security-critical systems is based on a set of well-known counteractive measures (i.e., protocols, algorithms) for which the correctness has been proved.

In this paper we give an overview of our approach to the model driven realization of security-critical inter-organizational workflows in the context of web services and web service orchestration. The description of security requirements is performed at a high level of abstraction. Security relevant artifacts are generated for a target architecture. A detailed description of the different aspects can be found in [10], [11].

Our approach provides a specification framework for the design of collaborating systems in the context of the platform-independent web service technology. It also supports the systematic transition from security requirements, via the generation of security artifacts, to a secure solution based on a web services platform. The specification of security requirements is performed in a platform-independent way and can thus be applied by domain experts without in-depth technical knowledge.

The structure of the subsequent sections is as follows. After providing an overview on web services composition, web services security and Model Driven Architecture in Section 2, we present a case study in Section 3, and describe our model driven approach in Section 4. Finally, section 5 gives an overview of related work and section 6 draws the conclusion.

2 Backgrounds

2.1 Web Services Technology

The emergence of web services technologies together with workflow composition languages allows for an easier and platform-independent collaboration between partners (.e.g.: governmental and local authorities). WS-BPEL [12] is a workflow composition language for web services and provides support for abstract business protocols and executable business processes. A business protocol specifies the public message exchange between parties and abstracts from how they are internally processed, while an executable business process models the behavior of a partner in a specific business interaction. WS-BPEL is an appropriate top layer standard to the web services protocol stack, including WSDL [13], SOAP, UDDI, WS-Transactions [14] and related standards. An alternative standard to describe business protocols is WSCI [15]. BPML [16] can be used to model executable business processes.

2.2 Web Services Security

As web services are often composed to carry out complex business transactions, not only the web service itself has to be secured, but also the message exchange between different web services. WS-Security [17] specifies a mechanism for signing and encrypting SOAP messages, and is used to implement message integrity and confidentiality. It also supports the propagation of the authentication information in the form of security tokens (e.g., Kerberos tickets or X.509 certificates). XACML

[18] provides access control mechanisms and policies within documents, while SAML [19] represents authentication and authorization decisions in XML format and is used to exchange this information over the internet (e.g., to support single sign-on).

2.3 Model Driven Architecture and Security

Model Driven Architecture (MDA) is an approach for the design and the implementation of applications that aims at cost reduction and application quality improvement [20]. At the very core of MDA is the concept of a model (i.e., abstraction of the target system). MDA defines two types of models, a Platform Independent Model (PIM), describing the system independently from the intended platform, and a Platform Specific Model (PSM) describing the system on its intended platform (e.g., J2EE or .NET). The process of converting a PIM into a PSM is called transformation. Models are described using a well-defined modeling language such as UML. Model Driven Security is based upon MDA in the sense that security requirements are integrated into design models, leading to security design models. Transformation rules of MDA are extended to generate security infrastructures [20].

3 Case Study

Our methodology for the systematic design and realization of security-critical inter-organizational workflows is illustrated by a portion of a workflow drawn from the use case "Processing of an Annual Statement" (Figure 1) describing the interaction between a business agent (the Tax Advisor) and a public service provider (the Municipality).

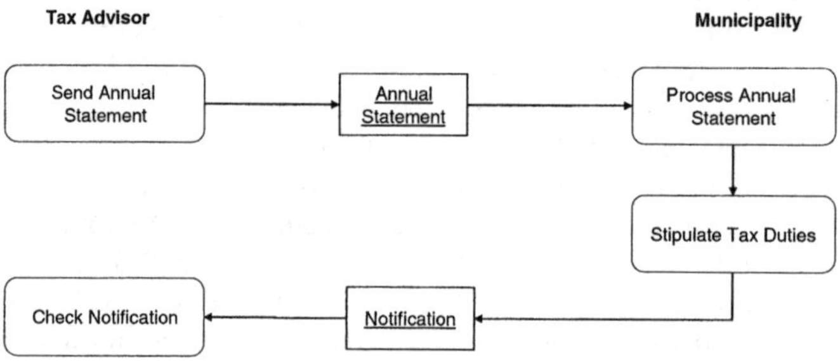

Fig. 1. Processing of an Annual Statement (Portion of Workflow)

The use case was elaborated within the project SECTINO, a joint research effort between the research group Quality Engineering at the University of Innsbruck and the Austrian Research Center Seibersdorf. It is based on a case study involving a major Austrian municipality. The project aims at the development of a framework supporting the systematic and efficient realization and management of innovative e-government related workflows with a special focus on security requirements.

In Austria, all wages and salaries paid to employees of an enterprise are subject to the municipal tax. Businesses have to send the annual tax statement via their tax advisor to the municipality which is responsible for collecting the tax by the end of March of the following year. The municipality checks the declaration of the annual statement and calculates the tax duties. A notification with the amount of tax duties is then sent to the tax advisor by mail. Ultimately, the workflow should allow the declaration of the municipal tax via the internet.

One of the project goals is to analyze security issues that may stem from the migration of the workflow to an e-government based solution and create the necessary run-time artifacts for the target architecture through model transformation.

4 Model Driven Security for Inter-organizational Workflows

In this section we present our approach to the management of security related aspects within the development process (Figure 2).

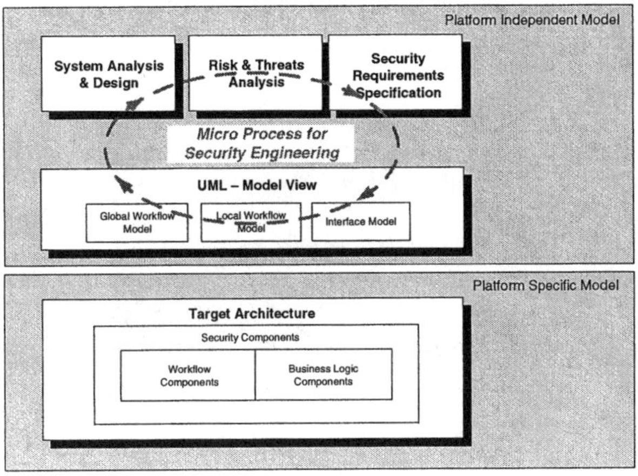

Fig. 2. Model Driven Security for Inter-Organizational Workflows

The development of security-critical inter-organizational workflows starts with the analysis and the design of the workflow, followed by a risk and threats analysis, and the security requirements specification (Section 4.1). Security requirements are then modeled in a platform-independent way at different levels of abstraction (Section 4.2). These four steps are executed iteratively, following a five step approach for security analysis called Micro Process for Security Engineering. The requirements are finally transformed into run-time artifacts for the target architecture (Section 4.3).

4.1 Security Analysis

Security related aspects within the development of inter-organizational workflows are tackled by a five step approach as illustrated in Figure 3 [9].

Table 1. Sample Scenario of a Security Analysis at the Global Level

1. The data exchange within the "Processing of an Annual Statement" has to comply with the requirements of integrity and confidentiality.
2. This workflow is open to the threat that a third unauthorized party may try to read and to modify the exchanged data.
3. The probability of occurrence is estimated as medium, the possible damage is estimated as substantial.
4. The measures to counter the threats involve encryption and digital signatures.
5. The proposed measures are checked. There remains the requirement that the two partners have to authenticate each other.

The Micro Process for Security Analysis is performed at different levels of abstraction (i.e., at the global, the local and the component level). Requirements and measures are explored and described at the appropriate level of detail based on given artifacts (e.g., the global workflow model). Table 1 illustrates the security analysis process using a sample scenario (Section 3).

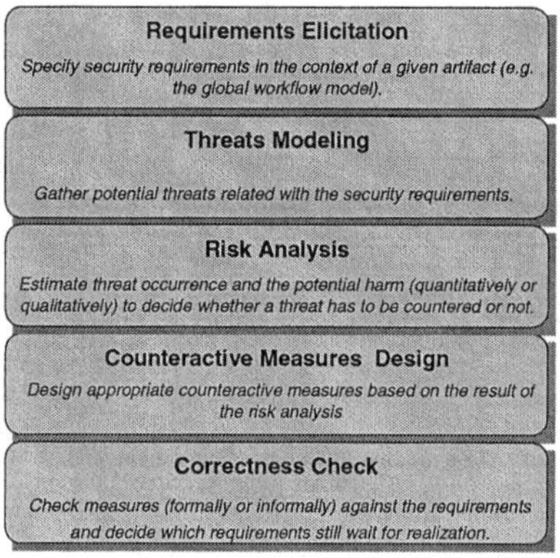

Fig. 3. The Micro Process for Security Analysis

In the early phases of design, security requirements are expressed in a textual way (e.g., by a security relevant section within the use case specification). In the context of the UML notation we provide extended notation techniques. Security requirements are related to each other so that they can be traced from one level of abstraction to the next (i.e., each requirement is transformed into one or several requirements or into some counteractive measures at the abstraction level underneath).

4.2 Model View

In the context of this paper a *workflow* describes a network of partners cooperating in a controlled way by calling services and exchanging documents. Our method of designing security-critical inter-organizational workflows is based on two orthogonal views: the *interface view* and the *workflow view*. The latter is further divided into the global workflow model describing the message exchange between cooperating partners, and the local workflow model describing the behavior of each partner. The application of these orthogonal perspectives allows us to combine the design of components offering services that may be called in different contexts.

This paper focuses on *programming in the large* [21] and assumes the business logic itself to be given. As there is no central control of the process, the inter-organizational workflow is designed by representatives of the partners involved in the workflow. Actions are allocated to specific partners in the global workflow model. Every action corresponds to some business logic implemented at a partner node.

Very often partners have already implemented some kind of application logic, maybe even made it accessible to customers as a web service. In this case, the development of an inter-organizational workflow requires an inside-out proceeding. The interface of the application logic is projected onto the interface model. The interface model of every partner's node describes the public part of the local application logic, which is accessible to the inter-organizational workflow and conforms to a uniform technical, syntactical and semantic specification the partners agreed upon. If for example, the partners agree to implement the global workflow based on web-services, some partners will have to provide a web services wrapper for their application logic; they may decide on parameter formats, interaction protocols, operation semantics or run-time constraints specification, information is typically published in WSDL files and technical Models (tModels) of UDDI Registries. Accordingly, in an outside-in proceeding, the interface model represents a specification of the functional requirements the partner has to implement at its node.

From a security perspective, the interface model deals with security requirements from the components' point of view, while the workflow model deals with the secure exchange of documents between different partners. In the sequel we briefly sketch the different models, followed by an explanation of the inter-model dependencies.

Global Workflow Model. The global workflow model describes an integrated abstract view of the workflow involving partners in autonomous organizations. The global workflow describes the interaction of partners abstracting from internal processing steps and does not contain any connection to the business logic.

The global workflow is modeled as an UML 2.0 activity diagram [22] describing sequences of actions, which represent web services. For each action, we specify which partner is calling the service, which partner offers the services and which documents are exchanged. We enrich the activity diagram of the global workflow by a qualification of the document exchange with security requirements. Figure 4 shows the document exchange between two public service providers requiring compliance to the security requirements of confidentiality and integrity. Security requirements are modeled in compliance with the UML 2.0 Metamodel by attaching a constraint, to the *ObjectNode*. The *ValueSpecification* of the constraint consists of attributes assigned a set of element nodes corresponding to the document parts to be encrypted and signed.

In our example, every part of the document sent from the Tax Advisor to the Municipality is meant to comply with confidentiality and integrity. At runtime, the Policy Enforcement Point, acting as a security gateway, will have to sign and encrypt the document at the company's boundary according to a security policy configuration file containing the above mentioned requirements (section 4.3).

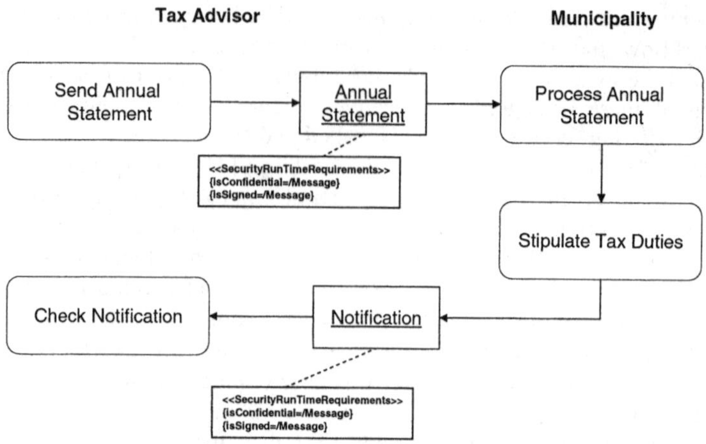

Fig. 4. A Sample Document Flow with Security Requirements (Global Workflow Model)

Local Workflow Model. The local workflow models define the portion of the global workflow each partner is responsible for. They are developed for each partner type. The local workflow is an executable process description that considers service calls from the outside, and contains internal actions as well as connections to the business logic. It is a direct input for a local workflow management system and is typically developed internally by partners. Referring to the sample process, the global workflow model captures the protocol between the online municipal tax component and the involved partners like the Municipality and the Tax Advisor, while the local workflow model describes the sequence in which the component accepts and processes incoming messages based on the services described in the interface model. The local workflow model describes the necessary processing steps to calculate the tax duties. These steps are performed internally and are invisible to the outside.

Interface Model. The interface model describes a component offering a set of services with given properties and permissions. Security requirements at this level of abstraction involve the support of a role model and the specification of access rights for particular web service operations. We describe access rights formally and platform-independently using OCL, a predicative sublanguage of UML [23]. The OCL specification is then transformed into an XACML-policy file via automatic generation. A more detailed description of the interface model can be found in [10].

Model Dependencies. Security requirements specified in the global workflow model have to be mapped in a consistent way to the local workflows of all cooperating partners, which reflect the business logic in their local environment.

Partner A in Figure 5 is responsible for the implementation of the business logic covering Actions 1, 2, 5 and 6 in the global workflow model. This can be seen as an abstract functional specification of the application logic a partner has to contribute to the global workflow. All the partners together agree on the signature format and naming conventions for the interfaces they provide to each other. These interfaces are visible to all partners and represent entry or exit points for data, messages or documents, either entering the local workflow for further processing or leaving it after processing (e.g., OP_1 (Msg1) := Msg4 in Figure 5).

In a second step, the partners map the interfaces of their local business logic to operations in the Interface Model (e.g., $LocalOP_B$ (LocalMsg1) in Figure 5). They are not visible to the partners and are used during the execution of their own local workflows in order to perform additional workflow actions.

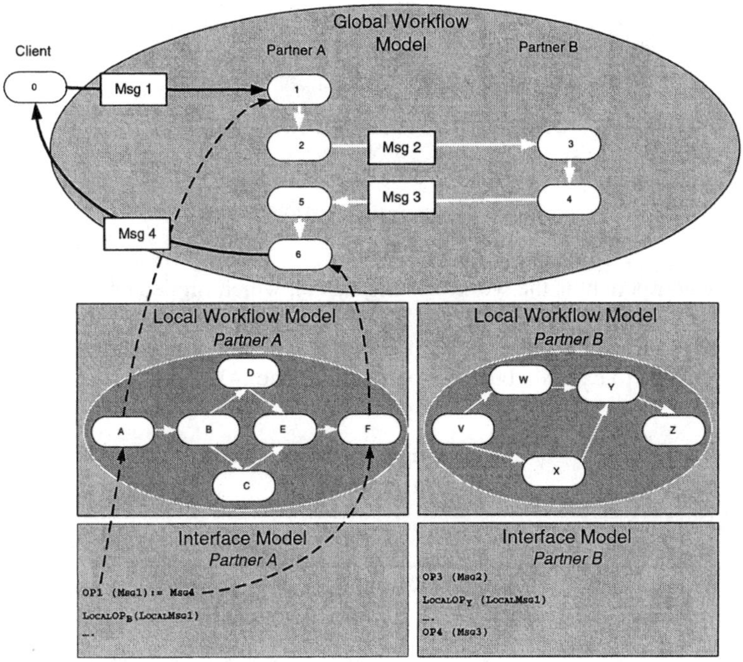

Fig. 5. Interface, Global and Local Workflow Model

In the global workflow model, either one or two actions are mapped to an operation in the interface model depending on whether the message exchange is asynchronous or synchronous. Van der Aalst et al. [24] present a formal approach based on Petri nets for the design of inter-organizational workflows guaranteeing local autonomy without compromising the consistency of the overall process. In our terms, this means that - in a peer-to-peer fashion – the local workflows should exactly realize the behavior as specified in the global workflow.

3.3 Target Software Architecture

In this section we present our target architecture for a partner which offers a portion of a distributed workflow. The architecture is based on the data-flow model of XACML as described in [18]. Figure 6 shows the software architecture in the view of a partner who implements his portion of the global workflow as a local workflow and offers an interface to its partners.

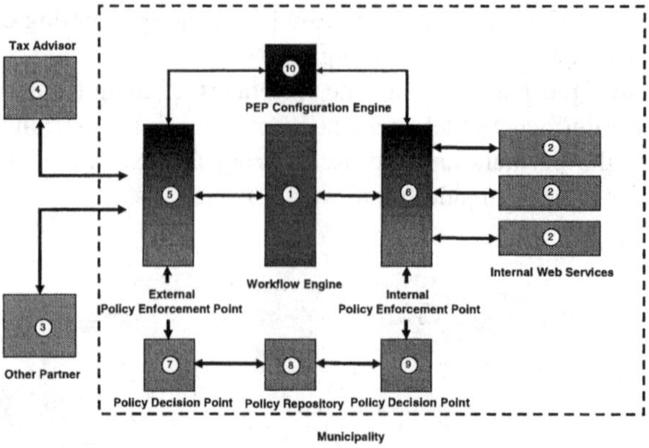

Fig. 6. Target Software Architecture

The core component is the workflow engine (1), which implements a choreography language such as WS-BPEL [12] or BPML [16] and aggregates and controls the sequence of existing Web services (2) to a composition that may be offered as a web service of its own to external business partners (3) and (4).

Table 2. Security Objectives and their Implementation in the PEP Component

Security Requirement	Security Component	Provided Functionality	Used Technologies & Standards
Authentication	External PEP Policy Decision Point Policy Repository	SOAP Firewall (Message Structure Processing) SOAP Firewall (Auhtorization Policies) Policy Archive	SAML, WS-Sec, XML-Encr.,XML-Sign, PKI, WSS4J, XML XACML, XML XACML, XML
Authorization	Internal / External PEP Policy Decision Point Policy Repository	SOAP Firewall (State-Dependent Permission Check,Mapping Global to Local Access Rights) SOAP Firewall (Auhtorization Policies) Policy Archive	SAML, WS-Sec, XML-Encr.,XML-Sign, PKI, WSS4J, XML XACML, XML XACML, XML
Confidentiality	External PEP PEP Configuration Engine	SOAP Firewall Check of Complimnace to Security Requirements	SAML, WS-Sec, XML-Encr.,XML-Sign, PKI, WSS4J, XML PKI, WSS4J, XML
Integrity	*refer to "Confidentiality"*	*refer to "Confidentiality"*	*refer to "Confidentiality"*
Non Repudiation	*refer to "Confidentiality"*	*refer to "Confidentiality"*	*refer to "Confidentiality"*

SAML	Security Assertion Markup Language (SAML)
XACML	Extensible Access Control Markup Language (XACML)
Sign	XML Digital Signature
Encr	XML Encryption
WS-Sec	Web-Services Security Specification
XSD	XML Schema Definition
WSS4J	Web-Services Security for Java
XML	Extensible Mark up Language
PKI	Public Key Infrastructure

Our prototypical generator is based on WS-BPEL, a workflow composition language for Web services. WS-BPEL is an appropriate top layer standard to the web services protocol stack, including WSDL [13], SOAP, UDDI, WS-Transactions [14] and a multitude of related standards. We use BPWS4J as a BPEL engine [25].

In order to provide a trusted domain atomic and composite web services are wrapped by security components. The Policy Enforcement Points (PEP) act as security gateways. The external PEP (5) implements security objectives like user authentication, confidentiality and integrity regarding data exchange with external partners, whereas the internal PEP (6) enforces access rights. It checks invocation requests from workflow partners to exposed services and then forwards requests to Policy Decision Points (PDP) (7) and (9) which check the requests according to some policy stored in the Policy Repository (PR) (8). The PEP Configuration Engine (10) supports the configuration of the security components acting as a repository for XML files that provide specific instructions to the Policy Enforcement Points.

Security requirements in the workflow models are implemented through basic concepts like keys, encryption, signatures and certificates based on XML and SOAP. Access control requirements are expressed in XACML, which is an XML based OASIS standard for a policy and access control decision language [19]. Table 2 gives an overview of the security requirements, the security components, the functionality the components provide and the underlying standards and technologies.

5 Related Work

Related work can be found in several areas. A number of approaches deal with secure document exchange and workflow management in a centrally organized environment. Among these are the Author-X system [26], PERMIS [27], and Akenti [28]. Often a central control is appropriate, but there are also many application domains requiring a local organization.

A whole community deals with inter-organizational workflow management systems [24], [29], [30], [31], [32], [33]. We do not aim to contribute a novel approach to this field. Instead, we rely on UML models for modeling workflows and existing workflow management systems based on web services technology. Security extensions at a low level of abstraction for workflow management systems are treated in [34], [35], [36], [37].

Model driven approaches that are close to the idea of our framework are [38], [39], [40]. Lodderstedt [20] introduced the notion of Model Driven Security for a software development process that allows for the integration of security requirements into system models and supports the generation of security infrastructures. These approaches deal with business logic, our approach deals with workflow management.

6 Conclusions and Further Studies

In this paper we have given an overview of our approach to Model Driven Security of inter-organizational workflows. Our framework is based on the idea of specifying security requirements at the abstract level of UML models and generating security components in the context of web services, web service orchestration and the upcoming related security standards.

At this stage, we have finished specifying the underlying concepts and evaluating adequate standards. Extension efforts are heading for several directions. We are working on the transformation functions and on an implementation of the core of the code generator for a run time architecture based on web services technology. We aim at the extension of the list of security requirements that can be expressed within our syntactic framework by considering additional features for basic security requirements (e.g., the distinction of documents signed by actors or by systems according to various legal requirements) and by introducing new types of complex, domain specific security requirements (e.g., transactional security requirements for electronic banking). Our case studies in the field of e-government show us an increasing demand for high-level development of secure workflow realizations.

References

1. Austrian Signature Act (Signaturgesetz - SigG), Art. 1 of the Act published in the Austrian Federal Law Gazette, part I, Nr. 190/1999.
2. Federal Act on Provisions Facilitating Electronic Communications with Public Bodies (E-Government Gesetz - E-GovG), Art. 1 of the Act published in the Austrian Federal Law Gazette, part I, Nr. 10/2004, entered into force on 1 March 2004.
3. Federal Act concerning the Protection of Personal Data (Datenschutzgesetz - DSG2000), published in the Austrian Federal Law Gazette, part I No. 165/1999, on 17. August 1999.
4. Austrian Security Manual, http://www.cio.gv.at/securenetworks/sihb/
5. OECD Guidelines for the Security of Information Systems and Networks, http://www.ftc.gov/bcp/conline/edcams/infosecurity/popups/OECD_guidelines.pdf.
6. P. Devanbu, S. Stubblebine: Software engineering for security: a roadmap. In: A. Finkelstein (ed.): The Future of Software Engineering, ACM Press 2000, pp. 227-239.
7. E. Ferrari, B. Thuraisingham: Secure Database Systems. In: M. Piattini and O. Díaz (eds.): Advanced Databases: Technology Design, Artech House, London 2000.
8. A. Hall, R. Chapman: Correctness by construction developing a commercial secure system. In: IEEE Software 19 (2002) 1, pp. 18-25.
9. The authors: Towards a Systematic Development of Secure Systems. In: Information Systems Security 13 (2004) 3.
10. The authors: Towards Model Driven Security of Inter-Organizational Workflows. Accepted for SAPS 2004.
11. The authors: Modeling and Realizing Security-Critical Inter-Organizational Workflows. In: W. Dosch, N. Debnath (Eds.): Proceedings IASSE 2004, ISCA, ISBN 1-880843-52-X, 2004.
12. BEA, IBM, Microsoft, SAP AG, Siebel Systems: Specification: Business Process Execution Language for Web Services Version 1.1, May 2003, http://www.ibm.com/developerworks/library/ws-bpel.
13. E. Christensen, F. Curbera, G. Meredith, S. Weerawarana: Web Services Description Language (WSDL) 1.1, http://www.w3.org/TR/wsdl.
14. BEA, IBM, Microsoft: Web services Transaction (WS-Transaction), http://www-6.ibm.com/developerworks/webservices/library/ws-transpec/
15. BEA, Intalio, Sun Microsystems, SAP: Web Service Choreography Interface (WSCI) 1.0, http://www.w3.org/TR/wsci/
16. A. Arkin: Business Process Modeling Language. San Mateo, CA: BPMI.org, 2002. Proposed Final Draft.
17. IBM, Microsoft, VeriSign: Web services Security (WS-Security), http://www-106.ibm.com/developerworks/webservices/library/ws-secure/
18. S. Godik, T. Moses: eXtensible Access Control Markup Language (XACML) Version 1.0 3 OASIS Standard, 18 February 2003, http://www.oasis-open.org/committees/xacml/repository

19. S. Cantor, J. Kemp, E. Maler: Assertions and Protocols for the OASIS Security Assertion Markup Language (SAML) V2.0, Last-Call Working Draft 17, 13 July 2004, http://www.oasis-open.org/committees/download.php/7737/sstc-saml-core-2.0-draft-17.pdf
20. T. Lodderstedt: Model Driven Security: from UML Models to Access Control Architectures. Dissertation, Univ. of Freiburg 2003.
21. F. Leyman, D. Roller: Production Workflow: Concepts and Techniques. Prentice-Hall 2000.
22. UML: http://www.uml.org.
23. OMG, UML 2.0 Superstructure Specification, http://www.omg.org/docs/ptc/03-08-02.pdf.
24. W.M.P. van der Aalst and M. Weske: The P2P appraoch to Interorganizational Workflows. In K.R. Dittrich, A. Geppert, and M.C. Norrie (eds.): Proceedings of the 13th International Conference on Advanced Information Systems Engineering (CAiSE'01), Springer, Berlin, pp. 140-156.
25. IBM: BPWS4J, http://www.alphaworks.ibm.com/tech/bpws4j.
26. E. Bertino, S. Castano, E. Ferrari: Securing XML Documents with Author X. In: IEEE Internet Computing 5 (2001) 3, pp. 21-31.
27. D. W. Chadwick: RBAC Policies in XML for X.509 Based Privilege Management. In: Proceedings of the IFIP TC11 17th International Conference on Information Security: Visions and Perspectives 2002, pp. 39-54.
28. M. Thompson, A. Essiari, S. Mudumbai: Certificate-based Authorization Policy in a PKI Environment. In: ACM Transactions on Information and System Security 6 (2003) 4, pp. 566-588.
29. W.M.P. van der Aalst.: Loosely Coupled Interorganizational Workflows: Modeling and Analyzing Workflows Crossing Organizational Boundaries. In: Information and Management 37 (2000) 2, pp. 67-75.
30. W.M.P. van der Aalst: Process-oriented Architectures for Electronic Commerce and Interorganizational Workflow. In: Information Systems 24 (1999) 8, pp. 639-671.
31. Z. Luo, A. Shet, K. Kochut, J. Miller: Exception Handling in Workflow Systems. In: Applied Intelligence 13 (2000) 2, pp. 125-147.
32. P. Grefen, K. Aberer, Y. Hoffner, H. Ludwig: CrossFlow: cross-organizational workflow management in dynamic virtual enterprises. In: International Journal of Computer Systems Science & Engineering 15 (2000) 5, pp. 277-290.
33. F. Casati and M. Shan: Event-based Interaction Management for Composite E-Services in eFlow. In: Information Systems Frontiers 4 (2002) 1, pp. 19-31.
34. V. Atluri, W.K. Huang: Enforcing Mandatory and Discretionary Security in Workflow Management Systems. In: Proceedings of the 5th European Symposium on Research in Computer Security 1996.
35. E. Gudes, M. Olivier, R. van de Riet.: Modelling, Specifying and Implementing Workflow Security in Cyberspace. In: Journal of Computer Security 7 (1999) 4, pp. 287-315.
36. W.K. Huang, V. Atluri: SecureFlow: A secure Web-enabled Workflow Management System. In: ACM Workshop on Role-Based Access Control 1999, p. 83-94.
37. J. Wainer, P. Barthelmess and A. Kumar: W-RBAC – A Workflow Security Model Incorporating Controlled Overriding of Constraints. In: International Journal of Cooperative Information Systems. 12 (2003) 4, pp. 455-485.
38. D. Basin, J. Doser, T. Lodderstedt: Model Driven Security for Process-Oriented Systems. In: 8th ACM Symposium on Access Control Models and Technologies. ACM Press 2003.
39. U. Lang.: Access Policies for Middleware. PhD Thesis, University of Cambridge 2003.
40. T. Lodderstedt, D. Basin, J. Doser: SecureUML: A UML-Based Modeling Language for Model-Driven Security. In: J.-M. Jézéquel, H. Hussmann, S. Cook (eds.): Proceedings of the 5th International Conference on the Unified Modeling Language, Springer 2002, pp. 426-441.

e-Government: A Legislative Ontology for the '*SIAP*' Parliamentary Management System

Carmen Costilla[1], Juan P. Palacios[2], José Cremades[3], and Jorge Vila[2]

[1] Titular Professor, *Information Systems and Databases* (SINBAD) Research Group
Technical University of Madrid (UPM)
costilla@dit.upm.es
www.sinbad.dit.upm.es
[2] Ph. Researchers at the SINBAD-UPM
{jppalacios, jvila}@sinbad.dit.upm.es
www.sinbad.dit.upm.es
[3] Founder Partner of CRC Information Technologies
jcremades@crcit.es
www.crcit.es

Abstract. The requirement of integrating, sharing and reusing legislative information is a research issue gaining priority for governments and institutions. The legal world is complex, heterogeneous and wide in scope. Therefore, we find convenient to define ontologies as a tool to decrease this complexity inherent to the legal domain. This paper is based on the *Parliamentary Integrated Management System* (*SIAP*) built for the *Asamblea of Madrid* and that is successfully running since 1999. In this context, we describe how *SIAP* manages the *Legislative Initiative (LI)* that arrives to a Parliament. Later, we propose an ontology in order to describe the *LI*, called *Legislative Ontology (LO)*. This *LO* conceptually models the *LI* including the structure of the Emendations to this *LI* and is connected with the act of making and passing laws. So, this *LO* makes easier the organizing task in the *LI* and, in general, all the Legislative procedural steps. Besides, this ontology could be offered as a basis for other parliamentary systems (as *SIAP*) to improve their *LI* procedures.

1 Introduction and Motivation

Nowadays, the legislative world is an important research goal. The requirement of integrating, sharing and reusing legislative information is a research issue gaining priority for governments and institutions. The *Asamblea of Madrid* is a clear example of governmental institution that had experienced this necessity. Currently, all documentary fonds of the parliament of Madrid are digitized, integrated and managed by the Parliamentary Integrated Management System (*SIAP*). *SIAP* was funded by the *Asamblea de Madrid* (1997-2000) and was built at our SINBAD-UPM research group joint to the Spanish businesses *CRC Information Technologies (CRC IT).* Nowadays, CRC IT commercializes *SIAP* (www.crcit.es/SIAP) and it is sponsored by the Technical University of Madrid (UPM), Oracle and Cronos entreprises.

As we know, the legislature is the democratically elected group of people who have the power to make and change laws. And the Legislative Ontology *LO* (proposed here) is connected with the act of making and passing laws.

M. Böhlen et al. (Eds.): TCGOV 2005, LNAI 3416, pp. 134–146, 2005.

Any Parliament has a double purpose. It makes possible to control the executive (the government) that has power over a concise society (country, autonomy, etc.). Also, it promotes laws as the legislative power basement.

This double aim is obtained through the Parliamentary Initiatives. One kind of Parliamentary Initiative is the *Legislative Initiative* (here after, *LI*). There are two kinds of *LI*: Law Project (LP), coming from the government's political party; and Law Proposition (LPROP), coming from another party. The main goal of any *LI* is the promulgation of the Law.

SIAP is successfully running at the *Asamblea de Madrid* since 1999. *SIAP* is composed of several modules and applications. It controls the documentary workflow in a Parliament and integrates and automates most of the parliamentary activity.

The *LI* automatic organization is an important application of *SIAP*. Its main objective is the automation of all *LI* procedural steps. That means, it includes all phases of parliamentary work, since the *LI* arrives at the Parliament until the Law is promulgated.

The *LI* procedural steps could be large and complex, even though they are perfectly regulated by the "Normative" of any Parliament [1]. Usually, the procedures of the *LI* carries out through the following stages:

- The *LI* (as document) is registered at the Parliament and arrives at the Parliamentary Table. This Table accepts its procedure and orders its publication on the Parliamentary Official Bulletin.
- The Parliamentary Groups register the emendations to the *LI* (in a fixed period). The emendations to the text of the *LI* could be total or partial.
- In general, the most important procedures of the *LI* start with the emendations and the *LI* text. Both are discussed and voted in the corresponding Committee. These actions produce an alternative text, merging the approved emendations.
- Finally, this new *LI* text is voted and approved by the plenary, in charge of the Law promulgation.

It is interesting to remark that this *LI* workflow, here summarized, could be applied to any Parliament. In the same way, the *LI*'s own organization (later described) also results very similar in any Parliament.

But the intrinsic richness of the legislative language implies that each *LI* is very complex in its content, with its own and specific structure, and with different workflow procedures. For example, the *LI* objective and the number and type of the *LI* emendations are completely different from other previous ones (even during the same legislature).

This heterogeneity makes difficult the exchange of information among different parliaments. Besides, the guarantee of consistency and integrity of the *LI* content in the actual legal framework is also a hard task. This problem becomes sharpen when the goal is the integration and the reusability of the legislative information that each Parliament admits, performs, promulgates and publishes, including its relations with other parliaments.

Fig. 1. SIAP is running at the Asamblea of Madrid

Apart from it, the semantic web provides ontologies describing a shared knowledge about a specific domain [7]. The ontologies allow to explicitly define structures and contents, coding the implicit rules of a part of reality. These explicit declarations are independent of its goal or its target domain [16]. Each ontology tries to get a consensus in a common understanding to reuse and share it between applications. In this sense, we adopt the ontology as a paradigm to reduce the complexity inherent to the legal domain (semantics reduces complexity).

As previous works, we have developed two ontologies based on two international archival description standards: ISAD(G) [19] and ISAAR(CPF) [18]. In addition, thanks to the gained experience of *SIAP*, we have also developed a Parliamentary Digital Archive ontology, called SIAP-O [14], intended to describe the structure of a Parliamentary Digital Archive (from the one working in Madrid). Based on these three ontologies, we have proposed a web architecture [13] for the virtual and dynamic integration of several Digital Archives [12], with mediator and wrapper layers.

This paper describes how *SIAP* deals with the *LI* procedural steps and proposes a Legislative Ontology, *LO*, (mainly its taxonomy) in order to describe the *LI* organization. Also, this *LO* includes the structure of the Emendations to the *LI*. The final idea is incorporating this ontology to the *SIAP* module in charge of the *LI* management. The *LO* ontology could be the basis for the improvement of other parliamentary legislative information systems similar to *SIAP*.

The remainder of this paper is organized as follows: Section 2 deals with the *SIAP* Integrated Parliamentary Information System, Section 3 describes the proposed legislative ontology. Finally, in Section 4, the conclusions are given.

2 The Parliamentary Integrated Management System - SIAP

Thanks to *SIAP* (Integrated Parliamentary Management System) the *Asamblea of Madrid* has totally digitized its documentary fonds, since the beginning of our democracy. The *SIAP* management system is powerful and ideally advanced for the web. The Legislative Management System is running at the *Asamblea de Madrid* as an application included in the broader *SIAP* system.

SIAP manages and controls the workflow of overall parliamentary documentary information and automatically creates the many types of parliamentary document produced by political activity. The *SIAP*'s design main guidelines were: the proper political activity, the institutional normative, Political Initiative typology and the nature of political documentation. In order to provide *useful information*, as intelligent as possible, we follow the guidelines in [4], [24] and other developed previous systems [8], [9].

The *SIAP* system structures the Political Initiative and Parliamentary jobs (Plenary sessions, Committees, etc.). The *SIAP* workflow sends the document to be considered (established by the regulation) according to each type of political initiative. Moreover, it is controlled when a document is sent to be published into the Official Bulletin, the Sessions Journal and dynamic web pages automatically created for a specific user type. *SIAP* associates the document to the respective File, to the corresponding Daily

Agenda, to the pertinent Official Bulletin, to the previous scripted political sessions, etc. Besides, *SIAP* also knows where the original document is stored and where the multiple document copies are held.

2.1 Objectives and Architecture

SIAP models Parliament's overall structure and organization. It has demonstrated a high degree of security and effectiveness for those procedural steps in each political initiative type. The main goal of *SIAP* is to obtain a perfect integration of the parliamentary information with the proper activity of the Parliament.

SIAP controls input documents and produces a huge amount of output documents, some of them with a public nature. It makes the entire Parliament of Madrid Official Bulletin, and the greatest part of Sessions Journal. Besides, *SIAP* applies documentary searching to other external Official Bulletins (from foreign institutions). If it were convenient, all this information would be dynamically published on the web.

- *Management of information generated by political Institution' activity,*
- *Control of regulated workflow,*
- *Design and implementation of Parliament structure and organization and its perfect integration into the parliamentary documentary flow,*
- *Semantic control, applications and GUIs software.*

SIAP has an open architecture to be implemented into the Institution network. It has an underlying object-relational database running into the Database Server and its applications could also work on its own (Law Budget Project, Archive Management, Registers, Documentary information due to the daily political activity, etc.).

SIAP runs on Oracle in Client/Server (C/S, two tiers) and in Internet/Intranet (three or four web tiers). In C/S, for providing services to civil servants that update the information system (with a high degree of protection and security). In C/S, protocols SQL*Net8 and OCA and, in Web OAS (Oracle Application Server and IAS of Oracle 9i) are used. For both, IntermediaText for information retrieval (before Oracle Context) is used. Figure 2 represents the documentary workflow and *SIAP* open architecture; where BOAM means Asamblea of Madrid Official Bulletin and DDSS means Sessions Journal.

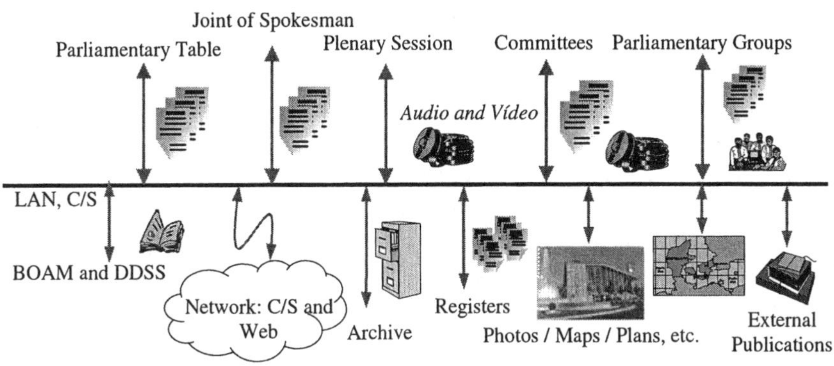

Fig. 2. Documentary workflow and ***SIAP*** open architecture (C/S and Web)

2.2 Capabilities

The daily activity in a Parliament produces documents tailored to many specific type of Parliamentary Initiatives. *SIAP* holds especially relevant information organized in *files* (descriptive folders) according to the initiative typology and objective. The *file* collects related information on political activity and marks the procedure type to schedule with all documents that are held inside it (initiatives, photographs, maps, graphics, audio, video, etc.).

Additionally, the file incorporates the following descriptive information: *Identification*, *Censure or judgment of the contained documents*, *Schedule*, *File Classification and its respective documents*, *Allocation*: topographical, informatics and address of Institution, departments, dependencies, etc., *File prosecution* (*workflow* with all states that must or should be adopted by the file, *Current status* and *History)* and, finally, *Relationships* between files by subject, type, date, state, descriptors, etc.

SIAP handles queries against the underlying object-relational database (SQL) and/or to the thesaurus with a powerful *information retrieval.* It searches thousands of publications and locates the subject of interest in a few seconds; locates the annexed document to the file in an almost instantaneous response, independently of the Legislature where it is stored [2]; and, finally, creates a lot of report results [10] (www.asambleamadrid.org).

SIAP controls the all of the information from any Legislature, knowing the topographical key signatures of its complete archive fonds. For example, The Madrilenian Court can instantaneously locate all files and documents dealing with *anorexia,* since the beginning of the Spanish democracy and can reproduce video fragments of the political sessions (Plenary and Commissions) in which this illness was discussed.

Through web applications, the parliament can negotiate the information exchange between similar institutions at any level, in an integrated and intelligent way. *SIAP* can offer *global information* produced by many others Institutions, as well as its own [15], [21], [22].

Fig. 3. The SIAP Parliamentary Activity Management at the Asamblea of Madrid

SIAP was introduced in many Spanish Parliamentary and Political Parties Conferences (since 1999), and it is considered a powerful and complete system. Figure 3 shows one of its main screen concerning to the Parliamentary Activity Management, through which the *LI* is automatically processed.

If other institutions could have similar information systems, then the web e-government information capabilities will grow in a spectacular way. We want to remark on how easy is to get dynamic interoperability on the web when data sources have the same Information System (same design and semantic control, similar software, etc.), as figure 4 represents.

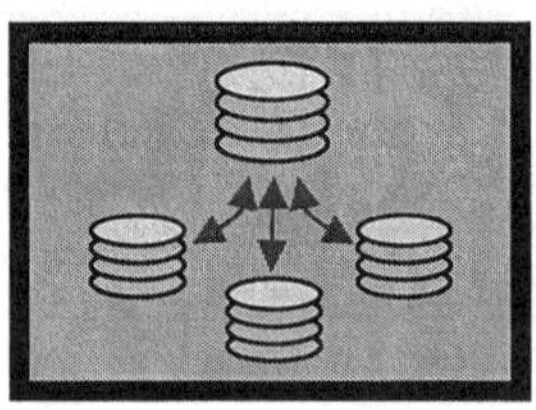

Fig. 4. Web Multi-parliamentary

However, in heterogeneous Information Systems environments it could be hard to provide easy and powerful access to a global e-government information.

2.3 Parliamentary Legislative Initiative

SIAP is organized in ten modules that can run in an integrated or independent way. These modules make use of four auxiliary applications. One of these applications is in charge of the *Legislative Initiative Organization (LIO)* we are dealing with.

The *LI* text (Law Proposition or Law Project) is organized in levels (Titles, Chapters, Sections, Articles, etc.). The *LIO* application allows to load the *LI* text from a file, organizes and publishes it. This organization could be applied manually (pointing out the content of Title I, art. 1, art 2., etc.) or automatically.

Fig. 5. The Budget Law Project Application of SIAP at the Asamblea of Madrid

Once the *LI* arrives to the Parliament, the *LIO* application can publish it on the Official Bulletin automatically. In order to do it, you only need to specify the format at any different level being present in the text of the *LI* (for example, the titles are in single line, capitalized and with roman numeration) and pushing a button to get it.

Figure 6 shows the hierarchical organization of the *LI*. These are optional levels (some of them can be empty), but the part bounded to the articled must be filled. So, *SIAP* organizes the *LI* in this way.

In order to publish the *LI* on the Official Bulletin, *SIAP* applies the format layout used at the Parliament.

SIAP manages the *LI* until the law is promulgated. It monitors all its procedures in

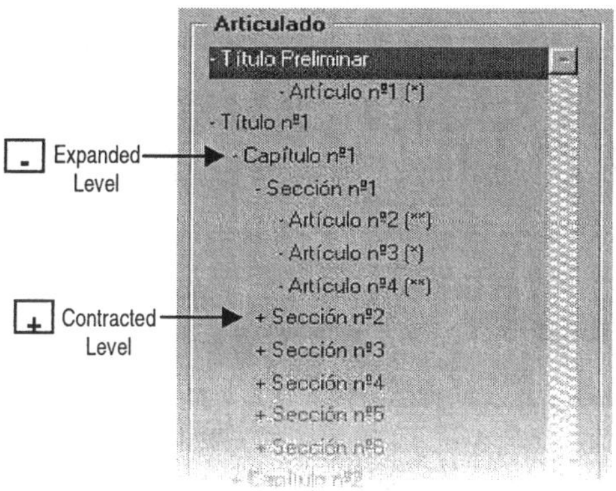

Fig. 7. Articled tree structure

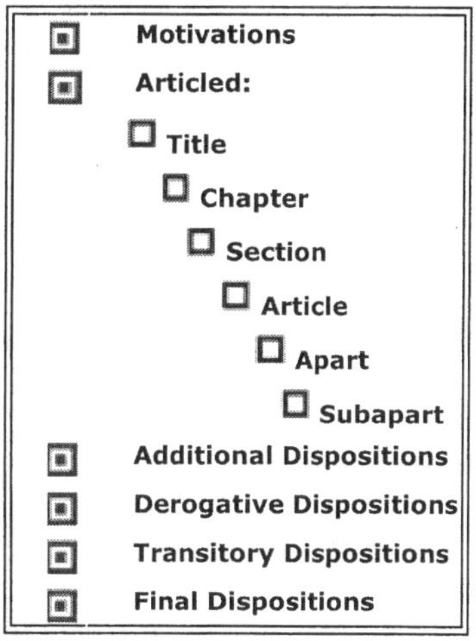

Fig. 6. *LI* Hierarchical Organization Levels

and produces many reports from the the related Committee, in the Plenary Session parliamentary activities related to this initiative.

This hierarchical organization is composed by syntactic elements on a tree, managed as directories. This syntactic layout of the *LI* elements helps for the automation and integration tasks of the legislative structures. So, if you are located on a parent level, its lower levels can be expanded (to be shown) or contracted (to be hidden), as figure 7 represents.

2.4 Legislative Emendations

Once a *LI* is published on the Official Bulletin, the parliamentary groups can register emendations in order to modify total or partially the *LI* text. *SIAP* manages and monitors the emendations. Each emendation registered (as a document) in the Parliament keeps related to the corresponding *LI* hierarchical level. *SIAP associates each emendation with the related level of the LI* and specifies the changes that emendation would produce in the text in case it were approved.

According to the presentation medium, the emendation typology is: *written*, *transaction* or '*in voce*'. And, the typology due to the kind of proposed changes is:

- *Addition* (to add text in some point or a new one).
- *Modification* (to modify all or part of the text in a point, or to modify a point and all its related sublevels. For instance, modifying an article and creating new sections inside it).
- *Deletion* (to delete parts of the text in a point or all the point, including all sublevels).

The emendation is linked to the *LI* text in different ways: a) several emendations are related to one point inside one *LI* level; b) one emendation can reference several parts of the text inside a point; c) one emendation can reference many points of the articled.

The *relationship between the emendation and the articled* is shown in a visual and intuitive way. Next to each *LI* point it is indicated the number of emendations linked. So, in figure 7, each asterisk '*' in one point, indicates that there is an emendation related to that point. From a menu at each level, we can get details about these emendations, and, in case you have the due grants, these emendations can be modified.

There are two *LI* reports involved in its procedural steps.

- *The publication of the LI in the Official Bulletin (OB)*, provides a homogeneous format to the *LI* text, as the Parliament's style specifies.
- *The two columns notebook*, intended to support the works carried out in the Committee. The left

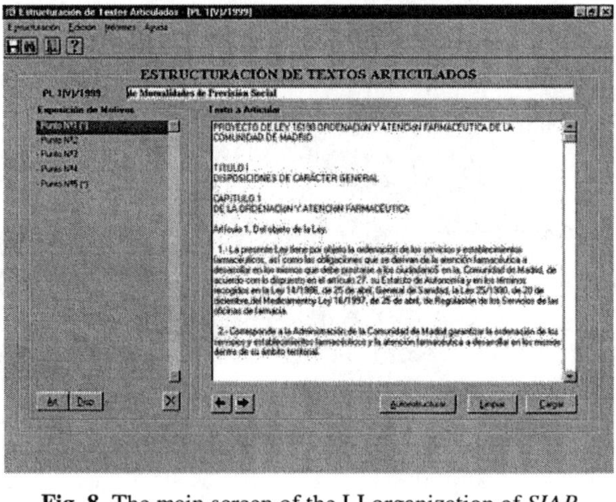

Fig. 8. The main screen of the LI organization of *SIAP*

column contains the initial *LI* text, and the right one shows the emendations. In such way that, for each point referenced by the emendations, it is indicated: author, type and text of each emendation.

This application stores the *original LI text* and supports the rest of the legislative modules (Committee and Plenary Sessions, etc.) Besides, at any moment, the *LI evolution* can be queried showing the *status* in which the emendations are up to date (approved, rejected or cancelled), and how they have affected the *LI* text. This way, *SIAP* manages the historical *LI* evolution.

Figure 8 shows the main screen of the *LI* management. It is divided in three frames. The upper one contains the identification data and the tittle into the text box. The left one shows the points of the *LI* organization (Motivation, Articled and Dispositions). The right frame shows the original *LI* text.

Once the emendation period is over, the *two columns notebook* is created and the Committee can start working on it.

We want to remark that *SIAP* automatically creates this *two columns notebook* report from the syntactic links between the *LI* text and the emendations. That means, the system is able to include, modify and remove elements inside a *LI* from the emendations.

Nevertheless, as the system lacks of semantics, it cannot 'understand' the changes it makes. Thus, it is impossible to automatically detect inconsistencies or integrity lacks inside the *LI* text. In fact, nowadays, the lawyer is the person in charge of assuring this kind of semantics among the original *LI* text and all the approved emendations.

As a consequence of this, we propose to build an ontology that monitors the semantics of the resulting *LI* text. After reaching this semantic objective, the next one will be the reusing and sharing of the legal framework produced in one Parliament, and the consistency with the laws promulgated by other democratic parliaments.

3 The SIAP Legislative Ontology

According to [23], the semantic conceptual models of legal domain are fundamental for the e-Government success. The incorporation of semantics in the legal structures could be very powerful.

This way, the computers will find the meaning of data following the *links* to the definitions of the terms and its key rules. It makes easier the automatic design of legislative services; because the main bottleneck is the inherent heterogeneity of the legal structure contents. To solve this problem and to be able to code the necessary information, we have XML and OWL ontologies as the best options [16].

We need to build ontologies [23] because the legal domain is not simple and it needs to be used for a wide audience.

An ontology describes shared knowledge on a specific domain in order to establish a communication way between humans and programs [2], [7]. Each ontology provides a precise definition of the terms (concepts) of a specific domain; that is, it provides a common language for sharing and re-using knowledge of some phenomenon in the domain of interest [16], [25] between applications and groups.

Consequently, applications can speak to each other and interpret, without ambiguity, the information they exchange. For this reason, they have been accepted as powerful description tools that allow to make explicit the semantic concepts. Since the early 1990s, a lot of research [3], [5], [6], [17], [25] deals with these semantic problems, where ontologies play a fundamental role.

3.1 An Ontology for the Legislative Initiative

The *LI* procedural steps are slow and complicated, due to the *LI* content complexity and the several emendations. Thus, the automation of the parliamentary work is sometimes inefficient and difficult to solve by intelligent information systems. Moreover, it seems to be important establishing a communication channel that allow the interoperability with other parliamentary systems [12]. In this context, there are current researches about web architectures [14].

This paper defines a *Legislative Ontology (LO)* in order to share, integrate and reuse parliamentary information, establishing a taxonomy among legislative concepts. Additionally, it makes possible the definition of semantic rules for the knowledge inference mechanisms. These rules are important to make possible interoperability with other different *LI* produced inside or outside the parliament.

Each concept of this *LO* is defined *'per se'* through properties and relationships to other concepts. Above this taxonomy, the knowledge inference mechanisms could be implemented.

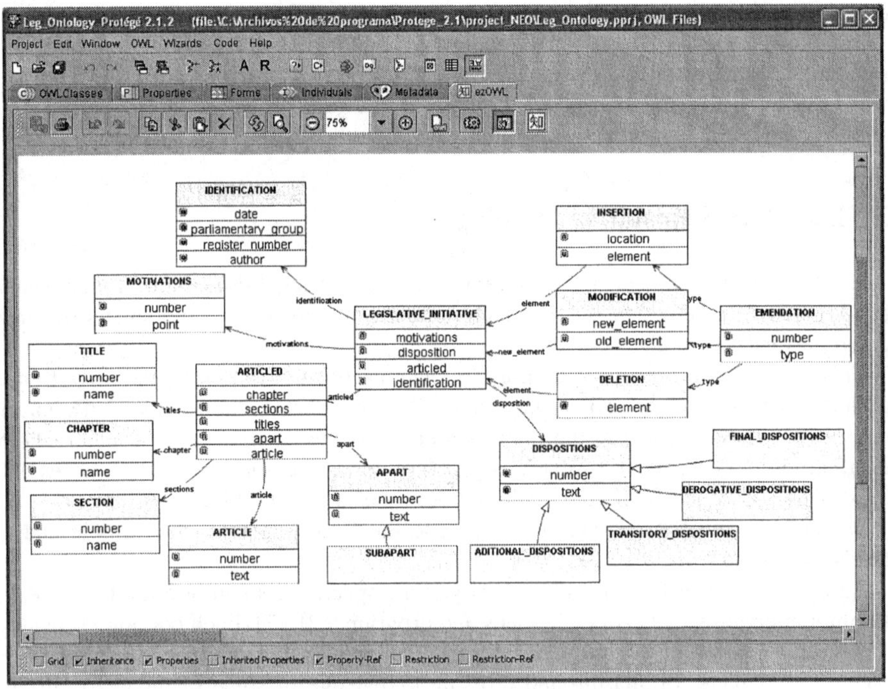

Fig. 9. Partial graph of the Legislative Ontology, *LO*

In addition, this kind of ontology enables the conceptual representation of the emendations and the support for the 'intelligent' *LI* procedural steps.

Through this *LO* different parts of the *LI* could be semantically connected. In the future, if many parliaments use this *LO*, it could also be possible the interoperability among many *LI* coming from different parliaments.

If the system understands the meaning of the managed concepts, then it will be able to infer the right actions (insert, update or delete) in order to integrate the emendation into the *LI* text.

```
...
<owl:Class rdf:ID="LEGISLATIVE_INITIATIVE"/>
<owl:ObjectProperty rdf:ID="identificacion">
  <rdfs:domain rdf:resource="# LEGISLATIVE_INITIATIVE"/>
  <rdfs:range rdf:resource="#IDENTIFICATION"/>
</owl:ObjectProperty>
<owl:ObjectProperty rdf:ID="motivations">
  <rdfs:range rdf:resource="#MOTIVATIONS"/>
  <rdfs:domain rdf:resource="# LEGISLATIVE_INITIATIVE "/>
</owl:ObjectProperty>
<owl:ObjectProperty rdf:ID="articled">
  <rdfs:range rdf:resource="#ARTICLED"/>
  <rdfs:domain rdf:resource="# LEGISLATIVE_INITIATIVE"/>
</owl:ObjectProperty>
<owl:ObjectProperty rdf:ID="dispositions">
  <rdfs:domain rdf:resource="# LEGISLATIVE_INITIATIVE "/>
  <rdfs:range rdf:resource="#DISPOSITIONS"/>
</owl:ObjectProperty>
...
```

Fig. 10. Partial definition of the LEGISLATIVE_INITIATIVE concept in the *LO*

SIAP is in charge of materializing (at the lower abstraction level) these changes to the *LI*. However, this *LO* adds intelligence to the *LI* procedural steps and helps to promulgate the Law. Besides, it makes easy to search, extract, represent and interpret the *LI* in a Parliament.

The *LO* definition is based on the flowcharts and in the analysis of the *LI* procedure realized at *SIAP* [11]. Figure 9 shows the partial *LO* OWL graph defined with Protégé 2000.

The *LI* is composed of 17 concepts. The two main ones are LEGISLATIVE_ INITIATIVE and EMENDATION. Figure 10 shows a part of the OWL definition of the LEGISLATIVE_INITIATIVE concept and figure 11 shows the OWL definition of the EMENDATION concept.

```
...
<owl:Class rdf:ID="EMENDATION">
  <rdfs:subClassOf>
    <owl:Restriction>
      <owl:cardinality
          rdf:datatype="http://www.w3.org/2001/XMLSchema#int">
          </owl:cardinality>
      <owl:onProperty>
        <owl:ObjectProperty rdf:ID="type"/>
      </owl:onProperty>
    </owl:Restriction>
  </rdfs:subClassOf>
</owl:Class>
...
<owl:ObjectProperty rdf:about="#type">
  <rdfs:range>
    <owl:Class>
      <owl:unionOf rdf:parseType="Collection">
        <owl:Class rdf:about="#INSERT"/>
        <owl:Class rdf:about="#UPDATE"/>
        <owl:Class rdf:about="#DELETE"/>
      </owl:unionOf>
    </owl:Class>
  </rdfs:range>
  <rdfs:domain rdf:resource="#EMENDATION"/>
</owl:ObjectProperty>
  ...
```

Fig. 11. Partial definition of the EMENDATION concept in the *LO*

The LEGISLATIVE_INITIATIVE concept describes the elements included in the *LI*, as:

- '*motivation*'. This concept gives an explanation about the reason why the *LI* is proposed.
- '*articled*'. It contains the hierarchical structure of the *LI*, composed of *Titles, Chapters, Sections, Articles*, etc.
- '*dispositions*'. This concept explains the final information that adds, summarizes and complements the articled part.

Also, it is described the EMENDATION concept, intended to *insert, update* or *delete* some element from the *LI*. Thus, this concept needs to be linked to the concise text point inside the *LI*, which is the updating target. This concept is categorized as follows:

- '#INSERT': adds information to the *LI* text, indicating the location of the new text.
- '#UPDATE': modifies total or partially the original text in a point and all its related sublevels.
- '#DELETE': deletes the text in a point or all the point, including all sublevels.

The *LI* organization that *SIAP* is running since 1999, enables to organize one particular *LI* in a given parliament.

However, *SIAP* does not understand the *LI* as a XML document, neither is able to semantically establish relationships among the conceptual terms defined in one ontology [20]. Therefore, the *Legislative Ontology* here proposed permits the following improvements: adds semantic to the *Legislative Initiative* procedural steps, makes possible the re-using and sharing of these kind of concepts, enables the knowledge inference in *SIAP* and, in the future, it will help to guarantee the integrity and consistency of the legal domain inside a parliament and with other similar ones.

4 Conclusions

We have taken as the starting point the *Parliamentary Integrated Management System* (*SIAP*), successfully running at the Asamblea de Madrid since 1999. *SIAP* makes the legislative organization allowing to work with one *Legislative Initiative* in one parliament. However, *SIAP* does not understand the *Legislative Initiative* as a XML document, neither is able to semantically establish relationships among the conceptual terms defined in one ontology.

This paper proposes a *Legislative Ontology* in order to manage the legislative procedural steps and to support its corresponding emendations inside a parliament.

This *Legislative Ontology* defines an OWL coded taxonomy, made through Protégé2000, to manage the *Legislative Initiative* and Emendations organization. Making use of this semantic tool and the *two columns notebook*, the *Legislative Initiative* and *Emendations* texts are merged to create a new legislative text.

Finally, we come up with some future applications of the *Legislative Ontology* here introduced.

Acknowledgments

This work is partially granted by the Ministry of Science and Technology (MCYT-TIC2002-04050-C02-02, DAWIS-UPM project), by Community of Madrid (07T/0056/2003/3, EDAD-UPM project) and by 'Spanish Network of Excellence Databases', RedBD, (MCYT-TIC2000-3250-E).

References

1. Asamblea Madrid, *Reglamento Asamblea de Madrid*, ISBN:84-451-1260-0, Madrid, 1997.
2. Baeza y Berthier, *Modern Information Retrieval.* Addison Wesley, 1999.
3. Berners-Lee T, Hendler J, Lassila O, *The semantic Web.* Scientific American 284(5): 34-43, May 2001.
4. Bernstein P, Halevy A and Pottinger R, *A Vision of Management of Complex Models.* ACM Sigmod Record, 29(4): 55-63, Dec. 2000.
5. Calvenese D, Giacomo de G and Lenzerini M, *A Framework for Ontology Integration.* In Proc.of the First Semantic Web Working Symposium, pp 303-316 – 2001.
6. Chandrasekaran B, Josepheson J, Benjamins VR, *Ontologies: What are they? Why do we need them?* IEEE Intelligent Systems, 14(1):20-26, 1999.
7. Clyde W, Hossapple, Joshi KD, *A collaborative approach to Ontology design.* Communications of the ACM. Vol. 45 n. 2, pp.42-47, Feb. 2002.
8. Costilla C, Bas MJ, Villamor J, *SIRIO: A Distributed Information System over a Heterogeneous Computer Network.* ACM Sigmod Record, 22(1): 28-34, March 1993.
9. Costilla C, Bas MJ, Villamor J, *The Object Data Model and its Graphical User Interface for an Object Database System.* Proc. Biwit, 161-172, IEEE Computer Society, 1995.
10. Costilla C, Calleja A, Cremades J, *SIAP: Sistema de Información para Ayuntamientos y Parlamentos*, Círculo Usuarios de Oracle, CUORE, Sección *'Vivat Academia'*, Oct. 2003.
11. Costilla C, *Análisis Funcional del Sistema Integrado de Gestión Parlamentaria*, SIAP Technical Report to *Asamblea de Madrid*, 144 pages, April 1999.
12. Costilla C, Palacios JP, Rodríguez MJ, Cremades J, Calleja A, Fernández R and Vila J, *Semantic Web Digital Archive Integration*, Int. Workshop on *Web Semantics*, 14th Int. Conf. on *Database and Expert Systems Applications*, DEXA 2004, IEEE Computer Society, ISBN: 0-7695-2195-9, pp. 179-185, Zaragoza, Spain, August, 2004.
13. Costilla C, Palacios JP, Rodríguez MJ, Fernández R, Cremades J and Calleja A, *Web Digital Archives Integrated Architecture*, in The 5th Int. Conf. on *Internet Computing* (IC'2004), Vol 1, Session: *Web Mining*, Arabnia H and Droegehorn O (eds.), ISBN: 1932415-44-0, CSREA 2004, pp.128-134, Las Vegas, USA, June, 2004.
14. Costilla C, Rodríguez M, Palacios J, Cremades J, Calleja A and Fernández R, *A Contribution to Web Digital Archive Integration from the Parliamentary Management System 'SIAP'*, Proc. of Sixth Int. Baltic Conf. on *Data Bases and Information Systems*, Barzdins J (ed.), ISBN:9984-770-11-7, pp. 481-496, Riga, Latvia, June, 2004.
15. Florescu D, Levy A and Medelzon A, *Database Techniques for the World Wide Web: A Survey.* ACM Sigmod Record, Sept. 1998.
16. Gruber, T. R. *Towards principles for the design of ontologies used for knowledge sharing.* Int. Workshop on Formal Ontology, 1993.
17. Guarino N and Welty Ch., *Evaluating Ontological Decision with ONTOCLEAN.* Communications of the ACM. Vol. 45 n. 2, pp. 42-47, Feb. 2002.
18. *International Standard Archival Authority Record for Corporate Bodies, Persons and Families,* 2nd edition, International Council on Archives , ISBN: 2-9521932-2-3, 2004.
19. *ISAD(G) General International Standardization Archival Description*, 2nd edition, ISBN 0-9696035-5-X, International Council on Archives, Ottawa 2000.
20. Kim, H. *Predicting how ontologies for the semantic web will evolve.* Communications of the ACM. 45(2): 47-51, Feb. 2002.
21. Mendelzon A, Mihaila G and Milo T, *Querying the World Wide Web.* JODL, (1,1) 1997.

22. Özsu MT, Valduriez P, *Principles of Distributed Database Systems*, Prentice-Hall, 1999.
23. Traunmuller R, *Legal Modelling as Part of Knowledge Enhanced e-Government*, in Proc. Of ICAIL03, Workshop on E-Government, Edinburgh, UK, June 2003.
24. Wand Y, Storey VC and Weber R, *An Ontological Analysis of the Relationship Construct in Conceptual Modelling*. ACM Transac. on Database Systems, 24(4):494-528, Dec 1999.
25. Zhong N, Liu J, Yao Y (eds.), *Web Intelligence*, Springer Verlag, 2003

No (e-)Democracy Without (e-)Knowledge

Giovanni M. Sacco

Dipartimento di Informatica, Università di Torino, Corso Svizzera 185,
10149 Torino, Italy
sacco@di.unito.it

Abstract. Citizens have never had complete and up-to-date information on all the laws, regulations and opportunities that concern them. Although the law does not excuse ignorance, information-publishing techniques, usually Official Gazettes on paper, make effective knowledge and awareness virtually impossible. One of the greatest opportunities of e-government is to overcome this information gap and to supply timely and complete information to everybody. The electronic availability of information is but a minor aspect of this problem. Rather, effective, timely and accurate ways of disseminating information must be found. We discuss several solutions, ranging from text retrieval to ontologies and agents, and focus on dynamic taxonomies, a model recently proposed for the intelligent exploration of heterogeneous information bases, that can provide guided browsing and personalized exploration for complex laws and regulations.

1 Introduction

Ignorantia legis non excusat - ignorance of the law does not excuse - is a centuries-old criminal law maxim familiar to everybody: all are presumed to be familiar with all the laws that concern them or face the costs of their ignorance. This principle usually extends to civil law and regulations in the large. Nowadays, European laws and regulations exist at several levels: at the town, province, region, nation level up to the European Union level. Despite many promises of reduction, the efficiency of the legislative machinery is excellent and corpora are constantly growing. In addition to law and regulations that limit the rights of individuals and corporations, there are legislative actions to grant new rights to special categories (e.g. handicapped persons) and financial aids or opportunities that are targeted to specific areas/subjects.

No real democracy or participation exists in practice, if the citizen is not fully informed of all the rights, duties, opportunities and law-making in-progress that concern her. Sir Cecil Carr remarked many years ago that "*as a collection, our statute books might be summed up as beyond the average citizen's pocket to purchase, beyond his bookshelves to accommodate, beyond his leisure to study and beyond his intellect to comprehend*". Internet and digital storage make purchasing and accommodating this vast amount of data a trivial endeavor. Finding what is needed is another story.

The problem studied in this paper is how to make citizens aware of all the laws, regulations and opportunities that concern them. Traditionally, access paradigms have focused on retrieval of data on the basis of precise specifications: examples of this

M. Böhlen et al. (Eds.): TCGOV 2005, LNAI 3416, pp. 147 – 156, 2005.

approach include queries on structured database systems, and information retrieval. However, most search tasks, and notably accessing large legal repositories, are exploratory and imprecise in essence: the user does not usually know precisely what he wants (e.g. a specific law), but rather he needs to explore the information base, find relationships among concepts and thin alternatives out in a guided way. Traditional access methods are not helpful in this context, so that new access paradigms are required. We show how dynamic taxonomies, a model recently proposed for the intelligent exploration of heterogeneous information bases, can provide guided browsing and personalized exploration for complex laws and regulations.

2 Traditional Information Access Methods

Since the vast majority of normative material is essentially textual and unstructured in nature, information retrieval techniques [20] were extensively used in the past both in pull and push strategies [16]. These techniques are quite appealing because, at least in principle, they require almost no editorial or manual processing of information. In addition to low costs, this also means the immediate availability of new material. Normally, full text is augmented by manually inserted metadata, such as year of publication, language, type of document (e.g. EUR-lex, http://europa.eu.int/eur-lex/en/index.html). Since laws and regulations quite often refer to and/or amend previous norms, many systems use some kind of hypertext linking [3] to make navigation through references viable for the user.

The limitations of commercial information retrieval systems have been known for some time. Blair and Maron [1] report a study on the use of IBM Stairs in a legal environment: they found that almost 80% of relevant documents were not retrieved. Although IBM Stairs is somewhat outdated, most search engines used to manage laws and regulations are even less powerful. The major problem in text retrieval is the extremely wide semantic gap between the user model and the system model. The user works at a conceptual level and is interested in retrieving complex concepts, while the retrieval system usually works at an extremely low level and usually only understands strings of characters. During the years, a number of improvements have been proposed: from inflectional normalization, to intelligent thesauri such as WordNet [2], to relevance ranking [6]. Despite these attempts, the semantic gap is still very large. Any user of search engines experiences low precision and recall for all but the most concrete queries.

In addition to these semantic problems, information retrieval systems have other shortcomings. First, they are extremely poor from the point of view of user interaction: the user has to formulate his query with no or very little assistance. This is usually difficult because the user often does not know precisely what the information base contains. Second, results are presented as a flat list with no systematic organization. Browsing the infobase is usually difficult or altogether impossible. The success of Yahoo as an alternative to search engines is a convincing proof of this statement.

Hypermedia [3] mainly addresses the problem of browsing/exploring, but it has a number of serious drawbacks. First, there is no systematic picture of relationships among infobase components. Second, exploration is performed one-document-at-a-time, which is quite time consuming. Third, building and maintaining a complex hypermedia network can be extremely costly.

The success of Yahoo makes traditional taxonomies appealing. Here, a hierarchy of concepts can be used to select areas of interest and restrict the portion of the infobase to be retrieved. Taxonomies support abstraction and are easily understood by end-users. However, they are not scalable for large databases. In fact, a normal taxonomy can be used for discrimination just down to the lowermost level of the hierarchy (terminal concepts, which are no further specialized): at that point, the list of items associated with the selected terminal concept must be inspected manually. The major problem here is that if the infobase is large, the average number R of the documents to be manually inspected will be too large for manual inspection. In fact, R = D/T, where D is the number of documents in the infobase and T is the number of terminal concepts in the index [9]. A small infobase of 100,000 documents with a reasonable subject index of 1,000 terminal concepts, already produces 100 documents per terminal concept on the average, too many for manual inspection. Traditional taxonomies are monodimensional: an item can be classified under one and only one concept. If we relax this assumption, and allow an item to be classified under j several concepts, things get worse because the number of documents to be manually inspected increases by a factor of j [9].

Solutions based on semantic networks have been proposed in the past [14] and are now addressed again in the current effort on ontologies and Semantic Web. This approach is quite expensive in terms of design and maintenance of complex conceptual schemata. General ontologies are more powerful and expressive than plain taxonomies, but they are better suited to programmatic access and much more difficult to understand and manipulate by the casual user. Usually, user interaction must be mediated by specialized agents. This increases costs, time to market and decreases generality and flexibility of user access. The solution we propose in the following can be seen as a complement, in addition to being an alternative, to complex ontologies: in section 5, we provide a preliminary discussion of how our taxonomy-based model can provide a user-understandable view on complex semantics.

3 Dynamic Taxonomies

Dynamic taxonomies [7], [8] are a general knowledge management model for complex, heterogeneous information bases. It has been applied to very diverse areas, including news archives, encyclopedias, multimedia databases [10], electronic commerce [11], and medical guidelines [19]. The intension of a dynamic taxonomy is a taxonomy designed by an expert. This taxonomy is a concept hierarchy (directed acyclic graph taxonomies modeling multiple inheritance are supported but rarely required) going from the most general to the most specific concepts. A dynamic taxonomy does not require any other relationships in addition to subsumptions (e.g., IS-A and PART-OF relationships).

In the extension, items can be freely classified under several topics at any level of abstraction (i.e. at any level in the conceptual tree). This multidimensional classification is a departure from the monodimensional classification scheme used in conventional taxonomies. Besides being a generalization of a monodimensional classification, a multidimensional classification models common real-life situations. First, an item is very rarely classified under a single topic. One reason is that items are very often about different concepts: for example a funding opportunity could be classified as Agriculture>corn, Agriculture>soybean, Location>Southern Italy, Company>Turnover>less than 1 million euro. Second, items to be classified usually have different independent features (e.g. Time, Location, etc.), each of which can be described by an independent taxonomy. These features are often called *perspectives* or *facets*.

By taking a "nominalistic" approach (concepts are defined by instances rather than by properties), a concept C is just a label that identifies all the items classified under C. Because of the subsumption relationship between a concept and its descendants, the items classified under C (*items(C)*) are all those items in the *deep extension* [17] of C, i.e. the set of items identified by C includes the *shallow extension* of C (i.e. all the items directly classified under C) union the deep extension of C's sons. By construction, the shallow and the deep extension for a terminal concept are the same.

There are two important consequences of our approach. First, since concepts identify sets of items, logical operations on concepts can be performed by the corresponding set operations on their extension. This means that the user is able to restrict the information base by combining concepts through the normal logical operations (and, or, not).

Second, dynamic taxonomies can find all the concepts related to a given concept C: these concepts represent the conceptual summary of C. Concept relationships other than IS-A are inferred through the extension only, according to the following *extensional inference rule*: two concepts A and B are related iff there is at least one item D in the infobase which is classified at the same time under A (or under one of A's descendants) and under B (or under one of B's descendants). For example, we can infer a (unnamed) relationship between Michelangelo and Rome, if an item that is classified under Michelangelo and Rome exists in the infobase. At the same time, since Rome is a descendant of Italy, also a relationship between Michelangelo and Italy can be inferred. The extensional inference rule can be seen as a device to infer relationships on the basis of empirical evidence.

The extensional inference rule can be easily extended to cover the relationship between a given concept C and a concept expressed by an arbitrary subset S of the universe: C is related to S iff there is at least one item D in S which is also in items(C). Hence, the extensional inference rule can produce conceptual summaries not only for base concepts, but also for any logical combination of concepts. In addition, dynamic taxonomies can produce summaries for sets of items produced by other retrieval methods such as information retrieval, etc. and therefore access through dynamic taxonomies can be easily combined with other retrieval methods.

Dynamic taxonomies work on conceptual descriptions of items, so that heterogeneous items of any type and format can be managed in a single, coherent framework. Finally, since concept C is just a label that identifies the set of the items classified under C, concepts are language-invariant, and multilingual access can be easily supported by maintaining different language directories, holding language-specific labels for each concept in the taxonomy.

Dynamic taxonomies can be used to browse and explore the infobase in the following way. The user is initially presented with a tree representation of the initial taxonomy for the entire infobase. Each concept label has also a count of all the items classified under it (i.e. the cardinality of items(C) for all C's). The initial user focus F is the universe (i.e. all the items in the infobase).

In the simplest case, the user can then select a concept C in the taxonomy and *zoom* over it. The zoom operation changes the current state in two ways. First, concept C is used to refine the current focus F, which becomes

$$F=F\cap \text{items}(C) \tag{1}$$

items not in the focus are discarded. Second, the tree representation of the taxonomy is modified in order to summarize the new focus. All and only the concepts related to F are retained and the count for each retained concept C' is updated to reflect the number of items in the focus F that are classified under C'. The reduced taxonomy is a conceptual summary of the set of documents identified by F, exactly in the same way as the original taxonomy was a conceptual summary of the universe. In fact, the term *dynamic taxonomy* is used to indicate that the taxonomy can dynamically adapt to the subset of the universe on which the user is focusing, whereas traditional, static taxonomies can only describe the entire universe.

The retrieval process can then be seen as an iterative thinning of the information base: the user selects a focus, which restricts the information base by discarding all the items not in the current focus. Only the concepts used to classify the items in the focus, and their ancestors, are retained. These concepts, which summarize the current focus, are those and only those concepts that can be used for further refinements. From the human computer interaction point of view, the user is effectively guided to reach his goal, by a clear and consistent listing of all possible alternatives.

Dynamic taxonomies can be integrated with other retrieval methods in two basic ways. First, focus restrictions on the dynamic taxonomy can provide a context on which other retrieval methods can be applied, thereby increasing the precision of subsequent searches. Second, the user can start from an external retrieval method, and see a conceptual summary of the concepts that describe the result. These two approaches can be intermixed in different iteration steps during a single exploration. The integration of dynamic taxonomies with information retrieval is especially important in the present context because dynamic taxonomies can be used to describe abstract, conceptual queries and information retrieval can be used to define concrete queries (for instance proper names). By offloading conceptual manipulation to the dynamic taxonomy component, the information retrieval component needs not be very sophisticated, and in fact, an efficient text retrieval system is usually adequate.

4 An Example

Giovanni, a farmer located in Cuneo, Piedmont, Italy is interested in opportunities (funding, etc.) in agriculture. These opportunities may arise from different sources (Cuneo, Piedmont, Italy, EU), may involve different crops, may have different requirements (perhaps, a minimum turnover), etc. With a conventional text retrieval system, finding the relevant documents is quite a difficult task. A query for agriculture is at the same time too broad (because it will retrieve all documents about agriculture, possibly thousands) and too restrictive (it will fail to retrieve tobacco-growing, if agriculture as a word is not mentioned in the document). How can Giovanni be sure he considers every relevant document? He can't, and he will probably find himself querying for a broad term, hoping it is all-inclusive but with no guarantee it is, and wade through a very long list of items that are mostly irrelevant to his needs.

Now assume that a dynamic taxonomy exists, whose top level is organized as:

- *Sector*, a facet describing sectors of activity (agriculture, chemistry, etc.)
- *Location*, a facet describing the location(s) to which a specific document applies
- *Subject*, a facet describing the subject(s) (e.g. persons or companies, public companies, etc.) to which a specific document applies
- *Document type*, a facet describing the type of document (law, regulation, opportunity, etc.)
- *Issuer*, a facet describing the issuer (town, country, etc.)

Each facet can be as articulated as required; the schema above is obviously quite simplified.

With this simple schema, Giovanni can explore opportunities by selecting *Sector>Agriculture* and then *Document type>Opportunity*, if this concept exists in the reduced taxonomy: if it does not, no opportunities for agriculture exists, and Giovanni is done. After this compound focus is set, the reduced taxonomy will show all the concepts related to it: specific Locations, Subjects, etc. Browsing is completely symmetric: the same result is obtained if he selects *Document type>Opportunity* and *Sector>Agriculture.*

Giovanni is also helped to discover new opportunities which involve changing something in his business: if he grows corn, he might discover that better opportunities exist for soybean crops, or that setting up a company increases his opportunities, etc. The simple translation of the labels for the concepts in the taxonomy, allows Jean, Johannes, John and Ivan to find relevant information in exactly the same way.

Note that a conventional taxonomy would not provide sufficient discrimination in thinning the result set: selecting *Sector>Agriculture* retrieves all the documents for Agriculture, including laws, regulation and other irrelevant material. Conversely, the selection of *Document type>Opportunity* retrieves opportunities in all sectors, not just Agriculture. In fact, result thinning in conventional taxonomies can occur only by specializing the current concept, and concepts in different branches in the taxonomy are not available.

5 Dynamic Taxonomies Applied to Laws and Regulations

The advantages of dynamic taxonomies over traditional methods are dramatic in terms of convergence of exploratory patterns and in terms of human factors. Sacco [9] provides analytical evidence that three zoom operations on terminal concepts are sufficient to reduce a 1,000,000-item information base described by a compact taxonomy with 1,000 concepts to an average 10 items. Experimental data on a real newspaper corpus of over 110,000 articles, classified through a taxonomy of 1100 concepts, reports an average 1246 documents to be inspected by the user of a traditional, static taxonomy vs. an average 27 documents after a single zoom on a dynamic taxonomy.

Dynamic taxonomies require a very light theoretical background: namely, the concept of a subject index (i.e. the taxonomic organization) and the zoom operation, which seems to be very quickly understood by end-users. Hearst et al. [4] and Yee et al. [21] conducted usability tests on a corpus of art images. Despite an inefficient implementation that caused slow response times, their tests show that access through a dynamic taxonomy produced a faster interaction and a significantly better recall than access through text retrieval. Perhaps more important are the intangibles: the feeling that one has actually considered all the alternatives in reaching a result.

Differently from most previous research, dynamic taxonomies cleanly separate the process of classifying documents from the use of the classification information in the browsing system. Obviously, the classification system and the design of the taxonomy must take into account the way classification is used, i.e. the extensional inference rule. First, dynamic taxonomies actually perform concept association mining. This simplifies index creation and maintenance since concept associations, which are often quite dynamic in time, need not be forecasted and accounted for in schema design. At the same time, the user is presented with associations the schema designer might not even be aware of (discovery). In traditional approaches, relationships among concepts must be explicitly described in the conceptual schema. Since only these relationships will be available to the user for browsing and retrieval, the schema designer must anticipate all the possible relationships among concepts: a very difficult if not helpless task. On the one hand, the designer will define relationships that do not actually occur in the corpus and are useless. On the other hand, some relationships will not be defined at all, either because they are not interesting for the designer (but they might be for the user) or because they have not occurred before and are unexpected. All these problems are solved because concepts relationships are automatically derived from the actual classification.

Second, since dynamic taxonomies synthesize compound concepts, these need usually not be represented explicitly. This means that the main cause of the combinatorial growth of traditional taxonomies is removed. Sacco [8] developed a number of guidelines that produce taxonomies that are compact and easily understood by users. Some of these guidelines are similar to the faceted classification scheme by Ranganathan [5], at least in its basic form: the taxonomy is organized as a set of independent, "orthogonal" subtaxonomies (facets or perspectives) to be used to describe data. As an example, a compound concept such as *Agriculture in Southern Italy* need not be accounted for, because it can be synthesized from its component concepts: *Sector>Agriculture* and *Location>Southern Italy*. Thus, one of the main causes of complexity in the design of comprehensive taxonomies is avoided: by synthesizing concepts, we avoid the exponential growth due to the description of all the possible concept combinations, and the resulting taxonomy is significantly more compact and easier to understand. In addition to minimizing the concepts in the taxonomy, breaking compound concepts into their base components allows the user to easily correlate concepts and explore such correlations. In the example, the user focusing on *Sector>Agriculture* will immediately find all the relevant locations related to agriculture (which include *Southern Italy*). If compound concepts were used, correlation cannot be carried out automatically, but it would require the manual inspection of labels. In addition, the excellent convergence of dynamic taxonomies allows the designer to define taxonomies that are much simpler and smaller than traditional ones.

Although the discussion above indicates that "minimal" taxonomies are desirable, there are situations in which additional concepts or facets actually improve user interaction. One of the problems of traditional taxonomies is that they require the user to perceive the world through the same concepts and understandings as the schema designer. However, as one of the referees remarked, a farmer does not probably think along the same lines as the legal expert coding the documents. With the inflexible monodimensional classification of traditional taxonomies, this problem has no solution. In dynamic taxonomies, additional facets can easily accommodate different, alternate perceptions of conceptual organizations, providing powerful personalization capabilities. In this case (farmer vs. legal expert), the two facets are not orthogonal and would not fit in a strict faceted classification [5]: just another proof that faceted classification systems are a subset of the multidimensional classification scheme proposed by dynamic taxonomies.

Both personalization and push strategies can be supported by dynamic taxonomies. In both cases, they can be implemented by using boolean expressions on the concepts in the taxonomy. In the case of personalization, such an expression defines a user profile, and can be automatically added to user queries in a way similar to query modification in relational database systems [15]. Farmer Giovanni's profile, for instance, could be *Location>Europe>Italy>Cuneo AND Sector>Agriculture*. User-friendly front-ends that shield Giovanni from the complexities of writing boolean expressions can be easily devised. Giovanni's profile will be considered as the initial context or focus, instead of the universe of discourse: when the initial reduced taxonomy is presented, only the concepts under which there are documents satisfying Giovanni's profile are preserved. Thus, Giovanni will not see documents and concepts for Latvia, nor documents or concepts for the automotive sector. This same user profile (or multiple versions of it) can be used to implement push strategies, since it provides an accurate statement of interests. In this way, the system acts in a proactive way and informs the user whenever new relevant material is available. Sacco [12] describes an efficient algorithm for dynamic taxonomy-based push strategies.

Two research topics are currently being investigated. The first one is the semantics of classification, and is especially important in the context of personalization and push strategies: what additional classifications can be inferred by the fact that a document d is classified under a concept C? Sacco [8] shows that the inclusion constraint implicit in subsumptions requires a *backward inheritance*, i.e. that a document classified under a concept C is also classified under all of C's ancestors. As an example, a document classified under *Rome* is also classified under *Lazio*, *Italy*, and *Europe*. Most systems based on dynamic taxonomies allow classifying documents under terminal concepts only. If we relax this limitation and allow a document d to be classified under a non-terminal concept C, backward inheritance still holds, but there might be implications on the descendants of C. For example, assume that d is a document describing funding for Agriculture and is consequently classified under *Agriculture*. Since d is not about some specific aspects of agriculture, it also applies to any of Agriculture's descendants, from corn to tobacco. Hence classifying d under C also implies that d is also classified under each of C's descendants. We call this type of inheritance *forward inheritance*, to distinguish it from the standard backward inheritance discussed above. Top-down (i.e. forward) inheritance is the standard inheritance rule for properties and methods in object-oriented systems. Extended inheritance (i.e., backward plus forward inheritance) also applies in a similar form to hierarchical structured material, such as video stories [13]. This notwithstanding, forward inheritance does not always apply. Often, especially in PART-OF relationships, a specific document may apply to a concept, but not to its components. A trivial example is a license plate that applies to a car, but not to its engine.

Forward inheritance is important when a) documents can be classified under non-terminal concepts, and b) when conceptual expressions are used to define a context for personalization or push strategies. In fact, with forward inheritance, Giovanni's profile *Location>Europe>Italy>Cuneo AND Sector>Agriculture* will retain all the documents classified under Italy, but not specifically under Cuneo: if only backward inheritance were used, these documents would be lost.

The second area of investigation is the automatic derivation of taxonomies from complex ontology schemata. The goal is to use dynamic taxonomies as a user-friendly front-end to complex information that is also available in a richer semantic form for agents and programmatic access. Sacco [12] shows that relational views can be translated into dynamic taxonomies by considering each tuple as a document, and transforming all the attributes of the view into facets. We are currently investigating how this mapping can be extended to cover schemata that are semantically richer than relational ones. However, we believe that in most practical cases, dynamic taxonomies coupled with information or database retrieval will be used as the unique access path to complex information. We feel that the current emphasis on ontologies and agents for search tasks is overstressed and that dynamic taxonomies often provide an efficient and effective alternative, which is easier to build and maintain, and much more transparent and intuitive for the casual user.

6 Conclusions

Dynamic taxonomies represent a dramatic improvement over other search and browsing methods, both in terms of convergence and in terms of full feedback on alternatives and complete guidance to reach the user goal. For these reasons, and because of easy personalization, multilingual access and push strategies, they give that kind of interactive knowledge management that is required for political awareness and participation. Systems based on dynamic taxonomies, such as Knowledge Processors' Universal Knowledge Processor [18], are currently available and offer real-time operations even on large information bases.

References

1. Blair, D. C., Maron, M. E: An evaluation of retrieval effectiveness for a full-text document-retrieval system. Comm. ACM, 28:3 (1985)
2. Fellbaum, C. (ed.): WordNet-An Electronic Lexical Database. MIT Press (1998)
3. Groenbaek K., Trigg R. (eds.): Hypermedia. Comm. ACM 37, vol. 2 (1994)
4. Hearst, M., et al.: Finding the Flow in Web Site Search, Comm. of the ACM, 45, 9 (2002)
5. Ranganathan, S. R.: The Colon Classification. Rutgers University Press (1965)
6. Robertson, S. E., Sparck Jones, K.: Relevance weighting of search terms. J. of ASIS. 27 (1976)
7. Sacco, G.M.: Navigating the CD-ROM, Proc. Int. Conf. Business of CD-ROM, (1987)
8. Sacco, G. M.: Dynamic Taxonomies: A Model for Large Information Bases. IEEE Transactions on Knowledge and Data Engineering 12, 2 , p. 468-479 (2000)
9. Sacco, G. M.: Analysis and Validation of Information Access through Mono, Multidimensional and Dynamic Taxonomies, Tech Report Dept. of Informatica, Univ. of Torino (2002)
10. Sacco, G. M.: Systematic Browsing for Multimedia Infobases, in Proc. CISST2003, Int. Conf. on Imaging Science, Systems, and Technology (2003)
11. Sacco, G. M.: The Intelligent E-Sales Clerk: the Basic Ideas, Proc. INTERACT'03 Int. Conf. on Human-Computer Interaction (2003)
12. Sacco, G. M.: Dynamic taxonomy process for browsing and retrieving information in large heterogeneous data bases. US Patent 6,743,349 (2004)
13. Sacco, G. M.: Uniform access to multimedia information bases through dynamic taxonomies, Proc. IEEE Int. Symposium on Multimedia Software Engineering (2004)
14. Schmeltz Pedersen, G.: A Browser for Bibliographic Information Retrieval, Based on an Application of Lattice Theory. Proc. ACM SIGIR Conf. (1993)
15. Stonebraker, M.: Implementation of integrity constraints and views by query modification. Proc. ACM SIGMOD Conf. (1975)
16. Story, G. A., et al.: The Rightpages Image-Based Electronic Library for Alerting and Browsing. IEEE Computer, 25:9 (1992)
17. Straube, D. D. & Ozsu, M. T.: Queries and query processing in object-oriented database systems, ACM Trans. on Information Systems, 8: 4 (1990)
18. Universal Knowledge Processor, www.knowledgeprocessors.com
19. van Rijsbergen, C. J.: Information Retrieval. Butterworths (1979)
20. Wollersheim, D., Rahayu, W.: Methodology For Creating a Sample Subset of Dynamic Taxonomy to Use in Navigating Medical Text Databases. Proc. IDEAS 2002 Conf. (2002)
21. Yee, K-P., et al.: Faceted Metadata for Image Search and Browsing, Proc. ACM CHI Conf. (2002)

Towards a Semantically-Driven Software Engineering Environment for eGovernment

Dimitris Apostolou[1], Ljiljana Stojanovic[2], Tomas Pariente Lobo[3], and Barbara Thoenssen[4]

[1] Planet S.A., Apollon Tower, 64 Louise Riencourt Str., 11523 Athens, Greece
dapost@planet.gr
[2] Forschungszentrum Informatik, Haid-und-Neu-Str. 10-14, 76131 Karlsruhe, Germany
Stojanovic@fzi.de
[3] INDRA, Avda. De Brusselas, 35, 28108 Alcobendas, Spain,
tpariente@indra.es
[4] University of Applied Sciences Solothurn, Riggenbachstrasse 16, CH-4600 Olten, Switzerland
Barbara.Thoenssen@fhso.ch

Abstract. As software processes for developing eGovernment services become more complex, it is necessary to provide computer-based tools to support the software engineering process. Furthermore, actions should be taken to limit the loss of critical knowledge during the life cycle of eGovernment services. In this paper we first illustrate the overall architecture of ONTOGOV, an under-development software engineering environment for developing and managing the life-cycle of eGovernment services. We then outline two ontologies upon which ONTOGOV is based. Finally, an application scenario is described and the paper concludes with the identification of further steps and research directions.

1 Introduction

In developing eGovernment services, problems arise from the gap and inconsistencies that exist between the perspective of policy makers and managers of Public Administrations (PAs) on the one hand and the technical realization of eGovernment services on the other hand. Moreover, large amounts of information can be derived in an eGovernment software development project. Such information may vary form policy-enforcement information to information related to programming objects (e.g. modules, classes). As software processes for developing eGovernment services become more complex, it is necessary to provide computer-based tools to support the software engineering process that spans, horizontally, many PAs and, vertically, several levels of software engineering – from decision makers to programmers.

In order to support today's fast software development approaches (e.g. iterative prototyping, extreme programming), software models and code must be easily reconfigurable. Reconfigurability demands consistent representations of software engineering information, homogeneous means of communication between software engineers (and other stakeholders) and tools, and support for managing changes in the

M. Böhlen et al. (Eds.): TCGOV 2005, LNAI 3416, pp. 157–168, 2005.

software lifecycle. Another dimension of the problem addressed relates to eGovernment systems' architectures: Recently, novel component-oriented runtime environments have paved the way for service oriented infrastructures [1]. In the eGovernment domain, since there may be a considerable number of service providers which offer very similar functionality, it is difficult to choose the most appropriate service by interpreting syntactic operation names as provided by state of the art Web service interface descriptions [2].

To deal on the one hand with reconfigurability and changes of eGov services and on the other hand with integration between services provided by different providers, we need a software engineering environment based on robust conceptual models. We have used Semantic Web technologies for constructing ontologies, which represent the meaning of processed data and resources and provided functionality of eGovernment services. In this paper, we first illustrate the overall architecture of ONTOGOV, an under-development eGovernment software engineering environment. We then outline the ontologies upon which ONTOGOV will be based. An application scenario is described then, and the paper concludes with the identification of further steps and research directions.

2 Pertinent Technologies and Related Work

2.1 Semantic Technologies in eGovernment

The eGovernment scenario is in some respects a more obvious and promising application field for ontologies than many other e-business areas, since legislative knowledge is by nature already "formal" to a big extent and it is by definition shared by many stakeholders. The e-POWER project [3] has employed knowledge modelling techniques for inferences for, e.g., consistency checks, harmonisation or consistency enforcement in legislation. The SmartGov project [4] developed a knowledge-based platform for assisting public sector employees to generate online transaction services by simplifying their integration with already installed IT systems. Similarly, the ICTE-PAN project [5] developed a methodology for modeling PA operations, and tools to transform these models into design specifications for eGovernment portals. Further there are a number of ongoing projects e.g. Terregov [6], Qualeg [7] that make use of semantic technologies for achieving interoperability and integration between eGovernment systems. Although such projects have convincingly demonstrated the feasibility of semantic technologies in eGovernment, they did not adequately address the matter of eGovernment service software engineering, and in particular the lifecycle aspects of eGovernment services.

2.2 Web Services in eGovernment

In developing the ONTOGOV, we assume and utilise Web Services as the executable application interfaces logically accessible using standard Internet protocols (WSDL and SOAP). Current languages for describing web services (WSDL) and their composition on the level of business processes (BPEL4WS[1]) lack semantic

[1] http://www-106.ibm.com/developerworks/library/ws-bpel/

expressivity that is crucial for capturing service capabilities at abstract levels. OWL-S[2] and WSMO[3]are the most salient initiatives to describe semantic web services. They aim at describing the various aspects of services in order to enable the automation of Web Services discovery, composition, interoperability and invocation. Both of the proposed approaches focus mostly on the service profile in order to support better discovery of services but they lack sufficient support for the process model itself. We argue that business process flow specifications should be defined at abstract task levels, leaving open the details of specific service bindings and execution flows. This abstract level enables the definition of domain-specific constraints that have to be taken into account during the (re)configuration of a process flow. In order to model this abstract representation of web services, we base our work on and extend the OWL-S and WSMO ontologies so that they are able to better support process and life-cycle modeling.

2.3 Semantic-Driven Software Engineering Environments

Software Engineering Environments (SEEs) are defined as integrated collections of tools that facilitate software engineering activities across the software lifecycle [8]. Deng et al. [9] have surveyed a number of knowledge-based software engineering systems: (i) most existing systems focus on a specific aspect of software development and do not support the whole lifecycle. In fact only two of the systems surveyed support the maintenance phase; and (ii) most existing systems aim to replace existing CASE tools and they do not support assertion of knowledge on top of existing CASE tools.

Ontologies are a promising means to achieve these conceptual models, since they can serve as a basis for comprehensive information representation and communication. Further ontologies can be used to address software engineering sub-domains, such as software versioning, change management, software quality, etc. Finally they can allow for involvement of non-technical people (e.g. public authorities' officers) in the software engineering process as ontologies can be used as coarse- or fine-grained models, therefore hiding or exposing details respectively and according to the intended audience.

3 ONTOGOV Architecture

eGovernment services have strict procedures that do not allow choosing but a concrete service among several of them that may offer similar functionality. In the eGovernment domain, it is difficult to select the most appropriate service by querying dynamically, at run-time (*late-binding*), a service description interface, as for instance a UDDI registry. This is particularly true when the selection of the service should be context-aware. This is the case for instance of some geographically-distributed services where multiple eGovernment providers (as local

[2] http://www.daml.org/services/owl-s/1.0/

[3] http://www.wsmo.org/

authorities) may offer the same type of service, but the law states how to choose the correct authority that must provide the service. The complexity that the late-biding approach puts on the service description interface pointed to an architecture that integrates a top level design of the process model of the services with the orchestration of the underlying atomic services that perform the whole process. In this architecture, the sequence of atomic services execution as well as the conditional paths of execution are being set in advance, during the configuration phase (*early-binding*). The proposed approach is a deviation from a pure Service Oriented Architecture, where the concept of process modelling does not exist, but a chain of autonomous atomic services that inter-relate ad-hoc, without supervision or guidelines. Advantages of the early-binding approach include: (i) Better control of the atomic service selection process and better runtime performance, as atomic services are set in advance to a Web Service implementation and thus the time for discovering the most appropriate service is considerably reduced. (ii) Less deadlocks during the service execution, as pre-setting atomic services to concrete implementations decreases the possibility of faults during the execution.

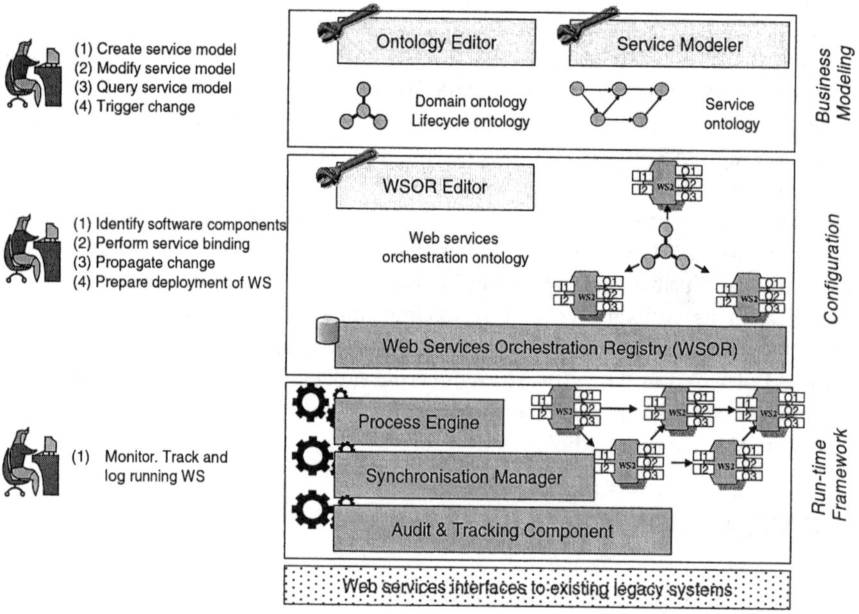

Fig. 1. ONTOGOV logical architecture

The proposed architecture (shown in Fig. 1) can be divided in three layers:

1. The Business Modelling layer is where a top level service model is drawn. Users of this layer will typically be PA domain experts that have sufficient knowledge of the domain. This knowledge includes the legislation that a service is based on, related directives, prerequisites etc.

2. The Configuration layer allows referencing the implementation of the business logic in actual software components. This task is carried out by the IT Consultant, who is responsible for the configuration and deployment of OntoGov services. In our platform, the software implementation will always be achieved through Web Services interfaces.
3. The Runtime layer should orchestrate and control the execution of the atomic services by making the correct invocations of the Web Services configured in the Configuration layer.

In principal, the lifecycle of an eGovernment service starts when PA Managers trigger the generation or the change of a service. In order to accomplish this task, PA Managers need to have a high-level view of service models, links to related laws, resources involved and inter-relations with other services. Such a high-level view is provided by the service models developed through the Business Model layer. The service ontology (or service model) becomes the main source of information for the Configuration layer. During configuration, the IT Consultant should identify the actual software components (Web Services) that enact the service model and the policy and security level that their SOAP messages should accomplish. The WS Orchestration Registry (described in detail in the next section) is an ontology-based repository that stores the mappings between atomic services defined in the service model and Web services that carry on with the task. According to the WSDL definition, these mappings comprise the selection of the WSDL operation (method) that should be called once the web service is invoked, and the linking of the WSDL parts (I/O attributes) to the atomic service inputs and outputs. A Runtime Framework should be properly installed in a broker machine to allow the execution of Web services. A key component here is the Process Engine that acts as an orchestration machine extracting the service ontology from the ontologies and proceeding to deliver the request to the first atomic service described in the process model. The engine relies on the use of a component called Synchronization Manager that hides the complexity of the synchronous or asynchronous behaviour of the Web services.

4 ONTOGOV Ontologies

In [10, 11], we introduced the following ontologies for modeling EGovernment services (Fig. 2): (i) Meta Ontology contains entities needed to describe services; (ii) Legal Ontology describes the structure of the legal documents; (iii) Domain Ontology contains domain specific knowledge; and (iv) Service Ontology describes a concrete service.

In this paper we extend our previous work aiming to resolve the two previously mentioned problems (reconfigurability and service integration) and to support the logical architecture outlined in section 3: (i) Lifecycle ontology that describes the information flow and the decision making process in the public administration; and (ii) Web Service Orchestration Ontology that allows binding of services during execution.

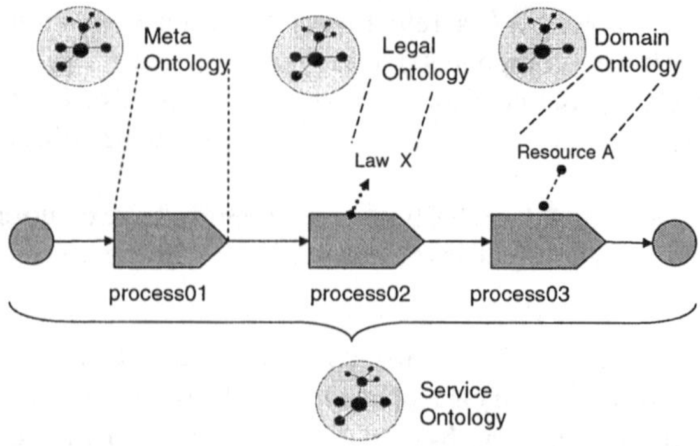

Fig. 2. Different ontologies used for describing semantic web services

4.1 Lifecycle Ontology

If an application aims at being useful, it is essential that it is able to accommodate the changes that will inevitably occur due to changes in the environment, users' needs or changes in its internal structures and processes. To avoid drawbacks of ad hoc management of changes, changes have to be applied on the model of the application. In order to do so, we developed the so-called *Lifecycle Ontology.*

The *Lifecycle Ontology* spans the range from the informal specification of requirements to a representation focusing on the realization of the service [12]. It is intended to support the transition from knowledge acquisition to implementation, i.e. the design phase. It includes entities for documenting design decisions and the underlying rationale. In this way it gives concrete clues on how a service has to be modified. Design decisions can be viewed as contributions to the satisfaction of requirements. Thus, the rationale of a design decision is its relationship to such requirements. Consequently, the *Lifecycle Ontology* is used for describing design decisions and their relationship to affected parts of the service as well as to the requirements that motivate the decisions.

In the *Lifecycle Ontology,* the design process is viewed as a succession of states of the service design. The transition between two adjacent states is effected by activities of the designer, i.e. by a design decision. Therefore, the main concept is the concept "*Design Decision*". The transition between states is modelled through two inverse properties "*hasReason*" and "*isReasonFor*" that are defined for the top concept of the concept "*Design Decision*" i.e. for the concept "*Reason*". The hierarchy of the concept "*Design Decision*" is shown in Fig. 3.

If the designer takes a design decision, s/he does so since a particular goal shall be reached, namely a requirement posed towards the service shall be met. Thus, the justification for a design decision consists of its connection to the requirements which the design decision helps to meet. This is modelled through the concept "*Requirement*" and corresponding properties (i.e. the properties "*isBasedOn*" and "*requires*") that establish references between a design decision and a requirement.

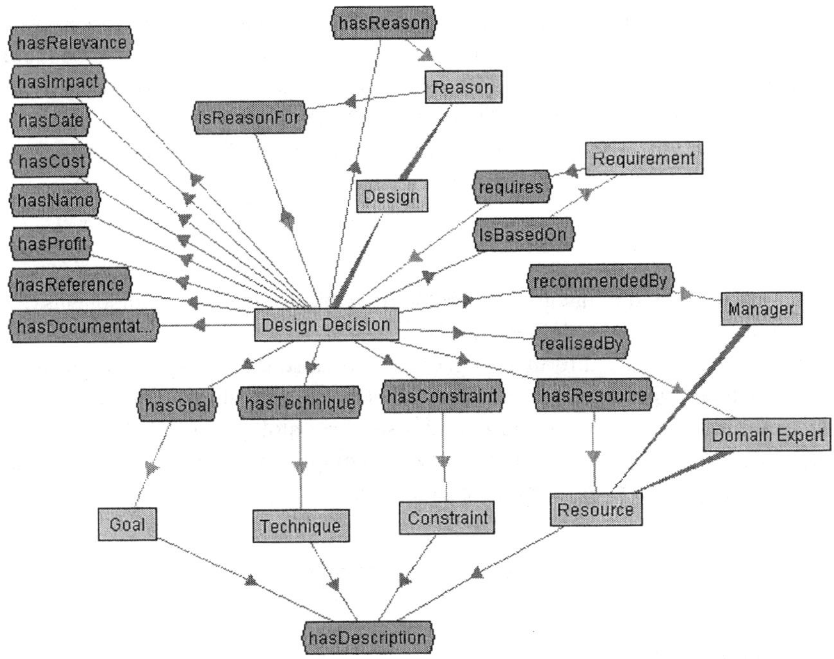

Fig. 3. A part of the Lifecycle Ontology

We identified many types of issues considered in the design process. We observed that decisions fell into one of these four categories:

- design *goals*, which are principles to be achieved through the decision process and that must be realized before the choice is considered complete;
- design *resources*, which are the resources --both physical and intellectual-- available to achieve the goal;
- design *techniques*, which are the strategies for achieving the goals using the design resources available;
- design *constraints*, which are outside influences that limit the use of resources and strategies to achieve a goal.

These elements of a design decision are modelled through the concepts "*Goal*", "*Resource*", "*Technique*", "*Constraint*" and a set of properties that relate each of them with the concept "*Design Decision*". These concepts share the property "*hasDescription*", which describes in more detail the concrete instance of the corresponding concept.

The *Lifecycle Ontology* also models the name of the design decision (the "*hasName*" attribute), when the design decision is made (the "*hasDate*" attribute), why it is required (the "*isRequiredBy*" property), why it is realized (the "*isRealisedBy*" property) etc. Moreover, it has a reference (modeled through the "*hasReference*" property) to the *Service Ontology* or its activity that is related to this design decision.

Finally, information supporting decision-making, such as cost, relevance, priority, impact, profit, textual description of the reason for a service etc. may also be included (not show in detail herein). A part of the *Lifecycle Ontology* is shown in Fig. 3. It can be concluded that the *Lifecycle Ontology* is a description of the service design process, which clarifies which design decisions were taken for which reasons, proves to be valuable for further development and maintenance.

4.2 WS Orchestration Ontology

In order to resolve the integration problem between software components and a service ontology, we have defined the *Web Service Orchestration Registry (WSOR) ontology*. It describes all information needed to finalise the configuration of the Web Services, which will be called during the service execution. This configuration consists in linking each atomic service of a service ontology to a WSDL description of real (existing) web services (i.e. software component). Moreover, it allows the dynamic binding of services during the execution.

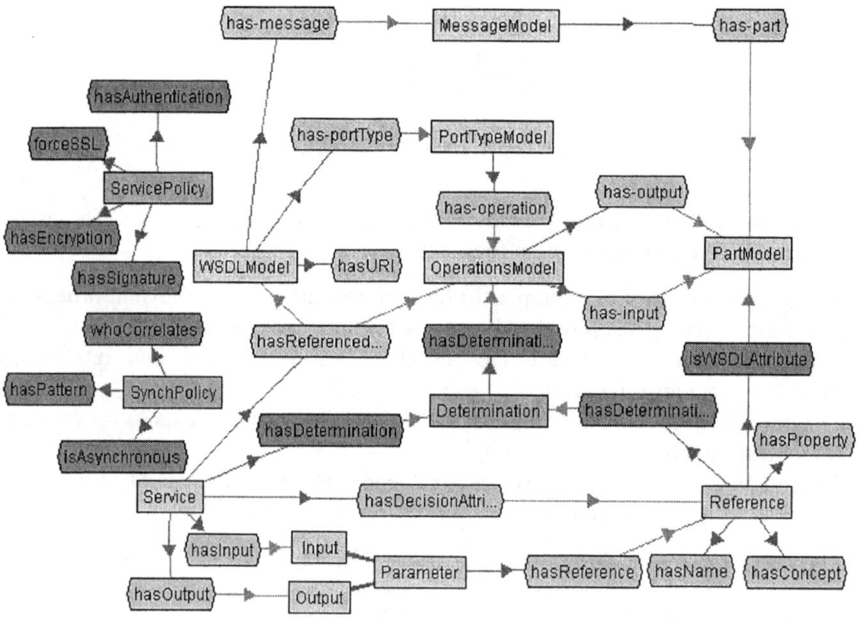

Fig. 4. The WSOR ontology

The *WSOR* is illustrated in Fig. 4. It includes the *WS ontology* that is shown in the upper part, the *Meta Ontology* shown in the bottom part. The middle part of this ontology shows entities that are defined in this ontology:

- The concept *"Decision"* represents the value that a Reference has to hold during the runtime in order to lead to a concrete software component (WSDLModel).
- *"hasReferencedSoftware"*, links the Service with its WS implementations (operations in a WS).
- *"isWSDLAttribute"* links the Reference concept with the PartModel.
- *"hasDecisionReference"* liks the WSDLModel with the Decision.
- *"hasDecision"* links the Service with the Decision, since one instance of the Service may have more than one Decision instance.
- *"hasDecisionValue"* links the Reference with the Decision.

The WSOR that describes a concrete service establishes the mappings between the instantiation of the WSDL ontology and the service ontology. Indeed, it comprises the selection of the WSDL operation (method) that should be called once the web service is invoked, and the linking of the WSDL parts (I/O attributes) to the atomic service inputs and outputs. This mapping cannot be completely automated, but at least some recommendations can be generated. We propose three levels of mappings:

- syntactical mappings –based on the string comparison. The names of the entities from the WSDL ontologies are compared to the lexical information about entities from the service ontology as well as to the synset [13] extension of them;
- structural mappings – take into account the all inputs and outputs information at the same time;
- context mappings – consider a set of activities in order to clarify the context in which an operation is used.

5 Application Scenario

In this section we illustrate how change detection and reconfiguration are addressed by ONTOGOV on the basis of an example using the service "Announcement of move". Today, the service provided is split into few separated tasks. De-registration has to be performed in one municipality, while several other entities, like telecommunication companies, have to be notified about the change of address. In addition, the person has to register in the new municipality. In order to improve service quality, there should be *one* task performed by the citizen regardless what and how much (technical) processes run behind. However, as a citizen may move from one municipality to any other – or even abroad – the change of address, deregistration and registration as well as the link between these processes can not be hard-coded because participating entities are changing every time the service is being performed.

The development of this (simplified) service with ONTOGOV will be as follows: The Domain Expert designs the service using the Service Modeler, based on the service ontology. Moreover, the domain expert adds more semantics by creating instances of the related ontologies:

- Domain ontology, comprising concepts like data (e.g. name, first_name, municipality_from, municipality_to) and documents (e.g. application form, administration leaflet etc.).
- Legal ontology, comprising instances of process relevant law or regulations, e.g. basis of the new process is a regulation about settlement. Then several instances

will be initiated in the legal ontology indicating the related law[4] (1_Landesrecht), the paragraph ('14_Bürgerrecht) and article ('142_Niederlassungsrecht').

- Organisational ontology, comprising instances of process relevant organizational units, e.g. involved in the new service are the organizational units 'Registration Office' and 'Administration Office' with its roles and personal.
- Lifecycle ontology, comprising instances of all (design) decisions relevant for the new service (e.g. technical or process immanent reasons), including instances of the legal and organizational ontologies.

Working only with instances of (meta-)ontologies allows for strong governance of the modelling as a whole. For example, adding the same organisational unit to two atomic services in a sequence will evoke a warning (as usually the activities will be performed as one) even though the process flow per se is correct. Up to now no framework (like BPEL, ivyGrid or others) allow for such semantically checks.

After the design process is completed, a machine readable version of the definition of the new service will be generated. The IT-Consultant uses the WS Orchestration Registry in order to finalise the configuration of the web services. S/he links each atomic service of the service ontology to the WSDL description of real (existing) web services (e.g. of the municipality of Olten), performs the mappings between the WSDL and the attributes used in the service ontology and stores the links and the mappings in the WSOR.

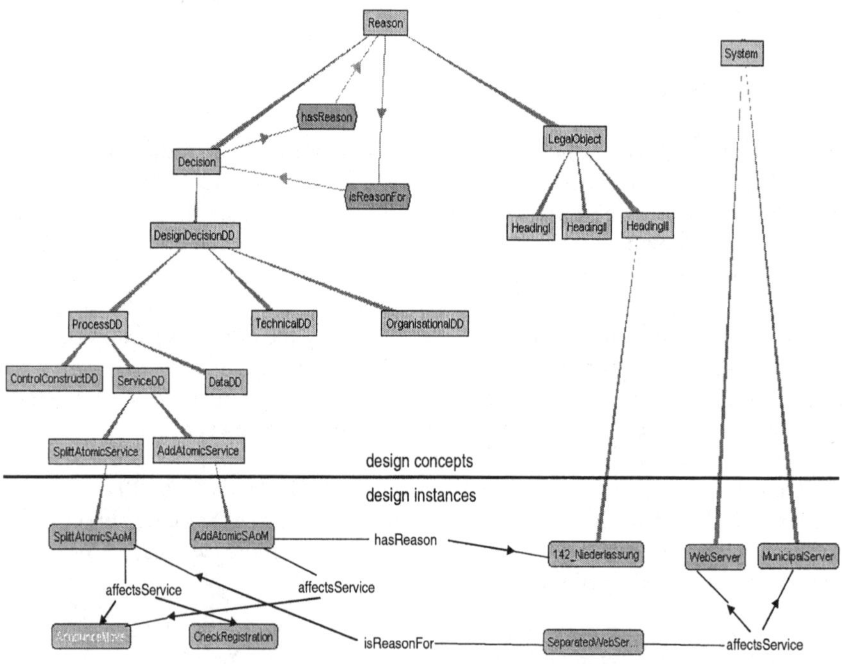

Fig. 5. Links between design decisions

[4] Note: example is taken from the Swiss legislation.

In case a service needs to be modified at a later stage e.g. due to changes of a regulation, it is important to detect all affected services, respectively activities. That is why for every service component (activity or control construct), design decisions data are modelled using the lifecycle ontology. In our example, "announce move" (checks, if all information required is filled in) and "check registration" (checks if the applicant is registered) are based on various decisions (Fig. 5). One decision is legally grounded: what data PAs need to know are defined by law (e.g. the applicant must give his/her name, current address, civil status etc.); another decision is technically grounded: due to security issues the activity "announce move" will be performed by a web server whereas the "check registration" activity will be run on a legacy system. A further decision is based on organizational reasons (e.g. activity 1 is performed by an organizational unit A (e.g. registration office) whereas activity 2 is performed by an organization unit B (e.g. administration office). Yet another decision is taken because of service-immanent reasons (e.g. activities are spited in order to make them reusable in other processes).

In case of a change of a law the ONTOGOV system can be queried to retrieve affected activities. Assume that the change affects all processes related to article '142_Niederlassungsrecht'. ONTOGOV searches for all decisions based on this legal reason. As a result, all affected services and activities are listed and proposed for modification. In the example, this is the service "Announcement of Move" with its activity "AnnounceMove".

6 Conclusions and Outlook

In this article, we highlighted a novel application of semantic technologies in the eGovernment domain: utilising semantics to drive and support the software engineering process for the development of eGovernment services. We considered the eGovernment domain, since eGovernment services are under the continual adaptation to the political goals of a government and to the needs of the people. Our approach (i) covers all the phases from definition and design through to deployment and reconfiguration of eGovernment services); (ii) provides the basis for designing lower-level domain ontologies specific to the service offerings of participating public authorities; and (iii) provides the basis for limiting the loss of critical knowledge during the life cycle of the software engineering process, in which a number of stakeholders (from policy-makers to developers) is involved.

In the near future, we will work to develop the actual software engineering environment and test it in three real-life governmental pilots. Future research directions include addressing adaptivity: extending this approach so that its implementation is capable of suggesting changes that can improve services. This can be done (i) by monitoring the execution of EGovernment services (e.g. the activity that causes the delay is a candidate for optimisation) and/or (ii) by taking into account the end-users' complaints (e.g. end-users might not be satisfied with the quality of services, since they have to supply the same information several times).

Acknowledgement

We would like to thank the European Commission for funding the OntoGov project through the IST programme.

References

1. M. Endrei, J. Ang, A. Arsanjani, Patterns: Service-oriented Architecture and Web Services, IBM Redbook, April 2004.
2. A. Paar, W. F. Tichy, "Semantic Software Engineering", in proceedings of AMS 2003.
3. T. van Engers, J. M. Patries, J. Kordelaar, J. den Hartog, E. Glasséee (2002). Available at http://lri.jur.uva.nl/~epower/
4. N. Adams, S. Haston, A. Macintosh, J. Fraser, A. McKay-Hubbard, and A. Unsworth, SmartGov: A Knowledge-Based Design Approach to Online Social Service Creation, in Bramer, M., Ellis, R., Macintosh, A; (eds.). 'Applications and Innovations in Knowledge-Based Systems and Applied Artificial Intelligence XI'; Proceedings of AI-2003 the 23rd Annual International Conference of the British Computer Society's Specialist Group on Artificial Intelligence ; Peterhouse College, Cambridge, UK, 16th-17th December, 2003
5. E Loukis, S. Kokolakis, Computer supported collaboration in the Public Sector: the ICTE-PAN Project, in preceedings of eGOV 2003 / DEXA 2003.
6. N. Benamou, "Terregov project overview", IANOS conference, Budapest, 2004.
7. C. Tatsiopoulos "QUALEG approach to intra-government interoperability", in Workshop on Technological and architectural challenges, eGOV04 Conference, Zaragoza Spain, 1st September 2004.
8. R. S. Pressman, "Software Engineering: A Practitioner's Approach", 5th Edition, New York, McGraw-Hill, 2000.
9. D. Deng, P. C.-Y. Sheu, T. Wang, H. Maezawa, F. Tsunoda and Akira K. Onoma, "DPSSEE: A Distributed Proactive Semantic Software Engineering Environment", The Fifth IEEE International Symposium on Multimedia Software Engineering (MSE 2003), Taichung, Taiwan, ROC, December 10-12, 2003.
10. L. Stojanovic, A. Abecker, N. Stojanovic, R. Studer, An Approach for the Change Management in the EGovernment Domain, In Proceedings of Second International Conference on Knowledge Economy and Development of Science and Technology (KEST'04), Beijing, China, 2004.
11. L. Stojanovic, A. Abecker, N. Stojanovic, R. Studer, On Managing Changes in the ontology-based EGovernment, to appear in Proceedings of the 3rd International Conference on Ontologies, Databases and Application of Semantics (ODBASE 2004), Larnaca, Cyprus, October 2004.
12. D. Landes, Design KARL – A language for the design of knowledge-based systems, In Proceedings of the 6th International conference on Software Engineering and Knowledge Engineering (SEKE'94), Jurmala, Lettland, pp. 78-85, 1994.
13. C. Fellbaum, WordNet - An electronic lexical database, MIT Press, 1998.

Towards Requirements for a Reference Model for Process Orchestration in e-Government

Jeffrey Gortmaker, Marijn Janssen, and René W. Wagenaar

Delft University of Technology, Faculty of Technology,
Policy, and Management, Delft, The Netherlands
{jeffreyg, marijnj, renew}@tbm.tudelft.nl

Abstract. A big challenge for governments all over the world is to improve the service provisioning to their clients, citizens and businesses. One way of improving service-provisioning is by means of a a one-stop-shop that integrates services that are performed by different semi autonomous agencies. This requires the coordination of service-delivery processes that run across different agencies. This is also called process orchestration. As little is known about process orchestrators, governmental decision-makers need support in designing them. This paper investigates the applicability of existing reference models from domains that are closely related to process orchestration, the Workflow Reference Model and the extended SOA reference model, to governmental decision-makers for implementing process orchestration in e-government, and identifies several main requirements for a reference mode for process orchestration, based on a case study performed at a business counter.

1 Introduction

A big challenge for governments all over the world is to improve the service provisioning to their clients, citizens and businesses. This is partly motivated by the aim to reduce the administrative burdens for citizens and businesses [1, 2], but is also demanded by its clients, whose expectations regarding service delivery will continue to rise as they get more and more accustomed to on-line trading and communicating at any time of the day [3].

A first step to satisfy this demand is offering access to governmental information and services on-line via the Internet. A next step is the provisioning of 'one-stop-shop'-services [4], where services of different governmental agencies are combined or integrated. An example is a business counter that functions as a single point of contact for interaction with different kinds of governmental agencies.

Both steps in improving the governmental service-delivery process have to deal with the problem of fragmentation of governments [4], as these service-delivery processes often include activities or sub-processes that are performed by various public agencies [5, 6, 7]. This requires the coordination of service-delivery processes that run across different agencies. This is also called process orchestration.

M. Böhlen et al. (Eds.): TCGOV 2005, LNAI 3416, pp. 169–180, 2005.

This problem of coordinating cross-agency service-delivery processes is not specific to the public sector; also in the private sector, businesses are looking for ways on how to coordinate their inter-organizational processes. Specific for the public-sector is, however, the strong emphasis on transparency, consistency, and non-discrimination of the service-delivery processes. Maintaining transparent processes is particularly important when service-delivery processes run across multiple, semi-autonomous agencies. This large number of more or less autonomous agencies involved in a particular service-delivery process is also a particular characteristic of the public sector.

A potential technological solution to the problem of coordinating sub-processes that run across different agencies is web service orchestration. Web-Service technology is based upon the notion of a Service-Oriented Architecture (SOA), an architectural paradigm according to which application functionality is not provided by large monolithic information systems, but by means of web-services.

Coordinating these different web services by means of a process flow in which the web services are invoked according to a predefined sequence is called web service orchestration, and the standard language for web service orchestration is Business Process Execution Language for Web Services (BPEL4WS, or BPEL for short).

If all governmental agencies that are involved in the service-delivery process provide access to their sub-processes and information systems by means of a web-service-interface, BPEL-based orchestration is a promising technological solution to the problem of coordinating processes that run across different agencies.

Within governments, little is known about how to coordinate cross-agency service-delivery processes, the advantages of web service orchestration-technology [8], and how web service orchestration-technology can be applied to support in coordinating cross-agency service-delivery processes. This indicates that there is a need for a reference model that can support governmental decision-makers in implementing process orchestration in e-government.

The *goal* of this paper is to investigate the applicability of existing reference models from domains that are closely related to process orchestration, the Workflow Reference Model [9], and the extended SOA reference model [10] to governmental decision-makers for implementing process orchestration in e-government, based on requirements for a reference model identified at a case study.

2 Existing Reference Models

A Reference Model can be defined as "(a) generally accepted abstract representation that allows users to focus on establishing definitions, building common understandings and identifying issues for resolution. (..)" [11]. A reference model for process orchestration in e-government would contribute to gaining insight in how to implement process orchestration, guide the design process, and recommend addressing certain issues.

As workflow technology also concerns the automation of processes, its resemblance with web service orchestration is clear. Also, some researchers claim

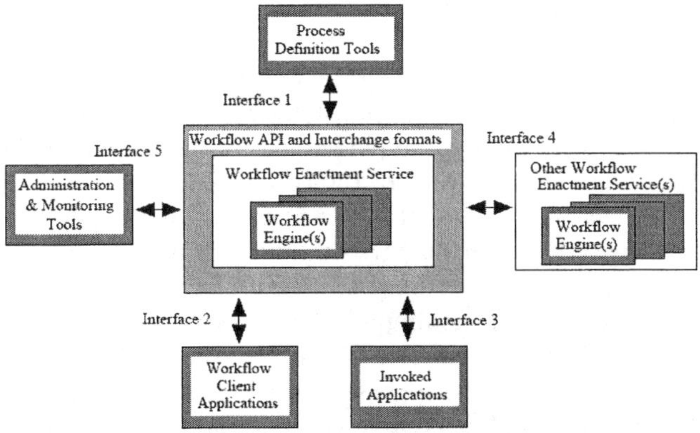

Fig. 1. Workflow Reference Model

that web service orchestration should take more notice of the lessons coming from workflow-research [12, 13]. For this reason, the existing workflow reference model may be relevant to decision makers facing the problem of implementing process orchestration in e-government.

As web services and web service orchestration are the main technologies for realizing a SOA, the extended-SOA reference model may also be relevant to governmental decision makers looking for guidance in implementing process orchestration.

2.1 Workflow Reference Model

The Workflow Management Coalition (WFMC) developed a reference model for Workflow Management Systems (WFMS) in order to promote standardization of, and interoperability and connectivity between the WFMS that have arisen over the years [14].

Figure 1 shows the Workflow Reference Model that defines the generic components and interfaces that make up a WFMS. This model aims at promoting the interoperability between different WFMS. We will discuss the components of a WFMS based on this Reference Model.

Central in the reference model is the workflow "enactment service" that consists of one or more workflow-engines. These engines execute the workflows, start new processes, select the people or applications that have to perform a task, send the necessary documents to the right people or applications, etc.

The first interface concerns the process definition tools. The processes that are executed by the WFMS can be defined 'at design time' by means of a graphical process-editor for the process-flow, and with program-code or scripting for invoking external applications. This interface is implemented by means of XPDL, the XML Process Definition Language [15]. This is a standard language for defining and interchanging processes designed by the WFMS. By means of XPDL,

WFMS can implement process-definitions that are designed by third party process definition tools.

The second interface is with the workflow client applications. A client application is usually implemented by a graphical interface that consists of a 'worklist' with the work items that have to be performed by the employee. The workflow engine does the assignment of tasks to the employees.

The third interface allows the WFMS to start external applications, either to perform automated tasks, or to support employees in executing their own tasks. A standard template with the address of a customer filled in can be started to support the employee task of sending a letter.

The fourth interface allows different WFMS to communicate with each other, i.e. that at a certain point in the process, the WFMS can start a (sub-) process on another WFMS. Although it is possible to consider the development of very complex interoperability scenarios in which a number of different WFMS, possibly of different vendors, cooperate to deliver a single enactment service, this scenario is difficult to realize, as it requires that all engines can interpret common process definitions and maintain a shared view of process states across the different WFMS [9]. More realistic is a form of cooperation where parts of the process are transferred to another WFMS. The interfaces 1, 2, and 4 can be implemented by means of Wf-XML, a standard by the WFMC [16].

A last interface with the workflow engine is used by different administrative and monitoring tools. These tools can be used to control issues like status, progress, and workload, and to add new users and roles.

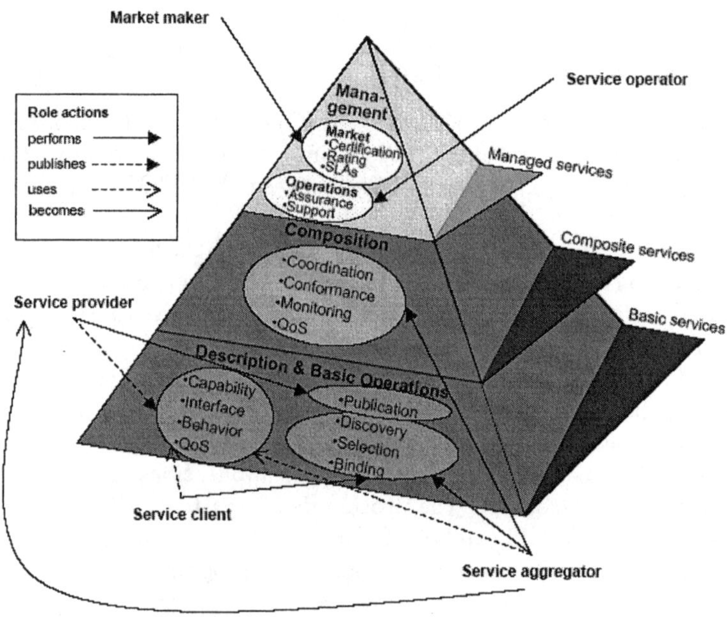

Fig. 2. Extended SOA Reference Model

2.2 Extended SOA Reference Model

The extended-SOA reference model was developed by [10] to provide support for service composition and management to the basic SOA operations of publishing, discovering, selecting, and invoking a service.

Figure 2 gives an overview of the extended-SOA pyramid, with the basic SOA-functionality at the bottom, and the higher-level functionality on top. Whereas in the basic notion of a SOA only the roles of service-provider, service-requester, and service-directory were involved, the extended SOA adds the more advanced roles of service aggregator and operator, and replaces the service-directory with the more advanced role of a market-maker.

Composite services are services that are composed out of other services, which on their turn also can be provided as services themselves. Web service orchestration is one way of service composition, and realizes a composite service by invoking the different subservices in a sequence according to a predefined process-flow. An overview of other ways of WS-aggregation is given by [17].

Service aggregators bundle services and by doing this become service providers themselves. Typical tasks performed by a service aggregator are controlling the execution of the component services and managing the dataflow (coordination), subscribing to events or information produced by the component services, and publishing higher level composite events (monitoring), ensuring the integrity of the composite service (conformance) and leveraging, aggregating, and bundling the component's Quality of Service (QoS) to derive the composite QoS (Qos).

On top of these aggregated services, the extended-SOA reference model identifies so-called managed services in the service management layer depicted at the top of the SOA pyramid of figure 2. In this level, the higher-level functionality concerning the management of all the different (aggregated) services is situated.

The functionality in the managed-service-layer can be divided into two categories: market and operation. Certification of services, rating services, and guarding and monitoring service-SLA's are typical management activities performed by a market-maker, supporting the buying and selling of services on a market. Another kind of managed services concerns operation management activities such as providing assurance and support are performed by the service operator.

2.3 Comparison of the Reference Models

Both reference models can hardly be compared to each other, as they are completely different. This huge difference can however be explained by looking at important factors underlying both reference models.

The first important factor is the *initial goal of both reference models.* The goal of the workflow reference model was "to promote standardization of and interoperability and connectivity between the WFMS that have arisen over the years" [14]. The goal of the extended-SOA reference model is more to de-mystify the concept of Service-oriented Computing (SOC) and to list and categorize all the needed functionality that is needed in successfully building systems using the SOC-paradigm. This explains why the Workflow Reference Model consists of parts of a WFMS, and the extended-SOA reference model consists of layers, roles, and functionality.

A second important factor is the *subject of the reference model.* The subject of the workflow reference model is the WFMS. The reference model prescribes the components it should be made of, and the interfaces between the components and the central workflow engine. The subject of the e-SOA reference model is the whole constellation of services, service-users, service-suppliers, and different kinds of third parties. This is a huge difference, but not so surprising when we consider that according to a SOA, systems are built out of many small functional services.

A third factor on which both models differ is the *level of aggregation* on which the models are situated. Where the Workflow Reference Model has components and interfaces as its objects, the e-SOA reference model has roles and functionality as its objects. Functionality and roles are situated on a business-level, whereas components and interfaces are situated on the implementation-level.

Although both reference models differ tremendously, both may contain important elements for a reference model that supports decision makers in implementing process orchestration in e-government. The following section will present a case study at a business counter, where a prototype of process orchestration using web-service orchestration was built.

3 Case Study at the Business Counter

The business counter is located in a medium-sized municipality, and offers a one-stop-shop to its entrepreneurs, integrating sub-services performed by different other agencies and organizations. For several services that are provided by different agencies, it acts as an account-manager that integrates these different services into one 'overall'-service, but it also offers many 'singular' services that also involve multiple back offices. Figure 3 provides a high-level overview of the business counter.

3.1 Liquor-License Process

A liquor license is one of the most important permits for the Hotel- and Catering Industry. Every restaurant or café that pours alcohol is obliged to apply for a license. For requesting a license, an entrepreneur can contact the business counter. After an initial intake meeting, the entrepreneur has to fill in an application form and return it together with the needed official documents, for example a floor plan. Hereafter, the name and address of the applicant are checked, the justice department and the police are asked for advice about whether the applicant has a criminal record or not. Finally, the building department has to check whether the building meets all legal requirements and the application for a liquor-license is published in the municipal newspaper. On basis of these advices, the back-office employee draws up a license or a letter stating the reasons for refusing the license.

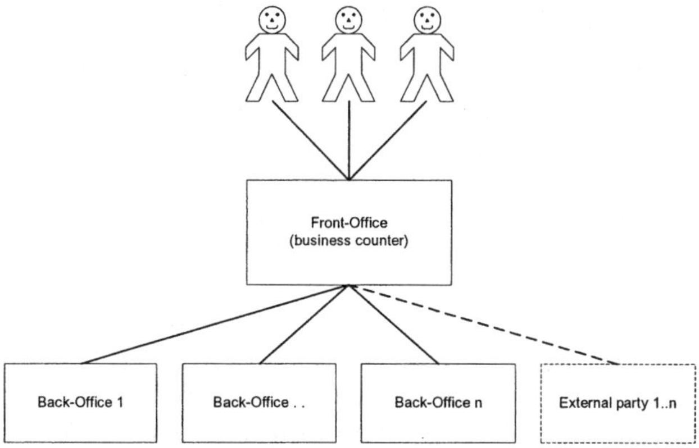

Fig. 3. High-level Overview of the Business Counter

3.2 Web Service Orchestration at the Business Counter

Currently, the business counter functions virtually without any ICT-support, but plans to automate the service-delivery processes at the Business Counter using web service orchestration-technology are being considered. To demonstrate the potential of web service orchestration for supporting processes like the liquor-licensing process, a BPEL-prototype was built using an early version of Collaxa Orchestration Sever, now Oracle BPEL Process Manager [18]. The process that was used in this prototype was inspired on a simplified variant of the liquor-licensing process. In the prototype, the overall liquor licensing process runs on a central orchestration server at the business counter, and tasks that are to be performed by other agencies are invoked as sub-services using a web-service-interface. An example of a web service that is invoked from the main liquor-licensing process is a web service at the police that checks whether the applicant is known in their database.

3.3 Requirements for a Reference Model for Process Orchestration at the Business Counter

As a process orchestrator, the main task of the business counter is coordinating the cross-agency service-delivery processes. As can be seen in the previous section, web service orchestration offers a promising technological solution to automate these cross-agency service-delivery processes. Web service orchestration is capable of supporting the whole cross-agency service-delivery process, but web service orchestration-technology does not solve the coordination-related issues that governmental decision-makers are currently facing when implementing process-orchestration.

Examples of the coordination issues that should be addressed by a reference model for process orchestration in e-government are ensuring the correct and in time execution of the process, information-sharing, and accountability.

Ensure Correct and In-Time Execution of the Process
As the process orchestrator is responsible for the overall service-delivery-process, one of the main coordination tasks a process orchestrator must perform is ensure that every sub-service in the cross-agency service-delivery process is completed in the right way, in time. At the business counter, for example, there is a problem guarding the lead-times of the overall liquor-licensing process, as some of the required sub-services sometimes take a long time to complete, or are even not completed at all. This way the required lead-times of the overall-process are not met.

Coordination-mechanisms like service-levels can help in ensuring correct, and in-time execution of every sub-service, but simply agreeing beforehand upon service-levels between the business counter and the different agencies is not enough. The service-levels need to be constantly monitored, and mechanisms that respond when a service fails, when a service does not produce the required answer, or does not answer in-time, should be put in place.

Information Sharing
Another coordination-related problem is the sharing of information between the different governmental agencies. When different agencies are all involved in one service-delivery process, they should all have access to the customer-data that is relevant to them. Within a single organization this can relatively easy be solved, for example by means of a large data-warehouse, but in a governmental setting, where many of the involved agencies have their own autonomy, this is not feasible. As the responsibilities are fragmented among many different governmental agencies, so are its information-systems, making information-sharing between multiple agencies even less straight-forward.

Agencies performing sub-services, need the business counter to provide them with information about the customer, as they need this data in performing the process. At the business counter, the building-department for example needs information about the applicant of the liquor-license, about the kind of restaurant it is requesting the liquor-license for, etc. This 'one-way' sharing of data is relatively straight-forward, but when different agencies start updating data that is required by other agencies, the process orchestrator should provide robust information-sharing mechanisms.

The issues of information-sharing will become even more important when the law comes into effect stating that citizens cannot be asked to provide personal data that is already available somewhere else in the government, aiming to reduce administrative burdens for citizens and businesses [1].

A major issue with information sharing is privacy. Not all agencies need all available customer information. For privacy-reasons, every agency should only have access the information he or she needs. An example is the information resulting from the check of the criminal record at the justice department. This data is not relevant for, and therefore should not be provided to other parties, such as the building department. Privacy-issues should explicitly considered when designing information-sharing mechanisms.

Accountability
Accountability is an important requirement for the whole public sector. For governmental service-delivery processes, it is especially important that the processes are transparent, non-discriminating, and consistent, and that the decisions made in the process are well motivated. Citizens and businesses do no longer accept a black-box view of the service delivery process, but want to know what steps have to reach the final decision.

Ensuring accountability for governmental service-delivery processes that run across different organizations is especially difficult, as it has to cope with different (semi-) autonomous agencies that are involved in the process. The decision not to grant a liquor license, because the police have strong suspicions against the applicant, should for example be very well motivated.

Ensuring accountability of cross-agency service-delivery processes requires specialized coordination mechanisms that ensure that the outcome of every process step is recorded, and that the overall process has run the way it was supposed to.

4 Applicability of Existing Reference Models for the Business Counter Case

The case study at the business counter provided us with an idea of the requirements for a reference model supporting governmental decision-makers in implementing process orchestration in e-government. The coordination issues that were identified in the previous section give an idea of the main issues that governmental decision-makers are facing, but are not exhaustive. This section will evaluate whether the two existing reference models meet the requirements that were identified in the previous section.

4.1 Applicability of the Workflow Reference Model

To evaluate applicability of the Workflow Reference Model, it will have to be translated into orchestration-concepts. The obvious link is on the level of with web service orchestration, instead of process orchestration. Analogous to workflow management, in web service orchestration there also exists a central 'orchestration server' to enact the process-flow. Examples are Oracle's BPEL Process Manager [18], formerly known as Collaxa Orchestration Server, Microsoft Biztalk 2004 [19], and IBM Websphere Business Integration Server Foundation [20]. Analogous to workflow, process definition and monitoring tools are also needed. External applications can be invoked by means of their web service-interface and human tasks can be supported by invoking a web service interface to someone's e-mail client. Web service orchestration also relies on invoking web services for interfacing with other orchestration servers. A process that is defined in BPEL can be made available as a web service itself, and thus be called by a process on another orchestration server.

From this translation of the Workflow Reference Model into web service orchestration-terms can be seen that there is quite a large resemblance between workflow and web service orchestration. The coordination issues that governmental decision-makers are facing, however remain unaddressed when decision makers rely only on this reference model when implementing process orchestration for their inter-agency processes. The reference model does not indicate how to guard lead-times, or how to facilitate information-sharing. Instead, the reference model seems to focus on what technical components, and kinds of technical interfaces are needed when implementing web service orchestration. This is, analogous with the initial goal of the workflow reference model, more relevant to vendors of orchestration technology, than to governmental decision-makers.

4.2 Applicability of the Extended-SOA Reference Model

The first thing to notice when looking at the extended-SOA reference model is that this reference model is rather 'business-oriented' in its roles and functionality. The model identifies a service-provider, service-requester, service-aggregator, service-operator, and even a market maker. Several of these roles can of course be performed by the same organization, but the model seems to be more tailored to situations where service requesters buy or rent services from service-providers on a services market.

Having said this, large parts of this reference model are still relevant to the situation of implementing process orchestration at the business counter. Especially the composite services layer is very relevant, as offering a service as a liquor-license where sub-processes at different agencies are incorporated into the overall service-delivery process, is an example of composition. The managed-services-level appears to be less relevant in the case of the business counter, but may become so in the future, when web service orchestration is adopted on a larger scale.

The business counter translates to the role of service aggregator in the reference model. It aggregates services that are provided by other agencies (service-providers), and provides these aggregated services to the customer. The reference model does address many of the issues that the decision-makers are facing by means of the tasks that the service-aggregator must perform.

The functionality in the composite services layer: coordination, monitoring and conformance-checking, and agreeing on service levels of the incorporated services matches quite well the requirements that were identified at the business counter. Although it does address these issues, it does not provide guidelines about how to fill them in. Decision makers can use this reference model only to identify the roles and functionality that they need to consider, but will have to fill these in themselves.

5 Conclusions

The goal of this paper is to investigate the applicability of two existing reference models to governmental decision-makers for implementing process orchestration in e-government, based on requirements for a reference model identified at a case study.

The case study showed that governmental decision-makers are looking for support in designing coordination related mechanisms like ensuring the correct and in-time execution of the process, information sharing, and accountability.

When comparing the both reference models to these requirements, it is clear that neither one can provide governmental decision-makers with enough support. The workflow reference model is too much focussed on technology, and therefore fails to address the non-technical coordination issues, and although the e-SOA reference model does address many of the issues, the model remains rather descriptive, only pinpointing the required functionality, but not indicating how this should be filled in.

To support governmental decision makers in implementing process orchestration in e-government, a new reference model is needed, focussing on the role of a process orchestrator, and prescribing how this role can be best filled in with respect to the needed coordination mechanisms. Further research will focus on designing such a reference model.

References

[1] Dutch Government. Actieprogramma andere overheid, 2003. (in Dutch).

[2] Dutch Government. Meer ruimte voor ondernemers door minder lasten - van lastenproductie naar lastenreductie, 2004. (in Dutch).

[3] Ronan McIvor, Marie McHugh, and Christine Cadden. Internet technologies: Supporting transparency in the public sector. *International Journal of Public Sector Management*, 15(3):170–187, 2002.

[4] Maria A. Wimmer. A european perspective towards online one-stop government: the egov project. *Electronic Commerce Research and Applications*, 1(1):92–103, 2002.

[5] Marcello Castellano, Nicola Pastore, Francesco Arcieri, and Valerio Summo. An e-government interoperability framework for cooperation among public administrations. In Dan Remenyi, editor, *Proceedings of the 4th European Conference on e-Government*, pages 159–170, Dublin Castle, Ireland, 2004.

[6] Mariangela Contenti, Alessandro Termini, Massimo Mecella, and Roberto Baldoni. An e-service-based framework for inter-administration cooperation. In M.A. Wimmer, editor, *Proceedings of the 4th IFIP International Working Conference on Knowledge Management in Electronic Government: KMGov 2003, Rhodes, Greece*, volume 2645 of *Lecture Notes in Computer Science*, pages 13 – 24. Springer-Verlag Heidelberg, 2003.

[7] Jeffrey Gortmaker and Marijn Janssen. Business process orchestration in e-government: A gap analysis. In Mehdi Khrosow-Pour, editor, *International Resources Management Association (IRMA)*, New Orleans, 2004. Idea Group Publishing.

[8] Jeffrey Gortmaker, Marijn Janssen, and René W. Wagenaar. The advantages of web service orchestration in perspective. In Marijn Janssen, editor, *6th International Conference of Electronic Commerce, ICEC 2004*, Delft, The Netherlands, 2004.

[9] Peter Lawrence, editor. *Workflow Handbook 1997*. John Wiley & Sons LTD, Chichester, 1997.
[10] M.P. Papazoglou and D. (eds.) Georgakopoulos. Special section: Service-oriented computing. *Communications of the ACM*, 46(10), 2003.
[11] The Open Systems Joint Task Force. Terms and definitions, 1999. [Online]. Available: `http://www.acq.osd.mil/osjtf/html/terms.htm`.
[12] W. M. P. Van der Aalst. Dont go with the flow: Web services composition standards exposed. *IEEE Intelligent Systems*, 18(1), 2003.
[13] Giacomo Piccinelli and Scott Lane Williams. Workflow: A language for composing web services. In M. Weske (Eds.) W. van der Aalst, A. ter Hofstede, editor, *Proceedings of the International Conference on Business Process Management*, volume 2678 of *Lecture Notes in Computer Science*, pages 13–24, Eindhoven, The Netherlands, 2003. Springer-Verlag Berlin Heidelberg.
[14] WFMC. About the wfmc - introduction to the workflow management coalition, 2004. [Online]. Available: `http://www.wfmc.org/about.htm`.
[15] WFMC. Workflow process definition interface – xml process definition language. Technical Report WFMC-TC-1025, 2002.
[16] WFMC. Workflow management coalition workflow standard - interoperability wf-xml binding. Technical Report WFMC-TC-1023, 2001.
[17] Rania Khalaf and Frank Leymann. On web services aggregation. In *Technologies for E-Services*, volume 2819 of *Lecture Notes in Computer Science*, pages 1 – 13. Springer-Verlag Heidelberg, 2003.
[18] Oracle. Oracle bpel process manager, 2004. [Online]. Available: `http://otn.oracle.com/products/ias/bpel/index.html`.
[19] Microsoft. Microsoft biztalk server home, 2004. [Online]. Available: `http://www.microsoft.com/biztalk/`.
[20] IBM. Websphere business integration server foundation, 2004. [Online]. Available: `http://www-306.ibm.com/software/integration/wbisf/features/`.

A Distributed Architecture for Supporting e-Government Cooperative Processes

Mariangela Contenti[1], Massimo Mecella[2], Alessandro Termini[2], and Roberto Baldoni[2]

[1] Università di Roma LUISS "Guido Carli", Centro di Ricerca sui Sistemi Informativi
mcontenti@luiss.it
[2] Università di Roma "La Sapienza", Dipartimento di Informatica e Sistemistica
{mecella, termini, baldoni}@dis.uniroma1.it

Abstract. In the last few years the e-Government discipline has attracted a growing attention both from practitioners and academics. Although the high number of action plan, projects and conferences spread all over Europe seems sanctioning the achievement of its maturity stage, several organizational and technological issues related with the modernization of service delivery are still far from a comprehensive solution and still require significant efforts. In this paper, the approach followed and the results so far achieved within the Eu-Publi.com research project, are presented. The discussion on the conceptual and design architectures of the Eu-Publi.com distributed, peer-to-peer system is enriched with results about the experimentation conducted on one of its core components.

1 Introduction

In the European Council held in Lisbon in 2000, the Government online was identified as one of the key actions to diffuse and widen the citizens' participation in the Information Society stimulating the use of Internet all over Europe. In its early stage, the enactment strategy for e-Government was then mostly focused on a rapid achievement and implementation of electronic service delivery. Many guidelines and benchmark frameworks were published (e.g., [1, 2]), and many projects started following new directions such as one-stop e-Government and life-events. Nowadays, researches and governmental activities are moving from e-Government to the emergent e-Governance: the achievement of a good governance in the Information Society require to exploit ICT resources, no longer only in the administrative activities, but also in the political and legislative ones.

Although this new impulse proves renewed and widened interests, some organizational and technological issues implied by the modernization of service delivery still require significant efforts, being far from a comprehensive solution. Above all, the back office integration for transactional cross-agencies services.

M. Böhlen et al. (Eds.): TCGOV 2005, LNAI 3416, pp. 181–192, 2005.

In the next sections the attempt of the Eu-Publi.com project to design and implement a cooperative system that, interconnecting at application level the several information systems, (semi-)automate inter-country complex *e*-Government services wil be discussed. More in details, in Section 2 the specific requirements driving the project are discussed, whereas Section 3 presents the proposed architecture for supporting cooperative *e*-Government processes, whose novelty lies in the distributed orchestration of different Web Services offered by the cooperating agencies. Section 4 presents the implementation and some preliminary performance tests; Section 5 compares our work with relevant research work, and Section 6 concludes the paper.

2 *e*-Government Requirements

The rapidly increasing number of conferences and projects as well as the first revolutions introduced in the European countries legal frameworks (e.g., the local implementations derived from the 1999/93/EC directive ruling the legal validity of well formed electronic documents) are all signs of the maturity reached by the discipline. At this stage, the core aspects and the more relevant hindrances appear as clearly identified [3]: prerequisites, for an *e*-Government enactment strategy, are the achievement of a technological interoperability of platforms and a deeper cooperation at organizational level; the constraints are related with the environment in which the public agencies operate, strictly constrained by norms and regulations and competitive and result-oriented at the same time.

On this purpose, the focus of the Eu-Publi.com project has been toward back-office integration and related interoperability issues: one of the first steps was to explicit the concepts behind complex *e*-Government services, through the definition of *macroprocess* as aggregation of processes to be jointly executed to satisfy the request of a service from a customer; the following the identification of the key functional requirements on the basis of the academic and end user partners consolidated experiences, enriched with desktop research.

On the hypothesis that each of the processes should be eventually (semi-)automated, the key functional requirement is the need for specific mechanisms, such as a process management systems, through which coordinate, control, monitor and audit the logical and temporal sequence of interdependency existing among the different process instances. Actually, among the several operational activities a complex business service is decomposable on, there is a plenty of control statements; their presence is motivated by the fact that an administrative procedure should exhibit transparency and equity of treatment under predefined conditions, enforcing in this way the citizens' confidence on the PA's operating.

As the introduction of technical and technological resources within organizations it not a so recent phenomena, the codification and enactment of procedures and modus operandi followed through years has been addressed with the more disparate organizational and technological solutions. The adoption of design methodologies and standards, being able to cope with legacy systems for providing reusable applications and platforms, represents the way through which establish a valuable cooperation and coordination among agencies. Issues to be addressed not only refer to the technological interoperability of ICT resources, but also to the semantic interoperability of business services, the latter reachable through the definition and adoption of linguistic and semantic support (e.g., ontologies). Actually, a suitable platform for *e*-Government cooperation and electronic service delivery should be able to provide support in the management of inconsistencies in the legal and administrative semantics that can occur in the cross border exchange of data, terms and concepts.

Another important requirement is the need, for each of the PA involved, to maintain, not only the autonomy, but also a well defined authority and responsibility on those steps and sub-processes each public agency is entitled for. The enforcement of this separation of concerns reflects the PAs need to maintain a well defined role, on the basis of which proceed in strategy definition and performance analysis. The outcome could be recursively adopted as a reference base for internal and global reallocation of resources and business process re-engineering.

These requirements, completed with valid solution enforcing the security of the system, and the privacy protection of personal and sensitive data exchanged and stored within the cooperative environment, apply to the design and development of the single composing processes as well as the overall process management system.

3 The Eu-Publi.com Architecture

In the Eu-Publi.com application scenario, each organization interfaces the others by offering specific application services independently from their realization, and the inter-organizational cooperation is obtained by sharing and integrating such application services. In this way the several interleaved organizations are loosely coupled and local internal processes re-engineering, being hidden by the service interfaces, does not impact on the overall cooperative process and related applications.

The foundation for the proposed architecture is the Service Oriented Architecture (SOA) model consisting of some basic operations and roles: in the case of Eu-Publi.com, each cooperating administration can act both as provider of its own services and as requestor for services available on other organizations. In addition, the Eu-Publi.com architecture extends the SOA model with further roles and operations. More in details *(i)* a layer supporting macro-process enactment has been introduced in order to cope with the previously highlighted process management needs; and *(ii)* behavioral notions have been developed in order to cope with general QoS for the system, e.g., reliability, and to develop dynamic capabilities of the system[1].

[1] In such a way, the Eu-Publi.com architecture not only resolves specific *e*-Government issues, but contributes also to the current state-of-art of the research by proposing an Extended Service Oriented Architecture.

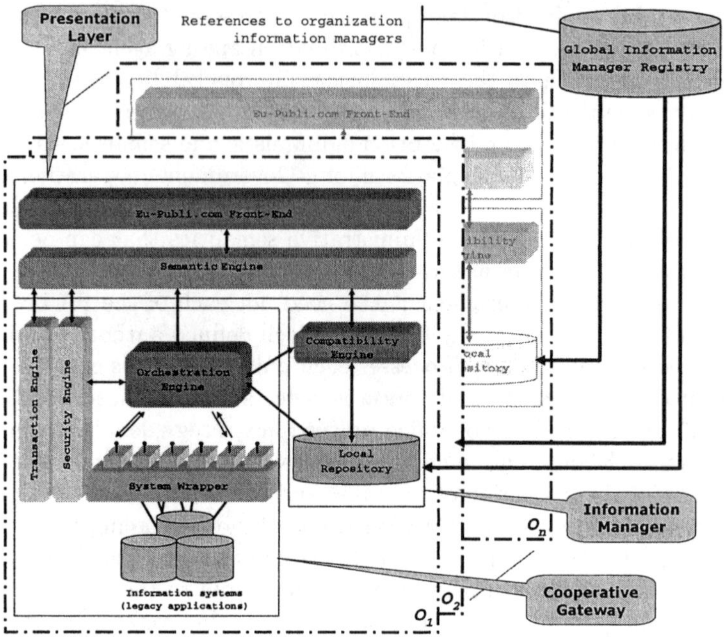

Fig. 1. Eu-Publi.com Architecture

The Eu-Publi.com architecture consists on the specification of how to realize a *cooperative layer*[2] that comprises the set of technologies, application protocols and services enabling the effective cooperation among administrations; it is designed as a peer-to-peer system, in which each organization deploys an instance of the three core macro-components (see Figure 1):

- the **Cooperative Gateway**, representing the back-end layer of the architecture: it *(i)* exports the set of data and application services offered by a single administration and *(ii)* includes the Orchestration Engine component, also deployed in a peer-2-peer fashion, that coordinates the services.
- the **Information Manager**, being the repository of the Eu-Publi.com peer, through which *(i)* service schemas, *(ii)* orchestration schemas and *(iii)* instance data are stored and made accessible.
- the **Presentation Layer**, responsible for the presentation to end users and representing the employees' front-end of the overall architecture.

In order to get the information distributed on all the organizations joining the Eu-Publi.com architecture, a further component, the ***Global Information Manager Registry***, is designed: it points to specific Information Managers containing specific information (as shown in Figure 1).

[2] As a prerequisite, the different organizations joining the Eu-Publi.com architecture must deploy a transport layer interconnecting each other, mainly based on standard Internet and Web protocols.

The cooperation of different agencies is achieved by making them responsible for exporting some views of its own information system as services; the *Cooperative Gateway* represents "where" and "how" services are deployed; it includes the definition on how different cooperating organizations are structured and connected and how pre-existing legacy applications (Local IS in the figure) can be integrated in a common cooperative process (the *System Wrapper* is the component wrapping the PA's legacy system).

The *Orchestration Engine* sub-system is responsible for coordinating all the services involved in a cooperative process; this component, working in a peer-to-peer fashion, acts at two different layers. Through "cooperative process definitions" (technically referred to as *orchestration schemas*) it dynamically finds and links suitable services; it also interacts with the different service instances deployed on the different cooperating organizations. Moreover, during the orchestration of a specific business process and whether needed, an Orchestration Engine can communicate with another Orchestration Engine deployed onto a different organization to move the responsibility of the process control (e.g., this could occur due to some legal constraints that oblige a particular administration to control the process).

The *Compatibility Engine* is in charge of managing service substitution during orchestration: this feature can be used in different scenarios, such as for handling different versions of the same service, in case of using a new service which offers improved functionalities with respect to the one currently used, during run-time substitution of an unavailable service with another one, and, in general, to enforce QoS to the system, e.g., load balancing [4].

The *Front-End System* is the component representing the GUI of the employees. This component works in a dynamic fashion: according to the specific process, it dynamically build the corresponding GUI.

The architecture also defines additional components that manage the set of non-functional requirements for the system:

- as Eu-Publi.com offers B2B integration to organizations located in different countries, the orchestration of the processes involves also cultural and linguist aspects. Therefore the existence of a component that will cope with the semantics of the exchanged information both in the presentation and the communication level is needed. With this aim, the *Semantic Engine* consists of mechanisms that enable the translation and the correspondence of terms.
- the *Transaction Engine* provides transaction and reliability features, which are mainly independent from the business domain. It adopts classical long running transaction models [5].
- the *Security Engine* is in charge of managing security-related issues, such as security and privacy of the data exchanged or communication security among the architectural components. This component also manages the access-policy for identification, authentication and authorization mechanisms envisioned by the architecture [4].

4 The Eu-Publi.com Prototype

The current implementation of the Eu-Publi.com architecture prototype relies on *Web Services technologies* [6], that can be viewed as the natural "software artifacts" of the service abstraction. Each PA joining the Eu-Publi.com system must export its functionalities as Web Services (in this case the Cooperative Gateway is the application server in which the PA's Web Services run); once an organization exports its services, an Orchestration Engine is needed in order to coordinate them into macro-processes. The implementation of such a component is based on BPEL4WS [7], i.e., the orchestration schema is a BPEL file. Moreover, in order to implement the distributed features of the architecture (not included in the BPEL specification), a specific protocol to "send" and "accept" the orchestration responsibility has been designed (see Section 4.2). The current implementation includes a simple Information Manager, based on UDDI, a Semantic Engine implementation based on OWL-S and UDDI, and a Front-End System implementation based on XForms. Finally, for what concern the Transaction Engine and the Security Engine, the W3C standards for security and transactions (i.e., WS-Security, WS-Coordination and WS-Transactions) have been considered.

In the following sections, some details about the current prototype are described; the focus is concentrated on the distributed orchestration mechanism, that is one of the most innovative result gained within the project.

4.1 Eu-Publi.com Architecture Deployment

As previously described, the Eu-Publi.com architecture is designed as a peer-2-peer system, in which each organization deploys an instance of the core components, namely the Cooperative Gateway, the Information Manager and the Front-End. As in a peer-2-peer system, there is no a clear separation between clients and servers: each organization can be both client and server.

In Figure 2 a simple process regarding the request of a license is shown; in the process three different administrations (organization A, B and C) are involved, each of them exporting some Web Services (WS_{A1} exported by A, WS_{B1} and WS_{B2} exported by B, and WS_{C1} export by C). It is supposed that the process is provided by the organization A, so the process started under organization A's responsibility from a client request (step 1). The organization A invokes the WS_{A1}, and then, for continuing the process, it passes the responsibility to the organization B (for example due to some legal or system restrictions for the access to the Web Services WS_{B1} and WS_{B2}). The Web Service WS_{C1} is then invoked by the Orchestration Engine running on the organization B (step 4-5, 8-9, 12-15) that sends back the responsibility to the organization A that concludes the process (step 18).

4.2 Orchestrator Engine Design

As previously pointed out, the implementation of the Orchestration Engine is based on BPEL4WS; unfortunately the BPEL specification does not cover all the aspects needed by this component: in particular no distribution of process is

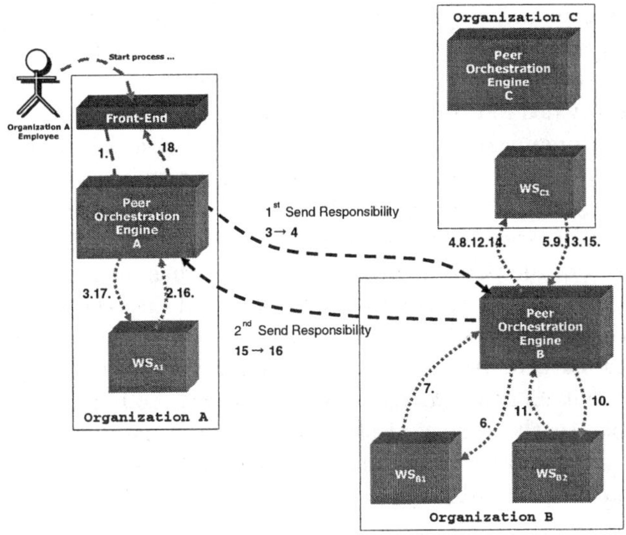

Fig. 2. An example process execution

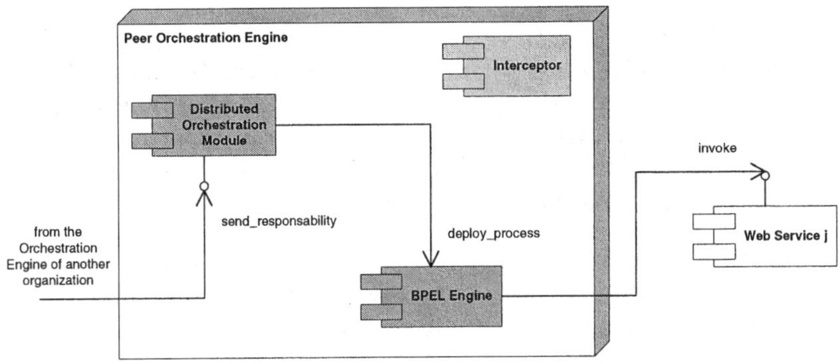

Fig. 3. Orchestration Engine Design

taken into consideration in the specification. This implies the need for a specific module managing the distributed orchestration. Figure 3 shows the design of the Orchestration Engine in the Eu-Publi.com architecture.

The **BPEL Engine** is the module containing the orchestration logic, i.e., it executes the scripts of the processes and it coordinates the involved Web Services, routing the messages in the correct order and maintaining the state of the process instances.

The **Distributed Orchestration Module** is the module implementing the distributed features not included in the BPEL specification The `send_responsibility` operation is implemented as a simple Web Service operation, i.e., this module is a Web Service exporting operations able to pass the responsibility or to accept the responsibility from another peer.

From a technological point of view, when a centralized process is created, it is deployed onto the engine of the initial organization; if there is any `send_responsibility` operation, i.e., the process is enacted in a peer-2-peer way, the process is divided into subprocess, and only the first of them will be deployed onto the initial organization. During the execution of a distributed process, the BPEL file describing the process is modified and transferred to a different Orchestration Engine, that *(i)* deploys the sub-process to execute, *(ii)* restores the state of the computation (explicitly sent by the old peer), and *(iii)* continues the computation from the point at which the old peer has interrupted its activities. From this point, the old peer is no longer involved into the process (excluding if another peer newly passes to it the responsibility for the orchestration).

Finally, the **Interceptor** is a module that analyzes the messages flow to/from the Orchestration Engine; the main feature of this module is to forward asynchronous reply to the correct destination in those cases in which the corresponding process instance is running on another Orchestration Engine, due to a previous `send_responsibility`.

4.3 Orchestration Engine Performance Analysis

Preliminary performance analysis carried out on the prototype are shown below.

Testbed Platform. The testbed environment consists of 4 Intel Pentium IV 2,5GHz and 1GB RAM workstations running Microsoft Windows XP Professional as operating system and equipped with Java Development Kit v.1.4.2_03, Apache Jakarta Tomcat Web Server v.5.0 as application server, and Collaxa BPEL Server v.2.0RC7 as BPEL Engine. The PCs are interconnected by a 100Mbit Ethernet LAN setted-up as a single collision domain.

Experiment Aim and Description. The aim of the experiment was to evaluate the overhead introduced by the `send_responsibility` operation in a process; the overhead is evaluated comparing the latency of the distributed orchestration with respect to the centralized one. In particular, the ratio between the average latency of the process execution with `send_responsibility` operation and the average latency of the same process with no `send_responsibility` operation is shown. In the experiment the number of `send_responsibility` operation in the distributed process, has been varied from 1 `send_responsibility` to 25 `send_responsibility`.

Moreover, two distinct sets of measure were conducted: the former measures the latency of the first instance of the process; the latter the latency of the other instances[3]; this separation is due to the run-time deployment of the distributed process pointed out in the previous section[4].

[3] For the first instances the average is evaluated by invoking 10 times the process, while for the other instances the average is evaluated by invoking 100 times the process.

[4] In the latency of the first instances is included the time for the deployment of the sub-process.

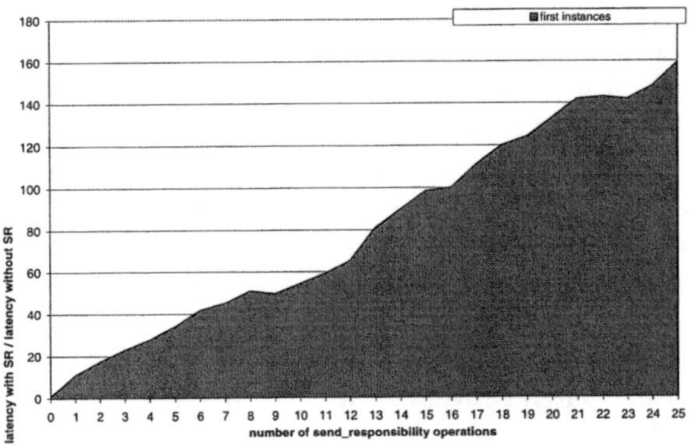

(a) Latency of the first instances.

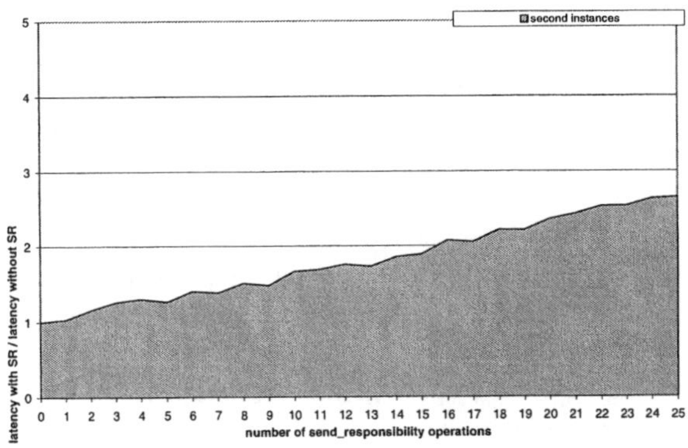

(b) Latency of the second instances.

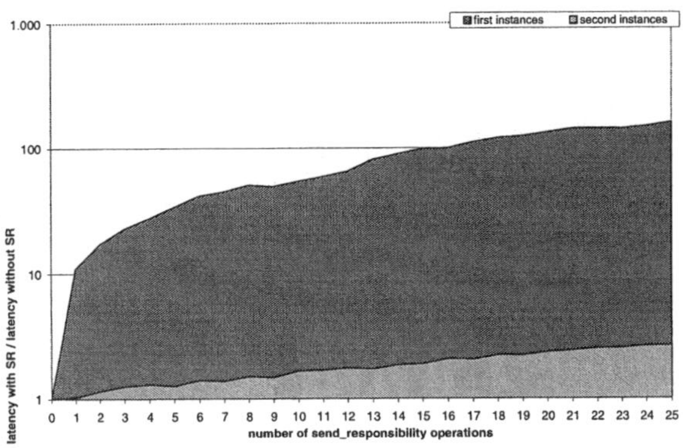

(c) Comparison between latencies.

Fig. 4. Experiment Results

Experiment Result. The tests results are depicted in Figure 4; in details whereas Figure 4(a) shows the latency for the first instance of the process used in the experiments, Figure 4(b) shows the latency of the second instance.

Both figures show that latency increases in a linear way, i.e., the overhead introduced by the `send_responsibility` operation is proportional to its number. This behaviour can be predicted because, from a technological point of view, the `send_responsibility` operation is an invocation on a Web Service (more the `send_responsibility` operations are, larger the distributed process is, and more the time required for its execution is).

Figure 4(c) (in logarithmic scale) also shows that the latency of the first instance of the distributed process is about 150 times slower than the latency of the second instance: this behavior is due to the run-time deploy of each subprocess (the deploy of a process involves many activities and it results very slow with respect to the invocation on a Web Service).

5 Related Work

The Eu-Publi.com architecture is based on the notion of Cooperative Information System (CIS); various approaches have been proposed in literature for the design and development of CIS's, e.g., schema and data integration [8], agent-based methodologies and systems [9], or business process coordination and service-based systems [10]. This last approach is the one adopted in the Eu-Publi.com project, and a general architecture focusing on those characteristics typical of the *e*-Government context has been designed.

Systems adopting such an approach are typically based on a SOA, in which a clear distinction is made between an internal architecture and an external one. The first is the one allowing back-end systems to be exported as Web Services; respect on this, the Eu-Publi.com architecture provides specific support in the presentation layer and in the system wrappers. But, as argued in [6], major research work is needed in the external one, which is the one allowing the peer-2-peer cooperation among different organizations; on this purpose, the Eu-Publi.com Orchestration Engine, implementing a distributed orchestration, is a novel proposal and a first, yet simple, solution to such an issue.

The issue of supporting cooperative processes based on Web Services is quite similar to the problem of inter-organizational workflows. In the last years, several systems and approaches has been proposed to support inter-organization workflows, by extending traditional workflow management system (WfMS) technology to distributed, Internet-based scenarios: CrossFlow [11], WISE [12], MENTOR-lite [13], e-ADOME [14]. The main difference is in that the Eu-Publi.com approach assumes that services offered by different organizations are "black boxes" to be coordinated. Conversely, all such proposals adopt a "white box" approach, in which the service internal workflow schemas are knwon and used for coordinating the overall process.

With respect to systems such as *e*-Flow [15], WebBIS [16] and AZTEC[17], the novelty of the Eu-Publi.com architecture is in the distributed nature of the orchestration engine; to the best of our knowledge, SELF-SERV [18] is the only system currently addressing a similar issue.

6 Conclusions

The paper presents the Eu-Publi.com architecture, specifically focused on *e*-Government service provisions based on orchestration of services. The approach is based on the concept of cooperative process, as unifying element among different inter-country agencies providing value-added services to European citizens.

The consideration and methodologies underlying this solution relies on a *technological improvement approach.* This approach, not requiring initial radical changes, allows to overcome the strictly constrains of norms and legal frameworks which hinder the rapid reconfiguration, in terms of interdependencies and involved actors, of business processes in the *e*-Government domain. The proposed architecture also enhances current state-of-the-art research in Service Oriented Computing, by providing a distributed orchestration mechanism which could be adopted also in many other scenarios and application domains. In *e*-Government, for instance, the distributed orchestration feature, relying on general considerations, could be reused and find applications also in other recent IST research projects such as TERREGOV [19] or SmartGov [20].

The preliminary test of the Eu-Publi.com prototype, strictly focused on the distribution feature of the Web Service orchestration, proves the approach feasibility in term of performances: an *e*-Government process in a real scenario is a long-running process and the overhead due to its distribution became negligible respect to its overall execution time; moreover, rarely, in the real world a macro-process would need tenths `send_responsibility` operations.

Acknowledgments

This work has been supported by the European Commission under Contract No. IST-2001-35217, Project Eu-Publi.com *(Facilitating Cooperation amongst European Public Administration Employees)* (`http://www.eu-publi.com/`). The authors would like to thanks the other project partners: ICE (Italy), IBERMATICA (Spain), ALTEC, NATH and CERTH/ITI (Greece). A special thank goes to Alessia Candido and Adriano Bernardini for their contributions to the development and experimentation of the prototype.

References

1. Australian National Audit Office, "Electronic Service Delivery, Including Internet Use, by Commonwealth Government Agencies", The Auditor-General, Audit Report No.18 1999-2000, 1999.
2. European Commision, "*e*-Government Indicators for Benchmarking *e*-Europe", 2001.

3. R. Traunmuller, Ed., *Electronic Government*, Springer Verlag, LNCS 3183, 2004.
4. The EU-Publi.com consortium, "Deliverable D2.1: The EU-Publi.com Architecture", 15th August, 2004 (please contact authors for a copy).
5. Morgan Kaufmann, Ed., *Database Transaction Models for Advanced Applications*, A. Elmargarmid, 1992.
6. Gustavo Alonso, Fabio Casati, Harumi Kuno, Vijay Machiraju, *Web Services: Concepts, Architectures and Applications*, Springer-Verlag, 2004.
7. "Business Process Execution Language for Web Services Version 1.1", Document. `ftp://www6.software.ibm.com/software/developer/library/ws-bpel11.pdf`.
8. M. Lenzerini, "Data Integration Is Harder than You Thought", in *SIGMOD/PODS 2002*, USA, 2002.
9. J. Castro, M. Kolp, and J. Mylopoulos, "Towards Requirements-driven Information Systems Engineering: the Tropos Project", *Information Systems*, vol. 27, no. 6.
10. U. Dayal, M. Hsu, and R. Ladin, "Business Process Coordination: State of the Art, Trends and Open Issues", in *Proc. VLDB 2001*, Roma, Italy, 2001.
11. P. Grefen, K. Aberer, Y. Hoffner, and H. Ludwig, "CrossFlow: Cross-Organizational Workflow Management in Dynamic Virtual Enterprises", *International Journal of Computer Systems Science & Engineering*, vol. 15, no. 5, 2000.
12. A. Lazcano, G. Alonso, H. Schuldt, and C. Schuler, "The WISE approach to Electronic Commerce", *International Journal of Computer Systems Science & Engineering*, vol. 15, no. 5, 2000.
13. G. Shegalov, M. Gillmann, and G. Weikum, "XML-enabled Workflow Management for *e*-Services across Heterogeneous Platforms", *VLDB Journal*, vol. 10, no. 1, 2001.
14. D.K.W. Chiu, K. Karlapalem, and Q. Li, "E-ADOME: a Framework for Enacting e-Services", in *Proc. VLDB-TES 2000*, Cairo, Egypt, 2000.
15. F. Casati and M.C. Shan, "Dynamic and Adaptive Composition of *e*-Services", *Information Systems*, vol. 6, no. 3, 2001.
16. B. Benatallah, B. Medjahed, A. Bouguettaya, A.K. Elmagarmid, and J. Beard, "Composing and Maintaining Web-based Virtual Enterprises", in *Proc. VLDB-TES 2000*, Cairo, Egypt, 2000.
17. V. Christophides, R. Hull, G. Karvounarakis, A. Kumar, G. Tong, and M. Xiong, "Beyond Discrete *e*-Services: Composing Session-oriented Services in Telecommunications", in *Proc. VLDB-TES 2001*, Rome, Italy, 2001.
18. B. Benatallah, Q.Z. Sheng, and M. Dumas, "The Self-Serv Environment for Web Services Composition", *IEEE Internet Computing*, vol. 7, no. 1, 2003.
19. TERREGOV project website, "`http://www.terregov.eupm.net/`", 2002.
20. SmartGov project website, "`http://www.smartgov-project.org/`", 2002.

eGovernment Service Marketplace: Architecture and Implementation

Elena Mugellini[1], Maria Chiara Pettenati[1], Omar Abou Khaled[2], and Franco Pirri[1]

[1] Department of Electronics and Telecommunications, University of Florence
{mugellini, pettenati}@achille.det.unifi.it, fpirri@ing.unifi.it
[2] Department of Computer Science,
University of Applied Science of Western Switzerland
omar.aboukhaled@eif.ch

Abstract. In order to provide citizens with quality services, respecting public administrations autonomy, we propose a new concept of eGovernment Service Marketplace (eGovSM). This paper presents an overview of the architecture and implementation of eGovSM easing the automatisation of administrative process involving several administrations and allowing the reuse of data. This architecture facilitates citizens' interaction with different public administrations by providing them a single and personalized access point to services. The eGovSM is formalized using a set of XML Schema models in order to support the realization of an interoperable and open system. The architecture is based on four main functional modules: UNICITIDM (UNIiversal CITizen IDentifier Manager) a module for the creation and management of citizen unique identifiers, LEM (Life Event Manager) for the management of all citizen interactions with the marketplace, DM (Document Manager) for the management of administrative process execution and SM (Service Manager) for the management of all public administrations interactions with eGovSM.

1 Introduction

The main e-government challenge is to facilitate citizen-public administration interaction enabling seamless services delivery to citizen through the network [1]. E-government services frequently need to link and use data from multiple and diverse information resources. Consequently, "interoperability" is the key word to address e-government challenges. Interoperability is not only a technical issue dealing with distributed computing, but it deals also with information sharing among different administrations and the redesign of administrative processes to support more effective delivery of e-government services. Three level of interoperability are relevant to e-government issues: technical, semantic and organizational [1]. The first one refers to technical issue of connecting computer systems, defining common communication protocols and data formats. The second one concerns the exchange of information in an understandable way even between applications that were not initially developed for this purpose. The third one refers to enabling processes co-operation. While interop-

M. Böhlen et al. (Eds.): TCGOV 2005, LNAI 3416, pp. 193 – 204, 2005.

erability requirements seem so obvious, today's reality is that information systems are not yet interoperable, different administrations are able neither to share and reuse data nor to cooperate for fulfilling e-government challenges.

Many e-government projects are being developed and various approaches have been proposed for the design and the development of an architecture to deliver e-government services to citizens; but, to our knowledge, the interoperability problem is not completely resolved yet [1].

The one that follows is a short analysis of three of the main e-government European projects (eGOV project [4], FASME project [7] and EU-PUBLI.com project [10]) together with a brief discussion of the differences between their proposed solution and our approach.

eGOV project proposes an architecture to enable "one-stop government" [6]. The architecture is made of a portal and a middleware component. The portal is the citizen access point to the system while the middleware is the component responsible for executing the requested service. In order to describe services a markup language (GovML) has been developed [5]. The GovML defines a set of metadata to describe public administration services and life events. The main advantages of the proposed solution are the provision of a single access entry to the system and the definition of a standard set of metadata to describe administration services. The main disadvantage is that each administration is obliged to implement the proposed architecture in order to provide the services and share data.

FASME project [8],[9] focuses on supporting citizen mobility across European countries by the integration of administrative process spanning among administrations belonging to different countries. In order to satisfy this objective a smart card is provided to citizen for the storage of all personal information and documents. Services are delivered through dedicated kiosk. The main advantage of the project is the idea of providing the user with a card that can authenticate him to the system while the main disadvantage is that citizens are obliged to reach the kiosk in order to access and use the system.

EU-PUBLI.com project [11],[12] defines a Unitary European Network Architecture. It proposes a middleware solution to connect heterogeneous systems of different public administrations and to enable a service-based cooperation between public administrations. The main advantage of this project is that the proposed solution respects the autonomy of each single administration and enables interoperability between different organizations. The main disadvantage is that it is a back-office solution and it doesn't provide support for documents delivery to citizens.

To make it easier for citizens to interact with administrations and to obtain services in a transparent way it is necessary to propose a system which both provides services according to citizen needs and respects public administrations autonomy and authority. The eGovernment Service Marketplace [23] proposes an architecture that:

- provides citizen oriented services (that is provide services to citizens every time they need, wherever they are and in a personalized way)
- respects the autonomy of the single administration (that is it doesn't obliged each single administration to deploy an instance of the proposed architecture)

- provides a single access point to government services via the web
- performs the necessary operations for collecting the information to deliver government services instead of the citizen

From the one hand the proposed marketplace provides services according to citizen needs, using "life event metaphor" [2] to hide the complexity of administrative process. From the other hand it integrates public administration legacy systems allowing public administration subscription to the marketplace according to four different interoperability levels. It is worth noting that in this first phase of system design and development we have decided to not take into account security and privacy issues since there are others projects that have already provided interesting solutions (for instance FASME project). Later on, we will better investigate the solutions proposed as well as the results obtained in these projects in order to evaluate a possible integration in our system.

2 The eGovernment Service Marketplace Concept

The eGovSM main purpose is to provide quality citizen oriented services facilitating citizen to public administration interaction. As it happens in a traditional marketplace, where a citizen can buy the products he needs without caring about production and delivery process, the e-government marketplace aims at providing e-government services to citizens without requiring the citizen to be aware of administrative process complexity. For instance, for the delivery of a document, citizens will not be concerned with administration responsibility or geographical location of information. The eGovSM purpose is not only to use technologies to increase the efficiency of administrative process. It aims also to make it easier for citizens to interact with public administrations rebalancing relations between citizens and administrations, and presenting e-government services according to citizen needs. For this reason the eGovernment Service Marketplace aggregates services according to "life event metaphor" [2],[3] that is services are organized around events that make sense for the citizen and the citizen doesn't need to be aware of various public administrations involved in the delivery of such services. The life of citizens is described providing a list of events that when occurring in citizen life result in a series of transactions between a citizen and different public sector organizations. Examples of life events could be "looking for a job", "moving home", "learning to drive", "pensions and retirement", "having a baby" and so on.

The marketplace concept of service is the communication (transmission or reception) of a document (official document or information). When a citizen requests a service, the marketplace correlates the requested service with the corresponding administrative process and executes this process to deliver the document to the citizen. In order to let the marketplace interact with a public administration it is necessary that this administration subscribes to the system. Each administration wanting to join the marketplace has to subscribe to it, declaring its availability to provide services and share data with the marketplace. In order to respect public administrations autonomy the marketplace offers four different subscription profiles [see Service Manager Paragraph].

Fig. 1 shows the entities involved in the marketplace and possible interactions between them. From the one hand citizens access the marketplace via a portal, from the other hand public administrations subscribe to the marketplace in order to share data and provide services. The figure highlights three different types of public administrations (PAs). PAs of "type A" represent administrations subscribed to the eGovSM that automatically provide data to the marketplace without requiring the citizen to interact with them. PAs of "type B" represent administrations subscribed to the eGovSM that, even if can automatically provide data to the marketplace, require a direct interaction with citizens (for example a hospital in case of a medical examination). Finally PAs of "type C" represent administrations that are not subscribed to the eGovSM and hence require a direct interaction with citizens to provide data.

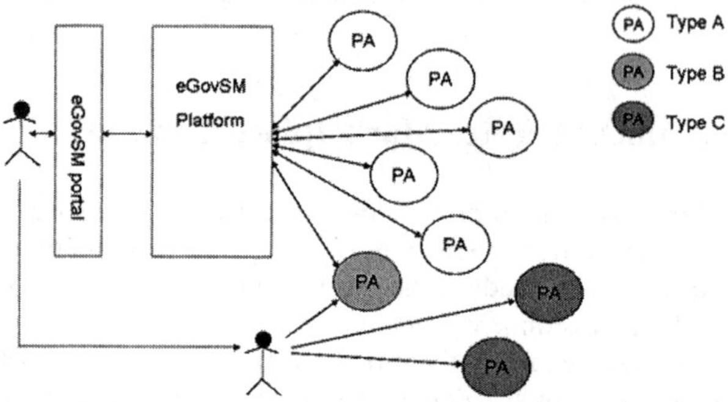

Fig. 1. eGovernment Service Marketplace, involved entities and interactions among them

The eGovSM is formalized using a set of XML Schema models [16]. This allows us to create an interoperable and open system. Public administration sector is a continuously changing world: public administration organization, responsibility and services are always in evolution. For this reason the design and development of an e-government system based on a set of formal models makes the system architecture more flexible and easier to extend in order to fulfill new public administration needs and requirements.

3 The eGovSM architecture

3.1 General Overview

The overall eGovSM architecture is shown in Fig. 2. The platform is based on four core components: the UNIversal CITizen IDentifier Manager (UNICITIDM), the Life Event Manager (LEM), the Document Manager (DM) and the Service Manager (SM). The UNICITIDM component creates and manages citizens' identifiers. The LEM component manages marketplace services creation and presentation to citizens and all the interactions with citizens. The DM component coordinates the execution of the administrative process. The SM component manages all the marketplace interactions with public administrations in order to retrieve the required data to deliver a specific service.

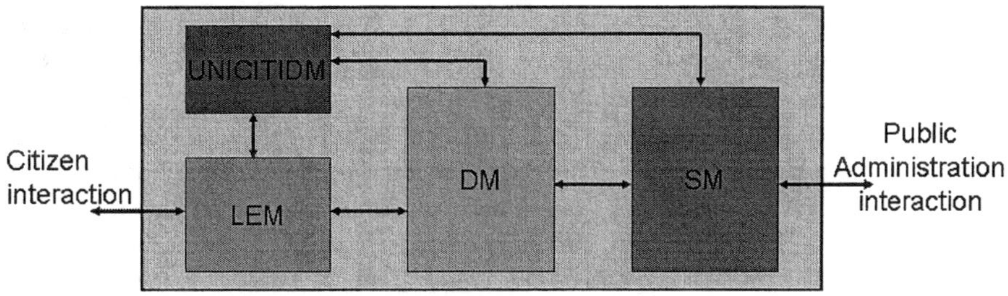

Fig. 2. Overview of eGovSM architecture

3.2 UNIversal CITizen IDentifier Manager

The UNIversal CITizen IDentifier Manager (UNICITIDM) is the module responsible for managing citizen identifier (UNICITID). The UNICITID is an identifier containing citizen personal information; it is unique and not variable. Its purpose is to allow eGovSM to find out the administrations responsible for citizen personal data. The UNICITID has a URN-like (Uniform Resource Name) structure similar to the one defined in the NIR Project [13],[14],[15] that allows identifying citizens of any country by providing a uniform, but adaptable, schema for defining country-specific identifier structure. The UNICITID is created the first time a citizen access the eGovSM platform and it is used only by the marketplace, remaining transparent to the citizen. The eGovSM provides only the basic structure of this identifier allowing administrations of different countries to extend and to adapt it to the specific public administration structure of their own country. As a consequence each eGovSM is able to interpret only identifiers coming from its country, but, thanks to the country identifier contained in every UNICITID, it can identify the eGovSM platform capable of managing a foreign identifier. The one that follows is an example of UNICITID:

- it:it:rossi.luca:1960-04-08:it.toscana.firenze:codicefiscale

The first field indicates the country responsible for the identifier (in this case "it"= Italy) and it is common for all the identifiers while the last one ("codicefiscale") represents a country-specific information. The eGovSM in order to retrieve, for instance, citizen address uses the birthplace information "it.toscana.firenze" and starts contacting administrations of "firenze", then of "toscana" and so on, until it finds the searched information.

3.3 Life Event Manager

The Life Event Manager (LEM) is the manager of all the interactions of a citizen with the marketplace (Fig. 3). It is the eGovSM component who presents available services to citizen and manages citizen service requests.

The LEM is responsible for creating, publishing and updating life events list in order to provide citizens with up to date and personalized list of available services in the marketplace. LEM is also responsible for citizen subscription and authentication as well as citizen service request management. When the eGovSM receives the citizen request, the LEM correlates the requested service with the corresponding administrative process creating a Process Descriptor. The Process Descriptor (PD) specifies the administrative process corresponding to the requested service; it describes the constraints to satisfy and the operations to do in order to deliver the service. A Process Descriptor is associated to each service provided by the marketplace, but depending on the citizen who is requesting it (where he lives, which are the administrations responsible to deliver the document) the number and the type of operations to do, for the service delivery, could vary. When the requested service concerns the delivery of an official document (that is a document with a well defined structure like a certificate), associated to the Process Descriptor there will be also a Document Descriptor. The Document Descriptor (DD) specifies the structure of this official document, i.e. the data it contains, constrains associated to that data and the way the data have to be aggregated in order to generate the document.

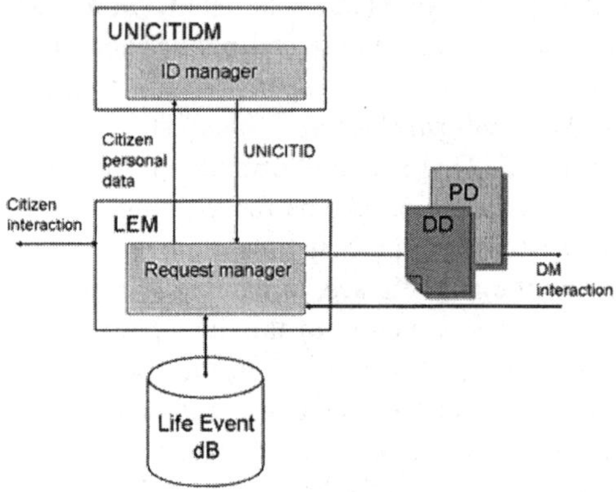

Fig. 3. Interaction between UNICITIDM and LEM modules

Finally the LEM tracks the process executed by the Document Manager in order to inform the citizen about the necessary time required to complete the service. For example, let consider that the citizen selects the service "getting your driving licence". The LEM has to create the Process Descriptor and Document Descriptor associated to this service. The Process Descriptor contains all the steps to be followed and the order in which they have to be executed to deliver the driving licence document. For example it establishes that before collecting the data and delivering the document to the citizen, the system has to check if the citizen has or has had problems with law, or if he has already passed the medical examination to obtain the driving licence. The Document Descriptor defines the structure of the driving licence document. It describes which information it is necessary to retrieve and how it has to be aggregated in order to create the document and which are the constraints associated to this information (for example it will check if the validity period of the document against the citizen age).

3.4 Document Manager

The Document Manager (DM) is the component responsible for administrative process execution (Fig. 4).

The DM main purpose is the management and coordination of all the operations necessary to collect the required data and to deliver the document the citizen has requested. In order to do this, it uses the Process Descriptor and Document Descriptor created by the LEM. The DM work is subdivided into two phases: in the first one it has to verify the fulfilment of prerequisites associated to the service while, in the second one, it has to coordinate all the operations to retrieve the necessary data. Finally DM uses a repository to register information regarding the process execution status. In case of a process interruption, due to logical or technical reasons, the system will be able to continue and finish the process later on.

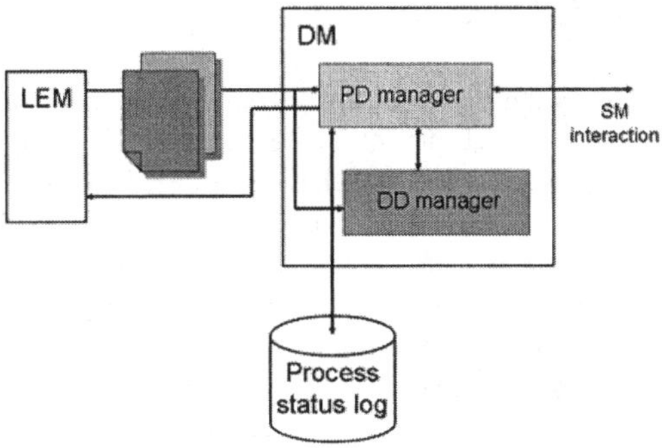

Fig. 4. DM module

3.5 Service Manager

The Service Manager (SM) is the coordinator and manager of all the marketplace interactions with public administrations (Fig. 5), providing DM with a homogenized access to the heterogeneous public administration information systems.

SM has also to mange public administrations subscription to the eGovSM. In order to allow public administrations to subscribe according to their capabilities it provides four subscription profiles. The basic profile (profile 0) refers to administrations that are not able to provide electronic data. The second profile (profile 1) refers to administrations that can provide elementary electronic functionalities (for example access and query to a database). The third profile (profile 2) refers to administrations that are able to provide a richer set of functionalities (for example implement web service technology). The fourth profile (profile 3) refers to administrations that deploy an instance of the eGovSM platform. This will enable future collaborations among eGovSM platforms of different countries or among administrations that will decide (without being obliged) to deploy their own eGovSM instance.

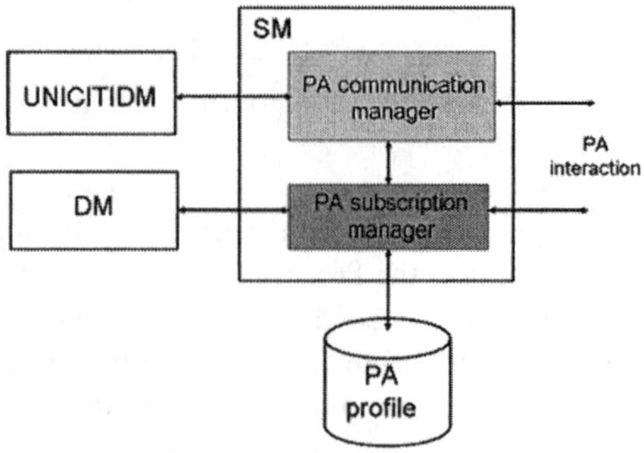

Fig. 5. SM module

4 eGovSM Prototype Development

At present a prototype is being developed in order to test and validate the proposed architecture. The prototype development is based on a .NET platform [17]. The choice of such kind of platform (.NET or J2EE) is dictated by the many offered facilities, for instance the rapidity of development process thanks to the set of provided APIs and high configurability possibilities (system issues, database access, security constraints, etc). Moreover, these platforms are based on the use of XML technologies which offers a high degree of interoperability. Finally, both the platforms fully support Web Services technology which represents the future of distributed developing approach. Our choice of using .NET platform was motivated by the following additional features:

- support of the Office suite, largely used in administrations, which facilitates administrations interaction with eGovSM system
- support of multi-language. .NET platform supports up to 20 different languages allowing the integration of already developed applications by different public administrations
- inclusion of a full API for the treatment of XML Schemas which eases the integration of our XML Schema models
- easy support of the deployment of applications compliant with .NET specifications and support for implementation on Linux ("Mono" project [18]) as well as Windows operating system

Figure 6 shows the citizen access interface to the eGovernment Service Marketplace. The interface is divided into three main parts:

- the first one, on top of the page (Fig. 6, reference 1) provides the service research by keywords and access policy management functionalities
- the second part (Fig. 6, reference 2) provides the complete marketplace life events list, its main purpose is to help citizen navigation in the marketplace
- the third part (Fig. 6, reference 3) is the principal one and it is used by the citizen to search a service, obtain detailed service information, ask for a service and obtain information on ongoing service requests

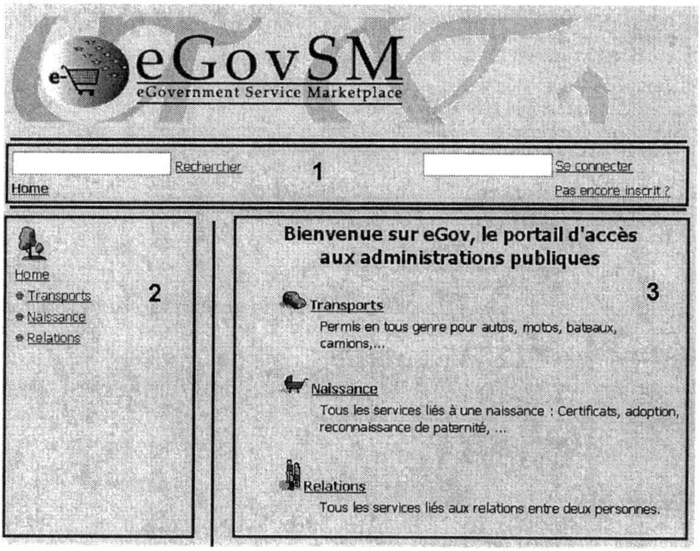

Fig. 6. Access interface of eGovSM portal

It is worth noting that even if the current version of eGovSM Portal is in French, thanks to the system modeling with XML technologies, multilingualism is easily supported. Moreover the system is highly flexible and easy extensible: inserting additional life events or services, for example adding the "marriage" life event, doesn't require to redevelop the application, but it only requires to add the information concerning the new life event in the database respecting the XML Schema specification and the new life event will be automatically included in the eGovernment Service Marketplace and displayed on the portal.

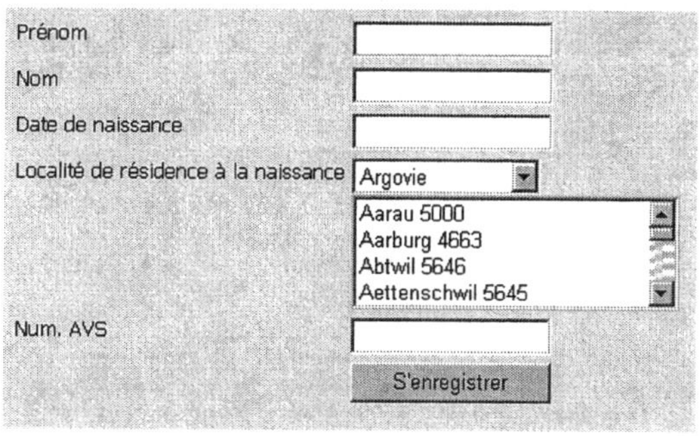

Fig. 7. Example of citizen subscription application form

In order to obtain a service a citizen needs to subscribe to the eGovSM i.e. he has to provide some personal data by filling in the proper subscription form (Fig. 7), and the system will use them to create the citizen UNICITID. Afterwards, the citizen, using this identifier, can connect to the eGovSM and ask for a service.

If a citizen doesn't subscribe to the eGovSM he can only navigate into the marketplace and access to service information but he cannot ask for a service (the "obtenir le service" command is disabled, see Fig. 8, reference 3).

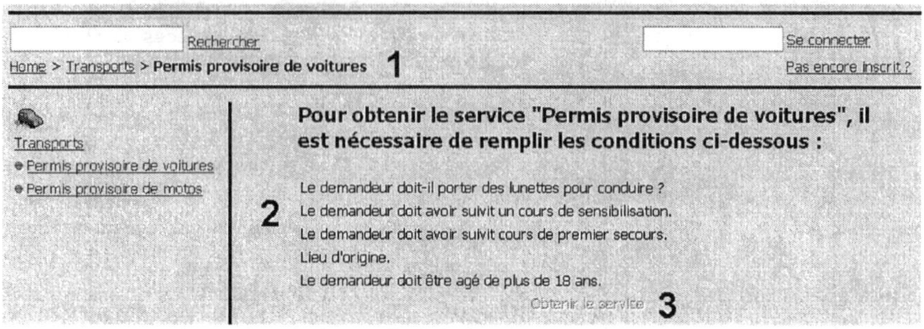

Fig. 8. eGovSM portal: example of service detailed description

In order to help citizen navigation in the eGovSM, just below the search by keyword functionality is displayed the navigation path, making easier for a citizen to "orientate" himself in the marketplace (see Fig. 8, reference 1).

4.1 Prototype Testing Scenario

As prototype testing scenario we have chosen the "obtain driving license" service (in figure 8 "permis provisoire de voitures"). This service requires both the collecting of information coming from different administrations (municipality, hospital and department of motor vehicle) and the satisfaction of different constraints (medical examination, moral requirements). All the information concerning such service (for instance service requirements and constraints) is provided to the citizen (Fig. 8, reference 2). Once the service request is sent, the citizen is informed about service delivery progress (Fig. 9).

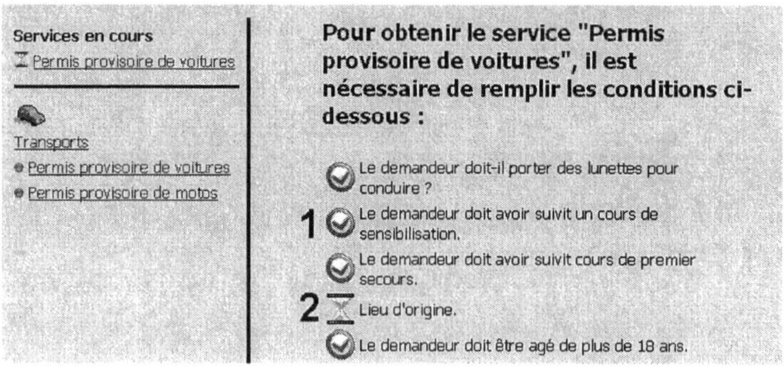

Fig. 9. eGovSM portal: example of service request execution

The "checked" icon (Fig. 9, reference 1) informs him that the specific task has been successfully completed, while the "hourglass" icon (Fig. 9, reference 2) informs him that the system has not completed the task yet. Two other possibilities are taken into account: a "cross" icon meaning that the task has not been successfully completed (for instance a constraints that has not been satisfied) and a "question mark" indicating that the system was not able to find the information among the subscribed administrations. Once the service has been successfully delivered, the marketplace sends a message to the citizen, informing him that he will receive the requested document by ordinary mail from the responsible administration. At present the prototype simulates also the generation of Provisional Driving Licence document (Fig. 10).

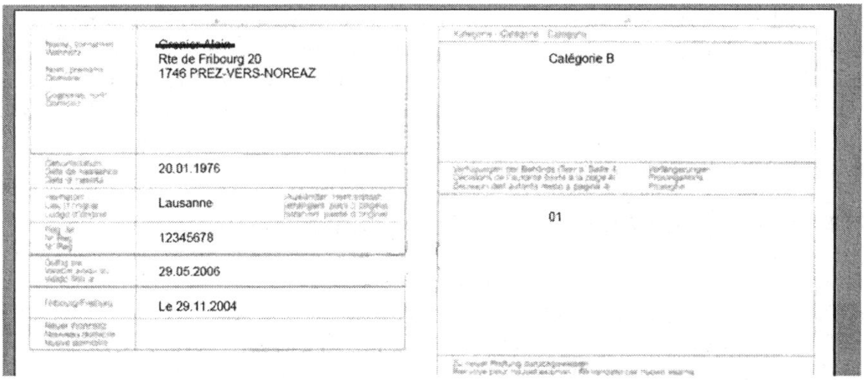

Fig. 10. Example of "Provisional Driving Licence" document generation

5 Conclusions and Future Work

This paper proposes a new approach to deliver services to citizen based on the concept of eGovernment Service Marketplace (eGovSM). The marketplace main objective is to provide quality citizen oriented services i.e. providing services according to citizen needs. In order to do this, the marketplace publishes services according to the life event metaphor, hiding to citizens the complexity of administrative process associated to each service. The eGovSM is formalized using a set of XML Schema models; the architecture itself is based on these models. An implementation of the eGovSM system, currently under development, will constitute the test-bed for further analysis and investigations to improve the architecture.

Further work is needed in order to investigate the use of Grid services to dynamically discover public administrations and their data resources.

At present we are envisaging the possibility of adapting and integrating in our system the results of GRACE European project [20]. The main goal of this project was to develop a Grid based search tool for digital library that is a service to search information through heterogeneous resources stored in geographically distributed collections [21],[22]. Our idea is to adapt the already developed searching mechanism into the e-government domain in order to discover public administrations information resources. This would eventually allow eGovSM platform to dynamically discover and locate relevant public administration resources; for instance, in case of replication of several eGovSM platforms across different countries, we can envisage the use of a Grid discovery service to locate foreign eGovSM platforms.

References

1. IDA report, "Linking up Europe: the Importance of Interoperability for eGovernment Services", European Commission 2003
2. Dipartimento per l'Innovazione e le Tecnologie Allegato n.1, "Front-office e servizi di e-government per cittadini ed imprese", Presidenza del Consiglio dei Ministri, 2002
3. Ireland life event classification: http://www.oasis.gov.ie/siteindex/by_life_event.html
4. The eGOV Project Website: http://www.egov-project.org/
5. G. Kavadias and E. Tambouris, "GovML: A Markup Language for Describing Public Services and Life Events", 4th Working Conference on Knowledge Management in Electronic Government, 2003
6. Deliverable D312 of eGOV project: "Platform integration and deployment report, description of the trials", 2003
7. The FASME Project Website: http://www.fasme.org/index-org.htm
8. Deliverable 6.1 of FASME project: "The Conceptual System Architecture of the FASME Project", 2001
9. Deliverable 6.2 of FASME project: "The FASME Prototype", 2001
10. The EU-PUBLI.com Project Website: http://www.eu-publi.com
11. M. Contenti, A. Termini, M. Mecella and R. Baldoni, "Supporting Inter-Administration Cooperation: The EU-PUBLI.com Approach", 3rd International Conference on Electronic Government, 2004
12. Deliverable D2.1 of EU-PUBLI.com project: "Report on EU-PUBLI.com Architecture Prototype", 2004
13. NIR Project Website: http://www.normeinrete.it/
14. A. Marchetti, F. Megale, E. Seta and F. Vitali, "Using XML as a mean to access legislative documents: Italian and foreign experiences", First European workshop on XML and knowledge management 2002
15. C. Biagioli, E. Francesconi, P. Spinosa and M. Taddei, "The NIR project: Standards and Tools for Legislative Drafting and Legal Document Web Publication", ICAIL 2003- Workshop
16. World Wide Web Consortium, "XML schema part 0: Primer", from http://www.w3.org/TR/xmlschema-0/
17. J. Sharp and J. Jagger, "Microsoft Visual C# .NET step by step", Microsoft press 2003 ISBN: 0735619093
18. Mono Project Website: http://www.mono-project.com/about/index.html
19. O. Zimmermann, M. Tomlinson and S. Peuser, "Perspectives on Web Services: Applying Soap, Wsdl, and Uddi to Real-World Projects (Springer Professional Computing)", Springer-Verlag, 01 October, 2003. ISBN: 3540009140
20. GRACE Project Website: http://www.grace-ist.org/
21. J. Siddiqi, B. Akhgar and M. Naderi, "Towards a Grid Enabled Knowledge Management Services", UK e-Science All Hands Meeting 2003
22. G. Haya, F. Scholze and J. Vigen, "Developing a Grid-Based Search and Categorization Tool", High Energy Physics Libraries Webzine 2003
23. eGovSM Project Website: http://www.eif.ch/projets/egovsm/

Towards Building E-Government on the Grid[1]

Ying Li[1,2], Minglu Li[2], and Yue Chen[1]

[1] Computer Science and Technology School, Soochow University,
Suzhou 215006, China
{ingli, cheny}@suda.edu.cn
[2] Department of Computer Science and Engineering,
Shanghai Jiao Tong University, Shanghai 200030, China
{liying, li-ml}@cs.sjtu.edu.cn

Abstract. This paper introduces the goal of ShanghaiGrid and its sub-project E-government on the Grid. The main existing problem of the E-government is how to integrate each government agency's resources to form cross-agency services for citizens. Grid technique provides an ideal way to solve this problem. The workflow middleware, transaction middleware, and the real-name citizen mailbox are discussed in detail.

1 Background

Shanghai has become the largest economic center and important port city in China, with a land area about 6,340 square kilometers and a population of 16 million people. Household PC penetration rate reached 60.4% and Internet user penetration rate reached 32% in 2003. It is the entrepreneur city of 2010 Shanghai World Expo. The municipal government is working towards building Shanghai into a modern metropolis and into a world economic, financial, trading and shipping center by 2020. It has been always paying attention to the development and establishment of information industry and society. The Information Service technology would enable the municipal government to integrate its information resources dispersed in different organizations and strengthen collaboration and information sharing.

2 The Current State of E-Government in Shanghai

With the development of Information technique, the E-government in Shanghai is developing rapidly and steps into the period of interactive government administration. The main achievements in 2003 are list below [1]:

[1] This paper is supported by 973 project (No.2002CB312002) of China, grand project (No.03dz15027) and key project (No.025115033) of the Science and Technology Commission of Shanghai Municipality. This is the development view, not the official document.

M. Böhlen et al. (Eds.): TCGOV 2005, LNAI 3416, pp. 205 – 212, 2005.

- Shanghai Public Affairs Network has been established and put into operation.
- The portal website of Shanghai-China offers 542 online service items as well as 653 forms for download. Users can personalize their portal and subscribe the information they need. Daily visit to the website reached 180,000 times.
- Four major databases such as population, legal identity, geographical information and macro-economics have taken shape and been put into use.

Although Shanghai's E-government is at the one of the top positions in China, it still has some weakness:

Current E-government infrastructure can not effectively solve the problem of "isolated island of information". The portal website provides more than 500 services, but most of them only provide simple tasks in certain area, cross-domain and cross-department services are rarely found. For the security and policy issue, the information and data can not be shared directly by each agency of the government, which leads to something could be done online must be done manually through each department agency. In some situation, citizens may file over more than ten different forms which download from the portal and manually hand in to several government agencies using traditionally approach, and each form contains similar data. The first reason that caused this situation from technique view is each government agency has its own database and for security and policy reason, the data can not be shared directly with each others, that we called "isolated island of information". The second reason is the trust issue. How can the government agency identify that the one who fill the form online is the right person?

The current web portal service is citizen-centered, which means through the web portal, citizens can get the information they need and feedback their suggestion and feelings back to the government. Using the web portal simplified the delivery of services to citizens. But the web portal service now mainly serves individuals, the Government-to-Business and the Government agency to agency should be further stressed. E-government is not good just for citizens - business benefits too. Like citizens, business wants government to deliver information and services in an easier, cheaper, more accessible and responsive, integrated, and customer-oriented way, so they can more easily meet their legal and regulatory obligations [2].

So how to provide coordinated, seamless and secure access to massive amount of data held across various agencies in a government in heterogeneous environment is a big problem in developing E-government. Another problem is how to build a shared platform to deliver all kinds of services to the user in the city.

3 The Shanghai City Grid Project

Grids offer us a new vision, infrastructure and trend for the coordinated resources sharing, problem solving and services orchestration in dynamic, multi-institutional virtual organizations. With the convergence of business and technology trends, Grid computing is rapidly moving out of its original home in High Performance Computing(HPC) and squarely into the business computing mainstream[3][4].

The Shanghai city Grid which called ShanghaiGrid was put forward in the end of 2003 to enhance the digitalization of the city and face the challenges and capture the opportunities of Grid by the science and technology commission of Shanghai municipality. The participants are Shanghai Jiao Tong University, Tongji University, Fudan University, Shanghai University, Shanghai Supercomputer Center, Shanghai Transportation Information Center, East China Institute of Computer Technology, IBM, Intel, etc. Several other grand fundamental research projects such as NHPCE (1999-2001), CNGrid (2002-2006), ChinaGrid (2002-2005), E-Science Grid (2002-2005), Spatial Information Grid (2001-2005), etc are also carried out in China [5]. The primary goal of ShanghaiGrid is to "develop a set of system software for the information grid and establish an infrastructure for the grid-based applications. By means of flexible, secure, open standards sharing and coordinating of computational resources, data information and dedicated services among virtual organizations, this project will build an information grid tailored for the characteristics of Shanghai [5]."

The ShanghaiGrid project has several sub-projects, E-government Grid is one of them.

4 E-Government on the Grid

4.1 Why Using Grid Technique

We believe that the grid technology would enable the municipal government to integrate its information resources dispersed in different organizations and strengthen collaboration and information sharing. This will be invaluable for improving the efficiency of government and its emergency response speed. Currently, we use Globus Toolkit 3 (GT3) [6] which is the de facto standard in Grid world as the basic infrastructure of the E-government. The main reasons that using the Grid technique and GT3 are listed below:

1. Grid is an ideal way to resolve the problem of "isolated island of information". The real and specific problem that underlies the Grid concept is coordinated resource sharing and problem solving in dynamic, multi-institutional virtual organizations (VO) [3]. If we regard each government agency as an individual VO, then we can apply sophisticated method used in Grid to coordinate each agency's resources which include databases, computational resources, storage resources, etc. Enabling integration of distributed resources is one of the important aspects in E-government.
2. General-purposed, open-standard protocols are widely used in Grid environment. For large distributed applications, it is one of the key issues.
3. GT3 is an open-source middleware for the Grid. Open-source is very important for the Government because government can really know what happens beneath the application, and it can be modified to meet the requirement of the E-government in which we have already designed a set of middleware to support the E-government applications. Moreover, GT3 provides good technical solutions for key problems such as authentication and authorization (implemented as GSI [6]), resource

discovery and monitoring service (implemented as MDS [6]), access and integration of data from separate data sources (implemented as Open Grid Services Architecture Data Access and Integration, OGSA-DAI [7]), etc. These services and libraries lower the complexity and technical threshold in development E-government.

4. Grid can provide super computational power. In most case, E-government do not need such computational power, but in some emergency conditions such as terrorism attack, nature disaster and basic facility misfortune, on the one hand we need real time data integration , on the other hand we need super computational power to quick response to these disasters.
5. Grid can reduce the Total Cost of Ownership (TCO) of the government; fully utilize the IT resources existing in the government.

4.2 E-Government Conceptual Framework

The E-government project was launched at 2003 as a part of the ShanghaiGrid project. Currently we put focus on the design of the middleware which provide common solution for ShanghaiGrid which we will discuss in the next section. The conceptive framework is shown in Fig.1.

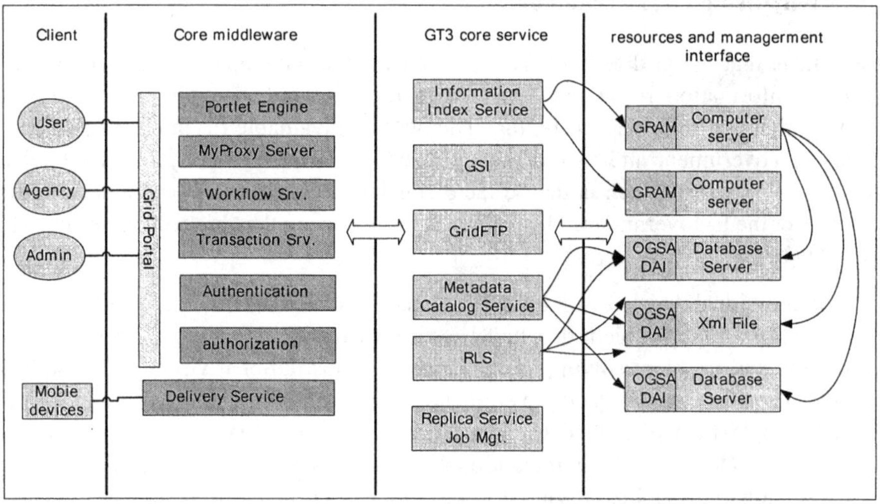

Fig. 1. Conceptual framework

Grid Resource Allocation and Management (GRAM) [13] is used to request and use remote system resources, to submit job and control them within a standard interface. The OGSA-DAI also provides common interface that can be used to access remote database which we will discuss later. GT is used to build Grid Environment, which provides a set of serivces and tools that facilitate the development such as the Metadata Catalog Service (MCS) [14], Replica Location Service (RLS) [15], Grid

Security Infrastructure and etc. A set of core middlewares such as workflow service, transaction service, information service are developed to meet the requirement of building E-government. The delivery service [16] is used to support the mobile device access the Grid environment.

5 The Implementation of Core Middleware

5.1 Workflow Service

First of all, we believe that workflow is very important for E-government. Workflow has grown to be a primary method in managing process. A well pre-defined workflow can provide efficient and easy-to-use service for end users. Users do not need to know the process, but only fill in information, and wait for the results. All the processes are transparent for users.

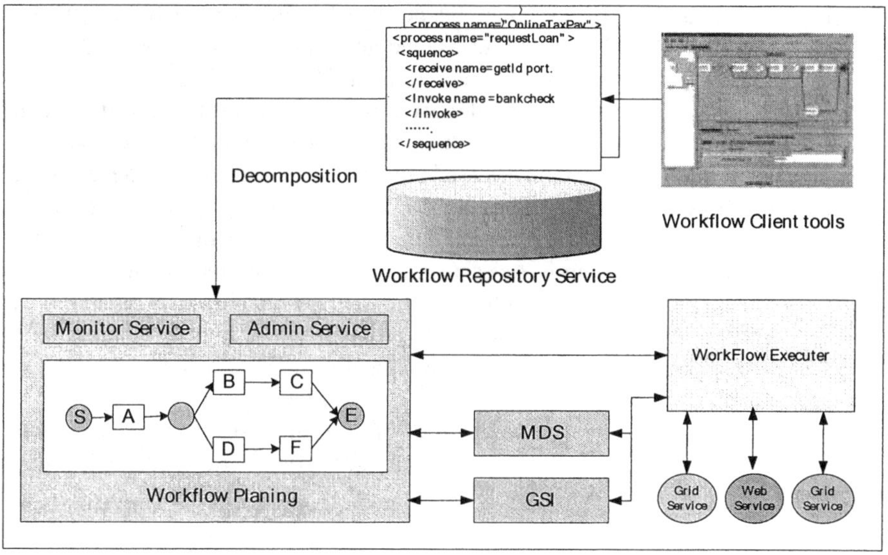

Fig. 2. Workflow middleware

Traditional workflow applications are widely used in government agencies. But they lack the ability of interoperation and rarely across agency. In Grid environment, we can compose Web Services or Grid Services distributed in various government agencies into one workflow. Fig.2 shows the framework of the workflow management system. More detailed work could be found in [8]. So far, workflows are composed by administrators using the existing Grid Services and web services with Business Process Execution Language for Web Services (BPEL4WS) [9] . A set of client tools were developed to support that mission.

5.2 Transaction Support

In Grid environment, transaction support is another big issue. We divide transaction as:

i) Atomic transactions (AT). AT is used to coordinate activities having short-lived application and executed within limited trust domains.
ii) Compensation transaction (CT). CT is used to coordinate activities having long-lived application. In order to improve the concurrency, a compensation model must be applied in CT.

The detail implementation of the transaction model can be found in [10].

5.3 Authentication and Authorization

Grid provides a common security infrastructure, but there still exists the problem of authentication: how we can justify Id with a real person?

The Real-Name Citizen Mailbox (RNCM) is now carried out by the Shanghai Government as well as the Real-Name Company Mailbox. Citizens in Shanghai can freely register a desired mailbox account, but he/she must go to certain place setting up by government agency to fill in some forms, and government officer there will manually checks the ID card to activate the mail account. Through this approach, government can use the mailbox account to identify a real person. Citizen can use his/her mailbox receives the bills, endowment insurances, medicare and other information. In the first ten days when this method released, about 60,000 citizens registered and activated the mail account [11]. This is valuable information in E-government. In future, if every person who registered the mailbox could get CA certification, much more applications could be applied in E-government. Currently, the user's mailbox account and password would be the basic authentication method for citizen. Although using real-name mailbox is a good way to solve the problem of the citizens' identification, privacy issue must be taken into account. Investigation shows 100% citizen show interesting in the mailbox and about 50% person consider the privacy issue [11].

MyProxy [12] is used in Grid environment as the repository storing Grid credentials. User using portal user name and password could get certain Grid credential through MyProxy.

5.4 Data Integration

To integrate various data among each government agency in a secure environment is a big challenge. Traditionally, government would like to build data warehouses to collect data from each government agency and present these read-only data to the public. But this approach limits the data exchange.

To do real time data integration, we use the OGSA-DAI to integrate data from each government agency. Fig. 3 shows a data proxy server used as a getaway of current existing database. The GT provides a basic grid environment such as security, authentication. Through the Grid data service factory, Grid applications can create a Grid data service, which could be used to query, update the data in the specialist database. Using these methods, the existing client system could not be modified and the policy could be easily maintained.

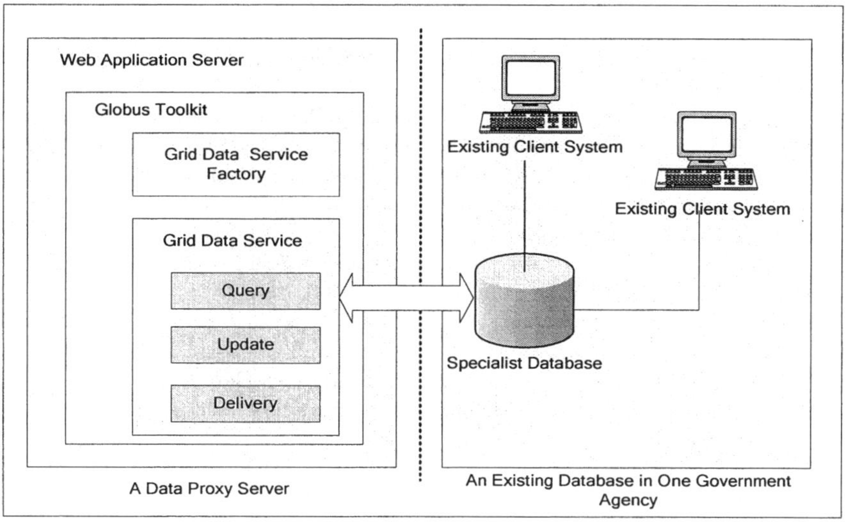

Fig. 3. Using data proxy server to share data among each government agency in Grid

6 Discussions

The frequent asked question about our model is why using Grid services and not Web Services? It is a difficult question. We know most work could be done in the same way by using Web services. But first of all, the project is about developing a Grid platform to support various Grid applications which include E-government. Second, we think that GT gives us a uniform solution or framework to meet the needs of developing such applications and we can use a set of open-source projects to avoid security issues such as potential 'back door' problem.

7 Conclusions

In this paper we introduce the ShanghaiGrid project and its sub-project E-government on the Grid. Some key middlewares are introduced in detail. Although Grid technique and the de facto standard Globus Tookit are developing quickly, we hold the confidence that Grid technique is an ideal way to build large distributed applications. A real-name citizen mailbox is introduced to solve the problem of how to identify real person with his electric id. The E-government project is ongoing project which we put much work on the common middleware currently that could be applied in Shanghai-Grid environment as well as E-government project.

References

1. Briefing on the Informatization Progress in Shanghai: www.sh.gov.cn
2. E-Government Strategy, http://www.whitehouse.gov
3. I. Foster, C. Kesselman, etc., Grid Services for Distributed System Integration. Computer, 35(6), 2002
4. Minerva Yeung, Intel and Grid computing, International Forum on Digital city and City Grid, Nov. 2003
5. Minglu Li, ShanghaiGrid in Action: The First Stage Projects towards Digital City and City Grid, The Second International Workshop on Grid and Cooperative Computing, 2003
6. V. Welch, F. Siebenlist, et al., Security for Grid Services, Twelfth International Symposium on High Performance Distributed Computing (HPDC-12), IEEE Press, June 2003
7. OGSA-DAI : http://www.ogsadai.org.uk
8. Ying Li, Minglu Li, etc., A workflow service model on ShanghaiGrid, 2004 IEEE International Conference on Services Computing (SCC 2004), 2004
9. Business Process Execution Language for Web Services Version 1.1, http://www-106.ibm.com/developerworks/webservices/library/ws-bpel/
10. Jiadi Yu, A Framework for Implementing Transactions on Gird Service, The 4th International Conference on Computer and Information Technology, 2004
11. http://www.smmail.cn
12. Novotny J, An online credential repository for the Grid:My Proxy, Proceedings 10th IEEE Symposiumon High-Performance Distributed Computing, 2001
13. GRAM: Key Concepts, http://www-unix.globus.org/toolkit/docs/3.2/gram/key/index.html, 2004
14. The Metadata Catalog Service, http://www.isi.edu/~deelman/MCS/, 2004
15. H. Stockinger, A. Samar, et al., File and Object Replication in Data Grids, Journal of Cluster Computing, 5(3), pp. 305-314, 2002

Applying the ISO RM-ODP Standard in E-Government

B. Meneklis[1], A. Kaliontzoglou[2,3], D. Polemi[1], and C. Douligeris[1]

[1] University of Piraeus, Department of Informatics, Karaoli & Dimitriou 80 Str., 185 34 Piraeus, Greece
{bmenekl, dpolemi, cdoulig}@unipi.gr

[2] National Technical University of Athens, School of Electrical & Computer Engineering, Heroon Polytechniou 9, Zografou, 157 73 Athens, Greece
akalion@softlab.ntua.gr

[3] Expertnet S.A., Security Research Department, Achilleos 1 Str. & Kifissias 244 Ave., Halandri, 152 31 Athens, Greece

Abstract. During the last years, governmental organizations have invested considerable effort and financial resources in the development and adoption of e-government services. In order to sustain the quality of their services, governmental organizations need to solve the problem of efficient and secure electronic exchange and processing of governmental documents and data. A major difficulty in this distributed deployment is the fact that these interconnected systems are heterogeneous and they may operate in multiple organisational domains. This paper demonstrates how the ISO/RM-ODP standard offers a general framework to design and develop an open distributed system attuned to e-government environments. This is subsequently supported by a high level case study of how this standard can be applied in the case of a system designed for small to medium sized European municipalities.

1 Introduction

During the last years, governmental organizations at all levels have invested considerable effort and financial resources in the development and adoption of e-government services. The first era of e-government activities included web site hosting and management. The more sophisticated of them even allowed limited transactions online. The next generation of e-government applications demand is for interactive service delivery, secure transactions, cross-border interactions and a homogenous framework for e-government systems communication. Moreover, the meaningful interaction between governmental organisations in order to provide more sophisticated services to citizens is an ever increasing demand. In order to sustain the quality of their services, governmental organizations need to solve the problem of efficient and secure electronic exchange and processing of governmental documents and data. It is of utmost importance that these services are provided in a way that is easily adoptable and accessible by all citizens, businesses and other public bodies.

Governmental organizations may be distributed within a small area (e.g. a town hall and other municipal offices) or a larger one (across a wider geographical area) and they have to interact with citizens and other organizations. Therefore, they need

M. Böhlen et al. (Eds.): TCGOV 2005, LNAI 3416, pp. 213 – 224, 2005.

distributed system architectures that address all of their specific requirements. The development of a distributed processing system is based on the understanding of the system's functionality and the efficient representation and structure of the system's fundamental information. A major difficulty in this distributed deployment is the fact that interconnected systems are heterogeneous and they may operate in multiple organisational domains.

ISO/RM-ODP (International Standard Organization/Reference Model of Open Distributed Processing) [1], OMG/CORBA (Object Modelling Group/Common Object Request Broker Architecture) [2] and OSF/DCE (Open Software Foundation/Distributed Computing Environment) [3] are examples of standards for open distributed processing that cope with distributed systems heterogeneity and openness. RM-ODP in particular offers a general framework to design and develop an open distributed system and has received an increasing acceptance by the scientific and commercial community over the last years [4], [5], [6], [7]. A recent proposal on an integrated framework for the development of open distributed systems is presented in [8]. This approach is based on UML and the Prototype Verification System (PVS) [9]. It extends the UML notation by assigning formal semantics to the graphical modelling constructs of UML notation. However, it focuses mainly on the system's state transitions, whereas RM-ODP is a more generic framework. Furthermore RM-ODP is closer to human natural language for specifications and thus it is easier to comprehend and use. Therefore, this paper proposes the selection of the RM-ODP standard for the design of an open distributed architecture attuned to e-government. A high level case study of how this standard can be applied in the case of a system for European municipalities is also presented.

The paper is structured as follows: Section 2 gives an overview of the RM-ODP standard and presents its fundamental characteristics; Section 3 presents the specific requirements of governmental organizations that have to be addressed by a system architecture tuned to this environment; Section 4 shows how RM-ODP and its features fulfil these requirements; Section 5 presents a high-level case study of how the RM-ODP standard is being used for the design of a system targeting municipalities and, finally, Section 6 draws conclusions.

2 An Overview of the RM-ODP Standard

ISO and ITU-T, have joined efforts to produce a common framework for developing Open Distributed Processing (ODP) systems that benefit from the distribution of information processing services in environments of heterogeneous technology resources and multiple domains. The ODP Reference Model (RM-ODP) is the result of this effort. RM-ODP creates an architecture that integrates support for distribution, interworking and portability and describes systems that support heterogeneous processing and information exchange between groups within an organization as well as between cooperating organizations [1].

RM-ODP defines the basic concepts of distributed processing, identifies the characteristics that qualify a system as an ODP system and introduces five viewpoints which are used in order to specify an ODP system. A viewpoint on a system is an abstraction of that system (or a part of it) that gives a specification of the whole (or part) of the system related to a particular set of concerns. RM-ODP also defines a viewpoint language that is used to describe each viewpoint. In effect, each viewpoint language provides a set of definitions of concepts and rules enabling the specification of the system from its corresponding viewpoint. Furthermore, RM-ODP provides a framework for checking the system's conformance to the specification and the consistency between the different viewpoints and defines certain functions that are required to support an ODP system. Finally, it presents a system architecture which provides distribution transparencies between system applications. Distribution transparencies enable complexities associated with system distribution to be hidden from applications when they are irrelevant to their purpose [1].

The five viewpoints and their corresponding languages, as defined in RM-ODP, that are used to specify an ODP system are the following:

- Enterprise Viewpoint, a viewpoint of an ODP system and its environment that focuses on the policies which define the behaviour of an object in the system as well as the system's purpose of operation and scope. This viewpoint describes the system from the aspect of what it is required to do. The Enterprise Language is used to describe the Enterprise Viewpoint.
- Information Viewpoint, a viewpoint which specifies and describes the information entities that are communicated, stored and processed in the system. The Information Language is used to describe the Information Viewpoint.
- Computational Viewpoint, a viewpoint which focuses on the way distribution of processing is achieved. The Computational Language is used to describe the Computational Viewpoint.
- Engineering Viewpoint, a viewpoint which focuses on the way different objects of the system use to communicate with each other and the resources that are needed to accomplish this communication. The Engineering Language is used to describe the Engineering Viewpoint.
- Technology Viewpoint, a viewpoint which focuses on the selected technology of a system. The Technology Language is used to describe the Technology Viewpoint.

The system specification of RM-ODP is based on an object modelling approach. This approach provides a formalization of well-established design practices of abstraction and encapsulation.

3 Architectural Requirements of E-Government Systems

This section presents the architectural requirements posed by the systems of governmental organizations wishing to engage themselves in e-government.

3.1 Interoperability

It is hard to achieve interoperability in a governmental organization system due to various forms of heterogeneity that exist in governmental environments. The interconnection of governmental organizations that use various platforms and systems is a difficult task requiring easily identifiable and publishable e-services, as well as clear interfaces for the establishment of secure and reliable connection points. Furthermore, even within the boundaries of a single public organization, a system may be spread across a geographical area. For example, in the case of a municipality, the administrative offices may be located further away from the cultural centre or the town hall. The fact that there is a large number of smaller public organizations makes interoperability between their systems even more challenging.

3.2 Scalability

Enhanced scalability is also a requirement that must be met by the infrastructure of governmental organizations due to the large number of citizens that need to be served with acceptable levels of quality of service. Furthermore, public administrations are continuously in the process of deploying electronically traditional paper-based services as well as new services. An e-government system should be able to host an increasing number of e-services.

3.3 Security and Trust

E-government services have to be secure so that government employees and users trust the system and feel confident in using it. Governmental organizations need to design, implement and operate a secure electronic environment for the exchange and processing of governmental e-documents, access to repositories of information for authorized public servants and hosting of shared applications.

3.4 User-Friendliness and Accessibility

A governmental organization environment has to be easily accessible by civil servants and citizens alike, with user-friendly interfaces covering the needs of various types of users. These requirements stem from the fact that governmental organizations have to serve a large number of citizens with diverse information technology training. It is very important that any complex operations be transparent to the end user. A governmental environment should also offer good international support for foreign citizens as well as support for disabled citizens.

3.5 Cost Considerations

Minimization of costs, both of deployment and of operation, is a very important requirement for the successful deployment of e-Government services. This issue is of even greater importance to smaller public organizations, which frequently do not have the same resources as their larger counterparts, in terms of finances and personnel.

3.6 Transparent Automated Processing

Automated processing is linked to the operational costs of e-Government services for governmental organizations, since they have to satisfy the requests of many people with only a handful of personnel under normal operation.

3.7 Cross-Border Characteristics

An ever increasing number of European citizens change their location to work in other countries. This means that there is a definite demand to support them in administrative procedures that include cross-border communication. In cross-border services there is exchange of information, data or documents between citizens and public administrations (C2G, G2G) in an international context and across administrative boundaries.

3.8 Limited Training

There is always a need for training of the government employees during and after the deployment of e-services. Especially in the case of larger governmental organisations that employ hundreds or thousands of people. Training could prove to be an extremely costly and complicated procedure. The provision of limited required training is of utmost importance for the minimisation of time that has to be invested by the staff before they operate any new system.

3.9 Compatibility with Existing Infrastructures

Citizens and governmental organisations have already established software, hardware and network infrastructures. These infrastructures nevertheless can seldom interoperate within a distributed architecture comprising of several organizations. Therefore, such an architecture must provide a compatibility layer with existing and legacy systems so that their current data can be used, since the complete replacement of legacy systems is usually prohibitively costly.

3.10 Mobility Aspects

Mobile access affords citizens the use of services detached from strict office hours and independent of locations. Mobility and independence add real value to these services. Services with mobile aspects are of interest to facilitate access to the era of mobile Internet services for governmental organizations, which means in particular a device-independent access to services (by cellular phone, PDA, etc.).

4 Suitability of RM-ODP for E-Government

The use of RM-ODP as a standard for designing a distributed system enables and supports the development of systems with certain desired characteristics. These characteristics, which are depicted in Table 1 and described below, satisfy all the requirements of a distributed governmental organization system.

Table 1. RM-ODP features against e-Government requirements

	Openness	Integration	Flexibility	Modularity	Federation	Interoperability	QoS	Security	Transparency
Interoperability	√	√			√				
Scalability	√					√	√		
Security/Trust								√	
User Friendliness/Accessibility							√		√
Cost Considerations		√		√					
Transparent Automated Processing			√						√
Cross-border Characteristics	√				√				
Limited Training						√			
Compatibility with Existing Infrastructures		√	√						
Mobility Aspects			√						

4.1 Openness

Openness of a system makes possible the change of the processing node at which a component is situated without the need for modification. This feature supports the scalability needs of governmental organization applications. Such applications must satisfy the demands of a continuously expanding group of citizens and so the machines that are used to host these applications should be upgraded on a regular basis. Openness of the system's design ensures that the migration of the applications to the new hardware and software will be achieved in a smooth fashion.

Openness also ensures the meaningful interaction between components, effectively covering the needs for interoperability and cross-border characteristics. The basis for interoperability is the communication and interaction between the different parts of the system. Furthermore, in order to achieve a satisfying interworking level between the different systems, cross-border characteristics must be integrated into them. The meaningful interaction of all components and the freedom to setup applications at any given node of the system (which are both provided by the system's openness) are essential in satisfying this goal.

4.2 Integration

Integrated systems incorporate various other systems and resources into a whole without costly ad-hoc solutions. Systems with different architectures and different resources are fine-tuned to work together. Integrated systems deal with the problem of heterogeneity and thus satisfy the governmental organization applications' demands for interoperability and compatibility with existing infrastructures. Furthermore, effectively incorporating existing systems and resources into new architectures lowers the cost of the migration procedure to the new solutions. This last feature is of great importance to governmental organizations since their financial resources are very often extremely restricted.

4.3 Flexibility

Flexible systems are capable both of evolving and of accommodating the existence and the continuous operation of existing legacy systems. A major requirement of a governmental organization is the use of the major part of its existing infrastructure when a new IT solution is introduced. Flexibility addresses the requirement of compatibility with existing infrastructure. Furthermore, changes in the system's architecture and topology are easily adopted when a system is flexible. The majority of modern e-Government solutions focus on the interaction with the citizens through more contemporary media (such as palmtop PCs or cellular phones) [7], [10], [11], which is a feature that requires mobile interfaces. Thus, flexibility helps to deal with transparent automated processing and mobility.

4.4 Modularity

The parts of a modular system are autonomous but interrelated. Modularity supports the reuse of previously developed software modules which in turn lowers the cost of a system's development. Governmental organizations can benefit dearly from this option since it comes in terms with their need for low cost solutions, especially when upgrading an existing system or trying to develop a completely new application for newly introduced services.

4.5 Federation

A federated system can be combined with other systems from different administrative or technical domains in order to achieve a single objective. Federated systems are satisfying the needs for interoperability and cross-border characteristics. Oftentimes, a governmental organization's offices and departments are not located in the same building or even the same area however the system of a governmental organization expands to all its premises and its components must interoperate effectively. Federation addresses this need successfully.

4.6 Manageability

ODP based systems are highly manageable. This means that they allow easy monitoring, control and management of resources and processes in order to support configuration, QoS and accounting policies. This directly affects the scalability of the system, since it allows easier management of the increasing number of users and helps with keeping the system operational in spite of the limited personnel training capabilities in governmental organizations.

4.7 Quality of Service (QoS)

Systems designed and implemented based on ODP take into serious account quality of service needs. They intend to cover provision of timeliness, availability and reliability in the context of resources (local and remote) and interactions, together with provision of fault tolerance that allows the remainder of a distributed system to continue to operate in the event of failure of some part. This means that ODP systems offer high availability, dependability and accessibility, which is very important when the system has to be continuously up and running to cover the diverse needs of a large number of citizens throughout the day. The QoS directly affects how users perceive the interaction with the services.

4.8 Security

ODP proposes a strong security framework for architectures, ensuring that system facilities and data are protected against unauthorized access and respect privacy. Certain functions are defined that are fundamental and widely applicable to the development of ODP systems. More specifically, ODP defines security functions (such as access control function, authentication function, integrity function and key-management function) which help organize and orchestrate the development and application of security policies within an ODP system. Security requirements posed by governmental organizations are generally strict and they are made often more difficult to meet in modern governmental infrastructures by the increasing needs for remoteness of interactions and mobility of parts of the system and of the system users.

4.9 Transparency

ODP has as primary goal the integration of transparency in systems. Transparency hides the details and differences in mechanisms used to overcome problems caused by distribution of applications. Aspects of distribution which should be masked (totally or partially) include: heterogeneity of supporting software and hardware, location and mobility of components and mechanisms to achieve the required level of QoS in the face of failures (e.g. replication, migration, checkpointing, etc.). RM-ODP introduces a set of distribution transparencies in order to support this need. Transparency is critical for a number of governmental organization requirements: user friendliness in order to hide application and processing details from users and automated processing so that a small number of civil servants and public workers can manage systems successfully.

5 The eMayor Case Study

The practical suitability of RM-ODP in e-government is demonstrated in this paper through an actual implementation. In the IST eMayor project [12], we have opted to use RM-ODP in the design and implementation of an e-government platform attuned to the environment of European Small to Medium Sized Governmental Organizations (SMGOs) [13], which in the eMayor case include several European municipalities. During the design phase we have applied RM-ODP concepts and principles in combination with UML to define a system that addresses the various needs of the municipalities, as they have been identified during the analysis and user requirements collection phase of the project [14]. This section presents the initial design concepts we have used in eMayor with examples from the first three RM-ODP viewpoints (Enterprise, Information and Computational).

As part of the Enterprise Viewpoint, eMayor has identified the main stakeholders in the municipality community domain and the roles they assume in the environment, such as the citizens and their delegates and the civil servants working in the municipalities or other organizations. Furthermore, we have identified the business processes that take place in the communities along with the activities of the various roles in them and we have described the policies and constraints related to the processes. This has led to the definition of Enterprise objects. One example is the PKI sub-community within the wider eMayor community that comprises the Regional CAs, a Pan-European CA, a Pan-European Validation Authority and the various registered Users (registered Civil Servant etc.) as shown in figure 1:

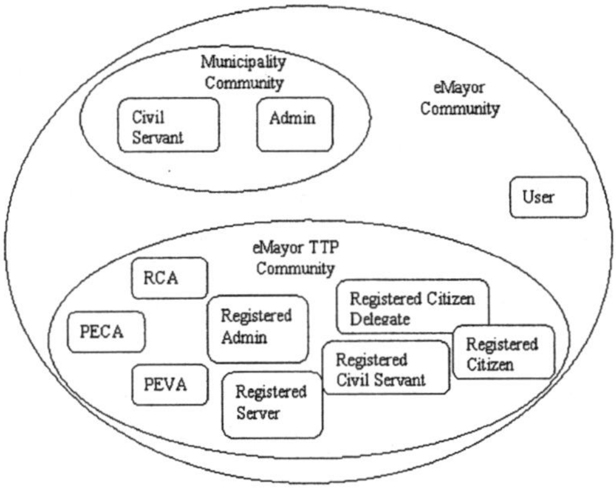

Fig. 1. The eMayor TTP community

The Enterprise Viewpoint defines all relationships among the entities and the processes they follow, e.g. for the PKI framework setup of an end-entity or the Certificate Validation. The specifications utilize free-form diagrams as well as UML diagrams (Use Case, Class, Collaboration and Activity diagrams) for the representation of the above concepts.

The Information Viewpoint has presented and analyzed various Information Objects that will be used by the eMayor platforms and communicated between them. Examples of such information objects are the User Credentials, User Profiles, Service Requests, a Registry etc. Class diagrams are used in order to represent the Information Objects, such as the one in figure 2 for the Service Request Information Object:

The Service Request object represents requests made for a specific service offered by the eMayor system such as certificate issuance, registration to the taxes services or a notification about the state of processing of another request. As can be seen in Figure 2, the subclasses of the Service Request Information Object are: Certificate

Request, Registry Request and Notification Request. Information Objects pass from various states as part of their life-cycle and the state transitions of the Information Objects are depicted in the Information Viewpoint using UML StateChart diagrams.

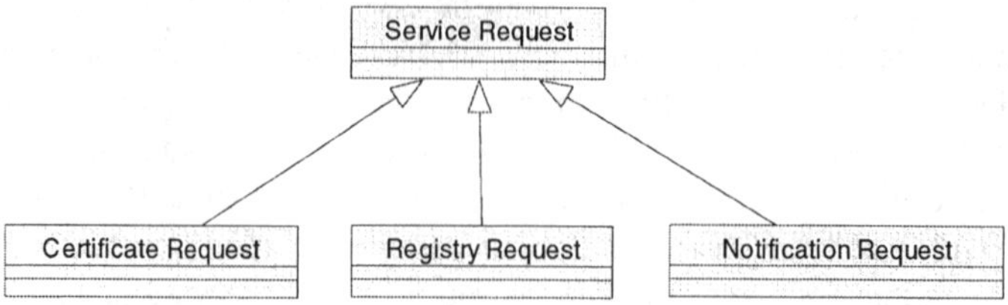

Fig. 2. Service Request Information Object

The Computational Viewpoint demonstrates the overall architecture of the eMayor system, divides the computational functionalities in distinct packages and depicts their interconnection and collaboration. The packages are elaborated with further details showing the Interfaces exposed by each package, as well as the internal mechanisms and modules. The computational packages identified so far are User Interface, Output Processing, Policy Enforcement, Format Transformation, Content Routing, Service Handling, Legacy Systems Adaptation and Persistent Storage as shown in figure 3:

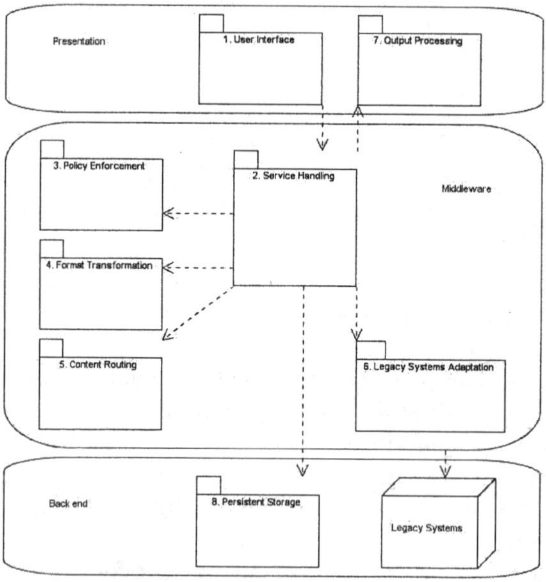

Fig. 3. The eMayor system architecture

The User Interface communicates with the Service Handling for the actual processing of the service and with the Policy Enforcement for access control, the security mechanisms and the policies of the municipalities' legal frameworks. Service Handling represents the core of the system and has dependencies to all other packages. It communicates with the Policy Enforcement (e.g. for access control, encryption and digital signature of documents and messages, etc.). The Format Transformation is responsible for transforming legal documents from a country-bound local format to a universal format for transport within the eMayor environment and vice versa. Content Routing provides the routing functionality for forwarding requests and legal documents to another municipality. The Legacy Systems Adaptation is the linking point with the legacy systems of the municipalities. The Persistent Storage modules handle storage to the file system or databases. Finally, Output Processing provides support for outputting information to devices, printing and notification services.

The specifications are supported by UML Component and Class diagrams for the presentation of Interfaces and Classes and Sequence diagrams for the presentation of sequences of actions involving multiple computational components.

6 Conclusions

In this paper we have demonstrated the suitability of the RM-ODP standard in the design of open distributed architectures attuned to e-government environments. The use of RM-ODP as the preferred framework encourages a clear separation of concerns (through the different viewpoint specifications), which in turn leads to a better understanding of the problems being addressed during the design of such a system. In the context of the eMayor project, we have applied RM-ODP concepts in order to design an e-government platform covering the needs of small to medium sized European municipalities. This paper has presented the initial status of the work towards this direction by giving a short overview of the first three viewpoints of the specification.

Acknowledgements

The authors would like to thank the E.C. for its support in funding the eMayor project (IST-2004-507217) and all the members of the project consortium for valuable discussions.

References

1. ITU-T Rec. X.901 | ISO/IEC 10746-1,2,3, "Reference Model for Open Distributed Processing – Part 1: Overview, Part 2 Foundations, Part 3 Architecture", 1996-98
2. Object Modelling Group/Common Object Request Broker Architecture, http://www.omg.org
3. Open Software Foundations / Distributed Computing Environment, http://www.osf.org
4. C.A. Costa, J.A. Harding, R.I.M Young, "The application of UML and an open distributed process framework to information system design", Computers in Industry, Elsevier Science, 2001, pp. 33-48

5. M. A. Nankman, L. J.M. Nieuwenhuis, "Specification of a distributed storage system", Computer Communications, Elsevier Science, 1996, pp. 30-38
6. M. Blinov, A. Patel, "An application of the reference model for open distributed processing to electronic brokerage", Computer Standards and Interfaces, Elsevier Science, 2003, pp. 411-425
7. German Federal Ministry of Interior, "SAGA - Standards and Architectures for e-government Applications, version 2.0", December 2003
8. I. Traore, D. Aredo, H. Ye, "An integrated framework for formal development of open distributed systems", Information and Software Technology, Elsevier Science, 2004, pp. 281-286
9. S. Owre, N. Sankar, J. Rushby, D. W. Stringer-Calvert, "PVS Language Reference v. 2.3", September 1999
10. Project "eGovernment for Development", 2004, http://www.egov4dev.org/topic4.htm
11. National Electronic Commerce Coordinating Council (NECCC), "M-Government: The Convergence of Wireless Technologies and e-Government", 2004, http://www.ec3.org/Downloads/2001/m-Government_ED.pdf
12. E.C. 6th Framework Programme, Electronic and Secure Municipal Administration for European Citizens – eMayor, IST-2004-507217, 2004. Available form: www.emayor.org
13. A.Kaliontzoglou, P. Sklavos, T. Karantjias, D. Polemi, "A secure e-Gorvenment platform architecture for small to medium sized public organizations", Electronic Commerce Research & Applications, Elsevier Science, 2004 (Article in Press)
14. eMayor consortium, "Deliverable D2.1: Municipal Services – Analysis, Requirements and Usage scenarios", eMayor project, IST-2004-507217, 2004, available from www.emayor.org

Quixote: Supporting Group Decisions Through the Web

J.A. Rubio, D. Rios Insua, J. Rios, and E. Fernandez

Decision Engineering Lab,
U. Rey Juan Carlos-DMR Consulting Foundation, Spain
jarubio@bayes.escet.urjc.es
{drios, jmrios, e.fernandez}@escet.urjc.es

Abstract. We describe a web-based architecture to support participation in group decision making. Emphasis is placed on security aspects related with our architecture, designed to enhance trust on the system.

1 Introduction

There is a current debate and many attempts to provide on-line support to democratic processes, so as to change the way people interact with governments. As an example, the URJC Strategic Planning Council is collecting feedback via computer from the URJC community (students, staff, lecturers) on how the university should be organized by year 2010.

Indeed, we view Internet as an opportunity to bridge the gap between governors and governees. Our current democratic institutions stem from times in which transportation and communications were difficult and time consuming. With the time, politics have evolved little and politicians have developed a style in which, except at political campaigns, they have little feedback from citizens.

We believe, however, that most ideas so far relating Internet and politics, are directed towards *facilitating* traditional political methods through new technologies: a political Internet discussion forum, rather than a political meeting; fundraising through the web, rather than through letters or telephone calls;... Our feeling is that there are ways to *transform*, rather than facilitate, politics: there are much more constructive and creative ways of involving citizens. Indeed, it is a tenet of ours that involving and communicating with the stakeholders at all stages of a decision making process leads to more consensual and better quality decisions.

Independently of Information Technology, many authors have discussed on pros and cons of increasing participation in political decision making, with the traditional debate between participatory and representative democracy. In [8] Pateman describes

> The current and widely accepted theory of democracy attaches very little importance to the concept of participation, and even emphasizes the dangers inherent in widespread popular participation in politics. The

M. Böhlen et al. (Eds.): TCGOV 2005, LNAI 3416, pp. 225–234, 2005.

> recent upsurge of demands for participation raises the question of its place in a realistic modern theory of democracy.

The discussion has indeed been enhanced by the perceived potentiality of new technologies to affect democratic processes. As an example, Brzezinski, see [1], even as early as in 1970, claimed

> We should increasingly ensure true participation in decisions which seem too complex and too far apart from the common citizen.

These ideas have been put to a extreme by the, now called, *cyberutopians*, one example of whom is Morris who, in his VOTE.COM, see [7], implicitly suggests a permanent e-referendum system:

> As direct democracy takes root, the American voter will become more involved and active. We do not have to wait anymore for the next election to express our view while the Congress makes decisions for us. We do not have to wait for a call from a pollster to speak our piece. We are going to take the Internet and tell our representatives what to do whenever we feel like it.

To counterbalance, we would like to just point out a recent note in *Wired*, referring to Bobbitt's *The Shield of Achilles* and entitled *Technology is killing democracy*!!!

We follow here an intermediate path, presenting a web based architecture aimed at distributing rationality to better resolve political decision making. By this, we mean helping groups through the web facilitating them the use of decision and negotiation analysis methods, see [2]. Ideologically, a close view is given in [5]:

> It's not a matter of allowing masses of individuals to vote instantaneously on simple questions posed by telegenic demagogues, but to promote collective and continuous elaboration of solutions and their cooperative solution, as close as possible to concerned groups.

The structure of the paper is as follows. In section 2, we provide a general description of our architecture and methods. We then provide a brief outline of its implementation. A crucial issue refers to trust and confidence in the system, which we promote through the use of cryptographically secure open truthful exchange (CSOTE) methods as compared with the FOTE and POTE frameworks described by Raiffa in [9]. We end up with a brief discussion.

2 Our Architecture

To some extent, we propose migrating to Internet the philosophy and methodology of decision conferencing, see [6], to support group decision processes. This may be seen as an asynchronous Internet based implementation of decision conferences. Note that standard decision conferences are synchronous and could be implemented, e.g., through videoconferences. But that would be yet another application of new technologies to standard political approaches.

In our architecture, QUIXOTE, the decision analysis would be carried out by a decision analyst or team of analysts on a master system for the decision making problem owner (the president of a government, the CEO of a company,...). The system would provide support for the entire decision making cycle, using computer aided brainstorming, problem structuring techniques and various quantitative modelling techniques such as probability assessment tools, multi-attribute utility elicitation or outranking methods, as appropriate to an application. At various stages of the process, some or all of the models would be fed onto a server, which could be accessed by different stakeholders and the general public. The level of access would vary from stakeholder to stakeholder and at different stages of the decision process. Initially, the server provides pages simply stating that an issue is being addressed and inviting comments and submissions via email. Later, pages are developed actively which allow users to interact with the model to explore the implications of their individual perspectives and judgements. These explorations could be kept private if the user so wishes, but more usefully provide the problem owner with a summary of the stakeholders' views in a format entirely compatible with the decision model. The interactions are supported by the Internet with confidence built in through a cryptographically secure open truthful exchange (CSOTE) approach.

Note that, typically, as the problem owner and various stakeholders would have different values and beliefs, they would opt for different alternatives. It might be beneficial, therefore, to enter into a negotiation round, in which a more consensual solution might be sought. This, again, is supported through the web. Finally, in some contexts, it could happen that no consensus is reached after negotiations: we may appeal to a voting scheme supported as a way to fix a course of action.

From a methodological point of view, the key part of our system is the negotiation module. We describe now the underlying methods. Specifically, we aim at supporting a group of n persons facing a joint decision making problem. Each person i, has to choose an action a_i from a feasible set A_i, $i = 1, \ldots, n$. This includes the case in which $A_i = A$, for all i, and parties should commonly implement the same alternative $a_i = a$. He also faces consequences $c_i(a_1, \ldots, a_i, \ldots, a_n, \theta)$, which depend on the actions of all persons and some common states of nature θ. We assume that each person has his own utility function u_i and probability distribution p_i and is a expected utility maximiser, see [2] for a full exposition on this. This means that, assuming that the other persons fix their actions $a_1, \ldots, a_{i-1}, a_{i+1}, \ldots, a_n$, the i-th negotiator will aim at solving the problem

$$\max_{a_i \in A_i} \Psi(a_i) = \int u_i(a_1, ..., a_{i-1}, a_i, a_{i+1}, ..., a_n, \theta) p_i(\theta) d\theta \tag{1}$$

Therefore, we have the expected utility of each joint action $a = (a_1, \ldots, a_n)$, obtained by each person and its optimal alternative.

In general, negotiators will not be able to maximise their expected utility simultaneously and we should enter into some kind of negotiation. We shall assume that the set of negotiators behave optimally in a Pareto sense. To wit, we

Table 1. This table shows the expected utility of each joint action a obtained by each person and its optimal alternative

		Negotiator			
		1	2		n
Action	a	$\Psi_1(a)$	$\Psi_2(a)$	...	$\Psi_n(a)$
Optimal Action		$a_1^\star$	$a_2^\star$		$a_n^\star$

say that the choice $a = (a_1, \dots, a_n)$ is dominated by the choice $b = (b_1, \dots, b_n)$ if $\Psi_i(a) \leq \Psi_i(b), \forall i = 1, \dots, n$, with strict inequality for one of the negotiators. When convenient, we shall use $\Psi(a)$ to designate $(\Psi_1(a), \dots, \Psi_n(a))$. In consequence, an agreement should be sought within the nondominated set, as it guarantees that there is no other alternative unanimously preferred by all the negotiators. Typically, the set of nondominated solutions does not, however, include a unique solution. To help the negotiators in reaching consensus within the nondominated set, we propose using a modification of Raiffa's balanced increment method, which we briefly summarise here, see [10] for full details.

To do so, we need the concept of bliss point associated with an alternative a.

Definition 1. *For a given solution a, and each negotiator i, $i = 1, \dots, n$, consider the expected utility Ψ_i^* of a feasible solution $x^i \in A$ which maximises the i-th's negotiator expected utility subject to $\Psi_j(x^i) \geq \Psi_j(a)$, $\forall j \neq i$. The bliss point associated with a is $(\Psi_1^*, \dots, \Psi_n^*)$.*

To fully associate it with a, we designate it as $(\Psi_1^*(a), \dots, \Psi_n^*(a)) = \Psi^*(a)$. Note that, in some sense, the bliss point represents the ideal expected utilities achievable, should the current alternative or status quo be a. The diagonal linking $\Psi(a)$ and $\Psi^*(a)$, which we designate by $[\Psi(a), \Psi^*(a)]$, provides a balanced improvement direction, there being a nondominated alternative $K[\Psi(a)]$ whose associated expected utilities are in such diagonal, under appropriate technical conditions.

We now define the concept of a balanced increment solution, see [9] for further details.

Definition 2. *The balanced increment solution $R_\alpha(\Psi^0)$ is the limit point in the utility set of the sequence $\{\Psi^t\}$ defined by:*

$$\Psi^t = \Psi^{t-1} + \alpha(\Psi(K[\Psi^{t-1}]) - \Psi^{t-1}) \tag{2}$$

where $\alpha \in (0, 1)$ and Ψ^0 represents the utilities achieved if negotiators fail to agree. A continuous version of the solution is obtained by letting $\alpha \to 0$, $R_\alpha(\Psi^0) \to R(\Psi^0)$.

Technically, the continuous BIM solution is obtained as a double limit. We implement it in the discrete version by starting at a given solution, computing its bliss point and moving a certain fraction, say one eighth, in the line segment between Ψ^t and $\Psi(K[\Psi^t])$. Also, at each step we may offer $K[\Psi^t]$, the nondominated solution in the diagonal with the bliss point, to reach a consensus if parties accept it. We also introduce, as stopping rule, that the process terminates when the parties agree on the solution $K[\Psi^t]$ offered, or Ψ^t is close enough, in terms of expected utilities, to the nondominated set, reaching no consensus.

To sum up, the modified balanced increment algorithm we implement is

1. Initialisation:
   - Start at a^0 with $\Psi^0 = \Psi(a^0)$, $t = 0$.
   - Compute $K[\Psi^0]$ (the nondominated solution in the diagonal with the bliss point).
2. Repeat
   - If parties agree on $K[\Psi^t]$, stop.
   - If Ψ^t is close to $K[\Psi^t]$, stop.
   - Ow, move fixed fraction α in $[\Psi^t, \Psi(K[\Psi^t])]$, obtaining Ψ^{t+1}.
   - $t = t + 1$
   - Compute bliss point of Ψ^t and $K[\Psi^t]$.

As indicated, when the algorithm does not lead to an agreement we may apply a voting scheme.

3 System Modules

The current implementation uses a web based system using the LAMP (Linux, Apache, MySQL, PHP) environment. There are three basic types of users:

- the problem owner, the entity which aims at solving a decision making problem, structures and publicizes it.
- the stakeholders or participants, who provide input (beliefs, preferences, votes) to the decision making process.
- the administrator, who takes technical care of the process development, from supporting the problem owner to structure the problem, to providing access rights to stakeholders, to defining time windows for voting.

Appropriate safety mechanisms are available, as we shall later describe in detail. In particular, participants will use secure validation mechanisms. The following system modules are included:

3.1 Problem Structuring

The system includes a module that allows the problem owner to build an influence diagram to structure the incumbent decision making problem, in terms of uncertainty, decision and value nodes. If needed, the problem owner may be aided by the administrator to build the diagram, which acts, in this case, as a decision analyst or facilitator. The module allows for:

- Adding and removing nodes.
- Adding and removing arcs.
- Editing and modifying the tables associated with the nodes.
- Saving a diagram for later evaluation.

The stakeholders will use the same structure to explore issues of interest concerning the problem.

3.2 Preference Modelling

The system includes a module that allows users to build their preference model. It is assumed that any user (problem owner, stakeholder) may build his own utility function, given the usability of the model developed. Each user will assess his utility function privately and communicate it to the system. Without much loss of generality, we assume that the users' preferences may be modelled through a weighted additive utility function, see [2] for details. The system allows for:

- Specification of basic properties of (multiple) objectives by the problem owner: number of objectives, their scale and range, whether the objective is to be minimised or maximised. It is assumed that all participants will share these objectives; some participants may disregard some of these objectives, by giving them zero weight.
- Assessment of each component utility function. For each objective, and each user, the utility of some attribute values is assessed with the probability equivalent method. Then, a concave-convex or convex-concave (piecewise exponential) utility function is fitted through least squares.
- Assessment of the weights of the additive utility function, again with the aid of the probability equivalent method.
- Saving the utility function for later purposes.

Users are expected to provide their preferences within a given time window. If agreed, summaries and or comparisons of utility functions may be obtained.

3.3 Problem Solving

Once with the preferences of a participant, we may proceed to compute his optimal alternative. For that purpose, the system includes a module that allows users to evaluate the influence diagram, based on his utility function, to obtain his preferred maximum expected utility course of action. The problem owner may find out his optimal alternative privately, as the stakeholders may do. If wished, they may make public their solutions. Alternatively, summaries of the obtained solutions may be provided.

3.4 Negotiating

Typically, the various parties involved (problem owner, stakeholders) will reach different optimal solutions. Consequently, a round of negotiations may be undertaken to try to reach a consensus. The negotiation is driven by our modification of the balanced increment method as explained above.

At each iteration, the system offers a solution to participants and, if accepted, it stops, that being a consensus. Alternatively, the procedure stops when two of the subsequent solutions offered are close enough. If the last one is accepted, a consensus is reached. At each iteration, users are expected to communicate whether they accept or not an offer within a given time window.

3.5 Voting

Our (automatic) negotiating scheme converges to a nondominated solution, but it is conceivable that participants may not accept such solution, neither the sequence of solutions offered. This deadlock could be solved through voting. For that reason, our system includes a voting module, which permits the design of a voting session, with several voting rules available, and its execution. Specifically, the voting rules implemented are:

- Plurality: Participants may vote for just one alternative. The winner is that receiving the biggest number of votes.
- Approval voting: Participants may provide at most one vote to as many alternatives as they feel like. The winner is that receiving the biggest number of votes.
- Cumulative voting: Each voter has m votes which he may distribute however he wants among the alternatives. The winner is that receiving the biggest number of votes.
- Borda count: Given that there are k alternatives, Borda count asks voters to rank them increasingly (k to the best,..., 1 to the worst alternative).The winner is that receiving the biggest number of votes.

Users are expected to vote within a specific a time window.

4 Csote Concepts in Quixote

It has been frequently discussed that a critical issue in applications related with e-democracy and e-government is the confidence and trust among system users. This is, for example, stressed in the recent report *Development of the Information Society in Spain (2002)*. For this reason, we have built on what we call the CSOTE framework, see [11] for details, in contrast with the FOTE and POTE frameworks described by Raiffa, see [9].

By CSOTE, we understand cryptographically secure open truthful exchange of information among participants and the system, enhancing reliability of all processes, achieved through:

- Confidentiality of system data, which will be accessible to only authorised parts.
- Communications security, therefore protecting bidirectional channels user-system.
- Data integrity, so that they are only modifiable by data owners.
- Accesibility, that is, potential ways of mitigating system attacks.

These issues may be achieved through cryptographical methods. Specifically, we shall sketch how public key cryptographical methods, see [3, 4], aid us in developing a more open, flexible and reliable framework for negotiations, in which the involved parts may reveal their real objectives and, possibly, achieve satisfactory agreements. This also aids us in automating negotiation processes as we may support all the issues we are interested in.

4.1 Interaction with the System

As we have mentioned, at various points, a participant must send his information to the system and, possibly, may wish to obtain a summary of the opinions of other users. For these purposes we use:

- *Partial secret revealing techniques.* They are based on the global knowledge of a function $f(x_1, ..., x_n)$, with each party knowing and revealing only a part b_i of the information about the domain of f and ignoring the rest, their aim being finding out the value of $f(b_1, ..., b_n)$. Two applications are:
  - Facilitate comparison of the utility functions of participants, should they wish to, with minimal revealing of information. For example, should they all have constant risk averse utility functions, they could find out which of them is more risk averse.
  - In a similar fashion, users could compare their weightings of various objectives, without revealing their exact values, to find out, e.g., which participant gives bigger importance to a criterion.
- *Zero knowledge techniques.* Specifically, we use ElGamal's cryptosystem as a basis to determine the equality or inequality of two discrete logarithms and build knowledge proofs to verify users' information. One application is:
  - The users may obtain any kind of partial information about other users' preferences, with them revealing no more than the necessary information, and therefore protecting the rest of it. The users might undertake these tests interactively, or not. In the latter case, the preferences and actions of the users could be verified publicly by system users.

4.2 Negotiation Phase

CSOTE is specially relevant during the negotiation rounds, the key part of our architecture. Once the users' preferences have been stored, we may proceed to look for alternatives satisfying the involved parts. For that purpose, we use the following methods:

- *(k, n)-threshold schemes.* An interesting piece of information (a secret) is divided in parts, in such a way that we only need to know $k < n$ of them to recover the secret. We can do this using modular arithmetic, the Chinese Remainder Theorem or Lagrange coefficients. We apply them, for example, to ensure that the choice of a certain action is made only if k users out of the existing n go for it.
- *Selling of secrets techniques.* With them, a buyer chooses what (secrets) to buy, with the seller not knowing what he has sold. We use the RSA cryptosystem, generating k cryptosystems, with special features, together with Jacobi symbols to enhance transparency in negotiations. To wit, with them, users may undertake exchanges and, moreover, negotiate over any set of elements or objectives in a transparent manner. Moreover, each user has the possibility of weighting their choices, as well the importance of the elements to negotiate.

- *Matching protocols.* We use ElGamal's cryptosystem, Diffie-Hellman's key agreement technique and zero knowledge proofs to check correctness of computations. For example, we undertake privately computations about users' objectives or preferences protecting locally the users' data. We could also use them to create groups with certain affinity in terms of their choices.
- *Verifiable public auction schemes.* We use mechanisms such as signatures to prove knowledge of a discrete logarithm as a mechanism for anonymous signatures, which serves us as anonymous certifier for all users. In such a way, for example, we induce auction schemes generating honesty, as, at each round, we would only need to know the highest stake. As the process would be totally blind to users, they would leave apart strategic behavior.
- *Strong proxy signatures.* With them, a user may delegate all his negotiation capacity to an agent, which would take care of such process within the system. Note that with the use of delegated signatures, we could condensate in a single agent the requirements of a large number of users, which may be specially relevant if many users take place in the negotiation process, as could happen, e.g., in a participatory budget elaboration.

4.3 Voting Phase

Again CSOTE supports the voting phase, in case no consensus is reached during negotiations. To undertake this process, we must take into account the transparency, the capacity of the user to verify his vote and, last but not least, the capacity to avoid that a voter is not able to give a proof of his vote to another entity, so as to avoid vote dealing.

Indeed, this is an area in which developers of e-voting systems are spending lots of effort. However, most known schemes are based on critical assumptions which make them vulnerable, including the existence of truthful communications and a truthful third part. Alternatively, we opt for using schemes which include a Tamper-Proof Randomizer (TPR), which allows us to randomise votes, leaving aside the need to use reliable third parts.

Once this randomisation has taken place, we prove to the voter the correctness of the process through re-encryptation proofs through a designated verifier, which, if appropriate, generates a valid vote certificate based on validity and difference proofs. Finally, these proofs and the final vote will be signed digitally by the voter's TPR to provide credibility to the vote.

5 Conclusions

We have outlined issues concerting trust and confidence, which are key in e-democracy applications, within a web based group decision support system. Case studies within the area of participatory budget elaboration will be reported in a forthcoming paper.

Acknowledgments

Research supported by grants from MEC(TSI2004-06801-C04-01), the Decision Engineering Lab (URJC - DMR Consulting Foundation) and the ESF-TED program.

References

1. Brzezinski, Z.: *Between two ages: America's role in the technotronic era.* Viking Press (1970)
2. French, S.,Rios-Insua, D.: *Statistical Decision Theory.* Arnold (2000)
3. Goldreich, O.: *Modern Cryptography, Probabilistic Proofs and Pseudorandomness.* Springer-Verlag (1999)
4. Lee, B.: *Zero-knowledge proofs, digital signature variants, and their applications.* PhD thesis, ICU University (2001)
5. Levy, P.: *L'Intelligence Collective.* Dunod (1995)
6. McCartt, A., Rohrbough, J.: Evaluating group decision support system efectiveness. *Decision Support Systems* **5** (1989) 243–253
7. Morris, D.: *Vote.com: How Big-Money Lobbyists and the Media are Losing Their Influence, and the Internet is Giving Power to the People.* Renaissance Books (1999)
8. Pateman, C.: *Participation and Democratic Theory.* Cambridge University Press (1970)
9. Raiffa, H.: *Negotiation Analysis.* Harvard UP (2002)
10. J. Rios and D. Rios-Insua. Negotiation over influence diagrams. Tech Rep on Statictis and Decison Sciences, Rey Juan Carlos University (2004)
11. Rubio, J. A.: Sobre métodos criptográficos en análisis de negociaciones. Master tesis, Rey Juan Carlos University (2004)

UNICAP*: Efficient Decision Support for Academic Resource and Capacity Management

Svetlana Vinnik and Marc H. Scholl

Department of Computer & Information Science
University of Konstanz, Box D 188,
78457 Konstanz
{vinnik, scholl}@inf.uni-konstanz.de

Abstract. Growing complexity of the data and processes to be managed, as well as the transition from strict governmental regulation towards autonomy make academic institutions a significant consumer of advanced software solutions. Strategic management requires a comprehensive analysis of large data volumes from heterogeneous sources, often imprecise and incomplete. Our aim is to assist university policy-makers in building strategic action plans in the field of resource distribution and teaching capacity utilization through explicit modeling and testing of diverse development strategies. The proposed decision support system (DSS), called UNICAP (acronym for university's capacity planning), is aimed at optimizing the academic decision making by allowing simulation and evaluation of strategic plans. We conclude by presenting a case study, carried by the planning experts of our university who used UNICAP filled with "real" university's data.

1 Introduction

Universities[1] throughout the world operate with large amounts of data, typically scattered across multiple, non-centralized information systems and applications. Support of administrative decision-making and knowledge discovery from such decentralized data flows require data-unifying OLAP-enabled applications [5] designed with close eye on the specific needs of the academic domain. The emergence of the Internet and other information technologies has been crucial in altering the operational environment of universities world-wide. Being public institutions and as such subject to governmental control, on the one hand, and exposed to globalization and economic accountability and performance challenges, on the other hand, universities turn into a significant consumer of e-government solutions, in particular of *intelligent systems* that provide advice to the policy-makers to assist in strategic and operational decision-making.

---

* Work reported in this paper is executed within a joint project of the University of Konstanz (Germany) and the Ministry of Science, Research and the Arts of the State of Baden-Württemberg (Germany).

[1] The term "*university*" is used here generally to refer to all types of public higher education institutions.

M. Böhlen et al. (Eds.): TCGOV 2005, LNAI 3416, pp. 235 – 246, 2005.

1.1 Background

Our research was inspired by the evolving reforms of the higher education system in Germany aimed at improving the performance of academic institutions in changing economic conditions [18]. Since similar challenges are faced by the universities throughout the world, we expect our contribution to be valid for the international academic community. Concerns about the efficiency of higher education have given rise to new models and systems aimed at facilitating strategic decision making, primarily concerned with resource allocation and performance analysis [3], [15]. Rapid globalization of the higher education enables a shift from individual solutions to more general strategic management models which can be appropriately adjusted to serve the needs of a particular institution. International comparative studies [8], [15], [20] have outlined a number of general performance descriptors (e.g. staff per student ratio, teaching load, student retention quote. etc.) which can parameterize such models.

Our proposed DSS is concerned with strategic planning of academic resources, their distribution and consumption. The common economic principle of demand-supply equilibrium builds up the core of the underlying computational model. *Educational supply* (ES) describes the available teaching capacities in terms of the amount of services (i.e., courses, supervision, etc.). *Educational demand* (ED) measures the consumption of those services by students according to their individual curricula.

Prior to the admission of new students, the *admission capacity* (AC) of every program, i.e. the upper bound on the number of beginners it can accommodate, must be announced. Accurate models and systems are necessary to avoid aggravating strategic errors which may lead to wasting expensive resources, long-term misbalance of the university's operation, and the failure to provide the required quality of education.

AC is derived from the educational resources released due to regular exmatriculation of some portion of the students and is distributed among all offered study programs according to the university's admission policy. Determining the AC from the available resources is called a *supply-oriented* approach as educational capacity is considered to be fixed. An alternative approach, called *demand-oriented*, reverses the computation by allowing the a-priori specification of the desired admission numbers and determining the required educational supply.

In Germany, a supply-oriented admission capacity model, introduced in 1972, is still enforced by the legislation. Its concept, trading-off accuracy and correctness for simplicity and rapid application with no software support, is obviously out-of-date and is being subjected to growing criticism in academic circles. The condition to fully utilize the available capacities implies adherence to the minimum staff-per-student ratios [18] disabling university-specific variations. Ensuring the general compatibility with the current approach, we propose a more flexible computational model.

The focus of our work has thereby been twofold: a) to propose the methodology for admission capacity planning, and b) to implement it in a software product. The remainder of the paper is structured as follows: in Section 2 we present the methodology for determining the admission capacity; Section 3 contains the requirements specification for the UNICAP architecture and functionality; implementation issues are presented in Section 4 followed by presentation of a case study in Section 5. We conclude by a summary of our contribution and proposals for future work.

1.2 Related Work

First efforts to develop academic planning applications go back to the 60-ies, with CAMPUS project [17] being an example of an ambitious multi-parameter simulation model which reached the marking phase in the 70-ies but had to be abandoned due to its overly complicated applicability and high input data requirements.

In the 90-ies, there was a renewed enthusiasm in developing software solutions for the academic domain. Decision support and expert systems were offered in the fields of course/exam/instructor scheduling [7], program assessment [6], resource allocation [3], [11], [15], admission policy [9], [12], managing university funds, academic advising, and strategic planning [2], [10], to name a few.

We expect the next generation of academic applications to increasingly incorporate OLAP and knowledge discovery functionalities and offer user-friendly interfaces in order to be adopted by larger target group of decision makers.

The major provider of academic software solutions in Germany is a non-profit organization HIS[2] [13]. However, HIS applications tend to target distinct administrative areas (e.g., personnel, finance, and facility management) related to the operational rather than to the strategic issues. We see a great potential for DSS with elaborate analysis and visualization techniques in the field of academic strategic management.

As for the computational model, similar approaches to determining educational capacities are apparently used in other countries [1], [2].

2 Methodology

To enable backward compatibility with the current practices for the purpose of "painless" introduction of the UNICAP in the hosting university and elsewhere in German legal environment, we used the official German admission capacity model as a starting point for the new approach. However, our concept has been made more generic by introducing multiple fine-tuning parameters, taking into account international indicators (as defined by authoritative organizations such as OECD [19] and CHEPS [4]) and ensuring the system's adjustability to varying conditions.

2.1 Basic Definitions

The hierarchal structure of a university is defined as follows: basic division units are the *faculties*, each responsible for one scientific discipline[3]. Faculties dispose of the teaching resources classified into *position groups*, such as professor, associate professor, research assistant, etc. Each position group has a *teaching load* assigned to it, which is the number of academic hours per week invested in curricular activities, denoted *semester periods per week* (SPW). The total of the teaching loads of a faculty, adjusted appropriately in case of special conditions (legal decrements, using external resources) and multiplied with the number of terms per academic year, expresses that faculty's annual educational capacity, or supply, denoted ES_{total}.

[2] HIS stands for Higher-Education Information System Corp.

[3] Multidisciplinary faculties are divided into sub-faculties to process each discipline separately.

Education is organized into *study programs* (henceforth addressed as *programs*) characterized by a *subject* and a *degree*. Some degree types allow multiple subjects (major and minor ones) to be combined. To account for this division we add a *priority* attribute with the value domain {major | secondary | N/A}.

Each faculty is said to "own" the programs offering its discipline and to supervise the students registered therein. Servicing the supervised students is called *self-contribution* of the faculty whereas services to the students from other faculties form its *exports*. Reversely, the parts of the program's curriculum referring to the services of other faculties form the *imports* of its supervising faculty. The increasingly popular class of *interdisciplinary* programs (i.e., coordinated by multiple faculties) has to be handled separately since the division of their costs is negotiated among the participating faculties. The total amount of services provided to supervised and non-supervised students describes the faculty's total educational demand, denoted ED_{total}.

Abstracting from different admission approaches (e.g., each term or once per year) we speak of the *annual* admission capacity. To determine the admission numbers for the faculty's programs from its ES_{total}, it is necessary to specify the admission scenario, i.e., the portion of each supervised program, called its *partition*, in the total number of the faculty's beginners (for example, 0.5:0.3:0.2 partitioning between bachelor's, master's, and PhD degrees, respectively).

Since most faculties have non-zero exports, it appears impossible to determine their admission numbers without considering the expected admission numbers of all importing faculties as the latter determine the amount of exported services. To balance the entire system one must construct the so-called *interdependency*, or export-import, *matrix* and solve the resulting system of equations.

2.2 Cost Model

We start out by describing balanced resource utilization for any single faculty:

$$ES_{total} = ED_{self-contribution} + ED_{exports} + ED_{interdisciplinary} \quad . \tag{1}$$

$ED_{self\text{-}contribution}$ measured in SPW is the portion consumed by the supervised students. To transform the available SPW into the number of students, $ED_{self\text{-}contribution}$ has to be divided by the costs of educating a student in a particular program, called the *curricular value* (CV)[4]. The CV of a particular program describes the necessary per-student teaching load for the entire duration of the study and can be computed from the program's curriculum. For example, if the curriculum consists of 100 SPW and the average teacher-student relation is 1:50, the resulting CV equals 2 SPW per student. Curricula consist of modules specifying the courses and other activities (internships, team projects, course papers etc.) to be attended or performed. For simplicity, we refer to all curricular activities as *courses*.

A course is characterized by its type T (lecture, seminar, tutorial, etc), volume in SPW and a *support relation* which upper-bounds the number of course participants.

[4] In Germany this value is called *standard-curricular-value* as it is assigned by the supervising ministries to ensure inter-university comparability of degrees offered in the same discipline.

The SPW of each course of type *T* are translated into the SPW of the teaching load by weighing the former with an adjustment coefficient adj_T, ranging between 0 and 1. adj_T is defined for each course type and expresses the preparation-intensiveness on behalf of the teaching staff for that type. For example, types such as lecture or tutorial are mapped in a straightforward matter whereas internship or laboratory supervision is multiplied with 0.5 due to expected lower preparation costs.

Curricular modules typically define domains of courses to choose from, not the courses themselves. Some modules are defined in a highly flexible way, for instance, allowing students to choose a lecture or a seminar, or a course of a non-supervising faculty. The costs of such modules will depend on the actually selected courses and may vary from one academic year to another. We suggest analyzing the course attendance and examinations statistics accumulated over previous years in order to make accurate assumptions for such uncertain cost areas.

We can now describe the per-student costs of attending a given course *C* of type *T* with the maximum number of participants *N*, which is the course's *curricular value*:

$$CV_{C_T} = \frac{SPW_{C_T} \times adj_T}{N_{C_T}} . \tag{2}$$

The CV of the entire program results from the sum of the CV of all the courses in its curriculum. Parts of this value, grouped by the supplier faculty, describe that faculty's *curricular quota* (CQ) in the program. The faculty's CQ in any supervised program is considered its *self-contribution quota*; other faculties' quotas are the program's *imports*. The sum of the self-contribution CQs of all supervised programs weighed with their respective programs' partitions produces the faculty's *weighted self-contribution curricular quota* $\overline{CQ}^F$ which is the weighted mean per-student costs of being educated in the faculty's programs.

2.3 Matrix-Based Solution

The AC of faculty *F* is obtained by dividing the self-contribution part of its resources, as defined in (1), by its weighted self-contribution curricular quota:

$$AC^F = \frac{ES^F_{total} - ED^F_{exports} - ED^F_{interdisciplinary}}{\overline{CQ}^F} . \tag{3}$$

The AC of a single supervised program *P* can now be computed as follows:

$$AC^{P\,in\,F} = \frac{AC^F \times Q^{P\,in\,F}}{LF^P} , \tag{4}$$

with $Q^{P\ in\ F}$ being *P*'s partition and LF^P as a *loss factor* (ranging from 0 to 1) to account for the fact that only a subset of the beginners will actually complete their studies while the rest change the program or quit. Division by the LF increases the admission numbers, thus preventing capacity under-utilization due to shrinking student numbers in higher semesters. We adopt the computationally correct *Hamburger Model* [21] for determining loss factors and will give no further explanations due to space constraints.

The problem of computing the admission capacity of a single faculty lies in the inability to evaluate the $ED^F_{exports}$ component in (3) as long as the admission numbers of each importing program are unknown:

$$ED^F_{exports} = \sum\nolimits_{\forall\ P\ not\ in\ F} \left(AC^P \times LF^P \times CQ^{F\ in\ P}\right). \tag{5}$$

The value of $ED^F_{interdisciplinary}$, however, can be estimated in a straightforward manner since the admission numbers of all interdisciplinary programs are known in advance:

$$ED^F_{interdisciplinary} = \sum\nolimits_{\forall\ interdisciplinary\ P} \left(AC^P \times LF^P \times CQ^{F\ in\ P}\right). \tag{6}$$

We proceed by constructing a system of linear equations which contains an equation for each faculty according to (1). The unknowns are the admission capacities of the faculties so that their number matches the number of equations. For any faculty F_i, i=1, …, N, with N as the total number of faculties, we denote F_i's AC as x_i (x_i, i=1, …, N, are the unknowns of the system) and rewrite (1) into a linear equation:

$$\sum_{j=1}^{N}\left(\sum\nolimits_{\forall P\ in\ F_j} CQ^{F_i\ in\ P} \times Q^{P\ in\ F_j}\right)\times x_j = ES^{F_i}_{total} - ED^{F_i}_{interdisciplinary}\ . \tag{7}$$

This just sets the total expected educational demand of F_i, summarized over all "demanding" programs grouped by supervising faculty, to match F_i's supply.

Within the demand-oriented approach, the desired AC^P is specified for each program P and the required AC of the supervising faculty F_i is determined as follows:

$$AC^{F_i}_{required} = \sum\nolimits_{\forall P\ in\ F_i} AC^{P\ in\ F_i} \times LF^P\ . \tag{8}$$

By substituting x_j in (7) with its specified value according to (8) and applying some reductions, we arrive at the computation of the required supply for faculty F_i:

$$ES^{F_i}_{required} = \sum_{j=1}^{N}\left(\sum\nolimits_{\forall P\ in\ F_j} CQ^{F_i\ in\ P} \times AC^{P\ in\ F_j} \times LF^P\right). \tag{9}$$

$ES_{required}$ of any single faculty can be calculated separately since (9) contains a single unknown.

The last step is to check the capacity utilization ratio for the specified admission numbers, which is the ratio between the required and the available educational resources. Full utilization will result in the value of 1.0 (i.e., 100%); under- and over-utilization are characterized by values less than and greater than 1, respectively. In German practice, a slight under-utilization (down to 80%) is considered even desirable. Generally, some deviation from the optimum can be acceptable. Exact bounds of the utilization tolerance interval should be set by the policy-makers. We suggest the default interval of [0.8, 1.1].

3 Requirements Specification

Among the target group's requirements, the basic one is for the system to be comprehensible and usable even for untrained users, familiar with the methodology, but not possessing any programming, database or other in-depth computer related skills.

The desired output of the program is a report containing the input data, the relevant interim results and the output in a form appropriate for decision support. Users should be able to modify the input and change the report's options in order to simulate various scenarios and to compare them. Decision support is realized by allowing the users to test their proposals "on the fly" and thus become aware of their effects and implications. Fig. 1 depicts the general procedure of creating a report. The two output options *5a* and *5b* stand for the choice between the supply- and the demand-oriented approaches, respectively, whereas simulation mode is realized by enabling repeated modification of the input data for iterating to an acceptable solution.

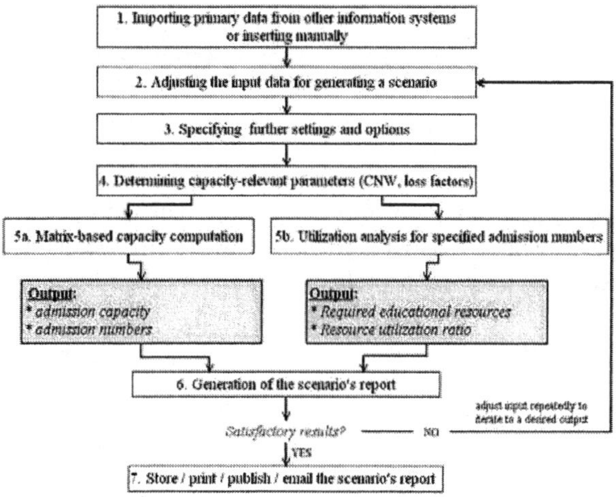

Fig. 1. Modeling the overall UNICAP's functionality

3.1 Data Management

Since the data is expected to be intensively queried and processed for simulation purposes, it is indispensable to back-end our tool with an efficient data management system. The required data originating from multiple sources has to be merged in the model's autonomous database. Once the actual data sources and formats are known, the required data transfer routines can be automated. Data centralization will also allow us to detect and fix contingent inconsistencies.

The relational model, extended to account for some German legislative implications, is shown in Fig. 2. Notice that the modeled data comprises a single computational period (i.e., academic year) which is appropriate for annual planning. To preserve and accumulate the data from previous years, the outdated data sets are placed each into its own database instance building up a data pool for data-mining purposes.

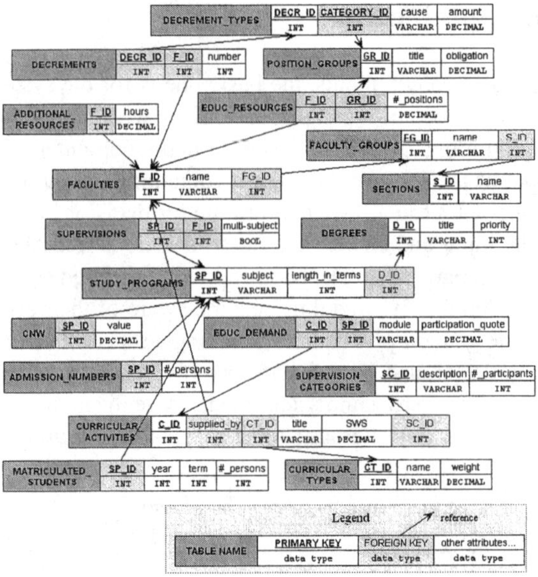

Fig. 2. UNICAP's relational data model

To prevent the central data pool from becoming damaged through unskillful manipulations, modifying access may be granted only to a competent user with administrative privileges. Ordinary users operate exclusively on their local data copies.

3.2 User Management

The target group is rather heterogeneous: the primary users are the experts who generate planning reports for external (supervising ministry and other institutions) and internal controlling; the primary beneficiaries, however, are the administrative policy-makers responsible for strategic planning; another target segment are the officials indirectly involved in capacity planning through related activities (e.g., constructing curricula, setting quality benchmarks, etc.) who altogether represent quite a large portion of the institution's officials.

To enable the heterogeneous user groups we pre-define respective access categories, such as *administrator*, *expert*, *guest*, etc., as well as *Administrator* and *Guest* user accounts in the corresponding categories for the extreme access privileges of full and read-only access, respectively. Other access aspects (e.g., storage limit per user) can be handled by defining new categories or editing the existing ones.

3.3 System Requirements

Multi-user support and database back-end imply network communication between the clients and the server. Data transfer is expected to be secured against unauthorized access. Appreciation of the application could be increased if it is implemented in a platform-independent manner abstaining from any commercial components. Ease of installation, configuration and administration as well as stable and reliable operation are crucial as otherwise the potential users might refuse to adopt the model at all.

4 Implementation Issues

To best fulfill the above requirements we have chosen a popular web-enabled client/server solution with database connectivity which offers a number of convincing advantages, such as availability of open-source platform-independent solutions, ease of installation and configuration, server-side maintenance and administration, etc.

Decision support is realized by efficient and interactive analysis of large heterogeneous data volumes. Typical operations are querying and manipulating the data as well as application of analytical tools and visualization of the results. Similar functions are imposed on OLAP applications [5]; therefore we opted for OLAP's (simplified) architectural scheme, as shown in Fig. 3. At this point, we leave out the employment of any OLAP tools for future work.

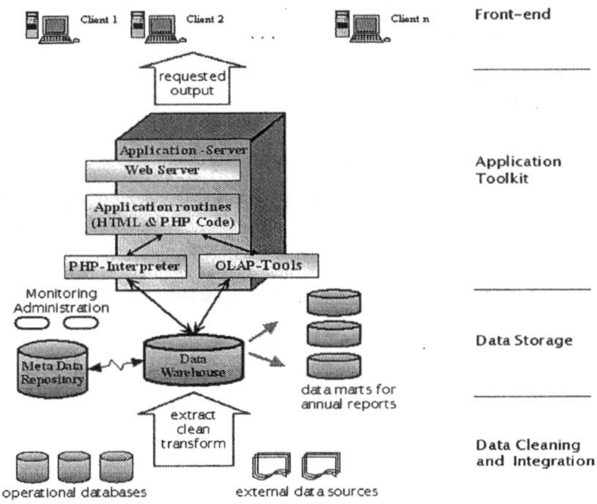

Fig. 3. Multi-layered software architecture

4.1 Database Back-End

The DBMS at the back-end manages two types of data: a) input data integrated from multiple sources into a centralized consistent set, and b) temporary data and interim results generated during simulations.

Compliant with the *data-warehouse* approach [14], the primary data is to be extracted, checked, transformed for migration, and, finally, transferred into the UNICAP's stand-alone database prior to any analyzing activities. *Data-cleaning*, i.e., bringing it into a consistent state, is essential for ensuring correct analysis results. Aware of the semantic constraints, we can incorporate integrity provisions directly into data manipulation routines. We have provided warnings against frequently occurring data conflicts as well as options as to how a specific faultiness should be handled.

4.3 Graphical User Interface

User interface is represented by a website front-end which displays the dynamically generated contents in a user-friendly form. Interactive elements enable the user to get acquainted with the computational concept, evaluate various scenarios and iterate to the desired output. The user is lead through the sequence of preparation, fine-tuning, simulation, and analysis steps, with context-specific assistance being offered throughout the interaction. To produce an impression of an application, every site follows the same layout with each functional area being at its fixed position, as shown in Fig. 4.

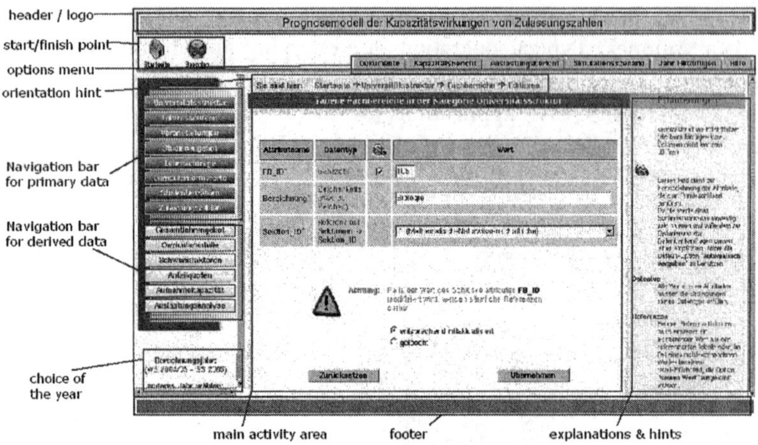

Fig. 4. Application's structural areas

Last not least, there is a separate user interface for the model's administrator which allows intuitive and comfortable monitoring and management of model's resources.

5 UNICAP in Action

To demonstrate the intuition behind using UNICAP we produce a fragment from one of the conducted case studies.

Task Definition. The Faculties of Biology (FB) and Computer Science (FCS) are setting up a new interdisciplinary Master's Degree in Bioinformatics with 30 beginners per year. Check if this plan can be supported with the available resources under the default capacity utilization tolerance interval of [0.8, 1.1].

Solution. We first generate the capacity utilization report for the initial data state. The overview in Fig. 5 (left) shows FB to be under-utilized with the ratio of 0.7647 whereas FCS is nearly balanced with the ratio of 1.0430. Having created our own simulation scenario, we adjust the input to accommodate the new program, its curriculum and the desired admission number. Analysis of the new state reveals FCS's incapability to service the desired number of beginners, as shown in Fig. 5 (right).

Testing the same setting with the admission number reduced from 30 to 20 (not shown here) leads to the utilization ratios of 0.81 and 1.0928 for FB and FCS, respectively, which are now both tolerable.

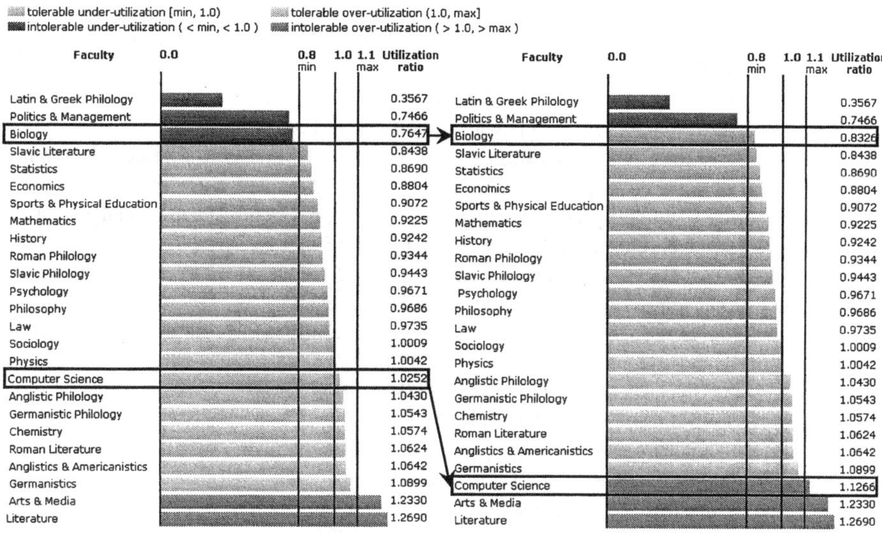

Fig. 5. Evaluating a user-defined scenario with UNICAP (fragment)

6 Conclusion

The presented UNICAP model is realized as a DSS for planning educational capacity in universities. The system integrates data from heterogeneous sources and allows users to interact with it in order to test various development strategies and become aware of their quantitative implications. Explanatory power of the user interface is assured by providing orientation aids, detailed instructions, graphical support and leading the user through the computation. Visually enhanced presentation of the output facilitates its perception and interpretation.

We consider UNICAP to be a starting point in building a more comprehensive DSS with OLAP functionality, designed with a close eye on the academic management needs. Such system should be helpful for optimizing the organization's internal process flows, but also for delivering an appropriate interface for inter-institutional controlling and knowledge discovery to be carried out by the supervising governmental bodies. Integration of the data from other sources and accumulation of the data from the past build up a base for refining and extending the analysis. Possible extensions would be visual analysis of teaching staff structure, educational supply, export-import relationships, as well as trend analysis from the accumulated historical data.

References

1. Aduol, F.W.O.: A model for estimating student unit cost and staffing requirements for university academic programmes with reference to Kenyan public universities, Higher education policy, 14/2 (2001) 117-140
2. Barlas, Y. et al.: A Dynamic Simulation Game (UNIGAME) for Strategic University Management, Simulation Gaming, 31 (2000) 331-358
3. Casper, C.A. and Henry, M.S: Developing Performance-Oriented Models for University Resource Allocation, Research in Higher Education, 42 (2001) 353-376
4. CHEPS Centre for Higher Education Policy Studies, University of Twente, Netherlands. http://www.utwente.nl/cheps
5. Codd, E. et al.: Providing OLAP (on-line analytical processing) to user-analysts: An IT mandate. Technical report, E.F.Codd & Associates (1993)
6. Deniz, D. Z. and Ersan, I.: Using an Academic DSS for Student, Course and Program Assessment, Proceedings of the ICEE 2001 Conference (2001)
7. Deris, S.B. et al.: University timetabling by constraint-based reasoning: A case study, Journal of the Operational Research Society, 48 (1997) 1178-1190
8. Education at a Glance: OECD Indicators - 2004 Edition. Centre for Educational Research and Innovation Education & Skills (2004)
9. Elimam, A.A.: A Decision Support System for University Admission Policies, European Journal of Operational Research, 50/2 (1991) 140-156
10. Eom, S.B. et al.: A survey of decision support system applications (1988–1994), Journal of the Operational Research Society, 49/2 (1998) 109-120
11. Franz, L. S. et al.: An Adaptive Decision Support System for Academic Resource Planning, Decision Sciences, 12/2 (1981) 276-293
12. Gottlieb, E.: Using Integer Programming to Guide College Admissions Decisions: A preliminary report, The Journal of Computing in Small Colleges, 17/2 (2001) 257-265
13. HIS Higher-Education Information System, Hannover, Germany. http://www.his.de/English
14. Hüsemann, B. et al.: Conceptual Data Warehouse Design, Proc. of the 2nd Intl. Workshop on Design and Management of Data Warehouses (DMDW'00), Stockholm, Sweden (2000)
15. Kwak, N. and Lee, C.: A Multicriteria Decision-Making Approach to University Resource Allocations and Information Infrastructure Planning, European Journal of Operational Research, 110/2 (1998) 234-242
16. Kaiser, F. et al.: Higher education policy issues and trends: an update on higher education policy issues in 11 Western countries, Higher Education Monitor Update Report, Enschede, Netherlands (2003)
17. Levine, J.B.: Application of the CAMPUS simulation models to the major planning decisions of a large university, Proceedings of the Second Conference on Applications of Simulations (1968)
18. Müller-Böling, D. et al.: University in Transition. Research Mission, Interdisciplinarity and Governance, Gütersloh, Verlag Bertelsmann Stiftung (1998)
19. OECD Organization for Economic Co-operation and Development, Paris, France. http://www.oecd.org
20. Salerno, C.: What we know about the efficiency of higher education institutions: The best evidence, Zoetermeer, Ministry of Education, Culture and Science, Netherlands (2003)
21. Seeliger, B.: Leitfaden zur Anwendung der Kapazitätsverordnung, Planning Department of Hamburg University (2001)

A Methodology Framework for Calculating the Cost of e-Government Services

Elias A. Hadzilias

IÉSEG School of Management, Catholic University of Lille, 59800 Lille, France
e.hadzilias@ieseg.gr

Abstract. This paper proposes a structured framework for calculating the cost of e-Government services, based on the complementary application of the IDEF0 modelling tool and the Activity-Based Costing technique. The motivation for this research effort was derived by the need to use an alternative method for the annual cost calculation of the TAXISnet e-Government services, since the relevant report published from the Greek Ministry of Finance in 2003 was based on traditional accounting approaches. The first step of the proposed methodology is the IDEF0-supported identification of the activities corresponding to the e-Government services and their initial classification as value-added or non value-added. Data collection follows, concerning cost elements and their activities using Activity-Based Costing. The paper concludes with a discussion concerning the added value of the proposed methodology framework and further research.

1 Introduction

E-Government has proven to be a durable and popular public management reform option over the last decade, attractive to elected officials and stakeholders who see its political benefits [1]. Public management scholarship on e-Government focuses on the beneficial effects of new technologies and examines the reasons why and how technology adoption occurs [2], [3], [4], [5].

Research in the e-Government field has not directly questioned the basic premise that using Information Technology (IT) in public administration is a positive and inevitable route to improvement, progress and cost effectiveness. Certain e-Government proponents argue that declining rates of trust in government can be reversed through the use of technology, either indirectly because of greater citizen satisfaction with more convenient services or directly through enhancing civic participation in the public sphere. The latter approach has been referred to as "digital democracy," "e-civics," and "e-democracy" [6] and argues that information technologies can enhance democracy by making public information more accessible and by enabling a range of civic discourse that otherwise would not occur: from facilitating citizen-initiated contacts through the Web [7], to enabling a representative and meaningful discourse that replaces complicated administration processes [8]. However, the potential of e-Government in this area has remained largely unfulfilled [9].

M. Böhlen et al. (Eds.): TCGOV 2005, LNAI 3416, pp. 247 – 256, 2005.

In the context of public sector reform, Heeks & Davies [10] identify four approaches to the use of IT in their entitled "four-eyes model". One of these is the "idolise" approach, in which public sector officials use computers but are "over-aware" of technology's potential. They believe IT can transform the business of government, and are dimly aware that information is something important. In consequence, the public sector becomes swamped in IT-driven projects, many of which have proved spectacular failures [11], [12]. The change expected has not occurred and the systems have fallen into disrepute and disuse, if indeed they ever worked in the first place – amounting to a gross waste of scarce resources.

Considering the struggle of public administration to maintain a high degree of transparency in the implementation of e-Government services projects, the justification of their budgets is realised through studies that describe comparative analyses of cost information between the traditional way of serving citizens and the IT-supported solutions. However, due to the lack of established methodologies for calculating the costs and assessing the benefits of implementing e-Government services, it is a common phenomenon for these studies to contain analyses that do not reflect the cost reality.

The motivation for this paper was a cost analysis report concerning the TAXISnet e-Government services project [13], published from the General Secretariat for Information Systems of the Greek Ministry of Finance [14]. In this report the traditional accounting approach has been followed to exhibit the value-added features of the project. TAXISnet offers a web-based interface, from which end-users (citizens, companies and public organisations) initiate transactions that provide electronic services [15]. This system is the evolution of a six-year IT project called TAXIS (TAXation Information System-named after the Greek word for order). It was initiated by the Greek Ministry of Finance, representing one of its strategic IT investments with an overall budget of approximately 90 million euros contributed by national and European Union (EU) funds and aimed at IT support to tax agencies all over Greece for carrying out tax filing, calculation and payment transactions with citizens and businesses.

Motivated by the afore-mentioned report for TAXISnet, the present paper proposes a structured methodology for calculating the cost of e-Government services projects, based on the complementary application of the IDEF0 modelling tool and the Activity-Based Costing technique. The next paragraphs refer to the description of these tools from a strategic point of view and their integration is presented afterwards in detail. Finally, the paper concludes with a discussion concerning the added value of the proposed methodology framework and further research.

2 The IDEF0 Modelling Tool

The IDEF0 modelling method is designed to model the decisions, actions, and activities of an organisation or system. It is not only the most widely used, but also the most field proven function modelling method for analysing and communicating the functional perspective of a system [16]. IDEF0 was derived from a well-established graphical language, the Structured Analysis and Design Technique – SADT [17]. The IDEF0 modelling method establishes the scope of analysis either for a particular functional analysis or for future analyses from another perspective. As a communication tool, IDEF0 enhances domain expert involvement and consensus decision-making through simplified graphical devices. As an analysis tool, IDEF0 supports the identification of the functions performed and what is needed to perform them.

The basic activity element of an IDEF0 model diagram is represented by a simple syntax. A verb-based label placed in a box describes each activity. Inputs are shown as arrows entering the left side of the activity box while the outputs are shown as exiting arrows on the right side of the box. Controls are displayed as arrows entering the top of the box and mechanisms are displayed as arrows entering from the bottom of the box. Inputs, Controls, Outputs and Mechanisms (ICOMs) are all referred to as concepts.

An IDEF0 model diagram is then composed of several activity boxes and related concepts to capture the overall activity. IDEF0 not only captures the individual activities, but also reveals the relationships among activities through the activities' related concepts. For example, the output of one activity may in turn become the input, control or even a mechanism of another activity within the same model.

A strategy for organising the development of IDEF0 models is the notion of hierarchical decomposition of activities. A box in an IDEF0 model represents the boundaries of an activity. Inside that box is the breakdown of that activity into smaller activities, which together comprise the box at the higher level, as shown in Figure 1. This hierarchical structure helps the analyst keep the scope of the model within the

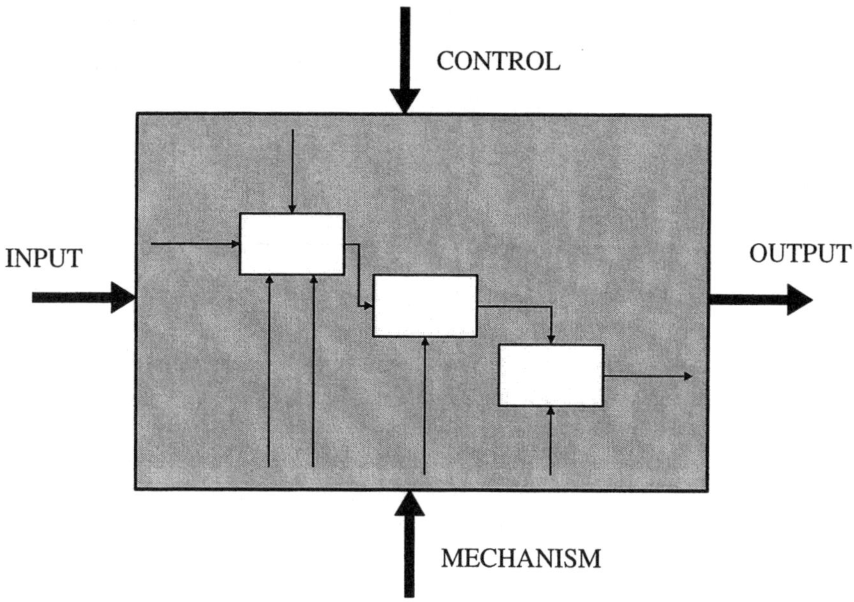

Fig. 1. Hierarchical decomposition of an IDEF0 model diagram

boundaries represented by the decomposition of the activity. This organisation strategy is also useful for hiding unnecessary complexity from view until a more in-depth understanding is required.

3 The Activity-Based Costing Technique

Activity-based costing (ABC) was introduced by Cooper & Kaplan [18] as an alternative to traditional accounting methods. It models the relationships between products/services and the resources used in their production at all stages, as depicted in Figure 2. In recent years, academics and management accountants have demonstrated a great interest in ABC [19]. However, surveys have shown that the diffusion process for ABC has not been intense [20], [21], [22].

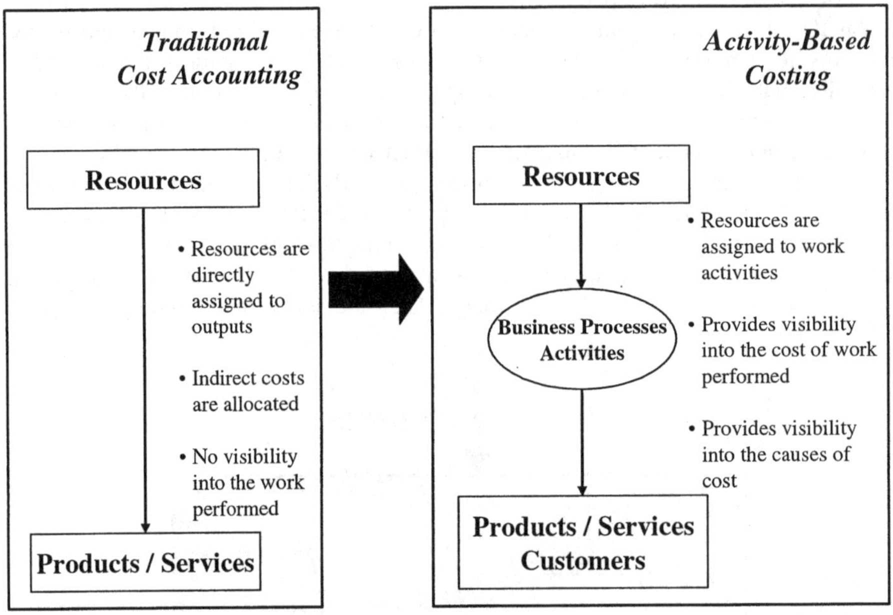

Fig. 2. Comparison of Traditional Cost Accounting and Activity-Based Costing

The ABC paradox lies in the fact that even though it has demonstrated strong benefits and advantages, it has not been employed by the majority of the organisations comprising both the private and public sectors [22], [23], [24]. A plethora of parameters have been tested in the literature in order to explain this paradox. These parameters include strategic posture and organisational structure [23], environmental uncertainty [25], the role of demand factors (e.g. percentage of overhead and product complexity) or supply factors (e.g. consultants and firm size), as well as factors that influence the diffusion of innovations, considering ABC as a form of administrative innovation (e.g. efficient choice, forced selection, fad and fashion perspectives) or the perception of relative advantage of the innovation over previous practices.

ABC is a technique that measures the cost and performance of activities, resources and costs objects, including overhead. The task of differentiating the organisation's activities as either value-added or non value-added is perhaps the most important theme in ABC. Non value-added activities are those that cause delay, excess, or variation, and therefore are targets for elimination or reduction in improving the business process. On the other hand, value added activities become targets for improvement, perhaps through streamlining or automated support.

4 Integrating IDEF0 and ABC

It is impractical to create an ABC model without a proper design tool that clearly identifies all the individual activities that take place in a system from the beginning to the end. Such a tool can greatly help to reduce time used for modelling and overcome the difficulties present in creating a cost model [26].

Documenting and understanding activities is necessary in order to calculate the cost of a business process, since activities are the building blocks of business processes. When employees understand the activities they perform, they can better understand costs based on the activities. Traditional financial information is reorganised by ABC into a form that makes sense to the functional user: in addition to the information that tells them how they allocate resources, it also tells them what to do with these resources. This ability to place costs on activities and their outputs provides a clear metric for depicting the real cost of the system and serves as a reference level for continuous improvement, whether for determining improvement priorities in the long-term or for measuring near-term success. ABC allows functional users to characterise the value of, or need for, each activity, eliminating the waste before automating (or reengineering) business processes.

A structured approach for the identification and analysis of the activities performed in the context of a certain business process can be provided by the IDEF0 function modelling technique. Even though ABC can be attempted without the use of IDEF0 modelling, it accomplishes the most complex task of identifying discrete activities and then defining the primary output measure for each activity.

Resources are assigned to activities so that they can be carried out: performing the activity results in a cost that can be priced, which can be assigned to the primary output. It is through ABC, that an organisation can visualise actual costs against individual activities, and find opportunities to streamline or reduce the costs, or eliminate the entire activity, especially if there is no added value.

The framework for calculating the cost of e-Government services, based on the complementary application of the functional modelling tool IDEF0 and the ABC technique, is comprised of the following steps: analysis of activities, cost collection, costs to activities assignment, definition of output measures and cost calculation.

4.1 Analysis of Activities

In the beginning, the scope of the activities to be analysed must be clearly defined. The depth and detail of analysis should be determined by activity decomposition, since the latter is complete when one common or homogeneous primary output per activity is reached. The IDEF0 function modelling tool is employed in this step to perform activities' analysis. Various data collection methods should be used (interviews, documentation, etc.) in order to provide the model with the correct input.

A decision is then made if an activity is value-added or non value-added. Additionally, whether the activity is primary or secondary, and required or not needed. An activity is considered as value-added when the output of the activity is directly related to the service requirements. Primary activities directly support the organisation's mission, while secondary activities support primary activities. Required activities are those that must always be performed while discretionary activities are performed only when allowed by the operating management.

4.2 Cost Collection

During this step costs are gathered for the activities which concern the e-Government services. These costs should be salaries, expenditures for software development, hardware infrastructure, leasing of communication lines, depreciation of fixed assets, etc.

These costs are used as the baseline activity costs. When documents for the costs incurred are not available, cost assignment formulas should be used. A classification of these cost elements is described in the Appendix.

4.3 Costs to Activities Assignment

The input for this step comes on the one hand from the results of activities' analysis based on the constructed IDEF0 models and on the other hand from the gathered organisational inputs and costs. Bringing all these elements together, results to the assignment of the input cost per activity. A simple formula for costs is used: outputs consume activities that in turn have consumed costs associated with resources. This reflects the philosophy of the activity-based costing technique.

During this phase of the proposed methodology, a simple method is utilised in order to calculate the total costs consumed by an activity - multiply the percent of time expended by an organisational unit, e.g. branch, division, on each activity by the total input cost for that entity.

It is important to point out that during this phase of the methodology, the origin of the costs takes places and not their calculation.

4.4 Definition of Output Measures

In this step the actual activity unit cost is calculated. Even though activities may have multiple outputs, only one is identified as the primary output. Activity unit cost is calculated by dividing the total input cost, including assigned costs from secondary activities, by the primary activity output volume: the primary output must be measurable and its volume or quantity obtainable. From this, a bill of activities can then be calculated which contains or lists a set of activities and the amount of each activity consumed. The amount of each activity consumed is extended by the activity unit cost and is added up as a total cost for the bill of activities.

4.5 Cost Calculation

In the final step, the calculated activity unit costs and bills of activities are used to identify the actual costs. A Pareto analysis is recommended to follow, in order to calculate the percentage of activities that consume the majority of costs. The confirmation of the previously identified non value-added activities occurs during this step with a clarity that allows us to eliminate them. Furthermore, this classification of activities permits the e-Government services to be provided to the citizen with greater efficiency.

5 Discussion

E-Government services should be characterised by:

- Ubiquity: offering services to citizens at any place (workplace, domestic, public), any time (24x7 availability), through multiple communication channels (Internet, phone, fax) and independently of IT skills (e.g. ability to type).
- Uniqueness of reference: single point of service for all cases, single sign-on for all services, single session for any service, transparent complexity, virtual integration.
- De-materialisation: no paper documents, no physical transport, no physical waiting in queues.
- Quality and cost effectiveness: maximum reliability of results, maximum quality of service, minimum time of completion, minimum difficulty of access, minimum cost of use.

It is deduced from the description of the proposed methodology framework, that the combination of IDEF0 and ABC can be utilised as a toolkit for providing accurate cost information concerning the operation of e-Government services. The IDEF0 maps all the activities performed for the delivery of these services and ABC proves to be a more credible costing system in comparison to traditional accounting, since it traces cost from resources according to the way they are consumed by the activities defined, rather than by some arbitrary basis.

Furthermore, this methodology provides more than an e-Government services specific pricing system. It serves as a reference model for future reuse when legislation is changed. It is a common phenomenon in Greece that taxation rules and laws are altered from year to year, according to government decisions and initiatives. Consequently, the activities supporting tax services provision to the citizens are enriched or lessened, resulting in a different workflow. For example, a circular was published [27] concerning tax refund, obliging the citizens who submitted their tax statement through TAXISnet and had a tax refund over 1.500,00 euros, to bring all documents to tax agencies within 10 days after receiving the relevant note. The number of citizens belonging to this category is close to 500.000. As a result, the cost of the e-Government services is highly increased due to the involvement of the tax agencies in the processing of the statements. It could also be argued that in this case, TAXISnet's role is limited from an e-Government services integrated system to a mere data collection intermediate with secondary information processing tasks after tax agencies enter the documented input from the citizens.

Therefore, the proposed structured methodology framework could face these legislative transformations, by simply adding or removing the corresponding activities from the IDEF0 model. Furthermore, it could serve as a tool for what-if scenario analysis in the legislation transformation process: before the introduction of a new tax law, its impact (cost or benefit) could be estimated on the whole taxation system, by arranging differently the workflows of activities in the IDEF0 model.

Another use of this framework would be in the launch of new e-Government services or design of new components. With its ability to relate investment to utilisation through various activities in which an individual might be involved, it could help justify such investments in the preliminary stage of such efforts. Concerning TAXISnet, the General Secretariat for Information Systems recently decided to deactivate some of its modules, because they were not as efficient as initially planned, although their development cost was over 70 million euros [28], [29], [30].

In the context of further research, a dedicated information system could be developed that would support the process mapping of the e-Government services with the IDEF0 tool and the allocation of costs using ABC technique. That could be used as a decision-support system for the various needs and requirements of public administration: accurate cost calculation of e-Government services, strategic management, automated what-if scenario analysis for legislation transformation purposes and development of organisational knowledge.

References

1. Coursey, D., Killingsworth, J.: Managing Government Web Services in Florida: Issues and Lessons. In Garson, D. (ed.): Handbook of Public Information Systems, Marcel Dekker, New York (2000) 331–344
2. Abramson, M.A., Means, G.E.: E-Government 2001. IBM Center for the Business of Government Series, Rowman and Littlefield, Lanham (2001)
3. Fountain, J.: Building the Virtual State: Information Technology and Institutional Change, Brookings Institution, Washington (2001)
4. Moon, M.J.: The Evolution of E-Government among Municipalities: Reality or Rhetoric? Public Administration Review 62(4) (2002) 424–433
5. Ho, A.T.-K.: Reinventing Local Governments and the E-Government Initiative. Public Administration Review 62(4) (2002) 434–445
6. Fountain, J.: Electronic Government and Electronic Civics. In Wellman, B. (ed.): Encyclopedia of Community, Great Barrington, Berkshire (2003) 436– 441
7. Thomas, J.C., Streib, G.: The New Face of Government: Citizen-Initiated Contacts in the Era of E-Government. Journal of Public Administration Research and Theory 13(1) (2003) 83–101
8. Shi, Y., Scavo, C.: Citizen Participation and Direct Democracy through Computer Networking. In Garson, D. (ed.): Handbook of Public Information Systems, Marcel Dekker, New York (2000) 331–344
9. West, D.M.: E-Government and the Transformation of Service Delivery and Citizen Attitudes. Public Administration Review 64(1) (2004) 15–27
10. Heeks, R., Davies, A.: Different approaches to information reform. In Heeks, R. (ed.): Reinventing Government in the Information Age: IT Enabled Public Sector Reform, Routledge, London (1999) 22-48

11. Hackney, R.A., McBride, N.K.: The efficacy of information systems in the public sector: issues of context and culture. International Journal of Public Sector Management 8 (6) (1995) 17-29
12. Heeks, R., Bhatnagar, S.: Understanding success and failure in information age reform. In Heeks, R. (ed.): Reinventing Government in the Information Age: IT Enabled Public Sector Reform, Routledge, London (1999) 49-74
13. Official website of TAXISnet e-Government Services of the General Secretariat for Information Systems, Greek Ministry of Finance: http://www.taxisnet.gr
14. Logothetis, I.: Cost analysis of submitting and processing income statements E1/E1A. General Secretariat for Information Systems, Greek Ministry of Finance, Athens (2003) The full Executive Report is also available at the website http://www.e-oikonomia.gr/meletes/executive_summary.pdf (last accessed 20/09/2004)
15. Stamoulis, D., Gouscos, D., Georgiadis, P., Martakos, D.: Revisiting public information management for effective e-government services. Information Management & Computer Security 9 (4) (2001)146-153
16. Malhotra, R., Jayaraman, S.: An Integrated Framework for Enterprise Modeling. Journal of Manufacturing Systems 11(6) (1992) 426-441
17. Marca, D.A., McGowan, C.L.: SADT: Structured Analysis and Design Technique. McGraw-Hill, New York (1988)
18. Cooper, R., Kaplan, R.S.: Measure costs right: Make the right decisions. Harvard Business Review 65 (5) (1988) 96–103
19. Bjørnenak, T., Mitchell, F.: The development of activity-based costing journal literature, 1987-2000. The European Accounting Review 11(3) (2002) 481-508
20. Lukka, K., Granlund, M.: Cost Accounting in Finland: Current Practice and Trends of Development. The European Accounting Review 5 (1) (1996) 1-28
21. Chenhall, R., Langfield-Smith, K.: Adoption and benefits of management accounting practices: an Australian study. Management Accounting Research 9 (1998) 1-19
22. Innes, J., Mitchell, F., Sinclair, D.: Activity-based costing in the UK's largest companies: a comparison of 1994 and 1999 survey results, Management Accounting Research 11 (2000) 349-362
23. Gosselin, M.: The Effect of Strategy and Organizational Structure on the Adoption and Implementation of Activity-Based Costing. Accounting, Organizations and Society 22 (2) (1997) 105-122
24. Venieris, G., Cohen, S., Kaimenaki, E.: ABC in Greece: Adopters, Deniers and Supporters. Proceedings of the 2nd Annual Congress of the Hellenic Finance and Accounting Association, Athens, Greece (2000)
25. Gosselin, M., Paré, P.: Activity – Based Costing: A response to changes in organizational environment? Proceedings of the 21st Annual Congress of the European Accounting Association, Antwerp, Belgium (1998)
26. Spedding, T.A., Sun, G.Q.: Application of discrete event simulation to the activity based costing of manufacturing systems. International Journal of Production Economics 58 (1999) 289–301
27. Circular 1028034/771/A 0012/31.03.04, General Directorate for Taxation, General Secretariat for Information Systems, Greek Ministry of Finance, Athens, Greece (2004)
28. Express 08/09/2004, Greek Daily Business Newspaper: TAXISnet is being redesigned, (Also at: http://express.gr/showarticle.php?article=54622&categ=2&lang=1 last accessed 20/09/2004)

29. Express 01/06/2004, Greek Daily Business Newspaper: Upgrade of TAXISnet is necessary, (Also at: http://express.gr/showarticle.php?article=52100&categ=2&lang=1 last accessed 20/09/2004)
30. Express 27/03/2004, Greek Daily Business Newspaper: Radical redesign of TAXISnet is being planned, (Also at: http://express.gr/showarticle.php?article=50527&categ=2&lang=1 last accessed 20/09/2004)

Appendix: Cost Elements' Classification of e-Government Services

Cost Element	Initial Cost	Operating Cost
Hardware – Computing Platforms – Networking Devices – Security Devices – Data Storage Devices	Depends on whether, or how, existing infrastructure can be used to support e-Government application(s)	New hardware may be required as the e-Government system scales. Expected ongoing maintenance costs.
Software – Development – Security – Monitoring & Management – Data Access & Storage	Depends on whether, or how, existing infrastructure can be used to support e-Government application(s)	New software may be required as the e-Government system scales. Expected ongoing maintenance and license costs.
Facility Expenses – Physical Modifications for Hosting or Security – Electricity, Plumbing, Heating & Cooling	Depends on whether, or how, existing infrastructure can be used to support e-Government application(s)	Facility upgrade expenses may be incurred as the e-Government application scales. Expect ongoing maintenance costs.
Service Provider Costs – System Development – Application Hosting – Telecommunications – Transaction Processing		
Organisation Labour Costs – System Manager(s) – System Developer(s) – System Operator(s) & Maintainer(s) – User Support Staff – Customer Support Staff – Functional Manager(s) – Administrative & Contracting Support		

Good Practice in e-Government: Management over Methods?

Lee Anthony Eddowes

University of Manchester

Abstract. In considering good practice in relation to e-Government, this paper contributes to critical discussion on the value placed on methodologies in implementing e-Government programmes. Assessments are made regarding institutional, technological and organisational factors within the public sector, and the manner in which methodologies have been and are currently being applied. An exploration is made of emergent e-Government driven methodologies, and in drawing on the work of Wastell, Newman and Kawalek (2002) perceptions of e-Government good practice are illustrated by implementing agencies.

1 Introduction

Electronic Service Delivery (ESD or e-Government) is continuing in its role of enabling reform the public sector in the U.K. Information Systems (IS) are rarely introduced on such an ambitious scale of the current programme. As such, what use has been made, and value taken, of applying Good Practice in terms of modeling or methodology techniques in delivering such a diverse set of change and technology? Structured paths leading to the introduction of technology and change have existed in distinct forms for some time, and have been applied with mixed results across a range of projects in both public and private sectors. There are two perspectives that may allow for an examination of e-Government in terms of these paths:

- Considering the existing framework of models and methodologies at the disposal of bodies responsible for implementing e-Government;
- Assessing e-Government programmes and the value of relevant techniques.

These are considered through an e-Government case study. It provides an overview of the progress of an organisation in implementing e-Government, in contrast to discussion of e-Government in broader policy terms.

2 Government Motivation

A formalised definition of e-Government is presented by Becker et al (2004) in that electronic government entails the simplification and implementation of information, communication and transaction processes, in order to achieve, by means of information and communication technology, an administrative service, within and between

M. Böhlen et al. (Eds.): TCGOV 2005, LNAI 3416, pp. 257–267, 2005.

authorities and, likewise, between authorities and private individuals or companies. All public bodies are involved with implementing e-Government, using models for this purpose known as Pathfinder projects. Pathfinders are intended to provide best practice, but apply to complex or significantly different areas, acting:

- As a focus for learning to enable all councils to meet the 2005 ESD target;
- To enable those councils at the leading edge to further develop products and disseminate their learning and good practice more widely;
- To develop products for national roll out, whether by local councils themselves or with private sector partners.

Responsibility for e-Government delivery lies with the Office of the Deputy Prime Minister (ODPM). Organisations are required to notify the ODPM of progress through formal reports, Implementing Electronic Government (IEG) statements. Figure 1 illustrates notified progress up to January 2004 of progress based on these reports.

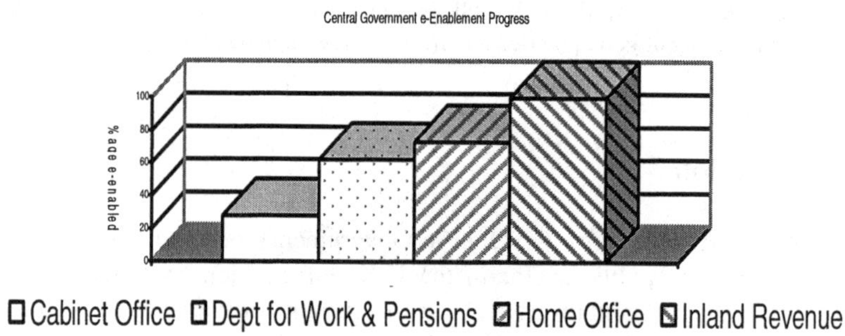

Fig. 1. Central Government e-Enablement Progress

3 An Established e-Government Context

The U.K. is not alone in being subject to the shifting nature of public services. The landscape of e-Government has seen the public sector across the continents at differing stages of implementing joined-up services. Has good practice been included in their scope? Can they be described as successes? Is it realistic to assess and contrast the projects and the techniques used to implement the e-Government concept with those applied in the U.K.? In 1959, the Association for Computing Machinery (ACM) was contemplating the progress of automated data processing across the U.S. Federal Government. The third and final paper noted that 'progress in developing and installing electronic systems varied considerably between installations'. A number of the issues that were identified in the paper reflected obstacles still occurring in IT projects today, including underestimating risk, time and the planning required.

The phases of progress in the US in terms of e-Government have been observed by Holden, Norris and Fletcher (2002) as being 1) catalogue, 2) transaction, 3) vertical integration and 4) horizontal integration. In order to provide an increasingly mature level of service, each phase has to be passed through in order to progress. They note the dearth of information and contemporary literature on e-government, including surveys and case studies. Their research did show that larger urban or industrial centers were more likely to adopt new technology. In addition, according to the local government respondents, the five greatest barriers to the adoption of e-government, in order of frequency of response, were: lack of technology or web staff; lack of financial resources; lack of technology or web expertise; issues regarding security; and the need to upgrade existing information technology.

4 Best Practice - Through Modeling and Methodologies?

Best practice, according to the Department for Trade and Industry, equates to showing how organisations have become more efficient and competitive. The scale of an undertaking may determine the relevance of applying some or all of these techniques in practice, but a pragmatic blend of these is often required in many instances. Looking at the implementation of e-Government, the majority of techniques are applicable given the scale of the undertaking. Models and methodologies provide a route to promoting consistency and best practice, and it is appropriate to note the relationship between successful projects and the valid application of such tools and techniques.

Approaches to the implementation of IST within organisations over the past forty years have been shaped by the emergence of 'hard' and 'soft' schools of systems thinking. The decisions taken in pursuit of objectives, definition of functional groups such as production, financial and marketing systems and the clear categorisation have lead to engineering of the subsystems to optimise each. Established methodologies apply a logical series of steps to analyse and redesign or rearrange the features of the subsystem, for example Boehm's description of (and later Sommerville (2000)) waterfall (and later spiral) approaches. Examples of commercial methods include Structured Systems Analysis and Design Method (SSADM), advocating a documented process to investigate, assess and reengineer an identified system or process. PRINCE 2 enables formalised control and oversight of an agreed project. The boundaries of procedural methods have been contrasted to a more holistic and integrated approach advocated by Checkland (1990). Factors noted by Bailey (1993) that would fall under such a more inclusive approach to introducing technologically linked change might include:

- Strategic planning;
- Existing procedures and systems;
- Cultural makeup;
- Accepted means of introducing new technologies.

With an increasing level of complexity in organisational life, Checkland (1999) continued to investigate the focus of broadening the inquiry into management where harder systems engineering techniques discovered limits and boundaries to their applicability. One drawback with a waterfall type approach is illustrated through the very objectives of a project utilising such a method – 'short circuiting' the steps in search of a reengineered system. This was illustrated by the action research project presented by Pardo and Scholl (2002), where short circuits to failure in a large project were identified and addressed in a live project, the New York State Central Accounting System Redesign Project. Management pressures came into play and the project risked failure through subsequently trying to take the identified 'short cuts' to project delivery.

The adoption of a suitable methodology in support of delivering the e-Government agenda therefore has to take into account the type of factors presented above through introducing a combination of change and technology at a varying number of levels both internally and externally. It may also follow that the methodology selected by an organisation may reflect the attitude and nature of the organisation to both its members and the communities it does business with, collaborates with and serves.

4.1 Modeling and Methodologies Toward e-Government

The statutory activities and responsibilities of public sector organisations are consistent across the UK. The public sector has a mixed record of using best practice when introducing IST. As mentioned previously, use of the Pathfinder projects has been made to provide consistent 'blueprints' for organisations undertaking projects which inherently address the same core requirements. These blueprints support all the activities involved in the development, deployment and continued operation of an IST project, which are all candidates for management through a relevant technique. The Government may have recognised a shortcoming of best practice. The combination of factors that sets e-Government apart (including change, new technologies, process reengineering and so on), may not be perceived as particularly onerous within a single project. However, the circumstances and scale multiply the complexity and brings into question the applicability and support offered by existing methods and tools.

One of the Pathfinder projects, intended to address new or complex areas of the e-Government agenda was the Salford Process Reengineering method Involving New Technology (SPRINT). The new methodology was designed to introduce programmes involving the level of complexity and risk presented by the implementation of e-Government. Few Local Authorities have publicly adopted SPRINT for their e-Government programmes. Current empirical evidence and fieldwork has suggested that the use of existing methods, particularly project management, are being employed to control the implementation of e-Government.

In addition, the Improvement and Development Agency (IDeA) has been in operation in support of local government to assist in the dissemination of best practice. This brief includes e-Government, where the central focus is on outcomes of saving time and money combined with achieving improvements. There is a clear if potted genealogy for the techniques used to specifically deliver e-Government in the U.K. and elsewhere. The application (or otherwise) of appropriate techniques and a reliance on control methods has really only served to throw into sharp relief the gap between established thinking and practice compared to new situations and circumstances arising from the change in systems and practice driven by e-Government generally.

5 An e-Government Case Study

The scope of public sector agencies involved in e-Government activity is all-encompassing in the U.K. The class of agency identified was Metropolitan Borough Councils (MBC), of which there are currently 36 Councils of this type across England. They preside over predominantly urban environments, and many provide key services including housing, education and social services. Demographically, they are comparable and the nature of the urban environment provides infrastructure more conducive to e-Government take up in both the civic and business communities.

5.1 Method of Approach

The development of suitable case studies and supplementary fieldwork involves both planning and preparation to support and aid involvement from the study participants. With the closer contact that a case study provides over a period of time, the execution will be monitored on a regular basis. The amendments, issues and factors having a bearing on the level of success will be noted and taken into account. The fieldwork component of the research is intended to provide an insight into usage of IS methods, and the results of their usage in the e-Government context. The MBCs will represent this sector, due to the level of IS usage and likely levels of change. The proposed approach utilises two types of fieldwork, intended to complement each other and provide supporting evidence for the research proposal.

Firstly, a case study will be developed in some depth to investigate key factors that will have a bearing on the successful introduction of e-Government within a target organisation. This will take the form of firstly recording the anticipated approach and assessing the likelihood of success. A series of structured interviews with senior staff central to the delivery of e-Government are central to the case study, supported by access to Council documents and material pertinent to the programme. The supporting fieldwork involves the use of surveys with similar organisations. A survey will be developed to probe related areas in order to compare the salient factors. This survey will also be followed up after a suitable period of time in order to track subsequent progress of plans and change in line with the case study.

5.2 Key Areas

For the fieldwork, the first set of materials for discussion with the participants was constructed around several core topics. These will comprise specific subject matter, with a set of specific questions or areas to be probed at this stage. The amount of time, level of access to the case study participants and other resources available required planning and management to take into account participant responsibilities.

The findings were reviewed closely and modified to prepare a suitable questionnaire for distribution to the wider response study group. In terms of introducing a major upheaval in terms of the focus and activities, the following topic headings were used to work with participants:

- Strategic direction, drivers and models for change;
- Methodologies applied to key projects and their structure;
- Anticipated outcomes and measures of success;
- Anticipated issues and management.

5.3 The Agency Profile

Council A is a traditionally mining and industrial area. The decline in these industries led to high unemployment in the 80s/90s, with 15% of its population in wards amongst the most deprived in England. The Executive was to be assessed in order to appreciate a specific delivery perspective in terms of decisions, goals and definitions of service.

The responsibilities for e-Government in Council A lay with a small executive team drawn from the Senior Management. Interviews were organised with members of the team, who were: the Head of IT Services, the Director of Finance and IT, the Deputy Director of Human Resources and the Head of Strategic Planning. The sub-headings below provide a selection of the key areas explored in the course of the case study. With many Directors approaching retirement, the contributors perceived that this is an opportunity for change in a number of areas.

5.4 Methodologies

The ethos at Council A regarding projects is 'evolution not revolution'. IS implementation is based around assessment of a pilot phase, whereby specific objectives are set and attainment of the pilot objectives moves a project into a further phase. Figure 2, Council A Phasing, illustrates the progression of pilots from exploratory phase to established implementation project.

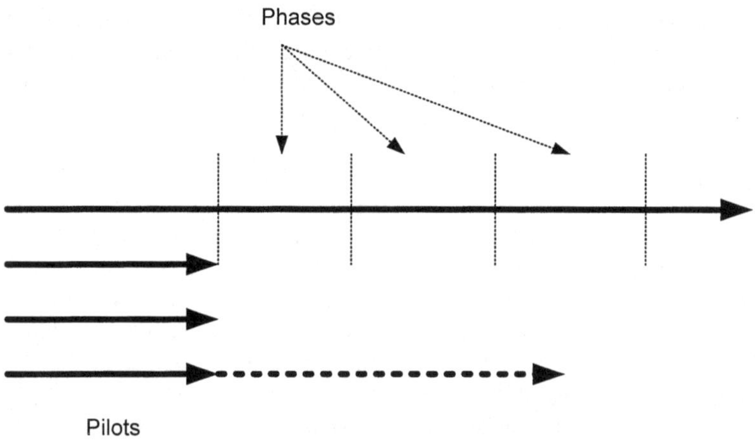

Fig. 2. Council A Phasing

The discarding of a pilot leads to a search for an alternative strategy: final business objectives are delayed not ignored. The methodology broadly reflects a 'waterfall' approach but is more of a 'house style' than a formalised and auditable means of implementing extensive IST programmes.

An example cited was the usage of electronic forms. Council A investigated the experiences of peer Authorities in this field. The piloting approach applied by Council A was used here. A single department was involved in the process for initial design to implementation. Feedback was incorporated and the system was introduced Council wide gradually. This may have been swifter but this is not the culture of the organisation. The Head of Strategic planning related the view of the Chief Executive in this respect – 'Speed is for others, getting it right is for us, irrespective of deadlines.'

5.5 IS Strategy and e-Government

Early in 2002, a new IS Strategy was issued. This centered on a replacement timetable for legacy systems based on three main drivers, being:

- Basing new systems around business processes and the ability to redesign;
- Technology linking front and back office systems enabling self service;
- Recording of transaction progress for performance assessment.

This movement of assessment to being a key component of Council systems is presented in Figure 3 below, New Auditing Paths.

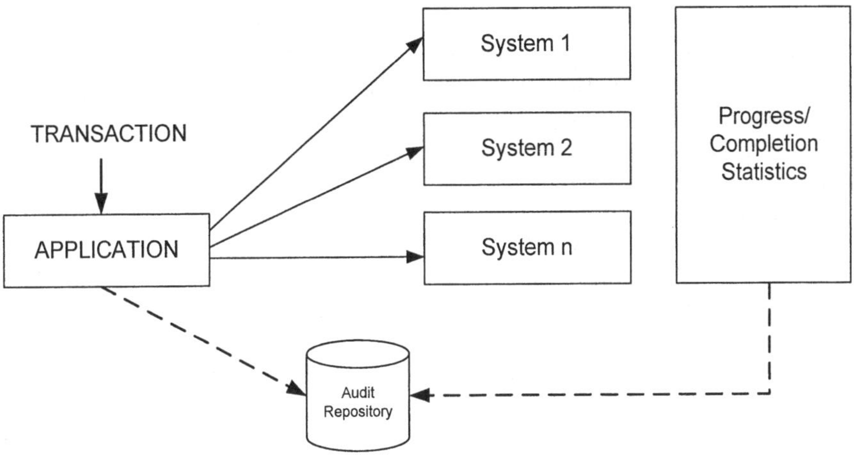

Fig. 3. New Auditing Paths

The e-Government initiative has resulted in a number of existing local bodies and new partnerships being allocated funds, without necessarily a clear remit on how these monies are to be best allocated. The experience of Council A, as a member of many of these local and/or regional groups, was the precedence of policy making over activity. The duplication of projects elsewhere was common given the lack of experience or direction in facilitating the bodies to deliver benefits.

5.6 Change

The executive committee referred to previously has responsibilities beyond e-Government. Where an initiative is deemed key to the Council achieving strategic or key objectives, resources and be suborned promptly given that the majority of changes are associated with the four Directorates represented on the committee. The approach to change within Council A in terms of inclusion and empowerment combined with technology and changing circumstances is illustrated through the ramifications of introducing a new cash receipting system across the Borough.

The project originally entailed closure of cash offices across the Borough, but the need for this was disputed by officers and members bringing political interests and pressures to bear. A review was initiated, which discovered an impact analysis had not been made regarding the closures. Service demands were for longer hours and Saturday opening. Subsequently, services were made available from libraries and through an innovative relationship where citizens could access facilities in Co-Op stores and Post Offices. Service access was improved and with savings of over £350,000 made.

5.7 Technology Transfer

Council A are unsure of their progress in regard to their peers and the overall government timetable. Comparators are not perceived as helpful, including the Society for IT Managers (SOCITM) reports on e-Government. No formal strategy exists in terms of technology transfer: the adoption of new technologies apparently just happening. Web site usage statistics are increasing, as are telephone channel contacts.

Significantly, IS projects are progressing on an ad hoc basis with poor regard to relevant circumstances and factors. For example, popular Libraries are to have staff trained and systems installed to allow processing of benefits claims. However, the creation of a trust to operate services meant staff were to be transferred under TUPE terms and as such would not be deemed eligible under Government legislation to undertake verification activities at that time.

Council A published a revised IS Strategy early 2002. This included appraisal of a number of initiatives undertaken by other Authorities, notably Beacon Councils. In terms of e-Government, Council A determined that it was not prepared to be a testbed for new technologies. The Director of Finance and IT observed that 'we do not want to be seen as bleeding edge in terms of technology…practical gains are what we seek'. The team was undecided over the appointment of a Service Delivery Manager to oversee such delivery. The examples they had witnessed did not reflect their circumstances enough to warrant an immediate programme of radical IST led change.

5.8 Assessment

Council A illustrated that although a central agenda is in place, the potential benefits that can be drawn from such a deceptively complex initiative need to be assured through the judicious use of meaningful parameters and/or directives. This type of agenda requires commitment through adequate resourcing and monitoring on the part of central government for the directive to be successfully implemented. This includes consistency of method, technology and application, and the case study highlights a number of points, presented below.

Interpretation: Council A exhibited a flexible interpretation of scope and timelines in common with numerous public agencies. In discussing this interpretation, Wastell et al (2002) have observed the focus on service applies not only to the type and nature of e-Government implementations, but also to the essential drivers of local government including the democratic process.

Focus: The IS Strategy clearly emphasised a replacement and upgrade approach. This approach has characterised other e-Government projects, i.e. projects instigated in isolation, projects being implemented on a minimalist basis to meet imposed targets, poor justification and limited or no joint agency approach to projects. Recent tendering through government agencies has indicated that significant numbers of agencies are only just commencing procurement of systems that are core to e-Government principles.

Service Users: Council A has noted an increase in take up of Internet based services, also of more established telephone services. This has come as a surprise, but consistent with a narrow approach to design, which would usually involve anticipating outcomes of projects that cross functional and operational boundaries.

Aggregation: Council A closely assesses technologies as part of a project, which in other circumstances would be quite appropriate. The use of Pathfinder projects was designed to bring a consistency of solution and method, but their purpose of indicating best practice has not been adopted at Council A or neighbouring peer authorities. The independence of local government in funding and implementing IST systems has allowed a plethora of technologies and to a lesser extent standards to proliferate based on a parochial view that proven national solutions do not apply to local needs.

Shared Approach: Council A promotes partnership working, intended to ensure a complimentary and joined up approach in delivering comprehensive and sustainable improvements within an area. This has worked well in a project with emergency services for a specific business process where issues around information management and sharing were not involved.

6 Conclusions

In preparing the paper, the chief concern involved the availability of best practice applicable to the implementation of e-Government. It is encouraging that there exists a range of proven methods and tools to support agencies in their efforts in this area (notably SSADM and Prince2). The documented application of these techniques has contributed to the quality and success of IST project implementations. This is supported by the case study and the progress of e-Government on an international scale.

However, the paper needs to highlight two specific issues. Firstly, the way in which established techniques and methods are being applied in terms of focus on the issues arising from e-Government. The case study highlighted the treatment of e-

Government as a project implementation, consisting of infrastructure, equipment and software. Current fieldwork and strong anecdotal evidence indicates that this approach is endemic across UK e-Government programmes.

Vassilakis et al (2003) commented on this in an assessment of electronic forms implementation by the Greek government, commenting on the development of electronic services was being treated as an isolated software project, thus information extracted from the involved domain experts is recorded as low level 'user requirements', rather than as high level organisational knowledge. This supports the thinking of Wastell et al (2002) who assessed the selective emphasis placed by implementing authorities on improving service than addressing more complex issues around local government that e-Government raises, including access to democracy and policy making. This strategy, albeit unwittingly perhaps, of shifting the focus of the e-Government effort removes the emphasis on change and evolvement of government services from the delivery level upwards.

The second issue relates to the nature of best practice in the shape of methodologies. Previous evidence indicates that existing methodologies provide a rich seam of support for organisations contemplating a major IST programme of a similar scale to e-Government. These have been utilised to good effect in many cases, but the unique nature of e-Government has begun to show the limitations of existing material. Becker et al (2004) highlighted the value of existing process oriented techniques leading to modernisation, contrasting to the reducing value of systems models in the face of rapid technology change, privacy and usage issues.

This is of little comfort to current and potential implementers of e-Government. The SPRINT approach, addressing introduction of new technology into an organisation, may provide a potential route for new methodologies to be developed. This growing emphasis on standards in a rapidly changing environment in order to ensure interoperability presents a potential shift in IS design. This shift indicates a more technological approach, as opposed to a more user centric view that was discussed by Moen and McClure (1994).

The previous successful application of methodologies for implementation of e-Government has coincided with a clear national framework firmly supported by the national government. These frameworks have specified specific targets, incorporated the change, service and democratic issues at their heart and been nationally co-coordinated and well funded. The issues surrounding implementation of e-Government in the UK has occurred not to a lack of supportive best practice examples or tools and techniques, but to a combination of lack of firm direction and steerage from central government tied to a local dilution of policy resulting in e-Government programmes becoming IT projects as opposed to change agents.

References

1. Bailey, J.: Managing People and Technological Change, Pitman, London (1993)
2. Becker, J., Algermissen, L., Niehaves, B.: Organizational Engineering in Public Administrations – A Method for process-oriented e-Government projects, 2004 ACM Symposium on Applied Computing, Pages 1386-9 (2004)
3. Boehm, B.: "A Spiral Model For Software Development and Enhancement" in Computer, Vol. 21, No. 5, May 1988 pp 61-72 (1988)

4. Checkland, P.: Systems Thinking, Systems Practice, Wiley (1999)
5. Deklava, S.: "Electronic commerce: a half-empty glass?" In Communications of the AIS, Volume 3, Issue 4 (June 2000), Article No. 6, Association for Information Systems Atlanta, GA, USA (2000)
6. "eGovernment indicators for benchmarking eEurope", (2001) http://europa.eu.int/information_society/eeurope/action_plan/pdf/egovindicators.pdf
7. Holden, S.H., Norris, D.F., Fletcher, P.D.: Electronic Government at the Grass Roots, Proceedings of the 36th Hawaii International Conference on System Sciences (HICSS'03), IEEE Computer Society (2002)
8. Corporate Author: UK Cabinet Office: Modernising Government White Paper (1999)
9. Moen, W.E., McClure, C.R.: The Government Information Locator Series: A User-Based Approach to Standards" in StandardView Vol. 2, No. 2, June pages 89-95 (1994)
10. Pardo, T.A., Scholl, H.J.: Walking Atop the Cliffs: Avoiding Failure and Reducing Risk in Large Scale E-Government Projects, Proceedings of the 35th Hawaii International Conference on System Sciences – 2002, IEEE Computer Society (2002)
11. Sommerville, I.: Software Engineering, Addison-Wesley, Reading, MA (2000)
12. "Survey of Progress and Trend of Development and Use of Automatic Data Processing in Business and Management Control Systems of the Federal Government, as of December 1957 III" in Communications of the ACM, Volume 2 , Issue 9 (September 1959), Pages: 34 – 43, ACM Press NY, USA (1959)
13. Vassilakis C, Laskaridis G, Lepouras G, Rouvas S, Georgiadis P, A framework for managing the lifecycle of transactional e-government services, Telematics and Informatics, Volume 20 , Issue 4 , Pages: 315 – 329, Pergamon Press, Inc. NY, USA (2003)
14. Wastell D, Kawalek P, Newman M.: Plus ca change: Defensive Translations and resistance to IT-enabled Change in Local Government (2002)

Participatory Budget Formation Through the Web

J. Rios[1], D. Rios Insua[1], E. Fernandez[1], and J.A. Rivero[2]

[1] Decision Engineering Lab,
U. Rey Juan Carlos-DMR Consulting Foundation, Spain
{jmrios, drios, e.fernandez}@escet.urjc.es
[2] Accounting Department, U. Rey Juan Carlos

Abstract. We describe a web-based system to support groups in elaborating participatory budgets. Rather than using physical meetings with voting mechanisms, we promote virtual meetings with explicit preference elicitation, guided negotiations and, only if consensus is not reached, voting.

1 Basic Concepts in Participatory Budget Formation

Participatory budgets constitute an attempt to allow citizens to have a word and aid in deciding and approving how public budgets, mainly in municipalities, are spent, whether (and how much) in transportation, culture, education, urban development, health,... They constitute a budget allocation model based on dialogue and citizen participation, which diverges from the current predominant representative model in which citizens choose representatives for four years, with practically no other direct opportunity to influence council policies.

In a sense, participatory budgets are transforming the idea of a representative democracy, in which the preferences of the citizens are considered just at the moment of elections, through voting, to move closer to a participatory democracy, based on direct participation and discussion of issues. In words of Souza, see [10]:

> Participatory budgets constitute a universal, direct and volunteer kind of democracy which gives population the opportunity of discussing about budgets and public policy, making relevant decisions. Citizens not only vote, but also get involved.

Among many potential benefits of participatory budgets, we would include:

- Legitimation
- Approaching decisions to citizens
- Public decisions made publicly
- Mitigation of alienation and apathy
- Transparency

M. Böhlen et al. (Eds.): TCGOV 2005, LNAI 3416, pp. 268–276, 2005.

Participatory budgets stem from the initial experience at Porto Alegre in 1988, which was definitely consolidated in 1992. Since then, participatory budgets are becoming increasingly popular in many other municipalities, all around the world, with nearly 200 municipalities undertaking them in 2003. As an example, in Spain villages like Cabezas de San Juan or Rubi, and cities like Albacete or Valladolid have now established such experiences.

Although they are all grounded in a relatively simple general principle, a comparison of participatory budget municipal regulations shows us a variety of participatory municipal council budget forms, with differences in the percentage of budget directly allocated, the number of participants, the number of rounds,... However, far from amorphous and disoriented, participatory budgets are set up along structured lines, including the necessary bodies, functional rules and principles embodied in municipal regulations. These are set down in manuals, which address the population and are reasonably clearly formulated. They are meant to ensure that regulations fixing the number of delegates to each body, the role of the public authorities, the prerogatives and powers of a participatory budget council and the discussion fora are clear and transparent.

There are, however, several criticisms to be made stemming from the experiences undertaken in such processes. From the conceptual point of view, we should stress that participation is frequently limited to a small fraction of the population, in part against the own concept of participation. From an information technology point of view, we appreciate that, except at a few experiences which use discussion fora to collect suggestions for projects to be implemented, there is little use of new technologies, as processes are based on discussion and physical meetings, and preferences are usually established through voting, very frequently just by raising hands. Among other things, this entails that it has turned out difficult to involve the youngest and poorest population; moreover, they have induced problems in neighbourhoods unable to articulate a common coherent investment plan. This is related with our final critique, from the point of view of the little decision technology employed: no formal modelling or quantification of the intensity of preferences of citizens is undertaken and no use of formal negotiation or group decision support tools is used. To sum up, there is little methodology available.

In this paper, we shall sketch a model and a web based system to support participatory budget elaboration processes. We essentially view them as a negotiation problem with budget constraints and describe an implementation of the balanced increment method to support such negotiations.

Many authors have dwelt on how Internet is changing the way people interact with governments. However, so far most ideas relating Internet and politics, are directed towards facilitating traditional political methods through new technologies, like electronic voting or Internet voting, instead of voting with a piece of paper. Our proposal here aims at transforming, rather than facilitating, politics, through the use of IT: it is a tenet of ours that involving and communicating with the stakeholders at all stages of a decision making process leads to better quality, more consensual decisions.

2 A Method to Support Participatory Budget Elaboration

We outline a description and a model of the participatory budget problem. A full description together with mathematical details may be seen in [7].

Suppose a group of m persons has to decide how to spend a budget b. There is a set of q proposals, $a_1, \ldots, a_q$. Proposal i has cost c_i, and is evaluated by the j-th individual with n_j criteria, with values x_{ijk}, $k = 1, \ldots, n_j$, $j = 1, \ldots, m$, $i = 1, \ldots, q$. We assume that all evaluations are under certainty, i.e. we have a fairly accurate estimate of each project costs and features.

We shall also assume that each participant is a (multiattribute) value function maximiser, see e.g. [1]. This allows us to associate with each participatory budget problem a matrix of entries v_{ij}, the value that individual j gives to project i, which he aims at maximising. We tray here to, somehow, provide a feasible solution that jointly satisfies the group of m participants.

A feasible solution for such problem is a subset of proposals, $F \subseteq I = \{1, 2, \ldots, q\}$, which satisfies the budget constraint, that is, such that

$$\sum_{i \in F} c_i \leq b. \tag{1}$$

To simplify matters, we shall assume that the value given by the j-th individual to each feasible solution, F, is the sum of the values of the objects in F assessed by the individual:

$$v_j(F) = \sum_{i \in F} v_{ij} \ , \ j = 1, \ldots, m. \tag{2}$$

Then, if $\{F^1, F^2, \ldots, F^s\}$ designates the set of feasible solutions, conceptually we may view the participatory budget problem as a negotiation table, see [8]. Note

Table 1. This table shows the value given by each individual to each feasible solution

	1		j		m
F^1	$v_1(F^1)$	...	$v_j(F^1)$	...	$v_m(F^1)$
F^2	$v_1(F^2)$	...	$v_j(F^2)$	...	$v_m(F^2)$
$\vdots$	$\vdots$		$\vdots$		$\vdots$
F^s	$v_1(F^s)$	...	$v_j(F^s)$	...	$v_m(F^s)$
	$F_1^\star$		$F_j^\star$		$F_m^\star$

that just obtaining this table may be prohibitively costly from a computational point of view, because of the combinatorial nature of the problem. The last row includes the optimal solution $F_j^\star$ for each individual, which may be obtained solving a knapsack problem, see, e.g., [4]. Clearly, if $F_1^\star = F_2^\star = \cdots = F_m^\star$, this feasible solution is obviously the group decision. However, typically, various individuals involved will reach different optimal solutions, and, consequently, a round of negotiations should be undertaken to try to reach a consensus. As the group will rank the alternatives partially, through the Pareto order:

$$F \succeq F' \iff v_j(F) \geq v_j(F') \ , \ \forall j \in \{1, \ldots, m\}, \tag{3}$$

the agreement should be sought within the nondominated set.

We shall assume that participants enter in the multilateral negotiation within the full open and truthful intermediary disclosure (FOTID) framework. This will imply, for us, that negotiators may communicate privately their preferences to an entity (our web system) which will know the preferences of all negotiators and, based on them, and some concept of fairness, will offer solutions to the negotiators until one is accepted. Participants have access to the alternatives of the feasible set. As we mentioned, their preferences over these alternatives are modelled by a value function. We denote by $S \subseteq \mathbb{R}^m$, the set whose points represent the value levels that each participant can reach through an outcome associated with a feasible solution, if they choose it jointly. The disagreement point is a vector $d = (d_1, \ldots, d_n) \in \mathbb{R}^m$, in which the j-th coordinate represents the value level that the j-th participant would receive if the negotiation breaks down.

Mathematically, given (S, d), the problem of selecting a reasonable nondominated point in S is known as a bargaining problem and it has been studied under arbitration schemes. For us, the solution for this problem is meant to produce a recommendation as an impartial arbitrator would make. There are different solution proposals, formulated by a list of properties or axioms, which embody normative objectives of fairness, see [11] for a summary.

For a bargaining problem (S, d), the highest value that the i-th participant can get from the disagreement point d without worsening the value of the other participants is known as the dictatorial solution for this participant, $D_i(d)$, and represents his preferred solution or his most optimistic expectation. This is

$$D_i(d) = \max_{d \prec x} x_i. \tag{4}$$

Given d, the bliss point will be $B(d) = (D_1, \ldots, D_n)$ and represents an ideal point, because participants can rarely get these values jointly through a feasible solution. The Kalai-Smorodinsky solution $K(d)$ lies where the diagonal linking the disagreement point and the bliss point crosses the set of nondominated solutions, as shown in Fig. 1a). See [3] for an axiomatic description of this solution. The direction of this diagonal represents a compromise direction in which joint value improvements are proportional to the participant's most optimistic expectation. Raiffa, in [6], proposed to compute a reasonable solution by beginning at the status quo and effects step by step improvements of the participants' utilities in the same direction of the line joining the point at the current solution with its bliss point, until a nondominated solution is reached. This limiting solution is known as *balanced increment solution.*

We propose such approach with the modification that, at each iteration, we offer parties the nondominated solution closes to the diagonal to see whether they accept it. Figure 1b) shows the first steps of our modified balanced increment method (BIM), see [9], for details. In the i-th iteration, the system offers

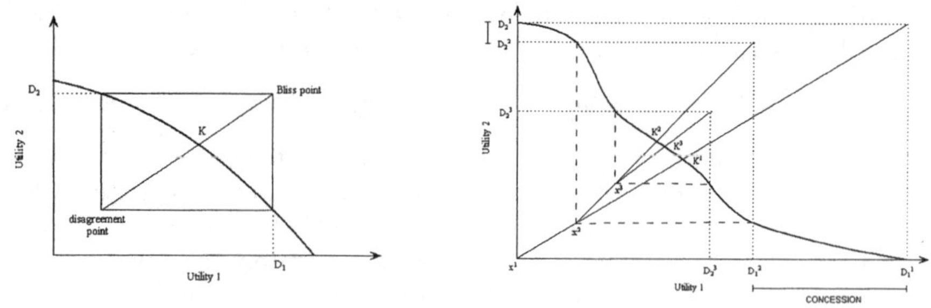

a) Kalai-Smorodinski solution **b)** First steps of BIM

Fig. 1. Balanced increment method with two participants

K^i, the Kalai-Smorodinsky solution from d^i. For participant 1, the value of K^i will be in the interval $[d_1^i, D_1^i]$, where d_1^i may be interpreted as the value of the dictatorial solution of participant 2, D_2^i, from the point of view of the participant 1. If participants do not accept unanimously the offered solution, the system offers another solution involving a concession in the participants' most optimistic expectation.

Initially, we propose helping the individuals to reach an agreement in the participatory budget problem using the balanced increment method (BIM), whose status quo shall be the solution which includes no proposals. With this initialisation of BIM, the set of nondominated solutions will not be constrained and all nondominated solutions can be considered potentially. In [8], we prove that such method leads to a nondominated solution with several nice properties from a group decision point of view. However, its implementation is extremely costly from a computational point of view, as it essentially implies precomputing the whole nondominated set in a combinatorial problem. Computation times will be unacceptable, when the number of projects is moderately big.

As an alternative, we propose using a greedy heuristic which we have found fairly powerful and proceeds in two stages. To wit, in a first stage we identify the set of nondominated projects; if this set does not exhaust the budget, we incorporate it to the solution and eliminate them from the set of project which participant will negotiate. We repeat until one layer of nondominated projects exhausts the remaining budget. At that point, we start the second stage, in which participants negotiate among the remaining projects with the BIM method. Specifically, we have

- Stage 1:
  - Compute set of nondominated projects
  - If budget is not exceeded, add to solution, else go to stage 2
  - Repeat with rest of projects after updating the budget
- Stage 2:
  - Negotiate over the remaining set of projects and available budget using the BIM method

As pointed out in [8], this heuristic does not guarantee a nondominated agreement.

It may happen, as well, that negotiators do not reach an agreement through negotiations. In such case, we would allow them, as usual in participatory budgets, to proceed through voting.

3 Supporting Participatory Budget Formation Through the Web

We implement through the web the previous model, integrating it in a complete system to support group decision making in the area of participatory budget formation. To some extent, the whole integrated process provides an asynchronous implementation of the philosophy and methodology of decision conferencing, see [5].

Among, many technological possibilities, we have adopted the LAMP (Linux, Apache, MySQL, PHP) environment. We distinguish three basic profiles:

- the *problem owner*, the entity which aims at solving a participatory budget problem, structures and publicizes it, which would be the mayor, in this case,
- the *stakeholders* or participants, which provide input to the decision making process, in our case, the citizens,
- the administrator, who takes technical care of the process development, from supporting the problem owner to structuring the problem, to providing access rights to stakeholders, to defining time windows for voting.

Safety mechanisms are available, with participants using appropriately secure validation mechanisms. The following system modules are included.

3.1 Proposal Elaboration

The system includes a module that allows the problem owner to structure the problem, if necessary with the aid of the administrator. The stakeholders will use the same structure to explore issues of interest concerning the problem. The module allows for:

- Defining the number of alternatives.
- Specify the alternatives and associated costs.
- Specify the budget.

We assume that the problem owner publishes a first draft of possible projects and invites citizens for comments and suggestions, and then consolidates, together with his technical staff, the final list of projects under consideration.

3.2 Value Function Assessment

The system includes a module that allows users to build their preference model. We assume that any user (problem owner, stakeholder) may build his own value function, as we have placed a lot of emphasis on usability. Each user will assess his value function privately and may communicate it to the system. Without much loss of generality, we assume that the users' preferences may be modelled through a weighted additive value function, see [2] for details. The system allows for:

- Specification of basic properties of (multiple) objectives by the problem owner: number of objectives, their scale and range, whether the objective is to be minimised or maximised. It is assumed that all participants will share these objectives. Some participants may disregard some of these objectives, e.g., by giving them zero weight.
- Assessment of each component value function. For each objective, and each user, the value of some attribute values is assessed with the probability equivalent method. Then, a concave-convex or convex-concave (exponential) value function is fitted through least squares.
- Assessment of the weights of the additive value function.
- Saving the value function for later purposes.

Users are expected to provide their preferences within a given time frame. Several facilities are included to provide convenient summaries of the value functions.

3.3 Individual Optimal Solutions

Once with the preferences of a participant, we may proceed to compute his optimal alternative. For that purpose, the system includes a module that allows users to evaluate the feasible alternatives, based on his value function, to obtain his preferred projects through the corresponding knapsack problem. The problem owner may find out his optimal alternative privately, as the stakeholders may do. If so, they may make public their solutions.

3.4 Negotiating

Typically, various parties involved (problem owner, stakeholders) will reach different optimal solutions. Consequently, a round of negotiations may be undertaken to try to reach a consensus. The negotiation is driven by our two stage heuristic, modification of the balanced increment method, as briefly explained above.

At each iteration, the system offers a solution to participants and, if accepted, it stops, that being a consensus. Alternatively, the procedure stops when two of the subsequent solutions offered are close enough. If the last one is accepted, a consensus is reached. Users are expected to communicate whether they accept or not an offered solution within a given time window.

3.5 Voting

Our (automatic) negotiating scheme converges to a solution, but it is conceivable that participants may not accept such solution, neither the sequence of solutions offered. This deadlock should be solved through voting.

For that reason, our system includes a voting module, which permits the design of a voting session, and its execution. Specifically, the rule implemented for voting is that of approval voting, with which participants provide at most one vote to as many alternatives as they feel like, the winner being that receiving the biggest number of votes. Users are expected to vote within a specific a time window.

3.6 Post-Settlement Module

If the system detects that the voted solution is dominated, we have the option of renegotiating an agreement starting again the negotiations taking the last solution as disagreement point, that is, as initial solution of the BIM.

4 An Experiment

An experiment has been conducted with a group of executives of a firm to decide in which projects invest the available budget for next year, with two criteria: the expected Net Present Value (NPV), the expected time of Pay-Back (TPB), that is the time to return on investment, labour costs and country risk. Twelve projects were considered. Participants were pleased with the session run.

5 Discussion

We have proposed a group decision support system implemented in the web to solve the participatory budget elaboration problem. To prepare the negotiation, the participants have to assess their preferences models privately. The negotiation is driven by the BIM. If the negotiation does not provide an agreement, the joint decision may be made by voting.

Rather than using new technologies to facilitate standard political decision making mechanisms, our scheme radically modifies them by allowing more participation from stakeholders, a more informed and transparent decision by the problem owner, and, even, a more consensual approach. The experiments performed have been successful.

The underlying model assumes equal importance to all participants. We should study negotiation methods in which participants can have different weights.

Acknowledgments

Research supported by MEC grant TSI2004-06801-C04-01, by the Decision Engineering Lab, URJC - DMR Consulting Foundation and the ESF programme on Electronic Democracy.

References

1. French, S.: *Decision Theory. An Introduction to the Mathematics of Rationality.* Ellis Horwood Limited, Willey, Chichester, GB (1986)

2. French, S.,Rios-Insua, D.: *Statistical Decision Theory.* Arnold (2000)
3. Kalai, E., Smorodinski, M.: Others solutions to nash's bargaining problem. *Econometrica,* **43** 3 (1975) 513–518
4. Martello, S., Toth, P.: *Knapsack Problems; Algorithms and Computer Implementations.* John Wiley (1990)
5. McCartt, A., Rohrbough, J.: Evaluating group decision support system efectiveness. *Decision Support Systems* **5** (1989) 243–253
6. Raiffa, H.: *Negotiation Analysis.* Harvard UP (2002)
7. Rios, J., Rios-Insua, D.: A framework for participatory budget elaboration. Tech Rep on Statictis and Decison Sciences, Rey Juan Carlos University (2004)
8. Rios, J., Rios-Insua, D.: Negotiation over influence diagrams. Tech Rep on Statictis and Decison Sciences, Rey Juan Carlos University (2004)
9. Rios-Insua, D., Holgado, J., Moreno, R.: An e-negotiation system to support edemocracy. *J. Multicriteria Decision Analysis* **12** (2003) 213–218
10. Souza, C. U.: Participatory budgeting in brazilian cities: limits and possibilities in building democratic institutions. *Environment and Urbanization,* **13** 1 (2001) 159–184
11. Thomson, W.: Cooperative models of bargaining. In Aumann, R. J., Hart, S. (eds.) *Handbook of Game Theory,* Vol II. North-Holland (1994) 1238–1277

On the Transition to an Open Source Solution for Desktop Office Automation

Bruno Rossi, Barbara Russo, Paolo Zuliani, and Giancarlo Succi

Center for Applied Software Engineering, Free University of Bolzano-Bozen,
Piazza Domenicani 3, 39100 Bolzano-Bozen, Italy
{bruno.rossi, barbara.russo, paolo.zuliani,
giancarlo.succi}@unibz.it

Abstract. There are many claims about the benefits of Open Source Software (OSS). However, these claims are seldom supported by empirical evidence, while on the other hand there are several impediment factors which might overcome the advantages deriving from the use of OSS in a corporate environment: cost of transition, personnel training and, interoperability and integration with existing technologies. These factors are often used by OSS opponents. In this paper we first report of a small-scale deployment of OSS for office automation in Public Administration bodies. We describe the environment, the process and the problems encountered. Next, we describe a proposal for a future experiment for empirically assessing OSS impediment factors, focusing in particular on personnel productivity. We again propose the deployment of OSS office automation tools in Public Administration bodies and we describe a system for monitoring the effect of the use of OSS on personnel productivity.

1 Introduction

Open Source Software (OSS) has grown a lot in popularity. Linux and the Apache web server are found in respectively 30% and 66% of the Internet's public servers, according to Netcraft's survey 1. We thus have some empirical evidence that OSS can work well, at least for the server side of a client-server architecture.

By assuming the fact above, supporters claim that OSS leads to a reduction in IT expenditure because:

- OSS is free, one does not have to pay any license;
- Source code is available, so it is possible to tune the software for specific needs by removing unnecessary, resource-consuming features. This translates in the possibility of using less powerful, thus less expensive, hardware.

The first reason is indeed true, while for the second reason we do not have any empirical study comparing OSS and proprietary solutions: proponents usually report common knowledge experience. Furthermore, such knowledge and experience are confined to very specific applications such as server architectures or software development. For example, in 2001 Amazon.com adopted Linux for most of its servers and reduced by 24% ($17 million) the IT expenditure, as reported by the IDG Group (2, 3). In August 2002, Verizon Communications, one the biggest telecommunication op-

M. Böhlen et al. (Eds.): TCGOV 2005, LNAI 3416, pp. 277–285, 2005.

erator in the USA, replaced the Unix and Windows workstations of its internal developers with systems based on Linux and OpenOffice. The average desktop cost dropped from $20,000 to $3,000 per developer and in the end the company saved $6 million 5.

It seems to be that the common feature of these success cases is that OSS has been able to penetrate the market only for applications which require more reliability and efficiency than user-friendliness and usability.

Therefore, it might be that OSS is not well suited for desktop and client applications, for which we know that Microsoft Office is the de-facto standard. If we think of a hypothetical deployment of OSS for desktop applications in a corporate environment, such as Public Administrations (PA), there are factors which might overcome the claimed advantages of OSS:

- Cost of transition from previous solutions.
- Interoperability and integration with existing solutions.
- Cost of training personnel for the new tools and hostility to change.
- Reduced productivity of the personnel.

The recent FLOSS project 6 funded by the European Union aimed at collecting data about the usage and development of OSS in Europe. Surveys were conducted between February and May 2002 on about 1,500 companies and public institutions, asking whether they were employing, or willing to employ, Open Source software. Four hundred of these were indeed using, or planning to do so in the near future, some kind of OSS.

There are two points of the FLOSS study 6 which are of interest for us:

- OSS for desktop applications (e.g. client operating systems, office automation, etc.) was employed only by the 20% of those four hundred establishments using OSS. If we further restrict to the use of OpenOffice that percentage drops to 10%. This confirms common wisdom that OSS is better suited for server and IT infrastructure tasks.
- It turned out that companies and public institutions were generally unable to quantify the benefits deriving from the use of OSS. They were also not even able to quantify benefits like license fees savings and hardware cost savings.

It is therefore important to empirically analyze and assess the benefits and the problems deriving from the use of OSS, in order to provide companies and public institutions with more significant data for their strategic decisions.

In particular, we focus on the OpenOffice suite: a set of key desktop applications which includes a word processor, a spreadsheet, a presentation manager, a drawing program, and an equation editor 7.

In this paper we first report of a small-scale deployment of the OpenOffice suite in several PA bodies. We describe the environment, the process and the problems encountered during the transition.

Next, building on that experience, we propose a future experiment for empirically evaluating the benefits and problems caused by the introduction of OpenOffice. The project aims at showing that OpenOffice allows personnel to produce as efficiently as Microsoft Office.

2 Small-Scale Deployments

The Consortium of the Townships of the Province of Bolzano-Bozen (Italy), in collaboration with the Centre for Applied Software Engineering of the Free University of Bolzano-Bozen, has performed a trial installation of OpenOffice in ten associate townships.

2.1 Environment

The trial installation of OpenOffice involved ten townships of the Alto-Adige region in Italy. Townships ranged from very small (five employees) to small-medium size (twenty employees). The activities performed are the usual office tasks: word processing, spreadsheet, *etc*. Microsoft Office was the only office automation tool used.

In the end, OpenOffice was installed on about one hundred desktop computers. The operating system was Microsoft Windows in all the cases.

We select a set of 16 PC computers uniformly distributed in the Townships. The end-users volunteered for the experiment belong to four different departments. In eight PC computers we have installed OpenOffice.

2.2 Process Transition

Transitions lasted from two to four working days and employed two instructors each. Personnel training was performed on-site and one-to-one.

Instructors first went to the site for "exploring" the environment and for collecting the most used documents by offices' personnel. The instructors then returned the day after with all the documents converted to OpenOffice's format. They then installed OpenOffice and train the personnel by working on the very same documents they were usually working on.

The conversion of more than two hundred documents from Microsoft Word to OpenOffice was performed without any particular problem and with great efficiency: the size of an OpenOffice document was generally one third of the equivalent Word document.

2.3 Problems

Personnel do not generally look positively at the introduction of new or different technologies and at the abandon of those which is used to: a phenomenon called "hostility to change". The most reported reason is the refuse to use tools different from those of colleagues or from those used at home. However, during the transition to OpenOffice we found only a few employees showing hostility to change.

We instead have found an inefficient use of resources: the personnel routinely used only the very basic features of Office, and did not consider little more complicate features which would have lead to better use of resources.

Users with good knowledge of Office have not had any problem in switching to OpenOffice. Most of the problems have been caused by personnel with little Office knowledge.

Personnel training has been usually performed on-site and one-to-one, but it has turned out that instructors have had to frequently interrupt training because of incoming phone calls, urgent documents delivering, *etc.*

3 The Experiment

The aim of the experiment is to studying, analyzing and evaluating the introduction of OpenOffice for all office automation tasks in the PA, while preserving existing proprietary solutions for desktop operating systems (*e.g.* Microsoft Windows). In particular, we investigate whether the use of OpenOffice does not significantly affect personnel productivity.

The experiment also aims at becoming a success case for the introduction of OpenOffice, and of OS desktop software in general, in companies and Public Administrations.

The experiment has been jointly conducted by Consortium of the Townships of the Province of Bolzano-Bozen, the Centre for Applied Software Engineering of the Free University of Bolzano-Bozen and a few local IT firms.

3.1 Design

The sample consists of 16 end-users. Eight of them volunteered to use OpenOffice. The rest continues to use Microsoft Office.

First we have drawn a picture of all the applications calling and called by the office automation tool used, and the macros used by each department.

Then we have monitored the use of the office automation tools for a period of seven weeks before the transition.

Soon after the transition we have monitored the use of both the old and new solution for a period of fourteen weeks.

Then we have configured the access to the documents to automatically opening them in OpenOffice. Although opening the documents with Microsoft Office is still possible, it requires a bit more complex procedure. Again we have monitored the use of Microsoft and OpenOffice for a period of three weeks.

3.2 Collected Data

We have selected data from two weeks before the transition, two weeks soon after the transition, and two weeks during the new configuration access to documents.

The data have been collected automatically in background with the PROM tool.

PROM is a software engineering tool originally developed for collecting process and product metrics in software development (9, 8). For example, it is possible to record the time lapsed in working on a Java source file, or the number of modifications applied. By the use of appropriate plug-in's we interfaced the PROM tool with Microsoft Office and OpenOffice, so that it is possible to collect process metrics for any kind of OpenOffice or Office document. For this preliminary study we have collected data on interaction of applications, on time of use of applications, and on number of documents daily used. We have not taken into account daily average time shorter than 5 minutes.

4 Data Analysis

In first seven weeks we have analyzed the calls between Word/Excel and the other Microsoft Office applications. We have selected the following applications

Table 1. Description of the applications considered

Called by	Description
CPCQM.EXE	Printer driver Canon
MSOHELP.EXE	MS Help Menu
EXPLORER.EXE	Folder viewer
DW.EXE	MS Error Reporting tool
EXCEL.EXE	MS Excel
IEXPLORER.EXE	MS web browser
MSACCESS.EXE	MS Access
MSTORE.EXE	Microsoft Clip Organizer
IFRUN60.EXE	Oracle Forms (Runforms)
OUTLOOK.EXE	MS Mail client
WINHELP32.EXE	MS Help guide

Table 2. Top score applications calling Word and Excel

Calling	Word	Excel
EXPLORER.EXE	80.74%	94.38%
OUTLOOK.EXE	14.61%	3.42%
DW.EXE	0.64%	0.92%
IFRUN60.EXE	0.11%	0.00%
IEXPLORER.EXE	0.19%	0.00%
EXCEL.EXE	0.04%	0.00%
UNKNOWN	3.68%	1.28%

Table 3. Top scores applications called by Word and Excel

Called by	Word/Excel
CPCQM.EXE	71.05%
MSOHELP.EXE	13.16%
EXPLORER.EXE	7.89%
DW.EXE	5.26%
EXCEL.EXE	2.63%
IEXPLORER.EXE	2.63%
MSACCESS.EXE	0.00%
MSTORE.EXE	0.00%
IFRUN60.EXE	0.00%
OUTLOOK.EXE	0.00%
WINHELP32.EXE	0.00%

The patterns expressed in the tables indicate the interoperability of the desktop applications that needs to be taken into account in the transition: customization and adaptation of the office tools impact on effort and costs.

In fact, despite the difference in percentage of calls all the applications that are in Table 1 need to be considered in the transition. For example we need to customize the call to an oracle DB as there has been at lest one call to this DB (IFRUN60.EXE).

For the same reason we analyze the existence of macros: for the accessible excel files it has been reported 43 macros for a total of 21,482 lines of code for 526 files inspected. No macros have been found in place for Word files.

We monitor the number of documents used and the daily time spent on the documents.

We derive a formula on daily productivity for each user

$$P_i = \frac{\#\text{Documents}}{\text{time}} \tag{1}$$

We have different types of productivity. The documents are Office documents (Docs (O)) or OpenOffice documents (Docs (OO)).

Docs (O) (or # Docs (OO)) is the total number of documents with extension Office (respectively Open Office) saved by an end-user in a day.

The time is the total time in a day of use of an application. So we have time for using the OpenOffice applications ad time for using Office applications – Open Office, time (OO) or Office, time (O).

Considering that OpenOffice files cannot be opened by Office there are three types of productivity.

$$P_{tot} = \frac{\#\text{ Docs (O)} + \#\text{ Docs (OO)}}{\text{time (O)} + \text{time(OO)}} \tag{2}$$

$$P_1 = \frac{\#\text{ Docs (O)}}{\text{time (O)} + \text{time(OO)}} \tag{3}$$

$$P_2 = \frac{\#\text{ Docs (OO)}}{\text{time(OO)}} \tag{4}$$

Then we average the daily productivity in each period of analysis, getting only one number for each end-user. The histograms below report of the three productivities in the three periods in the two groups.

Each bar in the below histograms represents the productivity of a single employee in the three different phase of the monitoring. The pre-transition phase corresponds to the nr. 1, the transtion phase to the nr. 2 and the post-transition to the nr. 3

The first picture represents the daily average productivity when documents are saved/modified as office documents (.doc, .xlm extension) disregarding the application used - within OpenOffice or Office (eq. 3). Therefore the productivity here is an upper bound of the productivity related to the solo use of Office: a user may have modified a file .doc with OpenOffice. Further analysis would consider this refinement (eq. 4).

The second picture displays the trends in the control group. From the picture we deduce that the first period of monitoring is characterized by a bigger productivity (eq. 3).

The third picture reports the productivity computed as ratio of number of files – indifferently Office or OpenOffice – and time spent with OpenOffice or Office applications (eq. 2).

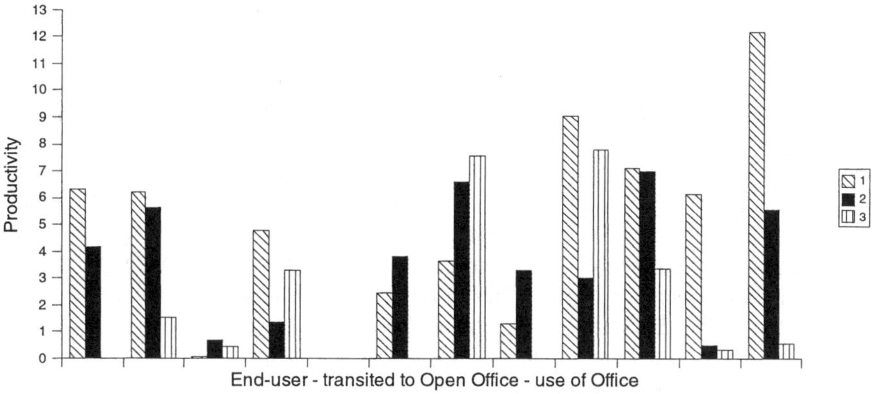

Fig. 1. Partial productivity (eq. 3) in the three periods in the group transited to OpenOffice

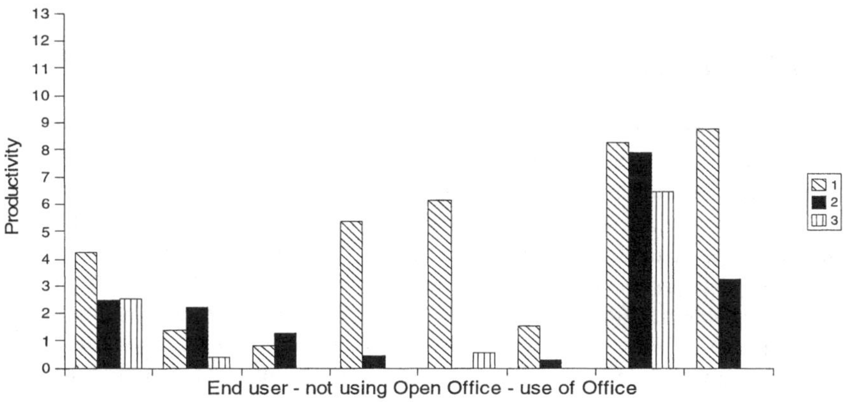

Fig. 2. Partial productivity (eq. 3) in the three periods in the group not using OpenOffice

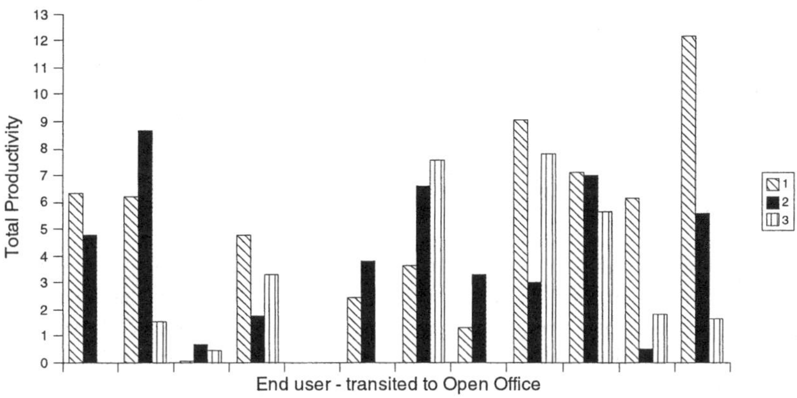

Fig. 3. Total productivity (eq. 2) in the three periods in the group transited to OpenOffice

5 Results

The preliminary analysis based on the groups comparison in the three periods of the experiment (Fig. 2), indicates that there is no lack of productivity in the group transited to OpenOffice.

Even more some of the members of the group transited to OpenOffice present a higher productivity when working both with only Office documents (eq. 3, Fig. 1 and Fig. 3 period n. 1) and with any kind of document (eq. 2, Fig. 3, period n. 3). In the transition, when the choice to use one or the other application is even (Fig. 1 and Fig. 3, period n.2), no increase of productivity has been registered: no documents new or saved as OpenOffice files have been produced.

In the third period the use of OpenOffice has increased as the path to access to Office applications has become more complex.

To facilitate the transition we have performed an analysis on application interoperability and existence of macros. This has helped to customize the new solution in terms of the needs of the end-user.

6 Analysis of the Problems

Again, the fact that Microsoft Office is by far the most used office automation tool raises the problem of training the personnel for OpenOffice. To this end, we have organized part-time courses on OpenOffice. The courses are held off-site, to avoid the disturbing factors experienced in the trial installation. In these courses, offices' personnel have been taught the basic and most used OpenOffice features, with the possibility of suggesting some particular topic of interest.

Another problem which might occur is the hostility to change. In this case, in order to maintain the efficacy of the training action, we might think of motivating the personnel by a series of "bonuses for change". Another solution is to train homogenous groups of people, that is, personnel coming from the same of closely related offices.

The choice of introducing OpenOffice while maintaining the same client operating systems is motivated by the need to minimize the training load for the personnel. That choice allows also a smooth transition, minimum interruption of public services and limits any possible hostility to change.

We will also establish: a hotline, a data base of success cases, a FAQ and a knowledge base. These services are aimed at PA personnel already trained and will offer user and technical support on various OS software of interest for the PA.

7 Limits of the Experiment

This is a preliminary experiment conducted on a small sample of public administrations. Results may only fit the context of this case study. Nevertheless the value of the experiment reported relays more on the identification of a suitable experiment design and few valid statistical variables rather than on comprehensive results. In any case although results are not the major issue here, they still indicate no loss of productivity in passing to Open Source solution.

The Open Source applications here are just desktop applications for office automation, further analysis will consider a wider/different set of open tools.

8 Conclusions

In the past years OSS has proved to be a very reliable solution for many server applications. However, the claims about the benefits and advantages deriving from the use of OSS are seldom supported by empirical evidence or studies.

We considered the use of OSS for office automation tasks, for which no significant success case is known. We described a trial installation of the OpenOffice suite, reported the problems encountered and describe a possible experiment design and data analysis.

The data collection has been made with a non-invasive tool working in background.

The good results of the trial installation motivate the instantiation of a more extended experiment aimed at studying, analyzing, and evaluating the introduction of OpenOffice in public institutions.

We suggest an extensive analysis of the application interoperability before a transition process. This would help the customization of the new solution according to the end-user needs.

Acknowledgements

This work has been done with the help of the Autonome Provinz Bozen - Südtirol under the extreme valuable supervision of Dr. H. Ladurner. The authors would also like to acknowledge the help and support provided by Dr. Hugo Leiter, Director of the EDP Unit of the Consortium of the Townships of the Province of Bolzano-Bozen.

References

1. Netcraft Survey, http://www.netcraft.com/survey/
2. Hochmuth P.: Amazon cuts costs with Linux. Computerworld, http://www. computerworld.com/softwaretopics/os/linux/story/0,10801,65674,00.html
3. Berger M.: LinuxWorld: Amazon.com clicks with Linux. ComputerWorld,
4. http://www.computerworld.com/softwaretopics/os/linux/story/0,10801,73617,00.html
5. Shankland, S.: Verizon switches programmers to Linux. CNET News.com, http://news.com.com/2100-1001-949913.html
6. Free/Libre/Open Source Software: Survey and Study. June (2002). http://www. infonomics.nl/FLOSS/
7. The OpenOffice project. http://www.openoffice.org
8. Humprey, W.: Introduction to the Personal Software Process. Addison-Wesley (1997)
9. Fenton, N.E. and Pfleeger, S.H.: Software Metrics: a Rigorous and Practical Approach. Thomson Computer Press (1994)

Public eProcurement in Action: Policies, Practices and Technologies

Catherine Hardy and Susan P. Williams

Discipline of Business Information Systems, School of Business,
The University of Sydney, Sydney, NSW, 2006, Australia
{c.hardy, s.williams}@econ.usyd.edu.au

Abstract. This paper examines how abstract governmental eProcurement policies are translated into practice. We adopt a social constructionist perspective on policy and argue that the processes of eProcurement in public sector organizations are interwoven in broader policy processes and heterogeneous networks. Using the case study method we provide an empirical illustration of how this perspective could be drawn upon to make sense of eProcurement in action.

1 Introduction

Public eProcurement research is underrepresented in the eProcurement literature. Whilst it has similarities with private sector contexts in terms of deriving economic value and quality it differs in terms of its social welfare implications [1]. Of further significance to this study is the limited attention to and perspectives on eProcurement policy. For example, policy has been discussed in terms of the technology to support its delivery [2], a driver in the design of the procurement process [1] or as an implication arising from eProcurement use [3]. Less attention appears to have been given to the role of policy itself in shaping eProcurement practice.

The objectives of public eProcurement, commonly found in government policy, are primarily focused on governance practices in terms of achieving better value for money, efficiencies and effectiveness and transparency in government procurement. While these are valid statements of the desired outcomes, they: offer limited guidance in terms of action (how the policy is implemented); may conflict with other policy areas because of competing objectives or priorities; and, prove hard to reach in the prescribed timeframe. Further, over time attention may shift to other priorities because of changing political landscapes and multiple layers of government. Consequently the goals articulated may bear little resemblance to what is happening in practice raising the question about the significance of policy, 'what is policy for' [4: 49].

That policy is a purposive course of action in terms of achieving some predetermined goals suggests that if the outcome differs significantly from the stated intentions then there has been some 'implementation failure' with the policy [4: 40-53]. Whether implementation is a problem and the type of problem it presents depends upon the perspective being applied [4:53]. While policy may be clearly

M. Böhlen et al. (Eds.): TCGOV 2005, LNAI 3416, pp. 286 – 297, 2005.

grounded in some conscious choice, its origins may exist in practice [4:15]. Therefore an alternative perspective is required that assists in addressing: How we arrive at these moments described as eProcurement policy implementation success or failure? What are the events that preceded them? What role does policy play in shaping these moments?

Our study addresses these questions by examining how abstract governmental eProcurement policies are translated into public procurement practices through adopting Colebatch's social construct of policy [4] and theoretical concepts from actor-network theory [14] serving two objectives. Firstly, by adopting these perspectives we argue that the processes of eProcurement in public sector organisations are interwoven in broader policy processes and heterogeneous networks. Secondly, we provide an empirical illustration of how this analytical lens is useful in making sense of eProcurement in action. We achieve these objectives through a case study analysis of three government agencies.

The study contributes to the eProcurement literature in two ways. Firstly the analysis makes visible the role(s) played by key actors in different settings, which assisted in translating eProcurement policy into practice. Secondly, the analysis provides us with a starting point for critically engaging with the notion of policy in eProcurement. We return to these themes in both, the analysis and case descriptions.

The paper is organised as follows. The next section discusses the policy construct. This is followed by an outline of our research design and methods. We then illustrate how the perspective could be employed to make sense of eProcurement in action through three case studies. The cases provide empirical evidence of the interplay between policy and eProcurement practice. Finally we discuss our conclusions and implications arising from this study.

2 A Social Constructionist and Actor-Network Perspective: Policy, Practice and Actors

Colebatch adopts a social constructionist approach influenced by structuration, instititutional organisation theory and governmentality in his analysis of the policy process. That is, neither policy nor the problems to which it addresses are natural phenomena with an existence of their own, but are produced by the policy participants. He recognises two dimensions to policy, the vertical and the horizontal which impact on the way that we understand and interpret policy. The vertical dimension views policy from a top-down perspective focusing on "instrumental action, rational choice and the force of legitimate authority". The horizontal dimension is concerned with the way policy structures action. That is, the relationships and nature of linkages within and between organisations, the interpretive frameworks used by policy participants in understanding policy questions and the "institutional formations within which these are mobilised" [4:24]. The two dimensions are mutually shaping in that the implementation of the authorised decision requires cooperation from "relevant others outside the line of hierarchical authority". Further the shared interpretive frames of meaning that arise from the horizontal dimension are given effect via "the instruments of the vertical dimension" such as policy directives. Complementing this with the actor-network perspective provides a socio-technical lens on the phenomena that emerges.

3 Research Design and Methods

The three case studies are drawn from a series of cases prepared for the Australian Government Information Management Office (AGIMO). Data collection consisted of documentary evidence and in-depth interviews. The documentary evidence analysed included official records (e.g. policy documents, annual reports, presentation materials), consultancy reports, reports from international bodies such as the European Union and newspapers. The material was collected over a period of four months (from May 2004 to September 2004). Interviews were conducted with key people from senior management levels as well as those in the eProcurement project areas in all three case sites. The interviews lasted on average one hour depending on the issues raised by the respondent.

The in-depth interviews had two objectives: to obtain a descriptive account of the eProcurement systems and to understand why the systems are what they are today. The latter objective required probing questions on issues relating to policy. During the fieldwork tape recordings of interviews were made, transcribed and reviewed. Where issues were unclear or required further elaboration follow up contact was made for clarification. Interviewees produced documents including reports to support their statements. This allowed a form of triangulation of research evidence, together with member checking of the case study write-ups.

We conducted a thematic analysis of the evidence collected. The analysis was focused at two levels. Firstly providing thick descriptions of the eProcurement systems and their impact. The concern was not merely to find evidence of the existence of particular practices but to gather detailed description of how these practices evolved. This analysis was a prelude for an interpretive analysis informed by the policy perspective to gain a richer and deeper understanding of how eProcurement was shaped in each context. Of particular importance were the historical circumstances of each agency and how these enabled an understanding of the eProcurement system.

4 eProcurement in Action: Empirical Illustrations and Analysis

This section is divided into two parts. First, each of the cases is described in terms of how they came about doing eProcurement (background and context) and how eProcurement was mobilised over time. The second part provides analyses of these findings in terms of the interplay between policy and practice.

4.1 Case Descriptions

4.1.1 Public eProcurement in Italy

Background and Context

Prior to 2000, the use of e-commerce and information technology (IT) more generally was considerably lower than comparable economies, notwithstanding that Italy had the highest mobile telephone usage in any industrialised country. Explanations for this included: “a dislike of the written, as opposed to the spoken word; the necessity of mastering English; and, a mistrust of fixed accounting systems” [5]. Further to this, requirements of the Italian Anti Trust Authority relating to fairer competition and audit recommendations regarding improving cost efficiencies in the purchasing of goods and services focused attention on strengthening public procurement practices.

With a view to reinforcing the "modernization" process of the public administration, [6] the responsibility for 'Il Programma di razionalizzazione della spesa' (The Program for the Rationalisation of Public Spending) mandated by the 'Legge finanziaria' (Financial Act), as amended, was delegated to Concessionaria Servizi Informatici Pubblici (CONSIP). CONSIP is a private company owned by the Ministro dell'Economia e delle Finanze (Ministry for the Economy and Finance (MEF)), which advises and assists public administrations with their procurement. Established in 1997, predominately as an information technology provider for the MEF, CONSIP created a second division in 1999, called the Direzione Acquisti in Rete della PA (DARPA) (Division of Online Purchasing). Of the 500 employees that work in CONSIP, approximately 170 are dedicated to DARPA.

DARPA was assigned the task of developing master conventions for "frame contracts" with suppliers to satisfy needs of Central and Local Administrations. It is structured into six key areas, namely: project management, monitoring and research and development; legal; purchasing; sourcing; eProcurement marketplace strategy; and eProcurement systems. Approximately half the number of employees are situated in the purchasing and sourcing sections to assist public administrations and suppliers in adopting and using eProcurement.

eProcurement has evolved as one of the main instruments for the rationalisation program, promoting the simplification and innovation of procurement procedures as well as macro level initiatives relating to the efficiency and transparency of government operations through IT enabled innovations. Further the goals of the rationalisation program and the eProcurement initiative were consistent with broader European Union directives and initiatives relating to public procurement, electronic exchange of information between public administrations and economic reform. However, whilst eProcurement was consistent with and drew attention to broader national and international strategies these were secondary to the primary objectives of reducing costs, simplifying purchasing procedures, and increasing transparency in public administrations.

How eProcurement was Mobilised

The business design of eProcurement is comprised of electronic catalogues, reverse-auctions and the electronic marketplace. It initially began with an electronic cataloguing system in July 2000 following the rationalization program being mandated by the 'Legge finanziaria' (Financial Act) 2000 earlier that year. Incorporated in the Financial Act was the use of common strategies in purchases supported by framework agreements negotiated by CONSIP [7]. Whilst it was compulsory for central government departments to join the program, local bodies, such as municipalities and schools needed only to take the frame contracts as a term of reference. The electronic cataloguing system replicated the specifications and terms of the frame contracts for public administrations to view online. During this period there was a major "ramp up of resources" to support the program. Further on, an online auction platform was developed for the use of CONSIP in awarding frame contracts for goods and services. This further enforced transparency in purchasing procedures of goods and services. The platform not only enabled suppliers to view and bid for the tenders but also informed them of the outcome.

CONSIP activities were also impacted by the creation of Presidential Decree 101 in 2002 regulating the use of digital procedures for public procurement in Italy. Whilst the Act was amended in 2003 to set out in further detail the statutory requirements for public administrations, it was subsequently amended maintaining the obligation only for the purchasing of goods and the supply of services characterised by high quality low labour intensity. However, the onus is still on the public administrations to demonstrate that they can negotiate a better position elsewhere if they choose not to use the system. Further enforcement had created "a little bit of rupture in the system." Resistance was experienced from both the public administration areas as well as the supplier side because of changing procurement practices and the need to use information technologies. As a result the program slowed in the earlier parts of 2004.

CONSIP conducted a major change management program to assist and educate the public administration bodies and suppliers about the "new model." Further, as a large portion of the economy in Italy is based on small and medium sized enterprises (SMEs), pressure was exerted from strong supplier associations for equitable access to government business. They were concerned that in deriving economies of scale through the aggregation of demand, SMEs were being excluded. CONSIP considered ways of tailoring the online environment so that SMEs could participate. The electronic marketplace was established in 2004 for smaller purchases and supplies in different geographical locations.

The economic and broader governance goals such as increased transparency appear to have been fulfilled. However challenges remain with respect to cultural resistance and technological issues, such as electronic payments. Making the system initially compulsory was seen as a necessity premised on the notion that suppliers would be more interested if they had certainty that someone would buy from the system. However, as the system is developed further, CONSIP are endeavouring to create an image that is more aligned with flexible services than obligations.

4.1.2 Public eProcurement in Western Australia

Background and Context

Prior to 2002, the responsibility for government tendering was with Contract and Management Services (CAMS). Following recommendations made from the Machinery of Government review a number of government agencies were rationalized. The Department of Commerce and Trade (DCT) and CAMS merged to form the Department of Industry and Technology (DoIT). Further to this a taskforce was formed to undertake a review into the effective delivery of government priorities. The Functional Review Taskforce (FRT) was required to examine the programs, functions, activities and services of each agency serving two purposes: (1) to determine their efficiency and effectiveness; and (2) to identify areas of expenditure where a whole of Government approach could produce a more effective outcome. In December 2002 the FRT reported its findings to Cabinet who subsequently endorsed the majority of the recommendations relating to procurement reform, corporate services reform, eGovernment, and capital asset management from a whole of government perspective.

Areas of interest in procurement reform included: reviewing inefficient processes; standardisation of systems and specifications; and exploring more aggregation opportunities across the public sector [8]. Reforms commenced in February 2003 with the DoIT being disbanded. The responsibility for government procurement was moved to a new Government Procurement Division of the Department of Treasury and Finance (DTF) and the IT innovation and policy area shifted to a new Office of eGovernment in the Department of Premier and Cabinet. Whilst the State Supply Commission has the broad policy role for Government purchasing, incorporating policymaking and regulation, the responsibility of procurement is devolved to individual public authorities or the DTF and the Department of Housing and Works for above threshold purchases.

The second phase of the review focused on the procurement function itself. Recommendations from the independent review [9] were endorsed in December 2003. Labelled as *Smarter Buying* the reform program serves two purposes. Firstly, to *harvest* savings, through strategic sourcing initiatives, while maintaining equitable access to government business. Secondly, delivering better quality procurement outcomes by enhancing the professionalism of procurement activities, the skills of procurement officers, processes and systems and streamlining procurement policy. These reforms are coordinated by the Procurement Program Management Office (PMO), located within the DTF.

How eProcurement was Mobilised

The Government Electronic Market (GEM™) electronic procurement system is comprised of: Gem Tendering; Gem Purchasing and Gem Contracting. Gem Contracting is a more recent initiative and so is not discussed further. The Gem Tendering system evolved from the Government Contracting Information Bulletin Board, which arose from the Commission on Government Review (1998-1999). It was created to advertise tenders and give early tender advice. The online tendering idea served to trigger interest by CAMS into the potential for electronic marketplace, electronic purchasing and electronic procurement systems.

Gem Purchasing was launched in early 2000 and supported by other initiatives of the time such as the WA Government Online Agenda. The initiative was kicked off with a buy local initiative and a budget of approximately \$3 million. The limited budget later proved to be a contributing factor to problems in the production environment and data corruption because of inadequate system testing.

Gem Purchasing became an instrument of state development in terms of: (1) encouraging business with government; and (2) maintaining market space following concerns expressed by the then Department of Commerce and Trade that business could be lost to the eastern states of Australia. However, while operational and functional issues were being addressed, there was a view that Gem Purchasing was evolving into a phenomenon that was extending to something further than what was initially intended. Gem Purchasing was intended to serve as a vehicle in transforming CAMS' core business of managing contracts. However CAMS endeavoured to change its procurement practices at one level whilst also trying to change contracting processes. This "resulted in elements of the agency practicing business as usual, while at the same time trying to change the paradigm" and as a result the "execution was fragmented"[10]. Secondly, when CAMS was later merged with DoIT it became part of a culture where the use of technologies was intrinsic to driving change.

The contract for supplying the IT platform for Gem Purchasing was awarded to a locally led SUN Microsystems consortium in August 2000 with other providers producing the catalogues and integrating the individual modules. The contractor faced a steep learning curve in understanding the IT architecture, which resulted in implementation delays and dissatisfaction in agencies. The system was fully functional by July 2001 coinciding with the commencement of the Department of Justice Prisons Supply Chain Management project. This project was completed in July 2002 with all WA prisons using the system.

Notwithstanding the number of agencies using Gem Purchasing, only the Department of Justice Prisons Directorate has embraced Gem Purchasing holistically and remains the only significant user of the system. The remaining users tend to be smaller agencies that do not have any purchasing system capability. The lack of uptake resulted in a review, conducted by AOT Consulting Pty Ltd which concluded in August 2003. During the course of the review no work could be done on the system as it was "frozen."

The review revealed in addition to the resource and implementation issues raised above, three other key issues. Firstly, increased interest from national and international government agencies were viewed as having distracted and diverted critical resources away from WA clients. Secondly, enlisting a large number of suppliers early was viewed as a key strategic error as there were a limited number of buyers in the marketplace. Finally, other reform and structural issues created competing priorities. The review concluded that Gem Purchasing should continue, subject to its recommendations being implemented.

4.1.3 Public eProcurement in Scotland

Background and Context

Public eProcurement in Scotland is shaped by broader UK public policies for improving government efficiency and delivering better value for money to taxpayers. In 1998, the UK Government report *Efficiency in Civil Government Procurement* [11] identified a series of targeted measures for improving public procurement. Following this, the 1999 *Review of the Civil Service in Government* [12] made recommendations for improvements in public procurement.
These included:

- improving procurement processes
- developing the skills and status of the procurement profession and
- exploring e-commerce and technology-enabled options for procurement.

Following Devolution in 1999, public procurement in Scotland became the responsibility of the new Scottish Parliament. In January 2000 the Minister for Finance established the Procurement Supervisory Board (PSB) to review public procurement issues including eProcurement. The PSB membership includes representatives from Central and Local Government, the Scottish Health Service and the private sector. The PSB proposed a strategy for eProcurement encompassing the whole of the Scottish public sector. The strategy received ministerial approval in

November 2000 and central funding was allocated to the National eProcurement Scotl@nd (NePS) programme.

How eProcurement was Mobilised

The NePS programme falls within the portfolio of the Scottish Procurement Directorate (SPD) and is the key agent for implementing the Scottish eProcurement strategy. The SPD has both a policy and an operational role. In addition to its responsibility for shaping public procurement policy and practice in Scotland the Directorate is also responsible for planning and coordinating the day-to-day procurement activities of the Scottish Executive.

In 2000 the Scottish Procurement Directorate conducted a review of business models for public eProcurement and concluded that no existing business model was completely suitable for use in the Scottish context. It was recognised that a holistic approach was required for eProcurement in Scotland where procurement process reform and the implementation of new technologies for procurement take place in a coordinated manner.

The NePS team took a broad interpretation; defining eProcurement as a business service as opposed to a technology solution, known locally as "little e, big P". The team developed a business model that emphasises the use of common methodologies for buyer-enablement and supplier-adoption and uses intermediary organisations to assist in providing the service and managing the technology platform.

The aim of the NePS programme is to establish a common platform and a common approach to eProcurement in the Scottish public sector that will result in efficiencies and cost savings for both buyers and suppliers.

The focus of the programme is to:

- provide a joined-up approach to public procurement in Scotland
- achieve efficiencies through improved procurement processes and deliver cost savings to government (and the Scottish taxpayer)
- raise the importance of procurement as a business activity
- improve the supplier experience of dealing with government (suppliers will be required to interact with one system when selling to the public sector)
- provide benefits to government agencies by developing common procurement processes, sharing of procurement knowledge and experiences and
- where appropriate, establish collaborative procurement practices.

The business design for the eProcurement in Scotland is a fully hosted and managed service that brings eProcurement into the reach of all Scottish Public Sector organisations through the initial investment of the Scottish Executive. The NePS programme team coordinates and supports the uptake of the service, which is provided by a private sector organization (Cap Gemini) and hosted on elcom's PECOS Internet Procurement Manager platform. The service is subscription-based and extends to Central Government, Local Government and the National Health Service Scotland. Buying organisations pay an annual management fee; there are no annual management fees for suppliers.

A Scoping and Readiness Assessment to establish the current status of the buying organisation in terms of readiness for adoption of the service is an integral part of the service. It includes activities such as spend profiling, analysis of supplier base and purchase-to-pay processes as well as an assessment of technology and human resource capabilities. The result is an implementation plan specific to the situation and context of each buying organisation.

The technology (the PECOS system) is a fully hosted application service that supports a range of buyer and supplier procurement functions including catalogue management, order cycle management, approval routing and electronic tendering and auctions. The PECOS system also provides financial settlement and invoicing functions and a range of reporting tools.

A key requirement of the NePS service is that it is accessible to all suppliers regardless of size and technology capability. The NePS team developed a range of procedures and supporting documentation for supplier adoption and enablement.

NePS has promoted a very holistic view of eProcurement as an end-to-end business service; requiring a multi-functional team with a good understanding of public procurement policies and practices and skills for re-engineering and benchmarking business processes. The NePS team assumes the role of an intermediary; supplying information and expertise to buyers and suppliers, coordinating change management activities and developing training programmes. They take a hands-on approach, using the implementation of the NePS service in the Scottish Executive (known locally as EASEbuy) to gather valuable experiential knowledge and to refine their support instruments and activities.

Broad economic goals and the provision of a whole of government eProcurement service have been realised. Going forward, procurement is a major theme of the *Efficient Government Initiative* announced in July 2004 [13]. The initiative promotes shared services, best practice and cross-sectoral working. Specific focus is on "back-office efficiencies" such as invoicing; the NePs team is now working towards offering "e-Invoicing" capabilities and moving the Scottish Public Sector closer to achieving complete e-Commerce solutions in government.

5 Analysis

Emerging from the three cases, the objectives of public eProcurement commonly focussed on governance practices in terms of achieving better value for money, efficiencies and effectiveness and transparency in government procurement. For example, Italy's rationalisation programme, the broader UK reform policy in Scotland and transparent tendering in Western Australia. While these are valid statements of the desired outcomes, they offered limited insight into how the policies were implemented and changed over time. Adopting Colebatch's policy perspective assisted in moving from the debate about whether objectives are meaningful or not, and whether they have been implemented or not, to understanding how the different images and business designs emerged and the influence of policy.

The cases reveal that the generic term of eProcurement groups different images and designs in a single concept. Further, while business designs of eProcurement reveal similarities amongst the different sites (with the exception of purchase to pay for Scotland) they evolved differently revealing the criticality of temporal context in policy design. Government priorities shifted arising from progress (or not) towards particular objectives or unintended consequences arising from practice. Thus, whilst the initial interpretation of eProcurement may have been shaped via instruments of policy directives, this varied in different social and temporal contexts. Of further interest is that while each site has its own history, culture and economic contexts that influenced the interpretation of eProcurement amongst the different cases, these differences do not 'explain' the specific directions taken in each site. We found that actor-network theory complemented Colebatch's policy perspective providing useful sensitising concepts in which to follow the series of moves relating to the development of eProcurement and the mechanisms by which site specific translations came about. Whilst we present these elements as sequential moments below, this is solely for the purposes of ease of analysis as it is more appropriate to conceptualise them as parallel dimensions in the social practice of organising.

Policy Inscriptions

eProcurement does not just begin as a blank slate but rather embodies social and economic relations and assumptions about meanings and uses of eProcurement. By viewing inscription over time we reveal how human and technical actors may affect the functionality of eProcurement and the form in which it evolves. For example, in Italy and Scotland broader government reforms were inscribed in eProcurement initiatives at the start and over the course of its development. This is in contrast to Western Australia, which initially adopted a narrower focus in terms of improving transparency in tendering. In the latter case competing policy priorities and objectives were more evident.

Translations and Intermediaries of Policy

Translations of eProcurement from abstract policy objectives to practice differed in each case evident by the multiple interpretations of eProcurement. In Scotland eProcurement was initially translated as a service for the whole of the public sector and as an instrument of reform in Italy. From its inception of improving transparency in the Western Australia government tendering process, the practice shifted towards a means of improving large volume government purchases through 'new' eProcurement technologies. A concomitant opportunity viewed by CAMS was that it could transform its own business and be seen as a leader in the area.

In each case there were structures and agents that mobilized these interpretations and designs. For example, in Scotland a heterogeneous network consisting of the National eProcurement Scotland Programme, technology providers and consultants, instruments and methodologies for buyer engagement and supplier adoption, buyers and suppliers in their own right, and databases of case studies were assembled to translate eProcurement policy into practice. The National eProcurement Scotland Programme and CONSIP in the case of Italy were obligatory passage points in enrolling key actors, such as government agencies, suppliers and IT providers and aligning their interests. In the Western Australia case the focus on technical functionality created difficulties in aligning the interests of different government agencies because of previous technology investments, continual structural changes and competing policy objectives. For example the "buy local" initiative influenced the engagement of a local technology consortium who had limited experiences with aspects of the technology architectures.

Irreversibility and stability

In the case of Italy and Scotland a convergent network emerged consisting of a body of allies in the form of government agencies and suppliers with a crystallized conception and mutual understanding of eProcurement. Hence the actors engaged in actions in support of the inscribed policies resulting in irreversibility. In contrast the Western Australia case did not stabilize in the form expected and different outcomes emerged largely due to issues relating to emphasis on the functionality of the 'new' technology versus existing functionality in established financial management systems and the changing identities and activities of the 'responsible' agencies. We are not stating here that irreversibility and stability are necessarily desirable, rather it was considered desirable in the context of Italy and Scotland. Further, it is part of ongoing change activities and so will not necessarily remain this way, for example with further policy reform.

6 Conclusion

The results highlight four key issues relating to public eProcurement policy. Firstly in the two cases (Italy and Scotland) where eProcurement is viewed more desirably, policies were based on broader government reform than on eProcurement itself. Secondly, the generic term of eProcurement is constituted of different images and designs. Hence designing policy in terms of a single concept may be misleading. Thirdly while business designs of eProcurement reveal similarities they evolved differently amongst the cases suggesting the need to take into account the temporal context when designing policy tools. Finally, at a theoretical level, this paper has illustrated the value of adopting a social constructionist and actor network perspective in exploring the complex terrain of eProcurement policy and practice. By utilizing this perspective, the policy processes which lead to the varying images of eProcurement become more visible. The design of eProcurement systems and practices are reflected in rules and procedures that persist over time and are both a shaper and an outcome of policy processes. That is in practice the policy process is not a systematic linear implementation of objectives.

References

1. Panayiotou, N.A. et al: An e-procurement system for governmental purchasing. International Journal of Production Economics. 90 (2004) 79-102
2. Carayannis, E.G and Popescu, D.: Profiling a methodology for economic growth and convergence: learning from the EU e-procurement experience for central and eastern European countries. Technovation. (2004) (in press)
3. Chu P-Y et al.: Exploring success factors for Taiwan's government electronic tendering system: behavioral perspectives from end-users. Government Information Quarterly. 21(2) (2004) 219-234
4. Colebatch, H.K.: Policy (Second Edition). Open University Press: Maidenhead (2002)
5. European Union: E-procurement/Italy: Catching up in Europe. Interchange of Data between Administrations (IDA) program E-Government Observatory Publications Available at: http://europa.eu.int/ida/en/document/686/197 (accessed on 27/8/04)

6. Ministero dell'Economia e delle Finanze: Italy's Report on Economic Reform – November 2000 (from European Commission, Economic and Financial Affairs, Economic Policy Committee Archives (2001) Available at: http://europa.eu.int/comm/economy_finance/publications/epc/it-report_en.pdf (accessed on 27/8/04)
7. CONSIP Rationalization Program on Public Spending for goods and services, Frame Contracts System participation information document provided during presentation of 25 June 2004
8. Department of Treasury and Finance - Procurement Reform Web Site Available at: http://www.dtf.wa.gov.au/cms/ref_content.asp?ID=792 (accessed on 3 September 2004)
9. Deloitte Touche Tomatsu: Business Solution and Implementation Plan (Deliverable C) report. Available at: http://www.dtf.wa.gov.au/cms/ref_content.asp?ID=792 (accessed on 3 September 2004)
10. AOT Consulting Pty Ltd.: Review of the GEM Purchasing E-Procurement Business System (2003) Available at: http//www.dtf.wa.gov.au/cms/pro_index.asp?id=454 (accessed on 15 July 2004)
11. HM Treasury & Cabinet Office: Efficiency in Civil Government Procurement. Published by The Stationery Office, July 1998. ISBN 0947819 592 (1998)
12. Gershon, P.: Review of the Civil Service in Government (1999) Available at: http://archive.treasury.gov.uk/docs/1999/pgfinalr.html (accessed on: 1st September 2004)
13. Scottish Executive: Efficient Government Initiative News Release (2004) Available at: http://www.scotland.gov.uk/News/Releases/2004/06/5713 (accessed on: 1st September 2004)
14. Law, J. and Hassard, J.: Actor network theory and after. Blackwell Publishers: Oxford (1999)

An Integrated Approach in Healthcare e-Procurement: The Case-Study of the ASL of Viterbo

Tommaso Federici

Università della Tuscia,
Dipartimento di Studi Aziendali Tecnologici e Quantitativi,
Via del Paradiso, 47 - 01100 – Viterbo – Italy
federici@scec.eco.uniroma1.it

Abstract. The size and growth of Italian healthcare spending for goods and services ask for prompt rationalization programs, with novel purchasing approaches (e-procurement), capable to provide significant reductions in purchasing and administration costs. If several interventions have not yet delivered the expected results, that's due to lack of problem segmentation and resistance to change of public structures. Health-related purchases require a segmented approach, to take into account the specific needs of different spending items and foster coherent organizational changes. It is therefore of interest to examine the e-procurement project undertaken by the ASL of Viterbo, for its scope, consistence and brilliant results[1].

1 Size and Peculiarities of Healthcare Spending for Goods and Services

A 20% share of public healthcare spending (2002, source ASSR[2]) is for the "purchasing of goods and services" (frequently named "intermediate healthcare consumptions"). Sizeable in percent, this component reaches huge absolute dimensions when referred to the whole Italian public healthcare sector. In one year (2002) the *National Healthcare System* spends about 17,5 €b for goods and services, a sum of money which is increasing both in absolute terms (it almost doubled from 1997 to 2002) and in percent (21,39%; in 1998, 21,68% in 1999, 22,46% in 2000).

The spending for goods and services largely varies in percent among the various Italian regions [5] and the market is further influenced by other complexity factors:

- about 350 diverse healthcare structures (ASL, AO and IRCSS[3]) with different procurement needs (thereby asking for a complex and strongly personalized offering);
- about 500 thousand, highly differentiated suppliers (multinationals, mid-size national Companies and local SME's).

---

[1] The gist of this paper is somehow similar to that of a recent article in bibliography [16].

[2] Agenzia per i Servizi Sanitari Regionali (Regional Healthcare Services Agency).

[3] ASL – "Azienda Sanitaria Locale" (local health authority), AO – "Azienda Ospedaliera" (hospital authority) and IRCCS – "Istituto di Ricovero and Cura a Carattere Scientifico" (shelter-and-care institute with also scientific purposes).

M. Böhlen et al. (Eds.): TCGOV 2005, LNAI 3416, pp. 298 – 309, 2005.

The main issue, however, is the composite structure of the spending, which includes standard supplies for the whole Public Administration (PA), together with highly specific purchases. Introducing e-procurement tools in the healthcare sector asks for a detailed analysis of spending variety, in order to match each purchase type with the appropriate electronic procurement tool, by clearly defining the nature of the need (e.g. operating room specific devices) and planning purchases without inconsistency, thereby supporting both healthcare performance and economy of procurement.

Healthcare spending for goods and services can be classified into three[4] items:

- *common* for the whole PA, independent from the type of buying Administration (e.g.: phone services, office materials). In 2002, this cost item for the Italian healthcare sector reached 4.2 €b (Consip, 2002), 23% of total (18 €b);
- *common-but-differentiated* (25% of total), existing for all the Administrations but highly differentiated by buying sector (e.g. in healthcare sector: hospitals building maintenance or cleaning);
- *healthcare-specific* (more than 50% of total), composed by drugs and medical devices[5].

This diversity – as well as the complexity factors indicated above – must be taken into account to devise innovative ways to manage procurement in order to rationalize and reduce spending, before choosing the most appropriate IT solutions.

2 e-Procurement Tools

The term "e-procurement" indicates the organizational solutions, as well as the supporting information and communication technologies, which offer on-line forms of procurement, more effective and efficient than traditional ones, to industrial, commercial and service Companies [15]. An e-procurement system, when correctly conceived, deals with the whole procurement process and not only its purchasing phase. It requires an overall redesign of the process, taking into account the whole life-time of a product or service [18]. When useful, logistic / *Supply Chain Management (SCM)* solutions might also be integrated, connecting IT systems of suppliers and clients.

e-Procurement solutions include widely different tools, in three areas: *e-sourcing*; *e-requisitioning* and *e-logistics* (the first two are alternative ways to deal with the purchasing phase, while the third one is a complement to both of them, to streamline the whole procurement process).

e-Sourcing, preferably applied to with medium / low-frequency purchases, includes web-based models and tools, which allow to perform on-line tenders and contracts, analyze spending and measure supplier performance, in order to optimize supplier, product ad service mix. It refers to both *e-auctions*, which allow to define a purchase price by accepting competitive on-line price reductions, and various types of electronic tenders, which reproduce the administrative procedures on the web. Auctions are particularly indicated to buy "well defined" supplies in terms of requirements, not requiring to provide and evaluate a specific project. For them, the criterion of lowest

4 This classification, formerly used to identify the economic aggregations of healthcare spending for goods and services, is very useful to single out the most suitable e-procurement tool.

5 Appliances and materials that, separately or jointly, are used in case of injury, disease, handicap, or during a physiological application.

price is suitable, without risk of adverse consequences in supply quality. On-line tenders, instead, are more suitable for non standard purchases, which ask to balance quality and price.

e-Requisitioning, yields its best results in term of savings when dealing with high-frequency supplies, with limited individual costs, and standardized non-strategic goods, with low consolidated technology [10]. It fully manages orders (from the issuing of purchase requests to the authorization of spending, to monitoring the order progress, up to the payment of supply), with the tool of *marketplace.* This collects and show the offers of goods and services proposed by admitted, even competing suppliers – with details on characteristics, prices and supply / payment term – to an audience of enabled buyers. With a single IT platform, it performs the whole purchasing cycle (from the choice of good and producer to the issuing of order, to the notification of the order to the supplier). For Italian PAs, this tool became – alternatively in *tying* and *untying* mode [1] – the *Electronic catalogue* of the goods and services which can be purchased at predefined conditions through the *Frame contracts ("Convenzioni Quadro")* negotiated by Consip and, more recently, in an experiment of true *Marketplace* [19], new tool for on-line negotiation useful for purchases of amounts lower than the threshold set by the European Union for public tenders.

e-Logistics is the optimized management of inventories (in healthcare structures, those of pharmacy and supply office) and of internal flows of purchased goods, based on Intranet/Extranet technologies, capable to directly link both internal and external players. Independently from purchase process, e-logistics can bring large advantages to the whole procurement cycle, particularly for repetitive supplies / continuous stock replenishment. It's an innovation closely linked to process redesign and supplier integration, the absence of which might severely reduce the scope of the benefits [12] coming from adopting e-sourcing or e-requisitioning innovative tools.

3 Correlation Between Tools and Spending Items

In the healthcare sector (more than in others) is paramount to safeguard – together with economy and timeliness of purchases, transparency of deeds and conformance to competition principles among Companies – high quality standards for many products and services purchased [21]. The large differences among spending items indicated above *(common, common-but-differentiated, healthcare-specific)* and the availability of diverse electronic solutions enforce a profound reflection on which solution suits most which type of good / service, according to a segmented approach.

Goods and services within the *common* spending can be standardized for the whole PA (large utilization, wide offering, repetitive purchasing quantities) and are perfectly compatible with *e-requisitioning* tools. The best opportunity – in terms of purchase price reduction, administrative costs and delivery time – is to link into a public marketplace, based on contracts negotiated by a single entity (at national, regional or local level). This would aggregate fractions of public demand, knock-down standard supply contracts of large overall amount, perform unified tender procedures for a number of "client" entities [14] "and – in the end – lower the final price".

The *common-but-differentiated* spending consists of supplies which must absolutely guarantee to the healthcare buyer the fulfillment of specific needs. It requires the presentation and evaluation of (even complex) projects, for which it's difficult to define criteria for automatic score attribution. The traditional procedure can be substituted by a tender partially performed on-line, moving onto the web the call, presentation, intermediate and final communications phases – with clear benefits in terms of administrative time and cost reduction – while keeping the offers evaluation phase off-line.

To reduce the *healthcare-specific* spending, a wider e-procurement approach must be used: looking just for the lowest price [12] can be counterproductive, since the requested goods and services are highly specific, and high quality levels are required as well. The maximum benefit can be obtained by reengineering the internal processes, merging several e-procurement methodologies and tools together – healthcare e-logistics, on-line tenders, evolved forms of marketplace – as well as providing adequate IT supports to the healthcare cost centers (e.g. hospital wards).

4 Case Study: ASL of Viterbo

The use of e-procurement tools in healthcare environments is based mostly on solutions pre-defined by external subjects, like the above indicated *Frame contracts* negotiated by Consip, which – as discussed – do not fully respond to the specific needs of a relevant share of healthcare purchases.

An interesting case – for its scope, early start and brilliant results – is the experience of the "Azienda Sanitaria Locale" (ASL) of Viterbo, which introduced well targeted and effective organization and IT solutions for e-procurement within a wider plan to more comprehensively rethink the procurement processes, set-up into various projects driven by the Procurement and Logistics (P&L) Department.

The ASL of Viterbo is organized in three areas: hospital services; territory services; administration services. With about 3.200 administrative and healthcare employees, it provides healthcare to the province of Viterbo (859 hospital beds), with a production value of about 350 €m, determined according to the individual spending allocated for each citizen of the province (297.686 as of December 31, 2001).

4.1 Activated Projects Approach

The e-procurement project of the ASL of Viterbo is characterized by a diversified and systematic approach, as well as a direct and decisive role assigned to the hospital wards: they actually deliver the health care and are the main final users of the new tools. The whole procurement cycle was resized, starting from a detailed analysis of the need for goods and services. Specific purchase characteristics were made explicit, spending was mapped in detail – divided among: *common, common-but-differentiated, healthcare-specific* – and an organic plan to link procurement needs and e-procurement solutions (according to theory).

The ASL relied heavily on the specialized competences of individual hospital wards and involved them in the definition of the new procurement processes, as a necessary complement to the cooperation with external Companies, capable to transfer their technology and management know-how. In the new process model, the wards, in their healthcare duty, assume a driving role, but not the responsibility to decide how to purchase each specific good. Working within a highly integrated procurement process (IT supported), they are informed of their overall consumptions and related stock levels[6] and can address the purchasing system directly, to signal specific emerging needs and issue very accurate orders in a very short time. According to experiences, about 2/3 of hospital stocks do not reside in hospital pharmacies (which essentially intermediate the order flow), but directly at wards: without adequate monitoring tools, it is difficult to know ward consumptions in a timely way and the chances of error increase when planning procurements centrally.

The use of public and private electronic catalogues for the *common* spending soon delivered the expected economic benefits, in line with the rationalization program promoted by Consip, with which the ASL of Viterbo instituted a reciprocal cooperation relationship, both to utilize the negotiated contracts for *common* goods and to test innovative initiatives like the *Marketplace*, to which the ASL of Viterbo took active part together with other 19 Italian PA's.

In order to improve the procurement and internal management of the *healthcare-specific* and *common* goods, from ward requests up to the purchasing channels, the ASL of Viterbo designed a fully IT-supported process, with procurement flows designed along two distinct routes, according to the type of goods to supply:

- for non-specific Medical Devices (MD), normally used in hospital wards for the routine healthcare activity, and office products (e.g.: ink, paper) the steps are:
  - *on-line tenders*, for products not in the hospital (never purchased or fully consumed), by transferring most phases of traditional tender onto the web – with minimal technological adjustments – while guaranteeing conformance to awarding criteria;
  - *e-logistics*, to automate the whole replenishment route of the product supplies awarded by tender, between pharmacy or supply office inventories and wards;
- for the Specific Medical Devices (SMD), used in surgical operations, the route activated is the *operating room e-procurement*, for materials which require an ad-hoc procedure, by designing a new on-line procurement process which optimizes the replenishment time and reduces the ward and inventory stock levels.

The wards activate the procurement process, which proceeds through the routes defined by the P&L Dept., according to the nature, availability and peculiarities of the requested devices. In this way, many management problems – related to the mutual understanding and coordination between specialized beneficiaries (ward personnel) and administration (Purchasing Department) – are overcome and do not slow down the performance of the healthcare delivery machine any longer.

The indicated distinction into two routes must be considered just a first experimental step. In the future, while continuing to pay attention on the differences among goods characteristics, the distinction could be overcome by extending the scope of the *operating room e-procurement* route that simplifies the process, as it integrates together supply and outsourcing of logistics.

4.2 Testing Methods

After characterizing spending categories, designing new processes and matching spending items with e-procurement tools, application tests were performed in internal

[6] To correctly evaluate this innovation, consider that 99% of Italian hospital wards do not reach the level of IT support needed for this kind of activities.

pilots. The sharing of results with involved professionals then preceded the implementation phase, which is still ongoing in the interested structures.

The test phase performed by the ASL of Viterbo on e-procurement solutions were conceived in order to track results in terms of innovation effectiveness and time and costs reduction, by producing:

- a detailed map of the existing process, with identification of micro-activities and number and type of human resources engaged, and quantification of working and elapsed time through interviews;
- a design of the new process flows, with embedded methods to automatically track the time spent in each activity;
- a comparison of volumes of goods, time spent and purchase costs between the existing and the new process.

The pilot phase performed an even more detailed analysis on cost elements for the *operating room e-procurement* (this is the main reason why only its data are exposed here), by identifying:

- the direct costs of the existing and the new process, quantified according to cost accounting (e.g. hourly pay per job position) and also by means of field surveys (e.g. squared meters actually occupied in the warehouses) or estimates, when precise measurements was not considered useful (e.g. costs of obsolete products);
- relevant indirect costs (e.g. general costs), estimated on the basis of fair criterion.

Time and cost savings reported are therefore actual, as results of an accurate analysis. Based on these data only, the ASL decided to implement the tested solutions fully.

4.3 On-line Tenders

The implementation of on-line tenders originates form a first experience with a private web portal in 2000 [2], which represented the starting point for the organization and technology innovation promoted within the ASL, aiming at reducing spending in constant growth with the introduction of novel tools, by that time rarely used in the public sector [17].

The electronic request for goods is satisfied by the hospital inventory, if the requested item is available; otherwise, the opportunity of a new purchase is evaluated by the specific Commission for that product typology. After approval, in case of non-specific MD's for example, the hospital pharmacy requests the opening of a tender to the Purchasing Department, according to the total hospital needs. The on-line tender route is reduced to a minimum vis-à-vis a traditional procedure [8]; it includes:

- *invitation*: when the tender is opened with related supply contract terms (goods / services characteristics and knock-down specifications), the ASL invites potential suppliers via e-mail and sends them an identifier and an access key to the system;
- *competitive price reductions and knock-down*: once invitation terms are expired, in the day and at time indicated, the offers received are filtered by the system according to products, technical specifications and price, and – after a further price reduction offer by participants – the supply is awarded;
- *award notification*: it is sent directly to the winner of the tender, with the related supply order approved by the ASL.

The ASL benefits from reduced time[7] and costs in carrying out the purchasing procedures and a database of all offers becomes available, to analyze the suppliers participation and winning patterns, the evolution of healthcare prices and the purchasing performance over time [22].

4.4 e-Logistics

The new e-logistics process outsources the management functions of hospital and supply office inventories to an external Logistics Service Provider (LSP), with significant reduction of the operating and economic burden on the ASL. After extending the IT support to all the hospitals of the ASL, the wards will be provided with an easy accessible product inventory, divided by categories, and a daily loading / unloading procedure with indication of actual stock levels.

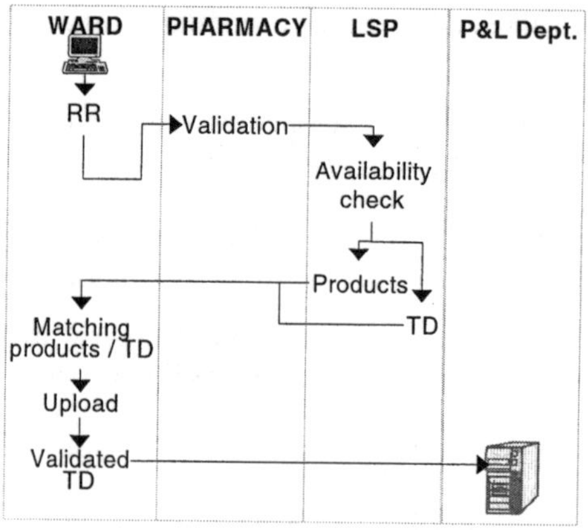

Fig. 1. Replenishment request internal flow

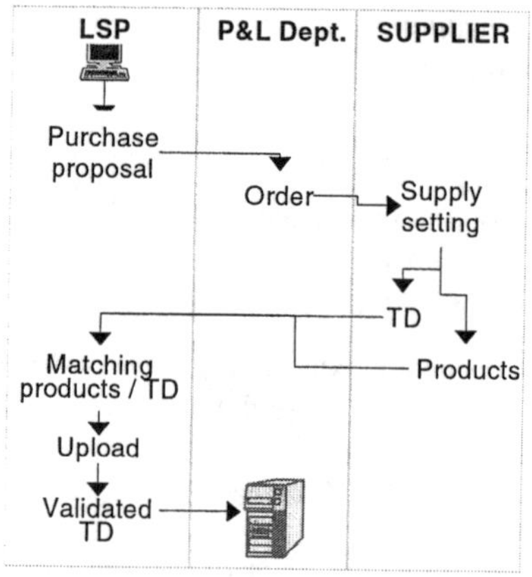

Fig. 2. Supply order flow

The process is activated by a ward need (see Fig. 1). Every day the hospital ward – in its healthcare duty – unloads the consumed goods from its inventory and issues a replenishment request (RR) when some good is beyond its minimum stock level. The RR of medical devices or supply office goods, through a software application linked to the hospital management information system, is sent to the LSP periodically (once or twice a week) by the ward sister, after validation by the hospital pharmacy. The LSP, if the good is available, replenishes the requesting ward inventory from its warehouse by sending the good together with electronic and paper transport documents (TD). The ward sister checks the conformity – in quality and quantity – of the received good with the TD and loads its electronic inventory. In this way, the P&L Dept. is informed centrally in real time about the stock levels of both the LSP and of the individual wards.

---

7 The invitation procedure is based on a supplier database; catalogued by technical specifications; the e-mail communication provides benefits already in the first phase, by reducing the invitation times by 50% (15 days vs. 30 in the traditional procedure).

The LSP is the sole procurement intermediary, but it cannot make any decision for new supplies, on behalf of the ASL, when a good is not available in its warehouse. The ASL outsources the management of central inventory and delegates the unloading of ward inventories, but does not externalize the purchasing function, which for obvious reasons remains exclusively in its hands. In case of stock-outs, the LSP sends a purchase order proposal to the ASL:

- when the goods are part of a still open supply agreement, after the validation by the P&L Dept., the order is sent to the awarded supplier (see Fig. 2), which sends the goods and related TD to the LSP, which will load its electronic inventory;
- when the supply agreement is closed (o for new goods), the P&L Dept. can decide to open a new (traditional or on-line) tender, at the end of which the illustrated route between awarded supplier and LSP is activated.

After the pilot experiment at Civita Castellana, the ASL of Viterbo planned a full roll-out of the system. With the technical support of Consip, the ASL is thus modeling a solution (centralization and outsourcing of the warehouse function) which might be extended to other ASL's. The initiative supports the thesis that savings in healthcare should be pursued through the IT support of the procurement processes of the wards and a profound review and integration of the logistics management [7].

4.5 Operating Room e-Procurement

The traditional planning of operating room provisioning is performed by hospital responsible and pharmacists, who manage the hospital inventories by periodically sending types and quantity estimates of goods to be purchased to the Purchasing Department, according to past consumption and future consumption forecast. This management approach, based on assumptions, generates problems in purchase planning when the hospital wards are not provided with adequate IT supports: the pharmacist unloads the goods allocated to a ward from the inventory, as if it were consumed at once; the good might remain instead unused in the ward for an unpredictable period of time, with no indication to the pharmacist and, least of all, to the Purchasing Department.

The pilot experience of "operating room e-procurement" has been carried out since 2001 at the hospital of Civita Castellana. The operating and technical staff of the General Surgery Department was directly involved in rethinking and redesigning the SMD procurement process from scratch. The model conceived is based on:

- a novel approach to provide the SMD's to the operating room, based on the type of surgical operation performed (actual data immediately available), and no longer on the SMD stock level that requires a huge administrative work;
- the definition of surgical protocols (SP) which indicate the type and quantity of the medical devices needed for each type of operation and allow to determine, after it has been performed, the quantities actually consumed to be reordered;
- the contractual allocation – with innovative paying terms – of the products supply and management to a single player.

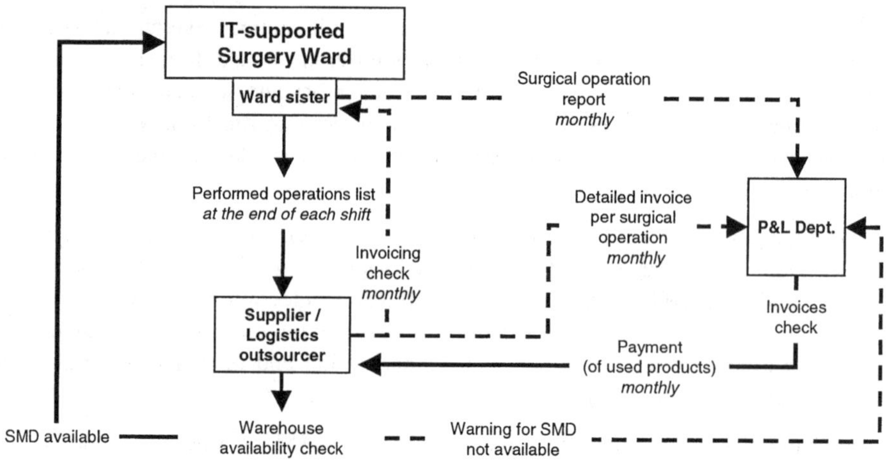

Fig. 3. Flow diagram of Operating room e-procurement process

The new procurement process (see Fig. 3) is supported by a shared application platform. At the end of each shift, the ward sister sends the list of the operations performed to the supplier. The supplier, according to the product quantities indicated by the corresponding SP's, knows product consumptions in real time and can thus replenish them. The goods are delivered directly to the ward which requested them and thus covers actual needs, with no intermediate steps, cost / time increase or stock-out risks.

The process ends monthly when the supplier, after a quick cross-check with the ward sister, issues a detailed invoice per surgical operation, which allows the P&L Dept. to activate the payment after a brief check and at the same time provides data for an effective periodical comparative analysis of ward needs.

The analysis performed at the end of the first semester of experimentation indicated that, to reduce spending, it is necessary to consider the whole supply cost and not only the purchase price, on which the procedure was focused before, in order to negotiate the lowest one.

Actually, the economic advantages were mostly concentrated in the administrative costs, which decreased from 100 €k per semester to only 20 (see Fig. 4).On the contrary, the purchase price of the operating room devices slightly increased (by 4%, due to their increase in market price); this witnesses that the project was aimed at not sacrificing the quality of supply at all[8]. With savings on the *total* final cost of the SMD supply of more than 73 €k per semester (30% less than the traditional approach), the experimentation of the ASL of Viterbo demonstrated that the e-procurement per surgical operation can provide substantial cost savings, not to be pursued by reducing the purchase costs (in order not to dangerously penalize the supply quality) but by redesigning the procurement process and thus reducing the administrative costs.

---

8 Particular attention was dedicated to both the supply range (purchased products increased from 92 to 141) and quality (by ordering the best products available on the market).

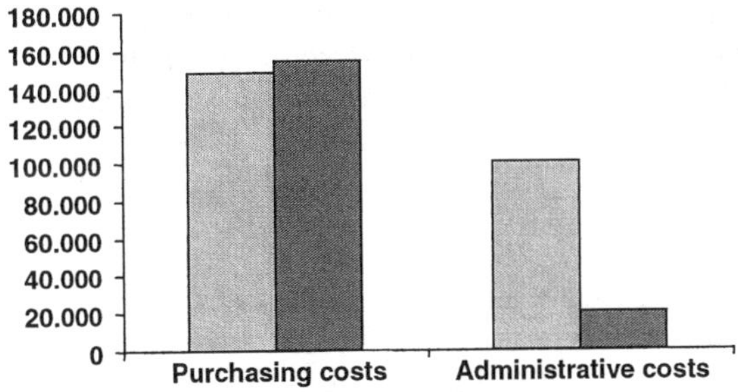

Approach	TRADITIONAL	INNOVATIVE	Difference	Diff. %
Purchasing costs	148.678,03	154.767,01	-6.088,98	-4,1
Administrative costs	99.927,29	20.232,60	79.694,69	79,8
Total	**248.605,32**	**174.999,61**	**73.605,71**	**29,6**

Fig. 4. Comparison between traditional and innovative procedure in Operating room e-procurement (1st semester 2001)

It may be of interest to examine the savings breakdown among the various cost items:

- 42% of savings came from reducing the fixed and financial inventory costs[9], by outsourcing logistics and shifting the payment terms after consumption. Stock-related costs were eliminated, as well as the losses from obsolete products; savings were then widened by end-of-the-month payments, after the goods were used;
- 26% of savings came from reducing personnel costs (of Hospital Pharmacy and Operating Room), for the fraction linked to inventory management[10], by outsourcing these activities to the LSP;
- 24% of savings came from reducing the administrative cost for purchasing and supply monitoring, by unifying sets of diverse medical devices into SP kits (instead of using a separate procedure for each type of device) and by being provided with detailed information directly, from the invoices per surgical operations;
- 8% of savings came from reduced order management and invoicing costs.

The objective of the experimentation was to verify the operating-economic impact that a specific supply system, based on on-line methodologies and provisioning *per surgical operation,* would provide vis-à-vis the traditional procedure [6]. According to the positive economic results achieved, together with a high level of healthcare performance (due to the reduction of stock-out risk in the hospital inventories), the ASL of Viterbo is now (end of 2004) opening a tender for the supply – through e-procurement – of the operating room specific devices for all the hospitals of the ASL.

---

9 As regards the pharmacy and the operating room inventories were measured: the *management cost per squared meter* of inventory premises; the *financial costs of the capital locked into stocks* (according to industry statistics, they were estimated at about 8% of average stock value) and the *cost of obsolete products* (estimated at 0,05% of purchases).

10 For comparison, personnel costs incurred for the following activities were considered: Bookkeeping; Product replenishment; Incoming goods inspection; Order / delivery expediting.

At the end of the project all the hospital wards will be provided with IT supports to directly perform the management of MD's (through e-logistics) and the procurement functions for SMD's (through the operating room e-procurement).

5 Conclusions

From the composite experience of the ASL of Viterbo, regarding the healthcare e-procurement, the following considerations can be derived or confirmed:

- healthcare structures (ASL and AO) provide critical and specialized services (vs. the rest of PA). The goods and services they need are frequently very specific and can have an impact on the service quality. Therefore, cost reductions should not be pursued on purchase prices [12], but on the whole procurement, logistics and administrative cycle;
- the goods and services needed are very diverse in terms of purchased quantities / number of suppliers, technical characteristics and peculiarities. Therefore, the e-procurement solutions must be segmented to properly respond to this variety;
- in order to obtain valid results when introducing e-procurement practices, a comprehensive perspective of the problem is needed, from which to proceed in order to design brand new purchase, logistics and administration processes and to integrate the various technical solutions available;
- for the most specific supplies it is paramount to involve wards doctors and technicians, as experts in the design phase and primary players of the redesigned process, since they only can define protocols and device characteristics on which depend the healthcare performances they are responsible of;
- on the technical level, it is necessary to provide a shared IT platform, linking the administrative offices, wards and external providers (when needed);
- a sound e-procurement introduction can provide significant savings for *common, common-but-differentiated*, and *healthcare-specific* spending items; as regards the last one (more than 50% of total), savings are mostly linked to administrative and financial costs [7].

The personnel seemed to positively participate in new e-procurement process. The main risk for a full implementation are therefore linked to the outsourcing of the logistics function (the core of the change) and could be minimized with the usual precautions used to grant a global service assignment (precise tender, accurate supplier selection, well defined contract terms, continuous performance monitoring).

References

1. Anton, J. and Yao, D., (1989). "Split awards, procurement and innovation", in *RAND Journal of Economics*, n° 30.
2. ASL di Viterbo, (2001). "eCommerce in sanità", participation form for "*Forum PA – SANITÀ 2001*". Available at www.forumpa.it.
3. Associazione Impresa Politecnico (AIP), (2002). "Emarketplace: quale ruolo nel B2B italiano?", in *Quaderni AIP* collection, Litogì, Milano.

4. Associazione Impresa Politecnico (AIP), (2003). "Dai Marketplace ai servizi di Sourcing, Procurement and Supply Chain Collaboration", in *Quaderni AIP* collection, Litogì, Milano.
5. Bertini, L. and Sciandra, L., (2001a). "La riforma del procurement della PA. Il nuovo modello di gestione e le estensioni alla Sanità", CTSP (Commissione Tecnica della Spesa Pubblica), Roma.
6. Bianchini, A., (2002a). La sperimentazione dell'e-procurement negli approvvigionamenti di Sala Operatoria, proceedings of *"Acquisti ed e-procurement in Sanità"* convention at FORUM PA 2002, May 8, Rome. Available at: www.forumpa.it/forumpa2002/convegni/archivio/S.7/1363-andrea_bianchini.pdf.
7. Bianchini, A., (2002b). I vantaggi conseguibili attraverso l'esternalizzazione della Logistica di un'azienda sanitaria, proceedings, November 5, 2002, Milano.
8. Bianchini, A., (2003). Il Progetto di eProcurement della ASL di Viterbo, proceedings of "*Gare on-line in Sanità*" symposium, July 1, 2003, Bologna.
9. Boni, Ma., (2001). Le problematiche attuali sugli acquisti di beni e servizi in sanità, proceedings of "L'evoluzione nei processi di acquisto di beni e servizi" symposium, June 1, 2001, Roma.
10. Boni, Ma., (2004). "e-Commerce: dopo tanta euforia ora serve più realismo", *Il Sole 24 Ore Sanità*, June 15/21, 2004.
11. Borgonovi, E., (2001). Stato dell'arte della Supply Chain Ospedaliera: dalla reingegnerizzazione dei processi ai portali Internet, proceedings of "FIASO, SIFO, FARE" convention, June 28, 2001, Milano.
12. Borgonovi, E., (2004). "E-procurement in sanità: dalla logica di modello alla logica di processo", *Mecosan*, n° 41, pp. 2-5.
13. Clerico, G. and Fiorentino, G., (2000). *I servizi sanitari in Italia*, Il Mulino, Bologna.
14. Consip, (2002). "Il Programma di razionalizzazione della spesa per beni e servizi della Pubblica Amministrazione", *Consip Annual Report* (house journal), April 2003, Roma.
15. Cotter, R., Mattei, U., Pardolesi, R., Ulen, U., (1999). *Il mercato delle regole: analisi economica del diritto civile*, Il Mulino, Bologna.
16. Federici T., Bianchini A., Morano T., (2004). "Le specificità dell'e-procurement in sanità: le esperienze dell'ASL di Viterbo", *Mecosan*, n° 51, pp. 41-57.
17. Federazione Italiana Aziende Sanitarie ed Ospedaliere (FIASO), (2001). "e-Com ed e-procurement in Sanità", *Fiaso News*, 3rd Year III n° 4, p 12.
18. Federcomin, (2001). *E-Business: realtà and prospettive* – Annual Report edited with IDC Italia.
19. Ferranti, F., (2003). "Il Marketplace bussa alla porta delle aziende del Ssn", *Il Sole 24 Ore Sanità*, October 21/27, 2003.
20. Mastrogregori, L., (2004). Il Programma di razionalizzazione della spesa and il Mercato elettronico della PA - Stato di attuazione e linee evolutive, workshop, Faculty of Economics, University of Tuscia, May 6, 2004, Viterbo. Available at: www.tommasofederici.it/convegni/releprmastr.pdf
21. Monteu, M. and Ruffino E., (2001). "E-procurement nelle aziende sanitarie", *Quaderni ASI* (Agenzia Sanitaria Italiana) collection - n° 17, p 25.
22. Ripa di Meana, F., (2001). "I fornitori non perdano il treno della tecnologia e l'Europa alzi la soglia", *Il Sole 24 Ore Sanità*, March 13/19, 2001.

Author Index

Abou Khaled, Omar 193
Apostolou, Dimitris 157

Baldoni, Roberto 181
Berntzen, Lasse 13
Blaschke, Thomas 25
Breu, Ruth 122
Bruschi, Danilo 112

Cantamessa, Marco 81
Chappelet, Jean-Loup 36
Chen, Yue 205
Contenti, Mariangela 181
Costilla, Carmen 134
Cremades, José 134

Dimitriou, Tassos 100
Douligeris, C. 213

Eddowes, Lee Anthony 257

Federici, Tommaso 298
Fernandez, E. 225, 268
Ferro, Enrico 81
Foteinakis, Dimitris 100

Gortmaker, Jeffrey 169

Hadzilias, Elias A. 247
Hafner, Michael 122
Hardy, Catherine 286

Janssen, Marijn 169

Kaliontzoglou, A. 213
Kilchenmann, Pierre 36
Kolsaker, Ailsa 70
Krek, Alenka 25

Lan, Ling 57
Lanzi, Andrea 112
Li, Minglu 205
Li, Ying 205

Macintosh, Ann 1
Märker, Oliver 48
McKay-Hubbard, Andy 1
Mecella, Massimo 181
Meneklis, B. 213
Michaelis, Susanne 48
Mugellini, Elena 193

Nai Fovino, Igor 112
Novak, Andrea 122

Palacios, Juan P. 134
Paolucci, Emilio 81
Pariente Lobo, Tomas 157
Pettenati, Maria Chiara 193
Pirri, Franco 193
Polemi, D. 213
Poppenborg, Annika 48

Rech Filho, Armando 91
Rios Insua, D. 225, 268
Rios, J. 225, 268
Rivero, J.A. 268
Roeder, Stefanie 48
Rossi, Bruno 277
Rubio, J.A. 225
Russo, Barbara 277

Sacco, Giovanni M. 147
Salz, Stefan René 48
Scholl, Marc H. 235
Shell, Danae 1
Steinmann, Renate 25
Stojanovic, Ljiljana 157
Succi, Giancarlo 277

Termini, Alessandro 181
Thoenssen, Barbara 157

Vila, Jorge 134
Vinnik, Svetlana 235

Wagenaar, René W. 169
Weber, Barbara 122
Williams, Susan P. 286
Winsvold, Marte 13

Zuliani, Paolo 277

Lecture Notes in Artificial Intelligence (LNAI)

Vol. 3416: M. Böhlen, J. Gamper, W. Polasek, M.A. Wimmer (Eds.), E-Government: Towards Electronic Democracy. XIII, 311 pages. 2005.

Vol. 3403: B. Ganter, R. Godin (Eds.), Formal Concept Analysis. XI, 419 pages. 2005.

Vol. 3398: D.-K. Baik (Ed.), Systems Modeling and Simulation: Theory and Applications. XIV, 733 pages. 2005.

Vol. 3397: T.G. Kim (Ed.), Artificial Intelligence and Simulation. XV, 711 pages. 2005.

Vol. 3396: R.M. van Eijk, M.-P. Huget, F. Dignum (Eds.), Advances in Agent Communication. X, 261 pages. 2005.

Vol. 3374: D. Weyns, H.V.D. Parunak, F. Michel (Eds.), Environments for Multi-Agent Systems. X, 279 pages. 2005.

Vol. 3366: I. Rahwan, P. Moraitis, C. Reed (Eds.), Argumentation in Multi-Agent Systems. XII, 263 pages. 2005.

Vol. 3359: G. Grieser, Y. Tanaka (Eds.), Intuitive Human Interfaces for Organizing and Accessing Intellectual Assets. XIV, 257 pages. 2005.

Vol. 3346: R.H. Bordini, M. Dastani, J. Dix, A.E.F. Seghrouchni (Eds.), Programming Multi-Agent Systems. XIV, 249 pages. 2005.

Vol. 3345: Y. Cai (Ed.), Ambient Intelligence for Scientific Discovery. XII, 311 pages. 2005.

Vol. 3339: G.I. Webb, X. Yu (Eds.), AI 2004: Advances in Artificial Intelligence. XXII, 1272 pages. 2004.

Vol. 3336: D. Karagiannis, U. Reimer (Eds.), Practical Aspects of Knowledge Management. X, 523 pages. 2004.

Vol. 3327: Y. Shi, W. Xu, Z. Chen (Eds.), Data Mining and Knowledge Management. XIII, 263 pages. 2005.

Vol. 3315: C. Lemaître, C.A. Reyes, J.A. González (Eds.), Advances in Artificial Intelligence – IBERAMIA 2004. XX, 987 pages. 2004.

Vol. 3303: J.A. López, E. Benfenati, W. Dubitzky (Eds.), Knowledge Exploration in Life Science Informatics. X, 249 pages. 2004.

Vol. 3275: P. Perner (Ed.), Advances in Data Mining. VIII, 173 pages. 2004.

Vol. 3265: R.E. Frederking, K.B. Taylor (Eds.), Machine Translation: From Real Users to Research. XI, 392 pages. 2004.

Vol. 3264: G. Paliouras, Y. Sakakibara (Eds.), Grammatical Inference: Algorithms and Applications. XI, 291 pages. 2004.

Vol. 3259: J. Dix, J. Leite (Eds.), Computational Logic in Multi-Agent Systems. XII, 251 pages. 2004.

Vol. 3257: E. Motta, N.R. Shadbolt, A. Stutt, N. Gibbins (Eds.), Engineering Knowledge in the Age of the Semantic Web. XVII, 517 pages. 2004.

Vol. 3249: B. Buchberger, J.A. Campbell (Eds.), Artificial Intelligence and Symbolic Computation. X, 285 pages. 2004.

Vol. 3248: K.-Y. Su, J. Tsujii, J.-H. Lee, O.Y. Kwong (Eds.), Natural Language Processing – IJCNLP 2004. XVIII, 817 pages. 2005.

Vol. 3245: E. Suzuki, S. Arikawa (Eds.), Discovery Science. XIV, 430 pages. 2004.

Vol. 3244: S. Ben-David, J. Case, A. Maruoka (Eds.), Algorithmic Learning Theory. XIV, 505 pages. 2004.

Vol. 3238: S. Biundo, T. Frühwirth, G. Palm (Eds.), KI 2004: Advances in Artificial Intelligence. XI, 467 pages. 2004.

Vol. 3230: J.L. Vicedo, P. Martínez-Barco, R. Muñoz, M. Saiz Noeda (Eds.), Advances in Natural Language Processing. XII, 488 pages. 2004.

Vol. 3229: J.J. Alferes, J. Leite (Eds.), Logics in Artificial Intelligence. XIV, 744 pages. 2004.

Vol. 3228: M.G. Hinchey, J.L. Rash, W.F. Truszkowski, C.A. Rouff (Eds.), Formal Approaches to Agent-Based Systems. VIII, 290 pages. 2004.

Vol. 3215: M.G.. Negoita, R.J. Howlett, L.C. Jain (Eds.), Knowledge-Based Intelligent Information and Engineering Systems, Part III. LVII, 906 pages. 2004.

Vol. 3214: M.G.. Negoita, R.J. Howlett, L.C. Jain (Eds.), Knowledge-Based Intelligent Information and Engineering Systems, Part II. LVIII, 1302 pages. 2004.

Vol. 3213: M.G.. Negoita, R.J. Howlett, L.C. Jain (Eds.), Knowledge-Based Intelligent Information and Engineering Systems, Part I. LVIII, 1280 pages. 2004.

Vol. 3209: B. Berendt, A. Hotho, D. Mladenic, M. van Someren, M. Spiliopoulou, G. Stumme (Eds.), Web Mining: From Web to Semantic Web. IX, 201 pages. 2004.

Vol. 3206: P. Sojka, I. Kopecek, K. Pala (Eds.), Text, Speech and Dialogue. XIII, 667 pages. 2004.

Vol. 3202: J.-F. Boulicaut, F. Esposito, F. Giannotti, D. Pedreschi (Eds.), Knowledge Discovery in Databases: PKDD 2004. XIX, 560 pages. 2004.

Vol. 3201: J.-F. Boulicaut, F. Esposito, F. Giannotti, D. Pedreschi (Eds.), Machine Learning: ECML 2004. XVIII, 580 pages. 2004.

Vol. 3194: R. Camacho, R. King, A. Srinivasan (Eds.), Inductive Logic Programming. XI, 361 pages. 2004.

Vol. 3192: C. Bussler, D. Fensel (Eds.), Artificial Intelligence: Methodology, Systems, and Applications. XIII, 522 pages. 2004.

Vol. 3191: M. Klusch, S. Ossowski, V. Kashyap, R. Unland (Eds.), Cooperative Information Agents VIII. XI, 303 pages. 2004.

Vol. 3187: G. Lindemann, J. Denzinger, I.J. Timm, R. Unland (Eds.), Multiagent System Technologies. XIII, 341 pages. 2004.

Vol. 3176: O. Bousquet, U. von Luxburg, G. Rätsch (Eds.), Advanced Lectures on Machine Learning. IX, 241 pages. 2004.

Vol. 3171: A.L.C. Bazzan, S. Labidi (Eds.), Advances in Artificial Intelligence – SBIA 2004. XVII, 548 pages. 2004.

Vol. 3159: U. Visser, Intelligent Information Integration for the Semantic Web. XIV, 150 pages. 2004.

Vol. 3157: C. Zhang, H. W. Guesgen, W.K. Yeap (Eds.), PRICAI 2004: Trends in Artificial Intelligence. XX, 1023 pages. 2004.

Vol. 3155: P. Funk, P.A. González Calero (Eds.), Advances in Case-Based Reasoning. XIII, 822 pages. 2004.

Vol. 3139: F. Iida, R. Pfeifer, L. Steels, Y. Kuniyoshi (Eds.), Embodied Artificial Intelligence. IX, 331 pages. 2004.

Vol. 3131: V. Torra, Y. Narukawa (Eds.), Modeling Decisions for Artificial Intelligence. XI, 327 pages. 2004.

Vol. 3127: K.E. Wolff, H.D. Pfeiffer, H.S. Delugach (Eds.), Conceptual Structures at Work. XI, 403 pages. 2004.

Vol. 3123: A. Belz, R. Evans, P. Piwek (Eds.), Natural Language Generation. X, 219 pages. 2004.

Vol. 3120: J. Shawe-Taylor, Y. Singer (Eds.), Learning Theory. X, 648 pages. 2004.

Vol. 3097: D. Basin, M. Rusinowitch (Eds.), Automated Reasoning. XII, 493 pages. 2004.

Vol. 3071: A. Omicini, P. Petta, J. Pitt (Eds.), Engineering Societies in the Agents World. XIII, 409 pages. 2004.

Vol. 3070: L. Rutkowski, J. Siekmann, R. Tadeusiewicz, L.A. Zadeh (Eds.), Artificial Intelligence and Soft Computing - ICAISC 2004. XXV, 1208 pages. 2004.

Vol. 3068: E. André, L. Dybkjær, W. Minker, P. Heisterkamp (Eds.), Affective Dialogue Systems. XII, 324 pages. 2004.

Vol. 3067: M. Dastani, J. Dix, A. El Fallah-Seghrouchni (Eds.), Programming Multi-Agent Systems. X, 221 pages. 2004.

Vol. 3066: S. Tsumoto, R. Słowiński, J. Komorowski, J.W. Grzymała-Busse (Eds.), Rough Sets and Current Trends in Computing. XX, 853 pages. 2004.

Vol. 3065: A. Lomuscio, D. Nute (Eds.), Deontic Logic in Computer Science. X, 275 pages. 2004.

Vol. 3060: A.Y. Tawfik, S.D. Goodwin (Eds.), Advances in Artificial Intelligence. XIII, 582 pages. 2004.

Vol. 3056: H. Dai, R. Srikant, C. Zhang (Eds.), Advances in Knowledge Discovery and Data Mining. XIX, 713 pages. 2004.

Vol. 3055: H. Christiansen, M.-S. Hacid, T. Andreasen, H.L. Larsen (Eds.), Flexible Query Answering Systems. X, 500 pages. 2004.

Vol. 3048: P. Faratin, D.C. Parkes, J.A. Rodríguez-Aguilar, W.E. Walsh (Eds.), Agent-Mediated Electronic Commerce V. XI, 155 pages. 2004.

Vol. 3040: R. Conejo, M. Urretavizcaya, J.-L. Pérez-de-la-Cruz (Eds.), Current Topics in Artificial Intelligence. XIV, 689 pages. 2004.

Vol. 3035: M.A. Wimmer (Ed.), Knowledge Management in Electronic Government. XII, 326 pages. 2004.

Vol. 3034: J. Favela, E. Menasalvas, E. Chávez (Eds.), Advances in Web Intelligence. XIII, 227 pages. 2004.

Vol. 3030: P. Giorgini, B. Henderson-Sellers, M. Winikoff (Eds.), Agent-Oriented Information Systems. XIV, 207 pages. 2004.

Vol. 3029: B. Orchard, C. Yang, M. Ali (Eds.), Innovations in Applied Artificial Intelligence. XXI, 1272 pages. 2004.

Vol. 3025: G.A. Vouros, T. Panayiotopoulos (Eds.), Methods and Applications of Artificial Intelligence. XV, 546 pages. 2004.

Vol. 3020: D. Polani, B. Browning, A. Bonarini, K. Yoshida (Eds.), RoboCup 2003: Robot Soccer World Cup VII. XVI, 767 pages. 2004.

Vol. 3012: K. Kurumatani, S.-H. Chen, A. Ohuchi (Eds.), Multi-Agents for Mass User Support. X, 217 pages. 2004.

Vol. 3010: K.R. Apt, F. Fages, F. Rossi, P. Szeredi, J. Váncża (Eds.), Recent Advances in Constraints. VIII, 285 pages. 2004.

Vol. 2990: J. Leite, A. Omicini, L. Sterling, P. Torroni (Eds.), Declarative Agent Languages and Technologies. XII, 281 pages. 2004.

Vol. 2980: A. Blackwell, K. Marriott, A. Shimojima (Eds.), Diagrammatic Representation and Inference. XV, 448 pages. 2004.

Vol. 2977: G. Di Marzo Serugendo, A. Karageorgos, O.F. Rana, F. Zambonelli (Eds.), Engineering Self-Organising Systems. X, 299 pages. 2004.

Vol. 2972: R. Monroy, G. Arroyo-Figueroa, L.E. Sucar, H. Sossa (Eds.), MICAI 2004: Advances in Artificial Intelligence. XVII, 923 pages. 2004.

Vol. 2969: M. Nickles, M. Rovatsos, G. Weiss (Eds.), Agents and Computational Autonomy. X, 275 pages. 2004.

Vol. 2961: P. Eklund (Ed.), Concept Lattices. IX, 411 pages. 2004.

Vol. 2953: K. Konrad, Model Generation for Natural Language Interpretation and Analysis. XIII, 166 pages. 2004.

Vol. 2934: G. Lindemann, D. Moldt, M. Paolucci (Eds.), Regulated Agent-Based Social Systems. X, 301 pages. 2004.

Vol. 2930: F. Winkler (Ed.), Automated Deduction in Geometry. VII, 231 pages. 2004.

Vol. 2926: L. van Elst, V. Dignum, A. Abecker (Eds.), Agent-Mediated Knowledge Management. XI, 428 pages. 2004.

Vol. 2923: V. Lifschitz, I. Niemelä (Eds.), Logic Programming and Nonmonotonic Reasoning. IX, 365 pages. 2003.

Vol. 2915: A. Camurri, G. Volpe (Eds.), Gesture-Based Communication in Human-Computer Interaction. XIII, 558 pages. 2004.

Vol. 2913: T.M. Pinkston, V.K. Prasanna (Eds.), High Performance Computing - HiPC 2003. XX, 512 pages. 2003.

Vol. 2903: T.D. Gedeon, L.C.C. Fung (Eds.), AI 2003: Advances in Artificial Intelligence. XVI, 1075 pages. 2003.

Vol. 2902: F.M. Pires, S.P. Abreu (Eds.), Progress in Artificial Intelligence. XV, 504 pages. 2003.